JOURNAL FOR THE STUDY OF THE OLD TESTAMENT
SUPPLEMENT SERIES
366

The Problem of Evil and its Symbols in Jewish and Christian Tradition

edited by

Henning Graf Reventlow and Yair Hoffman

T & T CLARK INTERNATIONAL
A Continuum imprint
LONDON • NEW YORK

Copyright © 2004 T&T Clark International
A Continuum imprint

Published by T&T Clark International
The Tower Building, 11 York Road, London SE1 7NX
15 East 26th Street, Suite 1703, New York, NY 10010

www.tandtclark.com

British Library Cataloguing-in-Publication Data
A catalogue record for this book is available from the British Library

Library of Congress Cataloging-in-Publication Data
A catalogue record for this book is available from the Library of Congress

Typeset by CA Typesetting, www.sheffieldtypesetting.com
Printed on acid-free paper in Great Britain by Cromwell Press, Trowbridge, Wilts.

ISBN 0-8264-6222-7 (hardback)

CONTENTS

PREFACE

The papers in this volume were originally read at the sixth symposium between the Department of Bible, Chaim Rosenberg School of Jewish Studies of Tel Aviv University, and the Faculty of Protestant Theology of the University of the Ruhr, Bochum, held in Bochum, October 2001.

The co-operation of the two departments has a long tradition. Our experience is that the exchange of scholarship in successive general topics generates for both partners new experiences and new insights and should be continued also in the future.

We have to thank again for their support the Chaim Rosenberg School of Jewish Studies and the Dean of Humanities, Tel Aviv University, the Evangelical Church of Westphalia, the Gesellschaft der Freunde der Ruhr-Universität Bochum and also the Faculty of Protestant Theology for hospitality received by the Israeli scholars.

The general topic of evil touches a problem that remains one of the deepest riddles of human existence and has been discussed both in the Bible itself and in the thinking of innumerable Jewish and Christian theologians and philosophers throughout the ages. We hope to have been able to contribute a little to these discussions by showing the different aspects of our ongoing research.

Henning Graf Reventlow and Yair Hoffman
Bochum/Tel Aviv, May 2003

ABBREVIATIONS

AB	Anchor Bible
ABD	David Noel Freedman (ed.), *The Anchor Bible Dictionary* (New York: Doubleday, 1992)
AJSReview	*Association for Jewish Studies Review*
AJSL	*American Journal of Semitic Languages and Literatures*
ATD	Das Alte Testament Deutsch
BA	*Biblical Archaeologist*
BHT	Beiträge zur historischen Theologie
BibInt	*Biblical Interpretation: A Journal of Contemporary Approaches*
BibOr	Biblica et orientalia
BKAT	Biblischer Kommentar: Altes Testament
BÖT	Beiträge zur Ökumenischen Theologie
BTSt	Biblisch-Theologische Studien
CBQ	*Catholic Biblical Quarterly*
CBQMS	*Catholic Biblical Quarterly*, Monograph Series
CChrSL	Corpus Christianorum, Series Latina
ConBOT	Coniectanea biblica, Old Testament
CRAIBL	*Comptes rendus de l'Académie des inscriptions et belles-lettres*
CSEL	Corpus scriptorum ecclesiasticorum latinorum
DJD	Discoveries in the Judaean Desert
EB	Encyclopedia Biblica
EncJud	*Encyclopaedia Judaica*
EvT	*Evangelische Theologie*
FKDG	Forschungen zur Kirchen- und Dogmengeschichte
FOTL	The Forms of the Old Testament Literature
FRLANT	Forschungen zur Religion und Literatur des Alten und Neuen Testaments
HAT	Handbuch zum Alten Testament
ICC	International Critical Commentary
IOS	*Israel Oriental Studies*
JANESCU	*Journal of the Ancient Near Eastern Society of Columbia University*
JAOS	*Journal of the American Oriental Society*
JBL	*Journal of Biblical Literature*
JCS	*Journal of Cuneiform Studies*
JJS	*Journal of Jewish Studies*
JSJ	*Journal for the Study of Judaism in the Persian, Hellenistic and Roman Period*
JSOT	*Journal for the Study of the Old Testament*
JSOTSup	*Journal for the Study of the Old Testament*, Supplement Series
KD	*Kerygma und Dogma*
KHAT	Kurzer Hand-Kommentar zum Alten Testament
OLZ	*Orientalistische Literaturzeitung*

OTG	Old Testament Guides
OTL	Old Testament Library
OTS	*Oudtestamentische Studiën*
PL	J.-P. Migne (ed.), *Patrologia cursus completus Series prima [latina]* (221 vols.; Paris: J.-P. Migne, 1844–65)
RB	*Revue biblique*
RevQ	*Revue de Qumran*
RHPR	*Revue d'histoire et de philosophie religieuses*
SBLDS	SBL Dissertation Series
SBLSS	SBL Semeia Studies
SBT	Studies in Biblical Theology
STDJ	Studies on the Texts of the Desert of Judah
THAT	Ernst Jenni and Claus Westermann (eds.), *Theologisches Handwörterbuch zum Alten Testament* (Munich: Chr. Kaiser, 1971–76)
ThWAT	G.J. Botterweck and H. Ringgren (eds.), *Theologisches Wörterbuch zum Alten Testament* (Stuttgart: W. Kohlhammer, 1970–)
TOTC	Tyndale Old Testament Commentaries
TRE	*Theologische Realenzyklopädie*
VT	*Vetus Testamentum*
VTSup	*Vetus Testamentum*, Supplements
WA	M. Luther, *Kritische Gesamtausgabe* (= 'Weimar' edition), *Briefe*
WABR	M. Luther, *Kritische Gesamtausgabe* (= 'Weimar' edition)
WBC	Word Biblical Commentary
WdF	Wege der Forschung
WMANT	Wissenschaftliche Monographien zum Alten und Neuen Testament
ZAW	*Zeitschrift für die alttestamentliche Wissenschaft*
ZTK	*Zeitschrift für Theologie und Kirche*

LIST OF CONTRIBUTORS

Professor Dr Franz-Heinrich Beyer, Ruhr-Universität Bochum, Germany

Professor Dr Christofer Frey, Ruhr-Universität Bochum, Germany

Professor Edward L. Greenstein, Tel Aviv University, Tel Aviv, Israel

Professor Dr Hans-Peter Hasenfratz, Ruhr-Universität Bochum, Germany

Professor Yair Hoffman, Tel Aviv University, Tel Aviv, Israel

Dr Yoram Jacobson, Tel Aviv University, Tel Aviv, Israel

Professor Dr Christian Link, Ruhr-Universität Bochum, Germany

Professor Dr Bilhah Nitzan, Tel Aviv University, Tel Aviv, Israel

Dr Yochai Oppenheimer, Tel Aviv University, Tel Aviv, Israel

Professor Dr Henning Graf Reventlow, Litt. D., Ruhr-Universität Bochum, Germany

Dr Osnat Singer, Tel Aviv University, Tel Aviv, Israel

Professor Dr Winfried Thiel, Ruhr-Universität Bochum, Germany

Professor Dr Klaus Wengst, Ruhr-Universität Bochum, Germany

Professor Dr Dietmar Wyrwa, Ruhr-Universität Bochum, Germany

Part I

THE BIBLE

'EVIL' IN THE BOOKS OF KINGS*

Winfried Thiel

I

The books of Kings are dominated by the theme of evildoing. This impression is obtained by the theological appraisals of many kings ('he did evil in the eyes of YHWH') which are spread over both parts of the literary complex (from 1 Kgs 14.22 or 15.20 to 2 Kgs 24.19), covering its surface. But the intention is also discernible in the narrative content. Being the last part of the Deuteronomistic history, the books of Kings throughout their whole conception offer a history of the decline of Israel and Judah up to the end of their national existence: from the last regnal years of David (1 Kgs 1) and the apostasy of Solomon (1 Kgs 11.1-13), the division of the kingdom (1 Kgs 12), the decay of the northern kingdom (2 Kgs 17) to the fall of Judah with the sack of Jerusalem, the burning of the Temple and the end of the Davidic dynasty.

It is tempting to pursue the topic in a phenomenological way. But to avoid covering the texts with a prejudice towards 'evil', a philological approach should be preferred. First of all the root רעע with its derivates, the feminine noun רעה and the adjective רע, will be considered.[1]

There are also numerous other words cognate with רעע. They belong to the same thematic range: רשע, פשע עשק, עון ועוה, עול, נבל, חמס, חטא and שדד.[2] These terms are not all contained in the books of Kings, and even those that are can be treated only marginally. The material containing רעע is very extensive in the books of Kings. With 63 occurrences of this root the books of Kings exhibit the highest frequency of examples within the Pentateuch and historical books.[3] Because 1–2 Kings constitute the final part of the Deuteronomistic history, we must look beyond the borders of these books to preceding sections of the Deuteronomistic work and to other parts of the canon as well. The theme cannot be treated exhaustively in the space available: only special aspects can be worked out.

---

*   In memory of Ilse von Loewenclau (1924–2001).

1.   The nouns מֶרַע, 'evil, crime' (only Dan. 11.27), and רֹעַ, 'bad quality, wickedness', likewise related to רעע, do not occur in the books of Kings.

2.   Cf. R. Knierim, *Die Hauptbegriffe für Sünde im Alten Testament* (Gütersloh: Gütersloher Verlagshaus Gerd Mohn, 1965, 2nd edn, 1967).

3.   Regarding the whole of the Old Testament canon, the amount of statistical instances within the books of Kings is less only than Jeremiah (146 examples), the Psalter (80 examples) and Proverbs (75 examples) according to the table in C. Dohmen and D. Rick, 'רעע', *ThWAT* VII (Stuttgart/Berlin/Cologne: W. Kohlhammer, 1993), 582–612 (esp. 585).

II

The root רע finds its antonym in טוב, 'good, beautiful, useful, efficient'. Both adjectives often occur as opposite expressions. Solomon asks from God as a manifestation of his governmental wisdom the ability 'to distinguish between good and evil' (1 Kgs 3.9). The king of Israel believes that Micaiah ben Imlah will not prophesy 'good concerning him, but ill' (1 Kgs 22.8, 18). The inhabitants of Jericho explain their situation to Elisha thus: 'Behold, the position of the city is good, but the water is evil/bad' – it is noxious, unhealthy. The land, watered by the spring of Jericho, causes miscarriages (שׁכל *pi.*, 2 Kgs 2.19). In 2 Kgs 4.41 an analogous assertion is intended (without the antithetical term טוב): Elisha removes the 'evil', that is, the harmful, unhealthy (דבר רע), in the meal which previously caused a bitter taste.

The expression is used in another way, namely theologically, in 2 Kgs 17.11. דברים רעים in this central Deuteronomistic text designates the many offences of the Israelites against YHWH and his will. They are enumerated in the context. This speech, after the fall of the northern kingdom, is one of the key texts to the understanding of evil in the books of Kings. The religious lapse of the Israelites in this connection is called 'your evil ways' (דרכיכם הרעים), from which the prophets have called Israel to return in vain (v. 13). The same phrase, now concerning Jeroboam I, is found in a Deuteronomistic or post-Deuteronomistic notice (1 Kgs 13.33).

The books of Kings contain another term antithetical to רע. The negative Deuteronomistic judgement 'he did the evil (הרע) in the eyes of YHWH' is opposed by the positive statement 'he did what was right (הישׁר) in the eyes of YHWH'. The evil is thereby qualified as what is not right, as what is wrong, as what contradicts the will and the direction of God. This theological horizon is supported by the comment 'in the eyes of YHWH', that is, 'in the sight of YHWH', in his opinion,[4] in addition to the content which characterizes an action as ישׁר, 'right'. With hardly any exception ישׁר refers to an attitude, being in accordance with the demands of YHWH, with his intentions and with his will, revealed in Deuteronomy. To do evil, wrong, is in contrast to that. This conclusion is confirmed by the details of the evil deeds of the kings in the negative appraisals.

III

The root רע(ע) signifies not only the evil that one does but also the calamity one suffers. If the misfortune is caused by God, and this is often the case, one can speak of disaster or mischief (רע) in contrast to שׁלום in Isa. 45.7 [in German the difference may be easier to express by the word *Unheil*]). If the active and the passive element, the doing and the suffering, are bound together in one expression, then according to the Israelite way of thinking a firm association between action and

---

4. On this issue cf. E. Jenni, in E. Jenni and D. Vetter, 'עֶיַן', *THAT* II (Munich: Chr. Kaiser; Zürich: Theologischer Verlag, 1976), 259–68 (esp. 266).

fate is to be assumed ('action-consequence-nexus', in German *Tun-Ergehen-Zusammenhang*).[5] (רע)רע represents what I call an 'integrative' term (like עָוֹן ו and *mutatis mutandis* צדקה and others).[6] Integrative terms can contain whole sequences in themselves, whose individual perspectives emerge from the particular contexts, without displacing each other completely. In some texts, the two aspects are so closely intertwined that they can be separated only with difficulty or even not at all (Jer. 4.18).

In the Deuteronomic and Deuteronomistic texts the connection between doing and suffering is caused by God. A 'synthetic view of life' (*synthetische Lebensauffassung*),[7] which preceded the religion of YHWH or which went by its side and worked automatically, is not provable from these texts. This holds good for the Old Testament as a whole, even for early wisdom.[8] Deut. 31.29 nicely shows the connection between doing and suffering and does not constitute counter-evidence:

> The disaster (הרעה) will meet you in the distant future, if you do what is evil (הרע) in the sight of Yhwh.

The coming of the calamity is expressed by indefinite terms; Yhwh is not directly mentioned as the subject of the events. However, it is strikingly explained by the further context that this is precisely what is meant.

The same matter of fact is obviously expressed in 1 Kgs 2.44. Solomon speaks to Shimei:

> You know yourself all the evil (הרעה)[9] that you have done to my father David; YHWH will now return your evil deed (רעתך) upon your head.

The evil deed of Shimei is his far-back-dating behaviour towards David (2 Sam. 16.5-10; 19.17-24; 1 Kgs 2.8-9). It is an offence between people which God will punish. Within the context of the section Solomon's reference to God's action indeed seems like a justification for his own death sentence against Shimei, which is executed immediately (v. 46a). Verses 44-45, like v. 32 that contains the same remarkable phrase,[10] are an addition at the end of ch. 2 which refers back to the

---

5.   Cf. basically K. Koch, 'Gibt es ein Vergeltungsdogma im Alten Testament?', *ZTK* 52 (1955), 1–42 = *idem*, *Spuren des hebräischen Denkens: Gesammelte Aufsätze 1* (Neukirchen–Vluyn: Neukirchener Verlag, 1991), 65–103. Koch uses the terms 'Tun-Ergehen-Zusammenhang' and 'schicksalwirkende Tatsphäre' synonymously.

6.   Other similar terms are found in Koch, *Spuren des hebräischen Denkens*, 89–90.

7.   K.H. Fahlgren, *ṣᵉdāḳā nahestehende und entgegengesetzte Begriffe im Alten Testament* (Uppsala: Almquist & Wiksell, 1932), 50–54 = *idem*, 'Die Gegensätze von ṣᵉdaqā im Alten Testament', in K. Koch (ed.), *Um das Prinzip der Vergeltung in Religion und Recht des Alten Testaments* (WdF, 125; Darmstadt: Wissenschaftliche Buchgesellschaft, 1972), 87–129 (esp. 126–29).

8.   On this issue cf. the argument of A. Scherer, *Das weise Wort und seine Wirkung* (WMANT, 83; Neukirchen–Vluyn: Neukirchener Verlag, 1999), 79–84, 148–49.

9.   MT: 'which your heart knows' is easily to be identified as an explanatory gloss.

10.   See H. Graf Reventlow, '"Sein Blut komme über sein Haupt"', *VT* 10 (1960), 311–27 = K. Koch (ed.), *Um das Prinzip der Vergeltung* (above n. 7), 412–31; K. Koch, 'Der Spruch "Sein Blut bleibe auf seinem Haupt" und die israelitische Auffassung vom vergossenen Blut', *VT* 12 (1962), 396–416 = *idem*, *Spuren des hebräischen Denkens*, 128–45; J.-M. Babut, 'Que son sang

secondary passage in vv. 5-9 and follows the intention to clear Solomon of his bloody deeds (cf. vv. 8-9).[11]

1 Kgs 14.9-10 as a whole introduces a theological pattern. Verses 7-11 form a Deuteronomistic speech, put in the mouth of the prophet Ahijah of Shiloh. This passage represents the theological appraisal, that the Deuteronomistic redactors usually place in the introductory regnal frame that is lacking in the case of Jeroboam I. God announces to Jeroboam by the mouth of Ahijah:

> (Because) you have done evil (רעע *hi.*) more than all who were before you and have gone and made yourself other gods...

> therefore I shall bring mischief (רעה) upon the house of Jeroboam and I shall cut off all males[12] belonging to Jeroboam, of age and under age, and sweep out (בער) behind the house of Jeroboam as one sweeps out dung until it is gone.

The evil behaviour of Jeroboam – disloyalty towards YHWH and the making of 'other gods' as molten images (namely, the golden bull statuettes of 1 Kgs 12.28-30) – calls up the reaction of YHWH: the announcement of the disaster which will sweep out the royal dynasty of Jeroboam. With regard to the style of both verses the change of address from the second person to the third person singular attracts attention. Obviously the Deuteronomistic redactors have inserted a traditional passage (vv. 10-11)[13] as announcement of the doom after the accusation (vv. 7aß-9), formulated by the redactors themselves. The announcement expresses the extermination of the dynasty.[14] It finds almost literal parallels in 16.3-4 (the dynasty of Baasha) and 21.21-22, 24 (the dynasty of Omri/Ahab). It is therefore inserted into later texts by the Deuteronomistic redactors as constantly repeated material with a retrospective view. In doing so, the redactors repeat the accusation which they expressed in varied forms (14.7*, 9/16.2/21.20b). The correspondence of evildoing (עשׂה הרע) and God's disastrous action (הבי א רעה) was preserved in 21.20b, 21; in 16.2-3 it was paraphrased.

The phrase 'sweep out behind' (בער אחרי *pi.*) appears in all of the three texts dealing with the announcement of disaster. It connects the prediction of the extermination of the dynasty with the commandments of Deuteronomy, which require Israel 'to remove the evil out of your midst' (בער הרע מקרבך *pi.* and similarly

---

soit sur sa tête!', *VT* 36 (1986), 474–80. The slight modification of the formula in 1 Kgs 2.44 (רעתו instead of דמו) was necessary, because Shimei did not shed anybody's blood.

11. The character of this portion as an insertion can be discerned by the new introduction to the speech of Solomon, which seems to be unmotivated. The relation to 2.5-9, both in form (for v. 44 cf. v. 5) and content, shows that these texts originated from one and the same hand. In contrast to 2.2-4, they are pre-Deuteronomistic (against E. Würthwein, *Das erste Buch der Könige Kapitel 1–16* [ATD, 11.1; Göttingen; Zürich: Vandenhoeck & Ruprecht, 2nd edn, 1985], 8–9, 26–27).

12. Lit.: 'who pisses against the wall'. The statement of completeness is not included in the text, but it is implied.

13. This is supported by the fact that vv. 10-11 possess characteristic, but no Deuteronomistic features of language.

14. Cf. W. Thiel, 'Deuteronomistische Redaktionsarbeit in den Elia-Erzählungen', in *Congress Volume Leuven 1989* (VTSup, 43; Leiden: E.J. Brill, 1991), 148–71 (esp. 159–65) = *idem, Gelebte Geschichte* (Neukirchen–Vluyn: Neukirchener Verlag, 2000), 139–60 (esp. 149–54).

Deut. 13.6; 17.7, 12; 19.19; 21.21; 22.22; 24.7).[15] Behind these demands the idea of the infecting power of evil possibly prevails. It can be defeated if the community removes the centre of infection[16] from its midst. In the focus of the texts from Kings, however, it is a matter of exterminating royal dynasties infected by the evil; it is not the community which has to do so. According to the Deuteronomistic judgement the people have been led into sin against God by the example of their kings (Jeroboam: 1 Kgs 14.16; 15.26, 30, 34 etc.; Baasha: 16.2, 13; Ahab: 21.22). In the eyes of the Deuteronomists, looking back from the exilic period, these eliminations of royal dynasties represent divine acts of doom. In this the Deuteronomistic redactors express their theological understanding.

In the traditions they incorporated, however, they found this understanding represented only in the case of the downfall of the Ahab family (2 Kgs 9.1–10.27*), especially in the narrative description of the designation of Jehu by the prophet Elisha or, more precisely, by one of his disciples (9.1-3, 4-6, 10b). Regarding the elimination of the families of Jeroboam and Baasha, the redactors had to hand only traditions about conspiracies, without traces of divine initiative (1 Kgs 15.27, 29a; 16.9-11). But they interpreted these as fulfilments of prophetic announcements (15.29b-30 → 14.10-11; 16.12-13 → 16.2-4) and accordingly as acts of punishment by God for evil committed against him by these kings (15.30; 16.13).

IV

People do not suffer evil caused only by their own deeds to which God reacts by bringing disaster upon them. They also do harm to themselves directly: hostile kings seek evil (1 Kgs 20.7) and commit it (1 Kgs 11.25 [text uncertain]; 2 Kgs 8.12), or a sovereign can ruin (רעה) himself due to his own drive for prestige and by misjudging the real limits of power (2 Kgs 14.10). Unlike the peoples surrounding Israel, especially in Mesopotamia, nowhere in the books of Kings and in the Old Testament as a whole is evil attributed to the influence of demonic creatures. In the popular religion of Israel there were doubtless demonistic conceptions, as is proved by the names of demonic beings, contained in the Old Testament.[17] But in the YHWH religion, reflected by the Old Testament texts, only traces remain. Creatures and phenomena originally belonging to the demonic sphere are subjugated to the power of YHWH or committed to his service.

---

15. Cf. U. Rüterswörden, 'Das Böse in der deuteronomischen Schultheologie', in T. Veijola (ed.), *Das Deuteronomium und seine Querbeziehungen* (Schriften der Finnischen Exegetischen Gesellschaft, 62; Helsinki: Finnische Exegetische Gesellschaft; Göttingen: Vandenhoeck & Ruprecht, 1996), 223–41 (esp. 236–37).

16. 'Ansteckungsherd', thus Fahlgren, *ṣᵉdākā*, 51 = *idem*, 'Die Gegensätze', 127 (above n. 7); cf. Rüterswörden, 'Das Böse', 228–29.

17. Cf. G. Wanke, 'Dämonen II. Altes Testament', *TRE* 8 (Berlin; New York: W. de Gruyter, 1981), 275–77, as well as the monumental work: K. van der Toorn, B. Becking and P.W. van der Horst (eds.), *Dictionary of Deities and Demons in the Bible* (Leiden: E.J. Brill; Grand Rapids; Cambridge: Eerdmans, 2nd edn, 1999).

The action of Elisha in reviving the dead boy (2 Kgs 4.34) is, according to Mesopotamian evidence, a magical ritual aimed at exorcizing noxious demons and stimulating vitality.[18] But before performing this rite, Elisha prays to God (v. 33b, doubtless an original part of the text). It is not the magical power of the wonder-healer, here even the wonder-reviver, that defeats death and brings back life. This is, however, not clearly expressed by the text, but indicated by the prayer that suggests authorization by Yhwh.

The spirit who according to 1 Kgs 22.21-22[19] offers himself as a lying spirit (רוח שקר), causing the prophets to utter a misleading prediction, is not a self-reliant being, but belongs to the divine council in heaven. He only replies to God's request in v. 20: 'Who shall deceive Ahab...?' His function as a lying spirit is the execution of a divine commission.[20] To be regarded in the same way are the evil spirit (רוח רעה) who induces Abimelech and the citizens of Shechem to their quarrel (Judg. 9.23), and the evil spirit who attacks and torments Saul (1 Sam. 16.14-16, 23; 18.10; 19.9). It is clearly expressed in all these cases that the spirit came from YHWH (1 Sam. 16.4: מאת יהוה; 16.15-16; 18.10: רוח אלהים רעה; 19.9: רוח יהוה רעה) and was sent out by him (Judg. 9.23). Hence, he is no more than a tool of doom employed by God himself. The same holds good for the 'destroyer' in Exod. 12.23 and even more with regard to the 'messenger' bringing the plague of 2 Sam. 24.17.[21]

A disastrous demonic power apart from, or opposed to, God never had a legitimate place in the Yahwistic religion. As a result, the possibility of defending oneself by magical rituals against misfortune supposed to be of demonic origin was not available to the people. Such actions may have survived in the popular faith, as shown by the allusions to apotropaic formulas and customs that are handed down. But in the more reflective faith that confessed the all-comprising power of YHWH, to them no space was left. Israel and the Israelites come face to face with God alone: 'Prepare to meet your God, Israel!' (Amos 4.12).

This was not only the concept of the prophets, but shared by the bearers of the tradition in the narrative passages within the books of Kings and later on by the Deuteronomistic redactors. Facing the disastrous invasion of the Aramaeans of

18. Cf. S. Daiches, 'Zu II. Kön. IV,34', *OLZ* 11 (1908), 492–93; and more recently B. Becking, *Een magisch ritueel in jahwistisch perspektief* (Utrechtse theologische reeks, 17; Utrecht: Faculteit der Godgeleerdheid, Rijksuniversiteit Utrecht, 1992). Among the commentaries cf., for instance, J. Gray, *I & II Kings* (OTL; London: SCM Press, 3rd edn, 1977), 498–99.

19. For this text cf. F. Lindström, *God and the Origin of Evil* (ConBOT, 21; Lund: C.W.K. Gleerup, 1983), 84–91.

20. 'Damit wird die Grenzaussage, daß JHWH-Propheten zu falschen Propheten werden und trotzdem dem Willen JHWHs entsprechend handeln, zur Möglichkeit' ('In this way the critical statement that the prophets of YHWH become false prophets and, nevertheless, act in accordance to the will of YHWH, becomes a possibility'). E. Noort, 'JHWH und das Böse', in *Prophets, Worship and Theodicy* (OTS, 23; Leiden: E.J. Brill, 1984), 120–36 (esp. 128).

21. Cf. W. H. Schmidt, 'Gott und Böses', *EvT* 52 (1992), 7–22 (esp. 17 with n. 37) = *idem*, *Vielfalt und Einheit alttestamentlichen Glaubens II* (Neukirchen–Vluyn: Neukirchener Verlag, 1995), 267–82 (esp. 277 with n. 37); W. Dietrich and C. Link, *Die dunklen Seiten Gottes*. II. *Allmacht und Ohnmacht* (Neukirchen–Vluyn: Neukirchener Verlag, 2000), 73–75.

Damascus who have arrived at Samaria and laid siege to the town (2 Kgs 6.24–7.20), the king of Israel[22] is at his wits' end, but by no means because of the superior strength of the hostile troops. Behind the military catastrophe he discerns a higher power at work: 'This is the disaster (הרעה) from YHWH. How shall I wait upon YHWH any more?' (6.33b). The king's hopeless despair is overcome by Elisha by means of a word of YHWH that predicts the restitution of normal life[23] and indicates the turning point of the distressing situation, the end of the siege and the retreat of the enemy (7.1). The continuation of the narrative reports how the word became true: as in the disaster (6.33), God is at work in the salvation. By a kind of divine terror (the term מהומה is not used, however) the Aramaeans were driven into flight (6.7, 28).

V

The fact that God is 'doing' (עשה) the mischief is never mentioned *expressis verbis* in the books of Kings.[24] But it is said that he has announced: that means he has planned the disaster (1 Kgs 22.23). More often it is stated that he is the one who brings (הביא) the mischief or has done so. Primarily the assertion is found in passages of the Deuteronomistic redaction. It is used as introductory formula for announcements of doom (1 Kgs 14.10, perhaps pre-Deuteronomistic; besides 1 Kgs 21.21; 2 Kgs 21.12; 22.16) in speeches, which are now put in the mouth of prophets: Ahijah of Shiloh, Elijah, prophets in general, Huldah. In prosaic form they follow the pattern of the prophetic word of doom: After the accusation, introduced by יען אשר (1 Kgs 14.7aß; 2 Kgs 21.11) or by יען alone (1 Kgs 21.20bß), follows the announcement, mostly beginning with לכן (1 Kgs 14.10; not in 21.21; לכן together with the messenger formula in 2 Kgs 21.12). In 2 Kgs 22.16-17 the redactors stick to the model in a less conventional way and place the announcement before the reference to guilt. In all these texts the phrase is frozen to a formula: הנני מביא רעה אל/על. This is obviously developed from pre-Deuteronomistic prophetic patterns, which do not yet show a stereotyped style and which originate in the Jeremiah tradition: Jer. 4.16; 17.18; 23.12.[25] In this respect again the Deuter-

---

22. According to the context of the books of Kings it refers to Joram, the last king of the Omri dynasty. His name, however, is not mentioned in the text. For several reasons, it has to be assumed that the tradition was linked to a king of the Jehu dynasty, perhaps Joash, and then was incorporated into the context at the wrong place. The Aramaean king Benhadad is the son of Hasael (cf. 2 Kgs 13.24). There is widespread agreement on that point. The (erroneous) identification of the Israelite king with Joram apparently caused some confusion to the text: vv. 31.32b introduce a kind of hostility between the king and Elisha, which is otherwise unknown to the text.

23. This is the reason for mentioning the price of food, referred to in 7.1.

24. The present phraseology is also rarely used outside the books of Kings, cf. H.-J. Stoebe, 'רעע', *THAT* II (above n. 4), 794–803 (esp. 800).

25. Most of the other examples in Jeremiah originate from the Deuteronomistic redaction of the book of Jeremiah: Jer. 6.19; 11.11, 23; 19.3, 15; 35.17; 36.31; 42.17; 44.2; 45.5. Cf. W. Thiel, *Die deuteronomistische Redaktion von Jeremia 1–25* (WMANT, 41; Neukirchen–Vluyn: Neukirchener Verlag, 1973); *idem, Die deuteronomistische Redaktion von Jeremia 26–45* (WMANT, 52; Neukirchen–Vluyn: Neukirchener Verlag, 1981). Jer. 49.37; 51.64; Ezek. 14.22 are of different origin.

onomists prove to be disciples of the prophets in language and theology, in particular as intellectual, but hardly physical, disciples of Jeremiah.

A special case is represented by 1 Kgs 9.9, which displays no introductory formula. The statement expresses no prediction of the future, but looks back to the doom (הביא רעה), which, having already occurred in the meantime, is now fictitiously placed in the narrative context of the time of Solomon. In this way the statement reveals the origin of the text as a whole within the exilic period. By means of a far-sighted admonition to Solomon, which actually is directed to their own contemporaries, the authors give an interpretation of the catastrophe of Judah, which has already come to pass. This is proved by the change of address from the second person singular to the second person plural in v. 6. Moreover, there are some Deuteronomistic texts, analogous in structure and very similar in vocabulary: Deut. 29.23-27 and Jer. 22.8-9 (on the structure cf. also Jer. 5.19; 9.11-15; 16.10-13). Considering these far-reaching agreements, we must assume that the texts reflect an important type of instruction, used by the Deuteronomistic circles of the exilic period. This instruction offers an answer to the question of the reasons for the disaster and interprets the catastrophe as a matter of punishment caused by disloyalty towards God and violation of the first commandment.[26]

Nowhere within the books of Kings is it stated that God repents (נחם ni.) of the disaster that he has planned or caused (contrary to the Deuteronomistic passages in Jer. 18.8; 26.3; 42.10, which are picked up in Jon. 3.10).[27] The root נחם and its derivates are not present in Kings. However, it can be stated that God postpones or moderates his decision to bring mischief. 1 Kgs 21.27-29 reports that God, after an act of penitence performed by Ahab, delays the calamity announced to the time of his son (v. 29). That is striking compared with the harsh condemnations and words of doom against Ahab expressed elsewhere (16.29-33; 21.19-22, 24, 25-26). In 2 Kgs 22.20 Josiah is assured that he will not see the forthcoming disaster. In spite of their peculiarities, these texts have much in common. As in 1 Kgs 21.27 acts of penitence are exercised by Josiah, too (v. 19, see especially כנע ni.). In their present form the statements correspond to the real course of events (with 1 Kgs 21.29 cf. 2 Kgs 9.16-26; with 2 Kgs 22.20 cf. 23.29-30). Only the end of Josiah in a military action is not taken into consideration.[28] We must assume that both texts are created or edited in accordance with the historical facts. 1 Kgs 21.27-29 had to explain the peaceful death of Ahab (22.40).[29] Verse 29 in its present form is a product of Deuteronomistic revision. Similarly the redactors have drawn the originally positive statement about Josiah nearer to the course of history by remodelling it (2 Kgs 22.19-20).[30]

---

26. Cf. Thiel, *Die deuteronomistische Redaktion von Jeremia 1–25*, 295–300.

27. Cf. J. Jeremias, *Die Reue Gottes* (BTSt, 31; Neukirchen–Vluyn: Neukirchener Verlag, 2nd edn, 1997).

28. How Josiah actually lost his life will probably remain a riddle for ever. At any case it did not happen בשלום.

29. The inconsistency with 22.34-38 is another problem.

30. More details in Thiel, 'Deuteronomistische Redaktionsarbeit' (above, n. 14), *Congress Volume Leuven*, 162–64 = *idem, Gelebte Geschichte*, 152–53.

All of these interferences in the tradition are based on the conviction that the God of Israel is planning and working mischief, but that at the same time he is also ready to reconsider his decision, and to delay, to moderate and even to remove the mischief. In this way God's sovereignty and freedom are preserved. The same God who is judge and mischief-maker is also the one who is prepared to forgive and remit punishment.

The punitive action of God is at work not only within the domain of national affairs, but in the more individual sphere of the family as well. In the secondary, but pre-Deuteronomistic, version of the tradition of the reviving of the son in 1 Kgs 17.17-24[31] the mother traces back the boy's death to her guilt (עָוֹן). She accuses Elijah of having brought her guilt to the attention of God by his presence in her house (v. 18). Elijah presents the facts before God in form of a question with accusatory connotations: 'O YHWH, my God, have you also brought calamity (רָעַע *hi.*) upon the widow, with whom I am sojourning, so as to bring death upon her son?' This sentence, written by a redactor who inserted 17.17-24 into the text,[32] refers to the broader context. The word 'also' (גַּם) shows that the author had in mind a wider circle of victims struck by the disaster, that is the Israelites, subjugated to the drought and its consequences (17.1-16). One single fate is picked out of this extensive catastrophe. But it is linked to the drought only slightly, by the context and by the word 'also' (גַּם). Originally, before it was connected to 17.1-16, the fate of the boy and his mother was an individual affair as in the case of 2 Kgs 4.8-37. God responds to the accusation of Elijah positively and in accordance with the request of Elijah causes the boy to revive (vv. 21-22).

VI

In the books of Kings the religious condemnation 'he did the evil in the eyes of Yhwh' attracts attention to a high degree. The phrase עָשָׂה הָרַע בְּעֵינֵי probably originates in the sphere of everyday life for which, however, only one example can be cited (1 Sam. 29.7). The opposite phrase עָשָׂה הַיָּשָׁר בְּעֵינֵי more often occurs in ordinary, non-theological contexts (Deut. 12.8; Judg. 17.6; 21.25; cf. Jer. 40.5).[33] עָשָׂה הָרַע בְּעֵינֵי יְהוָה is developed into a common theological pattern that appears in Deuteronomistic texts very frequently. As regards the books Deuteronomy–1 Samuel, it is related to Israel (Deut. 4.25; 9.18; 17.2; 31.29; 1 Sam. 12.17). The statement that Israel has done the evil in the sight of YHWH becomes a *leitmotif* within the Deuteronomistic layer of the book of Judges (Judg. 2.11; 3.7, 12; 4.1; 6.1; 10.6; 13.1). Throughout the books of Kings the statement serves as a criterion for judgement on the kings, generally placed within the introductory frame, but present in other Deuteronomistic elements of the text also. Similarly to the

31. The older version of the tradition is contained in the more extensive text of 2 Kgs 4.8-37.

32. A more detailed discussion is to be found in W. Thiel, *Könige. 2. Teilband. Lfg. 1* (BKAT, IX/2,1; Neukirchen–Vluyn: Neukirchener Verlag, 2000), 65–67.

33. Finally the verbs רָעַע, יָשַׁר and יָטַב and also the adjectives רַע, יָשָׁר and טוֹב are used in connection with בְּעֵינֵי, relating to people as well as relating to God.

shaping of the book of Judges, the accumulation of negative judgements puts the complete history of the northern kingdom under the sign of disaster.

In the phraseology of the framework the Deuteronomistic comments on the kings are combined with other data borrowed from the 'book of the chronicles (lit. "the events of the days")' or from other sources. These characterizations of kings are the Deuteronomists' own contribution to the introductory parts of the descriptions of royal government. They are theological assessments, for they expose the conduct of kings to divine judgement. Although they are shaped in a quite stereotyped manner, the comments do show certain modifications in their judgement. Without any exception the kings of the northern kingdom receive a negative attribution, for they all followed the 'sin of Jeroboam',[34] which means that they adhered to the statues of calves put up by Jeroboam I and to the sanctuaries of Bethel and Dan (1 Kgs 12.26-30). This, in the sight of the Deuteronomists, was a striking offence against the unique rank of the Jerusalem Temple and a case of idolatry. But there are also instances of qualifications of the harsh judgements against kings with regard to Joram, the son of Ahab, as well as Hoshea, the last king. Concerning Joram, his removal of the *massebah* of Baal is appreciated positively (2 Kgs 3.2). As regards Hoshea, reasons are lacking: Neither are we told in which way he committed evil, nor do we get any information why he should have been better than his predecessors (17.2). On the other side, Omri and Ahab are portrayed especially negatively. That he did evil, even worse than his precedessors, is stated only in connection with Ahab (1 Kgs 16.30-33), but not his father Omri who is characterized by the pre-Deuteronomistic data in the same way as the kings before him.[35]

The doing of evil provokes imitation and produces a string of fatal actions. In the books of Kings this is expressed in analogy to the book of Judges, but without the term 'continue' (יסף *hi.*). Here the disastrous influence of Jeroboam's sin (חטא *hi.*: 1 Kgs 14.16; 15.26, 30, 34; 16.19, 26; 22.53; 2 Kgs 3.3 etc.) and the guilt of other kings (Baasha: 1 Kgs 16.2; Baasha and Elah: 16.13; Ahab: 21.22; Manasseh: 2 Kgs 21.11, 16) is shown, by which they caused Israel and Judah to sin against God, so that king and people appear to be joined together in a kind of solidarity of addiction to guilt. Moreover, the sin of the northern rulers touches Judah by way of family bonds (2 Kgs 8.18, 26-27), or simply by the effect of bad examples (16.3-4). As a result, after the downfall of the northern kingdom a continuity of evildoing and bad conduct starts to develop in Judah also (21.2-6, 20; 23.32, 37; 24.9, 19). The only exception from this rule is King Josiah who is entirely positively qualified (22.2; 23.25). Because of the guilt accumulated by Judah for decades and centuries he was unable to stop the disaster (23.26-27) that put an end to the royal history of Judah.

---

34. Cf. J. Debus, *Die Sünde Jerobeams* (FRLANT, 93; Göttingen: Vandenhoeck & Ruprecht, 1967).

35. About Jeroboam I it is also said that he was worse than all who were before him (1 Kgs 14.9). But Jeroboam did not have any predecessors. Thus the introductory condemnation has obviously become a fixed formula.

In the presentation of the Judaean kings the Deuteronomists develop a modified kind of judgement, too. Only Hezekiah and Josiah are appreciated in an entirely positive way because of their reforming efforts over the cult (...עשׂה הישׁר: 2 Kgs 18.3-6; 22.2), and their superiority to all the other kings is clearly accentuated (18.5b; 22.25). Even King David, who in the eyes of the Deuteronomists was an exemplary king (1 Kgs 15.5), has been accused of blame in the affair of Uriah and Bathsheba. Though this story is told in a pre-Deuteronomistic tradition, it has been preserved within the Deuteronomistic history (2 Sam. 12.9). Those kings of Judah whose acting and conduct are commented on positively are criticized (except Hezekiah and Josiah) in a certain respect, mostly because of the existence of the 'high places' (במות), that is, the local sanctuaries, and because of the cult celebrated at these places (1 Kgs 15.14; 22.44; 2 Kgs 12.4; 14.4; 15.4, 35a). On Ahaz it is remarked that he 'did not do what was right in the eyes of YHWH' (2 Kgs 16.2b). In this case the term רע is avoided, but as the text continues (vv. 3-4), an enumeration of offences occurs which otherwise are described as 'bad' (רע: 2 Kgs 17.17; 21.6).

In connection with the negative judgements on the kings of Israel and Judah (1 Kgs 14.22; 2 Kgs 17.16-17; 21.9) the redactors characterize their conduct as 'evil, bad, ill' (רע). In most cases the charge refers to the offence against the first commandment: the disloyalty towards YHWH (שׁכח, עזב) and the worship of other gods. This accusation encompasses a wide variety, including the fabrication of idols (among others, the 'golden calves': 1 Kgs 14.9; 2 Kgs 17.16), acting according to the abominations of the nations (1 Kgs 14.24), the building of high places and the sacrifices offered upon them, the erection of altars for the hosts of heaven. The Deuteronomistic redactors took up some of this information from the 'book of chronicles (lit. "the events of the days")', for instance the building of the temple and altar of Baal and the erection of an Asherah in Samaria by Ahab (1 Kgs 16.30-31). The practices referred to in the accusation that some kings made their sons pass 'through the fire' (2 Kgs 16.3b; 21.6a; referring to Israel and children generally: 17.17a; to the abolition by Josiah: 23.10) also belong to the material handed down by tradition. The interpretation of this ritual is disputed. According to the Deuteronomistic redaction of the book of Jeremiah it was an act of burning children for Baal (Jer. 7.30-31; cf. 19.5; 32.35).[36]

Very rarely social offences are mentioned in connection with evildoing, thus for instance the crime of David against Uriah and Bathsheba (2 Sam. 12.9), already referred to above, or the spilling of innocent blood by Manasseh (2 Kgs 21.16). This social aspect is not completely passed over by the Deuteronomistic redactors. But it is extensively exceeded by the theological view, which was developed by the redactors in order to explain the doom inflicted upon Israel (2 Kgs 17*) and Judah: the failure towards the will of God (Deut. 31.29; 2 Sam. 12.9; 1 Kgs 11.6, 33; 2 Kgs 10.31; 17.16; 21.9, 22) and the striking offence against the first commandment and its implications.

---

36. Cf. Thiel, *Die deuteronomistische Redaktion von Jeremia 1–25* (above, n. 25), 129 and table on p. 131.

The Deuteronomistic redactors intend to show a way out of this involvement in guilt, which is still in process even after the punishment. The new perspective is made possible by the mercy and forgiveness of God (1 Kgs 8.30, 34, 36, 38, 50). The precondition for these is the turning back of the people to YHWH in repentance and prayer. The Deuteronomistic theologians put an invitation into the mouth of the prophets, which is an appeal to their own contemporaries: 'Turn back from your evil ways!' (2 Kgs 17.13).[37]

37. I wish to thank Peter Mommer, Henning Graf Reventlow and Andreas Scherer for correcting the English of my paper.

JEREMIAH 50–51 AND THE CONCEPT OF EVIL IN THE HEBREW BIBLE

Yair Hoffman

I

The entry 'evil' in a standard English dictionary[1] refers to two different aspects of this concept: moral-behavioral, on the one hand, and existential-physical, on the other. For the adjective we find: 'Bad, injurious, mischievous, worthless, morally bad, wicked; calamitous, troublous, sorrowful; unlucky, producing disastrous results; malicious, slanderous'. The noun 'evil' in the same entry is defined as 'An evil thing; that which injures or displeases, calamity, harm; sin, depravity, malignity'.

The same duality is reflected in modern Hebrew, which derives from biblical Hebrew. Thus, the root רעע is rendered in the BDB as 'evil' in its two aspects – 'ethical, evil, badness' and 'evil, distress, misery, injury, calamity'.[2] The same is attested also in some other biblical words within the immediate semantic field of רעע, such as עמל, אוֹן.

This duality could be found also in the French *mal* and the German *Böse*. Although perhaps less clear in German, Professor Wyrwa's study in this volume is nonetheless entitled (in German) 'Luther und Augustin über das Böse', with the title, as well as the whole study, patently referring to these two aspects of *Böse*.

It might have been very interesting to conduct a sociolinguistic research of whether all languages share this semantic feature, or whether it is typical only of monotheistic cultures in which divine justice is axiomatic. Such a seemingly obvious sociolinguistic study would have examined the possibility that the semantic duality of 'evil' is an application of the belief that the equation evil = sin necessarily leads to the equation evil = calamity, since evil in the sense of calamity is intuitively considered a punishment for evil in the moral sense.

I am not going to conduct such a semantic research, for two reasons. The first reason is that not being a sociolinguist, I am not qualified for such a task. This, in fact, makes any further reason unnecessary, but, nevertheless, I still want to mention a second one: such a study would have led the discussion astray to a narrow aspect of the problem of evil–theodicy in only one of its aspects: retribution,

---

1. *Cassell's English Dictionary*, completely revised and enlarged by A.L. Hayward and J.J. Sparkes (London: Cassell, 1971), 394.
2. F. Brown, S.R. Driver and C.A. Briggs, *Hebrew and English Dictionary of the Old Testament* (Oxford: Clarendon Press, 1966), 947–48.

namely, reward and punishment, and, mainly, the problem of the suffering right-eous and the prosperous wicked, which is not the subject of this volume.[3]

If I am not focusing on this aspect of evil, why mention it at all? Because it is still important, for our purposes in this paper, to mention the question of retribution in order to (a) differentiate it from my main subject and (b) nonetheless compre-hend it as an integral part of the more fundamental and provoking problem of Evil, namely, *its very existence* in our world. It is my intention to examine *whether the very existence of evil was considered a theological problem by the authors of the Hebrew Bible* [= HB] in which the issue of retribution has such crucial standing. One could wonder if this question is not superfluous, since, from a purely philoso-phical point of view, it seems improbable, even impossible, to think of divine retri-bution without viewing it in the general context of the existence of evil. However, not being a systematic philosophical book, the HB is free of philosophic exigencies, and one should avoid dismissing a priori the possibility of a biblical unawareness of the very existence of evil as a major theological question.

Along with its theological aspect, the topic of this paper also has a historical perspective. The very existence of evil is a dilemma that has troubled post-biblical, medieval and modern Judaism, as well as ancient, medieval and modern Christian-ity. In both cultures it has not only been the subject of theoretical debate, it also has had sociological implications, having been also a source of sectarianism.[4] Hence, in its historical aspect, the question would be: when did the existence of evil became a major theological problem within Judaic society? Was it so already in the biblical period, or only in the postbiblical era?

What is 'The Problem of Evil'? Why is the very existence of evil a theological problem? From among the many theologians, philosophers, and thinkers, believers and nonbelievers, ancients and moderns, who discussed the subject I have chosen to quote as a description of this problem a few lines from the work of Gottfried Wilhelm Leibniz. I consider his *Essais de Théodicée sur la Bonté de Dieu, la liberté de l'homme et l'origine du mal* published in 1710 one of the most interesting, sincere, and in a way courageous discussions of this subject. The quotations are from the English version[5] entitled *Essays on the Goodness of God, the Freedom of Man, and the Origin of Evil*.

For Leibniz, 'Evil may be taken metaphysically, physically and morally. *Meta-physical evil* consists in mere imperfection, *physical evil* in suffering, and *moral evil* in sin' (Section 21, 136).

Distinguishing between two classes of difficulties in relation to evil, he writes:

> The one kind springs from man's freedom, which appears incompatible with the divine nature… The other kind concerns the conduct of God, and seems to make him participate too much in the existence of evil…and this conduct appears con-

---

3. For this aspect, see the volume of the Second Bochum Symposium: H.G. Reventlow and Y. Hoffman (eds.), *Justice and Righteousness* (JSOTSup, 137; Sheffield: JSOT Press, 1992).

4. See: B. Nitzan, 'Evil and its Symbols in the Qumran Scrolls', below, 83–96.

5. G.W. Leibniz, *Theodicy: Essays on the Goodness of God, the Freedom of Man, and the Origin of Evil* (trans. E.M. Huggard; La Salle, IL: Open Court, 1985).

trary to the goodness, the holiness and the justice of God, since God co-operates in evil as well physical as moral… (Section 1, 123).

Referring to the first kind of difficulties, Leibniz writes the following:

freedom is opposed, to all appearance, by determination or certainty of any kind whatever

while

the foreknowledge of God renders all the future certain and determined… According to which it appears that man is compelled to do the good and evil that he does, and in consequence that he deserves thereof neither recompense nor chastisement (Section 2, 124).

As to the second class, he writes that since

all the reality and what is termed the substance of the act in sin itself is a production of God, since all creatures and all their actions derive from him… Whence one could infer not only that he is the physical cause of sin, but also that he [i.e., God] is its moral cause, since he acts with perfect freedom and does nothing without a complete knowledge of the thing and the consequences that it may have (Section 3, 124).

In short: God, the righteous, good God, is responsible for the existence of Evil – that is, sin, suffering, and wickedness, and this apparently annuls the moral justification for any divine retribution. Or, to quote a modern philosopher, J.L. Mackie:

In its simplest form the problem is this: God is omnipotent; God is wholly good; and yet evil exists. There seems to be some contradiction between these three propositions, so that if any two of them were true the third would be false. But at the same time all three are essential parts of most theological positions.[6]

Could the HB ignore such a profound theological dilemma? Of course, no one would expect it or even the immediate postbiblical literature – Jewish, sectarian, or Christian – to be as philosophically rigorous and meticulous as Leibniz, who was influenced by so many previous theologians and philosophers such as Saadiah Gaon, Maimonides, St Augustine and St Thomas Aquinas, to mention only a few.[7] But even on a very embryonic level, did the problem of evil, other than the aspect of divine retribution, really bother the biblical authors or their Israelite society?

6.   The quotation is taken from: J.L. Mackie, 'Evil and Omnipotence', in Michael L. Peterson (ed.), *The Problem of Evil: Selected Readings* (Indiana: University of Notre Dame Press, 1992), 89–101.

7.   For a theological-philosophical discussion of the problem, including its suggested solution from the perspective of a modern Christian theologian, see: John Hick, *Evil and the God of Love* (New York: Harper & Row, 2nd edn, 1978). An excerpt from this work appears in Peterson, *Problem of Evil*, 215–30. For a modern Orthodox Jewish perspective of the issue, see: David Birnbaum, *God and Evil* (Hoboken, NJ: Ktav, 1989). Both books contain up-to-date bibliographies on the subject.

II

Most biblical scholars have not touched upon this question, and when theological issues related to evil are discussed, divine retribution is the main, if not the only, topic that arises. One recent exception is Jon D. Levenson's *Creation and the Persistence of Evil*.[8] According to Levenson, not only was the HB aware of the problematic nature of the existence of Evil, but the struggle with this problem determined much of the Israelite ethos and cult in the biblical period. The presupposition for this view is that the main message of the creation story in Genesis 1 is that God *did not* create the world *ex nihilo,* but only subjugated the Chaos, the already existing primordial creatures, namely, the powers of Evil. Yet, as implied in other biblical texts:

> God's assumption of mastery is not complete and…the demise of the dark forces in opposition to him lies in the uncertain future.[9]

Because of the 'Survival of Chaos after the Victory of God' (the title of Chapter 2), 'God's ordering of reality is irresistible, but not constant or inevitable'.[10] Sometimes, therefore, YHWH is failing to exercise his magisterial powers over the world, so that those who revere him suffer the taunts and jeers of those who do not.[11]

Hence, the conclusion asserting 'The Vitality of Evil and the Fragility of Creation'[12] (the title of Chapter 4). If this was the belief, some action should possibly have been taken to ensure that the powers of evil would never again arise, which, claims Levenson, is the role of the cult. The most important cultic event in Israel, albeit not mentioned in the Bible, was the New Year Festival that lasted seven days, and was celebrated either once a year during Sukkot (the Feast of Booths) or Pesach (Passover), or perhaps even twice a year, during both Sukkot and Pesach. In this (or these) Festival(s) of the New Year (*ro'sh ha-shanah*), which included *yom ha-kippurim* – the Day of Atonement – just like in the Babylonian *akitu,* which was held on the fifth day of Nisan, the powers of evil were annually suppressed through the cult.[13] Hence the 'Conclusion: Chaos Neutralized in Cult' (the title of Chapter 9).[14]

Levenson's view leads to the conclusion that the authors of the HB and Israelite society as a whole were well aware of the existence of evil as a comprehensive theological problem, and therefore tried to solve it theoretically as well as practically. It is not my intention here to examine each of Levenson's assertions, with several of which I quite agree, only to argue that the following points in his presentation, which are crucial to this discussion, are at least somewhat unsound, if not

8. Jon D. Levenson, *Creation and the Persistence of Evil: The Jewish Drama of Divine Omnipotence* (San Francisco: Harper & Row, 1988).

9. Levenson, *Creation*, 7.

10. Levenson, *Creation*, 15.

11. Levenson, *Creation*, 21. Levenson infers this from Isa. 51.7-8, 12-13; 54.7-10.

12. Levenson, *Creation*, 47.

13. Levenson, *Creation*, 66–77.

14. Levenson, *Creation*, 121.

unproven: (a) the creation story presupposes that God did not create the primordial creatures; (b) those creatures, the embodiment of evil, were believed not to have been utterly annihilated; (c) a New Year Festival, that focused on helping Yhwh to fight the powers of Evil, existed, and played a central role in the Israelite cult.

Assuming that these claims are, at the least, not free from doubt, the question remains: was the very existence of evil a theological problem in biblical Israel?

III

I presume that, cognitively, the conceptualization of evil as a distinct entity is a prerequisite for awareness of the existence of evil as a comprehensive theological problem. It is impossible to discern how such a conceptualization arises within each individual culture; definitely not necessarily and automatically by a mere aggregation of a great amount of suffering, evildoers, cruel tyrants and calamities. The question to be asked, then, is to what extent one can identify in the HB alertness to the existence of evil as a major theological problem. I argue that a systematic review would show that the conceptualization of evil as a distinct entity is missing in most books of the HB. Since an exhaustive examination of this assertion cannot be conducted here, I shall demonstrate it by some examples. Take, for instance, the book of Job, wherein suffering, calamities, moral evil and wickedness are in sharp focus: nowhere in this book is there a comprehensive concept of evil as such, let alone awareness of a theological 'problem of evil'. Thus, for example, there is no conceptualization of evil in Job's pious words:

גם את הטוב נקבל מאת האלהים ואת הרע לא נקבל

'Shall we accept good from God and not accept adversity' (Job 2.10: 'adversity', as translated by the NKJV, and not 'evil', as rendered, for example, by Driver and Gray,[15] is the more accurate meaning of רע here). When cursing the day of his birth and sharply questioning God:

למה יתן לעמל אור וחיים למרי נפש

'Why does He give light to the sufferer and life to the bitter of soul?' (3.20) Job does not imply at all that he considers the very existence of evil a theological problem. Similarly, when he describes God's destructive activity, for instance:

המעתיק הרים ולא ידעו	אשר הפכם באפו
המרגיז ארץ ממקומה	ועמודיה יתפלצון
האמר לחרס ולא יזרח	ובעד כוכבים יחתום

'He shakes the earth out of its place, and its pillars tremble; He commands the sun and it does not rise; He seals off the stars' (9.5-7) reference is made to the omnipotence of God, His unlimited power, but not to His mastery of evil. The book of Job does not consider the very existence in the world of tribulation and suffering a

15. S.R. Driver and G.B. Gray, *The Book of Job* (ICC; Edinburgh: T. & T. Clark, 1921), 26.

theological problem, nor does it question the existence of the wicked; it only challenges the system according to which suffering is distributed among people.

Similarly, when the Psalmist describes the corruption of the wicked, he does not conceptualize all the aspects of evil into one abstract entity 'evil', he rather denounces the activity of the wicked, for example:

אלה פיהו מלא ומרמות ותך   תחת לשונו עמל ואון
ישב במארב חצרים   במסתרים יהרג נקי...
יארב במסתר כאריה בסכה   יארב לחטוף עני

'His mouth is full of cursing and deceit and oppression; under his tongue is trouble and iniquity. He sits in the lurking places of the villages; in the secret places he murders the innocent... He lies in wait secretly, as a lion in his den; he lies in wait to catch the poor' (Ps. 10.7-9).

With no conceptualization of evil, nor could there be any symbol of it, which is, indeed, to my mind, the case in the HB. Let us examine, for example, חשך (darkness), which has been claimed ever since to be a symbol of the powers of evil. It is definitely not a symbol of evil in the first chapter of Genesis, where God's separation between light and darkness, thus creating the day and the night, could not possibly be comprehended as a separation between good and evil, unless one adopts purely allegorical exegeses. The same notion, namely, that the darkness of the night is a constructive, necessary part of the world's order, is expressed in the creation hymn Psalm 104.[16] Even in texts in which darkness (חשך) is clearly a metaphor for something negative, it is not a symbol of evil power, but of distress, suffering, as opposed to אור (light), as a metaphor of salvation and well-being. For example,

העם ההולכים בחשך ראו אור גדול יושבי בארץ צלמות אור
נגה עליהם

'The people who walked in darkness have seen a great light; those who dwelt in the land of blackness upon them a light has shined' (Isa. 9.2 [MT 9.1]). Weinfeld, when trying to demonstrate that darkness,[17] not necessarily the word חושך, is a biblical symbol of the activity of the powers of evil, points to Gen. 32.27, where the mysterious איש with whom Jacob struggled pleaded שלחני כי בקע השחר ('let me go for the dawn is breaking'); this is hardly a proof that darkness symbolized evil. Such are also Weinfeld's other examples: Exod. 4.24; 12.13, 23; Job 3.4.

Do the primordial creatures תנין לויתן, function in the Bible as symbols of existential, presently active, evil? We cannot discuss here all the relevant texts needed to justify our negative answer to this question, but the following are two examples, once again taken from the book of Job. When Job asks הים אני (אסתנין כי תשם עלי משמר ('am I a sea or a sea monster that thou settest watch

---

16. For a discussion of Ps. 104 and its polemic against the Egyptian *Hymn to Athon*, see: Y. Hoffman, 'Psalm 104', in M. Fishbane and E. Tov (eds.), *Sha'arei Talmon* (Winona Lake, IN: Eisenbrauns, 1992), 13*–24*.

17. M. Weinfeld, 'God the Creator in Gen. 1 and in the Prophecy of Second Isaiah', *Tarbiz* 37 (1968), 105–132 (122) (Hebrew).

over me?', Job 7.12), he does not claim his innocence, his not being an evil power, but rather his utmost incompetence to endanger God as those creatures did in the primordial, not at the present, time. When God in His answer describes the בהמות (40.15) and ל ו י תן (40.25), He mentions them as monsters in the real world; there is no allusion there to their morality, and they by no means symbolize powers of evil.

IV

Against this background we shall now turn to the prophecy on Babylon (Jer. 50.1–51.58).

In the MT, this prophecy concludes the collection of Prophecies Against Foreign Nations (= PAFN) in the book of Jeremiah. The location at the end of the book is indicative of the importance the editor attributed to this prophecy, which is thus portrayed as the pinnacle of Jeremiah's prophecies, their logical and theological conclusion.[18] Although its main subject is the destruction of Babylon (77 verses out of 104) two other motifs are scattered throughout the prophecy in what seems to be quite a disorderly sequence: moral justification of the destruction (about 19 verses),[19] and proclamations of the salvation of Israel (8 verses),[20] presented as the direct and inevitable consequence of the destruction of Babylon.

Such a triple linkage between the destruction of a foreign nation, moral justification of this destruction, and the salvation of Israel is untypical not only of the genre of PAFN, but is also exceptional among Jeremiah's PAFN. There are only two short isolated verses in other PAFN of Jeremiah that contain explicit moral reasoning for the calamity that would befall the foreign nation: 49.1 (Ammon) and 49.16 (Edom). In all the other prophecies (Egypt: 46.1-12, 13-26; the Philistines: ch. 47; Moab: ch. 48; Damascus: 49.23-27; Kedar: 49.28-33; Elam: 49.35-39) this motif does not exist. The same holds true for the motif of Israel's salvation, that is presented as a consequence of the foreign nation's calamity: it comes only in one of Jeremiah's PAFN, and in a very brief hemistich – the prophecy on Ammon: 49.2b.

This literary and ideological uniqueness of the prophecy on Babylon, as well as its patch-like quality, is probably a reflection of the gradual process of its compilation. And, indeed, most modern commentators have correctly realized that the prophecy is a compilation of various literary units reflecting different periods of time.[21] This understanding naturally has a bearing on the dating of the prophecy: if

---

18. In the Septuagint the entire collection of PAFN in the book of Jeremiah is placed after 25.13a. Within this collection, the prophecy on Babylon is arranged after the prophecies on Elam and Egypt (chs. 27–28), in quite a nonstrategic position – neither the beginning nor the end of the collection.

19. 50.14b, 15b, 17-18, 24b, 28b; 51.5-10, 24, 33-36, 49-51, 56c.

20. 50.4-7, 19-20, 33-34.

21. 'Diese ist kein Stück von geschlossenem Aufbau, sondern zerfällt in eine Reihe von Einzelabschnitten' (W. Rudolph, *Jeremia* [HAT I.12; Tübingen: J.C.B. Mohr (Paul Siebeck), 1968], 297). See also J. Bright, *Jeremiah* (AB; Garden City , NY : Doubleday, 1965), 359–60;

it is not an original literary cast, then each of its units should be dated separately, and only then could we speak of the last stage of compilation. Be that as it may, most scholars have concluded that at least the final stage of the prophecy is post-Jeremianic. Holladay rightly draws a line between earlier and more recent commentators: 'earlier commentators regard the sequence [i.e., the whole prophecy] as a single oracle', and they all 'rejected the possibility that any of this material is authentic'.[22] On the other hand, recent scholars tend to consider the prophecy as a compilation of various layers, and most of them share the view that at least some of these units are Jeremianic.

I share this latter view. The authentic sections of the prophecy are attested by many typically Jeremianic stylistic and lexicographical features;[23] the amalgamated appearance of the prophecy, the absence of a clear logical sequence, the many redundancies, and the various literary styles are indications of its multi-stratification. Another feature that reveals the eclectic character of the prophecy is the large number of duplicates of previous sections in the book of Jeremiah: 50.30 = 49.26; 50.31 = 21.14; 50.40 = 49.18 ; 50.41-43 = 6.22-24; 50.44–46 =49.19-21; 51.15-19 = 10.12-16.

It is only natural that this eclectic, mosaic character, as well as the historical importance of the subjects in the prophecy, made of it a kind of a literary 'sponge' that easily absorbs insertions, interpretations and accretions. This nature of the prophecy tempted later editors to act accordingly, updating it by adding to the already eclectic compilation more material that was recent and relevant to their time. Thus, although the main parts of the prophecy are Jeremianic, and are therefore dated before the collapse of the Babylonian empire in 538 BCE, its final version is later.[24] In a way, the prophecy could be considered a kind of a 'rolling corpus', to use McKane's definition of the entire book of Jeremiah.[25] As such, it is very hazardous to date each of its literary components, mainly because most of them were intended to appear Jeremianic, and therefore had to conceal their actual late historical background. It is less perilous, however, to speculate about the time the 'rolling' of this corpus ended, and I would hazard as late a date as the second

R.P. Carroll, *Jeremiah* (OTL; London: SCM Press, 1986), 814–54; W. McKane, *Jeremiah* (2 vols.; ICC; Edinburgh: T. & T. Clark, 1986, 1996), II, 1249–1350; W. Holladay, *Jeremiah* (2 vols.; Hermeneia; Minneapolis: Fortress Press, 1989), 402–15; Y. Hoffman, *Jeremiah* (Mikra Leyisrael; Jerusalem and Tel Aviv: Am Oved and Magnes Press, 2001), II, 826–31 (Hebrew). Y. Kaufmann is one of the few scholars who deny any non-Jeremianic material in the prophecy. See: Y. Kaufmann, *Toledot Ha-Emumah ha-Yisraelit* (Jerusalem and Tel Aviv: Dvir, 1960), 422–23 (Hebrew).

22. Holladay, *Jeremiah*, II, 401. He refers to Duhm, Cornill and Giesebrecht. Some of these commentators propose a very late date for the prophecy, such as the Hasmonean period. See, e.g., B. Duhm, *Jeremia* (KHAT; Tübingen–Leipzig: J.C.B. Mohr [Paul Siebeck], 1901), XX, 360; D.C.H. Cornill, *Das Buch Jeremia* (Leipzig: Tauchnitz, 1905), 495.

23. See, e.g., the typical Jeremianic expressions: חתת\\לכד (50.2; 51.56); ש י ם (שו ם) לשמה (50.2; 51.56); מבלי (מאי ן) י ושב (50.3); the structure a + b יחדו (50.4); שבר גדול (50.22); עת פקדתם (50.27); ישם וי שרק על כל מכותי ה (50.13; cf. 19.8; 49.17).

24. This view is advocated by Holladay, *Jeremiah*, II, 402–13. However, I do not fully agree with his identification of the supposed expansions (50.17b-18, 30, 39-40, 41-43, 44-46; 51.11abb, 15-19, 28, 45, 46, 47, 48a, 57). See Hoffman, *Jeremiah*, II, 826–31.

25. McKane, *Jeremiah*, I, p. L.

century BCE, a date that could be inferred from a comparison between Jer. 51.46 and Dan. 11.5-4, 44.

Jeremiah 51.46	Daniel 11.4-5, 44
בשמועה הנשמעת בארץ ובא	ולא לאחריתו ולא כמלו
בשנה השמועה ואחריו בשנה	אשר משל ...
וחמס בארץ ומשל על־משל	ומשל ממשל ...ושמעות יבלה

| for the **rumour** that shall be heard in the land and **after** him a **rumour** shall come [one] year and after a year the **rumour** and evil in the land and a **ruler on ruler** | and not to his **posterity** nor according to his **rule** which he **ruled**... and he shall **rule** strongly his **rule**... and **rumours** shall trouble him |

The proximity between these two passages indicates an intentional dependency between them. If so, then the question to be asked is, which of them was influenced by the other: did the second-century author of Daniel use an ancient Jeremianic prophecy? Or, perhaps, he inserted into the old prophecy of Jeremiah some of his own words, in order to strengthen the ties between his 'prophetic' book and the prophecies of the prestigious Jeremiah? I suggest that the second option is more plausible.

The enigmatic nature of Jer. 51.46 corresponds with the mysterious style of the book of Daniel, rather than with Jeremiah's prophecies, or even with the non-Jeremianic sections in the prophecy on Babylon. This supports the assumption that the words in Jer. 51.46 were influenced by Daniel and inserted into the Babylon prophecy, and not vice versa.[26] The absence of this verse (in fact, of the whole section, Jer. 51.44b-49a) from LXX also supports the option of a very late addition.[27] The purpose of this very late insertion was probably to reinforce the connection between the two books and to suggest that Daniel's prophecy is the truthful divine interpretation of Jeremiah's. The same tendency is clearly reflected also in the 70 years prophecy (Dan. 9.24-27), but here the Jeremianic text (Jer. 25.11-12; 29.10) definitely antedates Daniel.

Returning now to the multilayer character of the prophecy on Babylon, it should be noted that the imperial city of Babylon outlived, not only the Persian, but also the Hellenistic occupation. Although it declined following Alexander the Great's death, it was not until the Parthian occupation in 124 BCE that the city finally lost its importance. Babylon's lengthy existence as a metropolis contradicted Jeremiah's prophecy, the transmission of which therefore called for theological and historical interpretations and adaptations.

---

26. The connection between these verses in the books of Jeremiah and Daniel was already mentioned by Rashi and R. David Kimhi in their interpretation to Jer. 51.46, although they obviously did not consider the possibility of a later insertion in the book of Jeremiah.

27. 51.46 is considered a later expansion also by Holladay, *Jeremiah*, II, 411, but he does not relate it to Daniel, and does not date the verse.

This was a dialectic process: on the one hand, it reflected the changing views about the city of Babylon; while on the other, its internal dynamics created new concepts of Babylon. The victories of Cyrus in the first half of the sixth century probably reinforced the expectations of a complete demolition of the city, and some vivid descriptions of its expected downfall were added to the prophecy. Such accretions created a monstrous picture of Babylon and its annihilation. Yet the city unceasingly prospered, thus endangering Jeremiah's reputation as a great and true prophet. Meanwhile, Persia became the oppressor, at least in the eyes of some factions within Israelite society, and a destruction of Babylon was no longer so relevant to the people's expectations. This led to typological interpretations, which caused the appellation 'Babylon' to lose its concrete historical meaning, and to symbolically represent any oppressive empire. At this stage, some additional sections were included in the prophecy, and solidified the two originally marginal motifs in the prophecy – the justification of Babylon's destruction and the salvation of Israel. Such are, I would suggest, sections in which the defeat of Babylon is presented as a defeat of its idols, with whom the city as a whole is identified: 50.2, 38; 51.15-19, 44, 52. In other passages Babylon was described as an entity that purposely and maliciously sinned against God and haughtily contended with Him: כי ביהה התגרית ('because you have set yourself up against YHWH', 50.24); כי אל יהוהח זדה ('for it has shown arrogance to YHWH', 50.29). Therefore, the battle against Babylon is considered נקמת יהוהח ('the vengeance of YHWH', 50.15, 28; 51.6, 36). The defeat of Babylon is described in terms related to cosmic upheavals and the primordial struggle (50.40; 51.34, 36, 41). Babylon is called by a variety of derogatory names referring to the moral as well as the physical aspects of evil. Moreover, the latter refer both to the destruction wreaked by Babylon on other nations and to the destruction that will befall Babylon as a consequence of its evil behavior. Thus Babylon is called: פטיש כל הארץ ('hammer of the whole earth', 50.23), which will eventually 'hammer' (= destroy) itself, too.

In a literarily independent and impressive poem Babylon is called מפּיץ (51.20) – 'a mace, a destroyer':

מפץ אתה לי כלי מלחמה
ונפצתי בך גוים והשחתי בך ממלכות
ונפצתי בך סוס ורכבו
ונפצתי בך רכב ורכבו
ונפצתי בך בחור ובתולה
ונפצתי בך רעה ועדרו
ונפצתי בך אכר וצמדו
ונפצתי בך פחות וסגגים

In translating this poem one faces the problem of rendering the anaphoric preposition בך, because here it has more than one import. It bears an instrumental meaning, 'with you',[28] as well as a locative meaning, 'inside you', which also contains the negative nuance of 'against you', expressing or implying an act of hostility:

---

28. BDB, 89, III.

Gen. 16.12…בו כל ויד בכל ידו.[29] How to retain in translation the same word, without losing its multiple nuances? None of the translations that I examined overcomes this problem, and they all render this preposition 'with you',[30] thus missing an important theological aspect of the poem. Without any literary pretensions as a translator, I used a slash to express this duality, and rendered בך as 'with/in':[31]

> You are my destroyer, weapon of war
> And I will destroy with/in you nations,
> And I will demolish with/in you kingdoms
> And I will destroy with/in you the horse and its rider
> And I will destroy with/in you a chariot and its charioteer
> And I will destroy with/in you man and women
> And I will destroy with/in you old and young
> And I will destroy with/in you the young man and the maiden
> And I will destroy with/in you the shepherd and his flock
> And I will destroy with/in you a farmer and his pair (of oxen)
> And I will destroy with/in you the governors and rulers.

Unfortunately, I found it utterly impossible to render in translation the double meaning of the verb נפצתי, which may be understood as being either in the past or future tense, or (after all, this is poetry), having both meanings.

Another harsh label for Babylon is הר המשחית, הר שריפה ('destroying mountain', 'mountain of burning', 51.25), that also refers to moral and physical aspects of Babylon's wickedness.

The most theologically loaded disparaging epithet for Babylon is the abstract noun זדון, 50.31 (LXX: ὑβρίστριαν [27.31], Targum רשיעא מלכא ('the wicked king'); מלכא ושיעאם: 'O you most proud'; Cornill:[32] 'Vermessenheit'; Rudolph:[33] 'Frechheit'; Holladay:[34] 'Sir Arrogance').[35] This epithet is explained by the *talion* words בכלאשו עשו לה כי אל יהוה זדה אל קדוש ישראל

---

29. BDB, 89, II.

30. Such is the translation of: KJV; NKJV; Carroll, *Jeremiah*; Holladay, *Jeremiah*; the Good News Bible waives the repetition of the verb and the preposition, but also translates only the instrumental aspect 'I used you to crash…to shatter…', etc. So, too, Luther: 'mit dir'; the same instrumental aspect, and only it, is reflected in the Spanish translation 'por tu medio' (*La Santa Biblia, Antigua Version de Casiodoro de Reina* [*1569*] *Revisada por Cipriano de Valera* [*1602*] *otras revisiones: 1862;1909; 1960*).

31. I have chosen to use the word 'destroyer' for מפץ, in order to use the same root for the repeated verb ונפצתי.

32. Cornill, *Jeremia*, 504.

33. Rudolph , *Jeremia*, 304.

34. Holladay, *Jeremiah*, II, 394.

35. As a noun זדון is typical of Jeremiah's PAFN. It is used in the prophecy against Edom (49.16) and twice in our prophecy (50.30; 31). The only other prophetic use of this abstract noun is Ob. 3, which is a doublet of Jer. 49.16. The two other appearances of the noun in the HB are Prov. 11.2; 21.24. As an adverb (בזדון) it is used in Dt. 17.12; 18.22; Prov. 13.10. In the Mishnah and the Talmud זדון is a technical term referring to sins that were done purposely, not by mistake (שוגג).

שמלו להכפעלה ככל (50.29), thus interpreting all the evils of Babylon – moral and physical – as one total act against God.

זדון here definitely has a stronger and more comprehensive meaning than it has in 1 Sam. 17.28 אני ידעתי את זדנך ואת רע לבבך which is the only verse in which זדון is interpreted by parallel wording, 'wicked heart'. The closest to Jeremiah's זדון is Ezek. 7.10:

הנה היום הנה באה יצאה הצפרה צץ המטה פרח הזדון

('Behold the day, behold, it is come: the morning is gone forth; the rod hath blossomed, <u>pride [wickedness??]</u> hath budded'), where it has an abstract meaning, though not one as comprehensive as in the prophecy on Babylon.

All these features reflect a clear intention of turning Babylon into a symbol of a universal, a-historical evil power. This propensity is probably the best explanation for the use of the mysterious non-historical names for Babylon לב קמי, ששך (Jer. 51.1, 41) written in a cryptic writing known as אתבי יש.[36]

The transformation of 'Babylon' from a historical entity into an unhistorical symbol, the metamorphosis of its historical defeat into a global a-historical annihilation of God's adversary, is both the cause and the consequence of the universal scope of Jeremiah 50–51.[37] No wonder that with the addition of the 'salvation to Israel' motif, it also acquired an eschatological interpretation, and the war against 'Babylon' was identified with the day of YHWH'S war, as clearly proven by משא בבל 'the burden of Babylon' (Isa. 13), that associates the battle against Babylon with the Day of the Lord (Isa. 13.9) and the punishment of the wicked universe (vv. 11-13).

Is Babylon then considered in Jeremiah 50–51 to be an embodiment of metaphysical, transcendental evil? No, it is not. It is a typology of the phenomenon of evil empires, but not of Evil. Thus, in the words הנני אליך זדון ('I am against you, Sidon', 50.31) it is not Evil as a distinguishable, autonomic power that is meant. The very need of authors and editors to paint the historical Babylon with this semi-historical typology attests to the lack of an abstract concept of Evil. Hence, there could not possibly be, and indeed there is no, awareness in the prophecy of the existence of evil as a theological problem. Yet, the desire to depict Babylon as an a-historical evil power, as reflected by the use of the abstract noun זדון for Babylon, is an important step towards the conceptualization of evil, which I argue to be a cognitive precondition to an awareness of the theological problem of evil. If so, then this, like other developments in Israelite thought, was motivated, not by abstract philosophical contemplations and discussion, as in the

---

36. א = ח, ב = ש, etc.: ששך is attested also in Jer. 25.26. The LXX to 51.1 has: *Xaldaious* for קמי לב, while ששך is represented in the LXX neither in 25.26 nor in 51.41. This latter datum is probably an indication of ששך being a rather late insertion to the MT. Carroll suspects the reading of קמי לב as a cipher for כשדים, but even he has to admit that ששך is a cipher for בבל. He suggests that the use of cipher 'may be no more than a vestige of incantatory practices directed against the enemy'. See: Carroll, *Jeremiah*, 838. If he is right, then the fact that this trick is employed only against Babylon testifies to the special status of 'Babylon' when these verses were written.

37. See, e.g., 50.22-25; 51.7-9, 20, 27-28, 41, 48.

Hellenistic culture, but, like other biblical ideas, by the typical biblical preoccupation with the meaning of history, both national and universal. This line of thought includes prophecies such as Isaiah 13 (on Babylon); 34 and 63.1-6 (on Edom), as well as some national psalms, such as Psalm 83, in which names of historical nations (Edom, Moab, etc.) should probably be interpreted typologically.

V

Was the absence of the conceptualization of evil in the prophecy on Babylon and in other biblical texts just a literary, internal biblical phenomenon, or did it indicate the common beliefs in Israelite society? An adequate answer to this question requires a study of various extra- and post-biblical sources, mainly some early Apocrypha, in which there is a clear awareness of the problem of evil, with consequent attempts to resolve it. I believe that those books have preserved concepts, which already existed in the biblical period, but nevertheless did not find their way into the Bible. The book of *Jubilees*, for example: it mentions the spirits of evil and impurity, headed by משטמה – Satan, the archangel of animosity and hatred – and Noah implores God not to let him and his evil angels rule the sons of the righteous people (*Jub.* 10.1-12). משטמה, not God, is responsible for morally questionable events, such as the order to slaughter Isaac (17.16), or the hardening of Pharaoh's heart (48.12-19). All these examples indicate that the existence of evil was considered a theological problem, which called for solution. I believe that such an awareness was not a complete innovation of late Persian–early Hellenistic Judaism, and its roots – only roots, not yet fruits – could be found already in the early post-exilic period, as echoed in some—though very few indeed – biblical texts. One prominent example is of course Isa. 45.5-7:

אני יהוה ואין עוד יוצר אור ובורא חשך	וזולתי אין אלהים... עשה שלום ובורא רע אני יהוה עשה כל אלה
I form light and create darkness I the Lord do all these things	I am the Lord and there is none else I make peace and create evil'

Since one cannot ignore the argumentative tone of this divine declaration and its proximity to the existence of evil, one has to decide with whom the prophet is arguing. Levenson,[38] following Weinfeld,[39] assumes that this maxim is in direct controversy with the creation story in Genesis 1. However, this assumption depends on many other unconvincing presuppositions regarding the Day of Atonement, the ancient Israelite calendar, and more. I therefore do not share the view that

---

38. Levenson, *Creation*, 123–25. He affirms the idea that the Creation story in Gen. 1 assumes that the darkness was primordial, and was not created by God; 'Light, which is God's first creation, does not [even – Y.H.] banish darkness. Rather it alternates with it' (123). On the other hand, according to Isa. 45.5-7 'No longer is darkness primordial and merely accommodated through creation into a new order of things' (125).

39. Weinfeld, 'God the Creator'. For a similar view, see: C. Westermann, *Isaiah 40–66* (OTL; London: SCM Press, 1969), 162.

Isa. 45.5-7 really challenges Genesis 1.[40] This polemic seems to me more of an antidote, an immunization, against non-Israelite, perhaps Zoroastrian dualistic beliefs, to which the exiles in Babylon might have been exposed.[41] In this case, then, one can deduce that within the Israelite society the conceptualization of evil was more prevalent than its direct manifestation in the biblical text. Be that as it may, these words of Deutero-Isaiah attest to his own comprehensive concept of evil. They do not, however, attest to an awareness of the existence of evil as a theological problem, neither by the prophet nor by his audience. Otherwise, we would have expected the prophet to confront the problematic logical consequence of his own dictum.[42] Yet, such a dictum, when read at a later period upon a different cultural background, could certainly produce an awareness of the problem of evil.

A different example is the role of the Satan in the story of Job, chs. 1–2. The Satan (not a proper name שׂטן, unlike משׂטמה in *Jubilees*) here is a sadistic, cruel, suspicious angel, who, with God's permission, does, indeed, possess much power, but he is by no means a counterpart to God, and this character's role in the story is not to solve the problem of evil in a Gnostic, dualistic manner. So, too, the Satan in Zech. 3.1-3.

Deutero-Isaiah and the Satan texts might well be only the tip of the iceberg of a popular belief in the existence of a nearly omnipotent evil power, which may be evidence of awareness of the problem of evil.

VI

We have distinguished three different streams flowing towards the river of the conceptualization of evil: Jeremiah's prophecy on Babylon, which represents the historical aspect of Israelite monotheistic thought; Deutero-Isaiah's maxim, which represents the more theoretical, reflective way of Israelite monotheistic thought, and the figure of the Satan, representing popular, perhaps even folkloristic and syncretistic trends within Israelite culture. A fourth stream whose flow determined to a great extent the Jewish culture of the post-biblical period was the Hellenistic culture. It was not until the confluence of these four streams that the problem of evil as a major theological issue, which called for theological solutions, emerged within the Jewish society of the last centuries BCE.

40. See: Y. Hoffman, 'The First Creation Story', in H.G. Reventlow and Y. Hoffman (eds.), *Creation in Jewish and Christian Tradition* (JSOTSup, 319; Sheffield: Sheffield Academic Press, 2002), 45–66.

41. See, e.g., B. Duhm, *Das Buch Jesaia* (HAT; Göttingen: Vandenhoeck & Ruprecht, 4th edn. 1922), 315; M. Buber, *Torat Haneviim* (Tel Aviv: Bialik Institute and Dvir, 1950), 195 (Hebrew).

42. Thomas Aquinas claims that these words do not raise any theological problem, since 'it would seem that the supreme God is the cause of Evil. For it is said', and here he quotes Isa. 45.5, 7 and Amos 3.6 אם תהיה רעה בעיר ויהוה לא עשה 'if there is calamity in a city, will not the Lord have done it?' But, he continues, 'These passages refer to the evil of penalty, and not to the evil of fault'. See: Thomas Aquinas, *Summa theologiae* (Cambridge: Cambridge University Press, 1964), I, Question 49, article 2.

Why was this such a late development in Israelite thought? How are we to explain the biblical inattentiveness to the comprehensive problem of evil over such a long period? Notwithstanding the rather pretentious character of such questions, and the intrinsic extremely speculative quality of their answers, I hesitantly express my reflections on this question. I suggest that it was the unqualified reign of theodicy in its narrow sense, namely, just divine retribution, that shunted this potential problem aside, and marginalized it in biblical thought. Indeed, from a purely logical point of view, even the certainty of divine justice does not offer a satisfactory thorough solution to the problem of evil, yet it reduces the dilemma to the degree of existential irrelevance. For if a society is overwhelmingly convinced that physical evil, that is, calamity, is always a justified consequence of a moral, behavioral evil, then the existence of evil is cognitively relegated to the degree of a mere abstract philosophical and theoretical problem, and problems of this sort can hardly achieve a central status that determines the cultural and political agenda of a society. Thus, the more precarious the concept of retribution became (as in books such as Job, Ecclesiastes) the wider the entranceway for the cognitive penetration of the comprehensive problem of evil. Only then did it come to be a powerful theological, political and sociological impetus, capable of creating new faiths, new sects and new religions.

THE WRATH AT GOD IN THE BOOK OF LAMENTATIONS

Edward L. Greenstein

Until fairly recently, the theology of the book of Lamentations has tended to be assimilated to the theology of Deuteronomy, the Deuteronomist, and the classical prophets.[1] The destruction of Jerusalem by the Babylonians in 586 BCE, and the ravages that it entailed, are explained theologically in the following, fairly paradigmatic way. The people of Jerusalem and Judah sinned against God; God became angry; as a consequence, God vented God's anger on Jerusalem and Judah. The venting of God's anger is, therefore, in this perspective, a just punishment for Judah's sins. 'Israel's admission of personal iniquity signifies the absolute exoneration of God.'[2]

Scattered throughout Lamentations are various admissions or allusions to the Judeans' transgressions. Take, for example, this admission from the words of a personified Zion in 1.18: 'YHWH is just, for I have violated his word'; or this from 5.16: 'The crown has fallen off our heads; woe is upon us, for we have sinned.' In fact, however, such references to Judah's trespasses are, in spite of the attention

---

1. Cf., e.g., C. Westermann, 'The Theological Significance of Lamentations in Prior Research', in *idem, Lamentations: Issues and Interpretation* (trans. C. Muenchow; Minneapolis: Fortress Press, 1994), 76–81; J. Hunter, *Faces of a Lamenting City: The Development and Coherence of the Book of Lamentations* (Frankfurt: Lang, 1996), 73–83; J. Renkema, 'Theology', in *idem, Lamentations* (trans. B. Doyle; Historical Commentary on the Old Testament; Leuven: Peeters, 1998), 58–62. For examples of such an assimilation, or of a tendency in that direction, see, e.g., N.K. Gottwald, 'The Key to the Theology of Lamentations', in *idem, Studies in the Book of Lamentations* (SBT, 14; Chicago: Allenson, 1954), 47–62; H.-J. Kraus, *Klagelieder (Threni)* (BKAT; Neukirchen–Vluyn: Neukirchener Verlag, 2nd edn, 1960), 15–18; B. Albrektson, 'The Background and Origin of the Theology of Lamentations', in *idem, Studies in the Text and Theology of the Book of Lamentations* (Studia Theologica Lundensia, 21; Lund: C.W.K. Gleerup, 1963), 214–39; R.K. Harrison, *Jeremiah and Lamentations* (TOTC; Leicester and Downers Grove, IL: Inter-Varsity, 1973), 200–203 and *passim*; S.P. Re'emi, 'The Theology of Hope: A Commentary on the Book of Lamentations', in R. Martin-Achard and S.P. Re'emi, *God's People in Crisis: Amos and Lamentations* (International Theological Commentary; Edinburgh: Handsel Press; Grand Rapids, MI: Eerdmans, 1984), 73–134 (76, 92–93 and *passim*); R.B. Salters, *Jonah and Lamentations* (OTG; Sheffield: Sheffield Academic Press, 1994), esp. 114–16; A. Berlin, *Lamentations: A Commentary* (OTL; Louisville, KY, and London: Westminster John Knox, 2002), 18–19. Note the revision of N.K. Gottwald, 'The Book of Lamentations Reconsidered', in *idem, The Hebrew Bible in Its Social World and in Ours* (SBLSS; Atlanta: Scholars Press, 1993), 165–173 (171).

2. J. Krašovec, 'The Source of Hope in the Book of Lamentations', *VT* 42 (1992), 223–33 (228).

they have drawn from many interpreters,[3] few and far between. There are a couple of small concentrations of them in ch. 3, the middle chapter of the book, but such references are scarce in chs. 1 and 5 and virtually absent from chs. 2 and 4.

Far more typical of the book as a whole, with respect both to content and tone, is a passage such as this from 2.11:

> My eyes are spent of tears, my insides churn;
> My heart (lit., liver)[4] is poured onto the ground
> Over the ruin of the daughter of my people,
> As children and infants faint (from hunger) in the streets
> of the city.

Any analysis of the meaning of Lamentations must take proper account, on the one hand, of the diversity of perspectives that one finds in the full text,[5] and, on the other, of the fact that the first, last, and overall impression one gets as a reader is that the book is not primarily a theological explanation of the catastrophe that befell Jerusalem in 586 BCE but a lament that expresses suffering, grief, and anger. Thus Gottwald, in his important 1954 study, already observes: 'Lamentations reveals a deep sense of desertion by men and God and it confronts suffering as a threat to God's purposes in history and to the very life of faith.'[6] Westermann, too, emphasizes the pervasive character of the book as a lament and as an accusation, pointed at the God who has wrought such disaster.[7]

Yet Gottwald tries to ease the degree of suffering that is expressed in Lamentations by attributing to it a 'basic purpose', which is to master 'pain and doubt in the interests of faith'.[8] This notion of controlling pain for the sake of holding on to one's faith is, of course, a superimposed message that finds no articulation anywhere in the book. Westermann, too, who asks us to appreciate the lamentational character of the book,[9] and who endeavors to interpret the thrust of the book

---

3.   E.g., M. Weiss, 'On the Book of Lamentations', מורי ישורון 3 (1966), 11–16 (14–15) (Hebrew); Krašovec, 'Source of Hope'; D.R. Hillers, *Lamentations* (AB; Doubleday: New York, 2nd edn, 1992), 5–6; Hunter, *Faces of a Lamenting City*, 113–20 and *passim*.

4.   It is emotion, rather than bile, that is spilled; see, e.g., I. Provan, *Lamentations* (NCB; London: Pickering; Grand Rapids, MI: Eerdmans, 1991), 70–71. For the word-pair לב־כבד in so-called 'synonymous' parallelism, in Hebrew, Ugaritic, and in Akkadian (*libbu-kabattu*), see, e.g., S.E. Loewenstamm, 'Notes on the Origin of Some Biblical Figures of Speech', in J.M. Grintz and J. Liver (eds.), *Studies in the Bible Presented to Professor M.H. Segal* (Jerusalem: Kiryat Sepher, 1964), 180–87 (182–83) (Hebrew); M. Dahood, 'Ugaritic-Hebrew Parallel Pairs', in L.R. Fisher (ed.), *Ras Shamra Parallels*, 1 (AnOr, 49; Rome: Pontifical Biblical Institute, 1972), 323–24.

5.   Cf. recently A. Cooper, 'The Message of Lamentations', *JANESCU* 28 (2001), 1–18. Gottwald ('Lamentations Reconsidered', 171–72) suggests a socio-historical reason for the diversity of theological response in Lamentations: in the wake of the national devastation, various 'streams of tradition were commingling and clashing'. For a psychological approach to the inconsistencies, attributing them to different stages in the grieving process, see P. Joyce, 'Lamentations and the Grief Process: A Psychological Reading', *BibInt* 1 (1993), 304–20.

6.   Gottwald, 'Key to the Theology', 52; cf., e.g., Renkema, *Lamentations*, 62–63.

7.   Westermann, 'The Theological Significance of Lamentations', in *idem*, *Lamentations*, 221–35.

8.   Gottwald, 'Key to the Theology', 52.

9.   Westermann, *Lamentations*, 78.

without ch. 3 – which he regards as a later addition[10] – cannot escape the charms of conventional theology. The wrath of God that saturates the book will, Westermann argues, subside. In the end, 'God's anger is punishment for people who admit their guilt.'[11]

A turning-point in the scholarly reading of Lamentations occurs in the 1983 article by Moore, who contends that Lamentations is less about theology than it is about suffering.[12] In its wake follow the commentaries of Provan and Renkema,[13] from the 1990s, and even more boldly, in the last decade, the articles and books of two younger American scholars, Dobbs-Allsopp and Linafelt.[14]

For Dobbs-Allsopp, 'there is genuine acknowledgment of sin in Lamentations, but that is not the whole story, or even the most important part of the story'.[15] Lamentations presents a vast human tragedy, 'reveal[ing] the dark side of existence'.[16] Considering the anger at God for bringing on the tragedy, the book, for Dobbs-Allsopp, deals in a profound way with the problem of evil.[17] I shall be returning to this point below.

Linafelt criticizes earlier scholars who insisted on locating the 'core meaning' of Lamentations in its middle chapter, by arguing that the middle is the center, and the center is the core.[18] This seemingly literary hermeneutic is, of course, an entirely arbitrary strategy. One could argue just as well that what is most important is what is reiterated most often, in one form or another; or that what is most important is what is presented at the end of the work, as a climax or conclusion of sorts. Linafelt attributes scholars' focus on Lamentations 3 to three chief factors:

Chapter 3 opens with the words אני הגבר ראה עני 'I am the man who has seen affliction'. Chapters 1 and 2 had featured the poet or elegist, who maintains a low profile by trying not to identify or call attention to himself, as well as a female

---

10. Westermann, *Lamentations*, 221, 227, 229.

11. Westermann, *Lamentations*, 224; cf., e.g., Renkema, *Lamentations*, 64–65.

12. M.S. Moore, 'Human Suffering in Lamentations', *RB* 90 (1983), 534–55.

13. Provan, *Lamentations*; Renkema, *Lamentations*.

14. F .W. Dobbs-Allsopp, *Weep, O Daughter of Zion: A Study of the City-Lament Genre in the Hebrew Bible* (BibOr, 44; Rome: Pontifical Biblical Institute, 1993); *idem*, 'Tragedy, Tradition, and Theology in the Book of Lamentations', *JSOT* 74 (1997), 29–60; *idem*, *Lamentations* (Interpretation; Louisville, KY: John Knox Press, 2002); T. Linafelt, 'Zion's Cause: The Presentation of Pain in the Book of Lamentations', in *idem* (ed.), *Strange Fire: Reading the Bible after the Holocaust* (New York: New York University Press, 2000), 267–79; *idem*, *Surviving Lamentations: Catastrophe, Lament, and Protest in the Afterlife of a Biblical Book* (Chicago and London: University of Chicago Press, 2000). See also K.M. O'Connor, *The Book of Lamentations: Introduction, Commentary, and Reflections* (New Interpreter's Bible, 6; Nashville: Abingdon Press, 2001), 1011–72.

15. Dobbs-Allsopp, 'Tragedy', 37.

16. Dobbs-Allsopp, 'Tragedy', 30.

17. Dobbs-Allsopp, 'Tragedy', 34.

18. For such a contention, see, e.g., J.H. Tigay, 'Lamentations, Book of', *EncJud* (1971), X, 1372 (1368–75); B. Johnson, 'Form and Message in Lamentations', *ZAW* 97 (1985), 58–73 (esp. 60). For the critique, see Linafelt, 'Zion's Cause', 268; *idem*, *Surviving Lamentations*, 5–6 with 151 n. 4, where a number of other offending commentators are also enumerated; cf. also Renkema, *Lamentations*, 69–70.

speaker, representing Jerusalem or Zion. Chapters 1 and 2 take a strongly emotional tone, while ch. 3 tends to be more reflective. Scholars, claims Linafelt, favor the more masculine and deliberate speaker of ch. 3 over the more feminine and emotional speakers of chs. 1 and 2.

Most scholars, most of whom are Christian, display a 'Christian bias toward the suffering man' of ch. 3, in whom they see a figure of Christ.

Linafelt finds in most biblical scholars, especially those of earlier generations, an inclination to interpret Lamentations as a means of 'reconciling' with God rather than as a vehicle for 'confronting' God.[19]

Linafelt himself prefers to set theological explanation aside and to seize upon chs. 1 and 2 in particular as 'presentations' of the suffering that has been witnessed and endured by survivors of the catastrophe. Making use of studies of the literature and testimony produced by survivors of the *Shoah* and other atrocities by Des Pres and others,[20] Linafelt examines the rhetoric of Lamentations 1 and 2 as survival literature.[21] The objective of the survivor, as opposed to the theologian, is 'to [bear] witness to pain rather than to find meaning in it'.[22] One of Des Pres's chief findings is that for the survivor, pain is not meaningful but senseless. Linafelt does not go to that extreme in interpreting Lamentations. He acknowledges that the personified Jerusalem and the poet both admit to some degree of guiltiness. But the question is: how much? And is the punishment – the divine reaction – proportionate and fair?

I will take as the point of departure for my own discussion of divine anger and the anger directed at God in Lamentations a comment made by Herion in an encyclopedia entry on the 'Wrath of God'. Herion observes: 'God's righteousness is…called into question when divine punishment seems disproportionate [as in the case of] Job… God's wrath can be viewed negatively, especially when it appears to be excessively cruel (Lam. 2:4) or unjust (Num. 16:22; Job 19:11).'[23] Divine wrath functions in ancient Near Eastern literature and beyond as a mechanism for initiating a process that leads to placating a deity.[24] The underlying assumption is that bad things happen as a result of a god responding to opposition to the divine will. People seeking to alleviate their suffering perform acts that in their understanding will mollify the angry deity. Divine anger in this scheme can be a just response to injustice. But it can also be excessive and irrational.[25] The book of Lamentations, in its very last words (5.22b), leaves the reader with the

19.   Linafelt, 'Zion's Cause', 268; cf. *Surviving Lamentations*, 5–13.

20.   T. Des Pres, *The Survivor: An Anatomy of Life in the Death Camps* (New York: Oxford University Press, 1976).

21.   Linafelt, *Surviving Lamentations*, 35–61.

22.   Linafelt, 'Zion's Cause', 274; *Surviving Lamentations*, 43–44.

23.   G.A. Herion, 'Wrath of God (Old Testament)', *ABD* (New York: Doubleday, 1992), VI, 991–96 (995); cf. Renkema, *Lamentations*, 158. For the comparison of Lamentations to Job, in this respect, see Dobbs-Allsopp, *Weep, O Daughter of Zion*, 55.

24.   See P. Considine, 'The Theme of Divine Wrath in Ancient Mediterranean Literature', *Studi micenei ed egeo-anatolici* 8 (1969), 85–159. For divine anger in the Mesopotamian laments, see, e.g., P.W. Ferris, Jr, *The Genre of Communal Lament in the Bible and the Ancient Near East* (SBLDS, 127; Atlanta: Scholars Press, 1992), 54–55.

25.   Considine, 'Divine Wrath', 114–15.

following address to God: קָצַפְתָּ עָלֵינוּ עַד־מְאֹד 'You have shown us your anger exceedingly.'[26] Some theologians simply posit that in the Bible in general, and even in Lamentations, divine wrath is no more than a temporary posture calculated to impose divine justice.[27] The question we will explore is whether God's wrath at Judah has gone too far, has crossed the line.[28]

Lamentations articulates a great deal of anger. Is this anger a medium by which the divine wrath is perceived as an overreaction and thereby provokes the poet's angry response? In what follows I shall examine a number of rhetorical strategies by which the wrath at God finds expression in Lamentations. If it turns out that the anger is multifarious and intense, then it may be concluded that the articulation of anger against the deity is a means of calling into question the justice of God's punishment and the justness of God.

One way by which the unfairness of God's punishment is suggested is in the way that the sin that is supposed to justify the punishment is described. As is well known, the lamentation over the destruction of a city and temple is a genre that is represented in full form in the ancient Near East in our book of Lamentations, on the one hand, and in (at least) six different laments that were composed in Sumerian after the fall of the Ur III dynasty at the turn of the second millennium BCE, on the other.[29] Whether there is any direct or indirect relationship between the biblical book and the much older Sumerian laments is a question that need not detain us here.[30] What is of interest to the present discussion is that, from a comparative

26. The verse as a whole is ambiguous, mainly on account of the opaque function of the opening particles כִּי אִם. Is the verse to be read indicatively, interrogatively, or as a conditional fragment? See T. Linafelt, 'The Refusal of a Conclusion in the Book of Lamentations', *JBL* 120 (2001), 340–43.

27. See, e.g., Westermann, *Lamentations*, 224; cf. A.J. Heschel, 'The Meaning and Mystery of Wrath', in *idem, The Prophets* (Philadelphia: Jewish Publication Society, 1962), 279–98.

28. Cf., e.g., O'Connor, *Lamentations*, 1038, 1043.

29. S.N. Kramer, *Lamentation over the Destruction of Ur* (Assyriological Studies, 12; Chicago: University of Chicago Press, 1940); M.W. Green, 'The Eridu Lament', *JCS* 30 (1978), 127–67; *idem,* 'The Uruk Lament', *JAOS* 104 (1984), 253–79; P. Michalowski, *The Lamentation over the Destruction of Sumer and Ur* (Winona Lake, IN: Eisenbrauns, 1989); S. Tinney, *The Nippur Lament* (Philadelphia: S.N. Kramer Fund, 1996). The sixth lament, over Ekimar, is not yet published; see, e.g., Michalowski, *Lamentation*, 5; Ferris, *Genre*, 24. For a survey, see W.W. Hallo, 'Lamentations and Prayers in Sumer and Akkad', in J.M. Sasson (ed.), *Civilizations of the Ancient Near East* (New York: Charles Scribner's Sons, 1995), III, 1871–81.

30. See, e.g., T.F. McDaniel, 'The Alleged Sumerian Influence upon Lamentations', *VT* 18 (1968), 198–209; W.C. Gwaltney, Jr, 'The Biblical Book of Lamentations in the Context of Near Eastern Literature', in W.W. Hallo *et al.* (eds.), *Scripture in Context II: More Essays on the Comparative Method* (Winona Lake, IN: Eisenbrauns, 1983), 191–211; Hillers, *Lamentations*, 32–39; Ferris, *Genre;* Dobbs-Allsopp, *Weep, O Daughter of Zion; idem,* 'Darwinism, Genre Theory, and City Laments', *JAOS* 120 (2000), 625–30; *idem, Lamentations*, 6–12; Westermann, 'The Dirge and a Lament over the Death of a City', in *idem, Lamentations*, 1–23; M. Emmendörffer, *Der ferne Gott: Eine Untersuchung der alttestamentlichen Volksklagelieder vor dem Hintergrund der mesopotamischen Literatur* (Forschungen zum Alten Testament, 21; Tübingen: Mohr Siebeck, 1998), esp. 290–95; E.L. Greenstein, 'Lament over the Destruction of City and Temple in Early Israelite Literature', in Z. Talshir *et al.* (eds), *Homage to Shmuel: Studies in the World of the Bible*

perspective, the Sumerian laments do not blame the destruction of Mesopotamian cities and temples by the high gods, An and Enlil, on the sins of the people. The gods have their own reasons or no reason at all. Some scholars contrast the biblical book of Lamentations with the Sumerian laments, underscoring the point that in the Bible, the devastation is a divine response to human sin.[31]

The point should not be overstated, however; for while sin is occasionally mentioned in Lamentations, that sin is never specified. Gottwald speaks for many in writing: 'As to the specific sins which constitute the great iniquity of Judah, we are surprised that more detail is not given.'[32] Consider, by contrast, an ancient Sumerian text that is closely akin to the laments over the destruction of cities – the Curse of Agade (or Akkad).[33] In this text, Enlil destroys Akkad because a prominent king of Akkad, Naram-Sin, had looted the temple of Enlil in Nippur.[34] The crime is explicit. In the biblical book of Lamentations, it is vague.

Contrast with the nondescript mention of sin in Lamentations the vivid detail in which the depredations of the catastrophe are described: the siege of the city; the famine and disease that kill many and lead the survivors to desperate acts.[35] The divine fire that burns temple and city in Lamentations, just as it does in the Sumerian laments, has no clear justification, almost as in the Sumerian laments. One may come to view the confession of sin in Lamentations as *pro forma* and of little real significance. In Lam. 5.16, as was said above, the people of Judah say, 'we have sinned' (חָטָאנוּ); but in the same chapter (v. 7) that claim would seem to be undermined:

(S. Ahituv Festschrift; Beersheva: Ben-Gurion University of the Negev Press; Jerusalem: Bialik Institute, 2001), 88–97 (Hebrew); Berlin, 'The Mesopotamian Context', in *idem*, *Lamentations*, 26–30.

31. E.g., Gwaltney, 'Biblical Book', 207–209; Ferris, *Genre*, 139–41; Dobbs-Allsopp, *Lamentations*, 9, 29.

32. Gottwald, 'The Theology of Doom', in *idem*, *Studies*, 63–89 (68); cf., e.g., Tigay, 'Lamentations', 1369; Alan Mintz, 'The Rhetoric of Lamentations', in *idem*, *Hurban: Responses to Catastrophe in Hebrew Literature* (New York: Columbia University Press, 1984), 17–48 (25); Provan, *Lamentations*, 23; Renkema, *Lamentations*, 476; F.W. Dobbs-Allsopp, 'Rethinking Historical Criticism', *BibInt* 7 (1999), 235–71 (255–57 n. 68). Harrison (*Jeremiah and Lamentations*, 209), in an obvious – and strained – attempt to identify some sin, reads Baal worship into the imagery of Lam. 1.8-9; cf. X.H.T. Pham, *Mourning in the Ancient Near East and the Hebrew Bible* (JSOTSup, 30; Sheffield: Sheffield Academic Press, 1999), 75.

33. J.S. Cooper, *The Curse of Agade* (Baltimore and London: The Johns Hopkins University Press, 1983). For the literary relationship between this text and the book of Lamentations, see Dobbs-Allsopp, *Weep, O Daughter of Zion*.

34. Cf. Dobbs-Allsopp, *Weep, O Daughter of Zion*, 53.

35. Cf., e.g., Moore, 'Human Suffering', 546–55; Dobbs-Allsopp, *Lamentations*, 41–44. The ravages of the siege are delineated in I. Eph'al, *Siege and its Ancient Near Eastern Manifestations* (Jerusalem: Magnes Press, 1996) (Hebrew); for a broader survey of military sieges and their effects, see P.B. Kern, *Ancient Siege Warfare* (Bloomington and Indianapolis: Indiana University Press, 1999); for an analysis of the depredations of the siege of Jerusalem as they developed in stages, and as described in Lamentations, see the excellent study of my student: Y. Miodovnik, 'The Motif of Famine in the Book of Lamentations and its Notional Setting in the Light of Ancient Near Eastern Literature' (MA thesis, Tel Aviv University, 2001) (Hebrew).

אבתינו חטאו ואינם ואנחנו עונותיהם סבלנו
נאבהיינוחטאוואינם ואנחנו עוחיהם

Our ancestors sinned and are no more;
And we – we have had to suffer their punishments!

The point of this verse bears emphasizing. Here the people do not confess their own sins. They call attention to their suffering. This suffering they do indeed interpret as a punishment for transgressions against God. But not for their own transgressions, but rather as punishments that should rightly have been imposed on their predecessors (cf. Jer. 31.28-29; Ezek. 18.2). We may wonder, therefore, how sincere is the people's admission of guilt in 5.16 and elsewhere?[36]

We may get a clearer answer to our question by considering yet another rhetorical strategy for expressing the sense that God has been unfair. In ch. 1, as is often noted, Zion is personified as a woman. The female image takes on several guises.[37] Here, she is a widow whose lovers abandon her, refusing to offer her comfort for her losses (vv. 1-2).[38] There she is a woman harassed, whose nakedness has been seen, leading to her dishonor (vv. 3, 8). Twice her sins are referred to (vv. 5, 8), but nowhere is her sin identified, and in no place is she described as an unfaithful woman or a whore.[39] The city can explain her afflictions only as punishment for her rebelliousness; but this is at most a subjective impression, not unlike the guilt that is sometimes felt by a battered woman, as O'Connor has suggested.[40]

In any event, whatever guilt the female figure may have to bear, it is severely mitigated in our text by two factors. For one thing, the image of a widow that is drawn at the beginning of the chapter, does not imply guilt.[41] It is not the widow's

36. Krašovec ('Source of Hope', 228) reads 5.7 and 5.16 in their textual sequence and seeks to derive the contrary interpretation: first, the people acknowledge their ancestors' sins, and then they come to acknowledge their own. It must be admitted by any reader of Lamentations, however, that the verses of each chapter do not conform to a chronological, or a progressive thematic, arrangement; cf., e.g., Harrison, *Jeremiah and Lamentations*, 202–203; B.S. Childs, *Introduction to the Old Testament as Scripture* (Philadelphia: Fortress, 1979), 594. Hillers (*Lamentations,* 164) compares Jer. 3.25, where the speakers explicitly confess their own sins in addition to those of their ancestors. In Lam. 5.7, however, there is a marked contrast; here, the speakers do not express their own sins; cf. Emmendörffer, *Der ferne Gott,* 70–71; O'Connor, *Lamentations,* 1069. Berlin (*Lamentations,* 120–21) discusses alternative interpretations of Lam. 5.7 but opts to minimize the significance of the term 'ancestors'. In any event, the bottom line for her is similar to the one developed here: the concern is less with sin than with suffering.

37. Cf., e.g., M. Biddle, 'The Figure of Lady Jerusalem: Identification, Deification, and Personification of Cities in the Ancient Near East', in K.L. Younger, Jr, *et al.* (eds.), *Scripture in Context 4: The Biblical Canon in Comparative Perspective* (Lewiston, NY: Edwin Mellen Press, 1991), 173–94.

38. For the precise interpretation of 'widow' in this context, see C. Cohen, 'The "Widowed" City', *JANESCU* 5 (*The Gaster Festschrift*; 1973), 75–81.

39. Cf. N.C. Lee, *The Singers of Lamentations: Cities under Siege, from Ur to Jerusalem to Sarajevo* (Biblical Interpretation, 60; Leiden: E.J. Brill, 2002), 85.

40. K.M. O'Connor, 'Lamentations', in C.A. Newsom and S.H. Ringe (eds.), *The Women's Bible Commentary* (London: SPCK; Louisville, KY: Westminster/John Knox Press Press, 1992), 178–82 (180); idem, *Lamentations,* 1032–33.

41. O'Connor, *Lamentations,* 1032–33; N. Graetz, 'Jerusalem the Widow', *Shofar* 17.2 (Winter

fault that her husband has died. For another thing, as Dobbs-Allsopp has remarked, just at the points where the reader might begin to frown with disapproval on the victimized woman, she is given voice – and her voice presents her situation with force and pathos.[42] While others may treat the woman as 'unclean' and shamed,[43] the reader sees her tears and hears her cries and empathizes with her.

The images of destruction that comprise the bulk of the book also produce empathy for the victims of the catastrophe – rather than for the God who has perpetrated it. A perusal of the depredations that are described reveals that several of them appear to be anticipated both in the curses that accompany the covenant laws in the Torah, in Leviticus 26 and Deuteronomy 28, and in the rebukes and indictments that are found are in the prophetic literature.[44] Some interpreters have, accordingly, drawn the conclusion that the destruction is the fulfillment of the covenant threats and the prophetic warnings.[45]

One can hardly deny the logic of this argument. However, one needs also to consider which of the covenant curses receives the most vivid realization in Lamentations. Of all the covenant curses of Leviticus and Deuteronomy that are reflected in the horrific descriptions of Lamentations, the one that most stands out is that of compassionate women driven by the starvation of the siege to cook their own children for food.[46] The image defines the grotesque: a monstrous borderline phenomenon that we would ordinarily suppress or deny.[47] This curse, which has a precedent in the elaborate vassal (or succession) treaty of Esarhaddon,[48] but not in other series of curses from the Neo-Assyrian period,[49] occurs both in Lev. 26.29-30

1999), 16–24. It is also not a woman's fault that she menstruates, as is implied by Lam. 1.9; see O'Connor, *Lamentations*, 1030. Lee (*Singers,* 104–107) attempts to resolve the problem by interpreting נִדָּה in Lam. 1.8 not as 'menstruant' but as 'wanderer', with a secondary meaning of defiled by rape.

42.   Dobbs-Allsopp, 'Rethinking Historical Criticism', 255–57 n. 68; *idem, Lamentations*, 64–65.

43.   Cf., e.g., S.M. Olyan, 'Honor, Shame, and Covenant Relations in Ancient Israel and its Environment', *JBL* 115 (1996), 201–18 (215–17).

44.   D.R. Hillers, *Treaty-Curses and the Old Testament Prophets* (BibOr, 16; Rome: Pontifical Biblical Institute, 1964).

45.   E.g., Albrektson, 'Background and Origin', 231–37; Harrison, *Jeremiah and Lamentations*, 218, 220, 235; G.H. Cohn, *Studies in the Five Scrolls: The Scroll of Lamentations* (Jerusalem: Ministry of Education, 1975), 52–56 (Hebrew); Re'emi, 'Theology of Hope', 122; Hillers, *Lamentations*, 148; Berlin, *Lamentations*, 21–22.

46.   Cf., e.g., E. S. Gerstenberger, *Psalms, Part 2, and Lamentations* (FOTL, 15; Grand Rapids, MI: Eerdmans, 2001), 498.

47.   Cf., e.g., W. Yates, 'An Introduction to the Grotesque', in J.L. Adams and W. Yates (eds.), *The Grotesque in Art and Literature: Theological Reflections* (Grand Rapids, MI: Eerdmans, 1997), 1–68.

48.   For Esarhaddon's vassal (or succession) treaty §69, see: S. Parpola and K. Watanabe, *Neo-Assyrian Treaties and Loyalty Oaths* (State Archives of Assyria, 2; Helsinki: Helsinki University Press, 1988), 52. Cf. Hillers, *Treaty-Curses*, 62–63.

49.   The curses that one finds in the bilingual (Assyrian–Aramaic) Tell Fekheriyeh inscription and in the eighth-century BCE Aramaic inscriptions from Sefire and Bukan, for example, parallel

and in Deut. 28.53-57. It is adumbrated in the prophets as well.[50] The great biblical Hebrew philologist Arnold Ehrlich remarks that it is the most terrible curse he has ever read of.[51] Twice the curse is described as reality in Lamentations (2.20; 4.10).[52] The terrible extreme that is delineated is rendered even more pathetic as it comes on top of other passages that describe the shriveled breasts that can no longer suckle the infants and the dying of children in the city (2.11-12, 19; 4.2-4). The starvation and cannibalization of the children is, as Dobbs-Allsopp says, the very 'paradigm […] of innocent suffering'.[53]

Johnson seeks to preserve a veneer of divine justice here by interpreting the starvation of the besieged to the point of cannibalism as measure-for-measure punishment for the Judeans' sin of offering up their children in a pagan ritual, the Molech rite.[54] I would respond to Johnson with two points. First, the sin is indeed reported by some of the prophets, but it is nowhere cited in Lamentations. Second, what justice is there in punishing the sins of the parents by causing their children to suffer and die (verses like Exod. 20.5 etc. notwithstanding)?[55] Rather, one may find in Lamentations' focus on the cannibalization of the children a case of divine wrath gone to the extreme – a terrible excess of 'justice', which is no justice at all. Gottwald observes that the accusation of God for perpetrating such an atrocity would be blasphemy were it not for 'the brutality of the circumstances it describes'.[56] The nefarious nexus between the afflictions of God and the suffering of the children is conveyed by an irony of language. The divine acts are repeatedly

the somewhat milder biblical curses of food scarcity that one finds in Lev. 26.26 and Deut. 28.38-39; see A. Millard, 'Hadad-Yith'i', in W.W. Hallo and K.L. Younger, Jr (eds.), *The Context of Scripture 2: Monumental Inscriptions from the Biblical World* (Leiden: E.J. Brill, 2000), 154b; J.A. Fitzmyer, *The Aramaic Inscriptions of Sefire* (BibOr, 19; Rome: Pontifical Biblical Institute, 1967), 14–15 (I A 21-24), 80–81 (II A 1-3); A. Lemaire, 'L'inscription araméenne de Bukân et son intérêt historique', *CRAIBL* (Jan.–Mar. 1998), 293–99 (ll. 5'-8'). Cf. Hillers, *Treaty-Curses*, 61–62.

50. E.g., Isa. 9.18-20; Jer. 19.9; Ezek. 5.10; Zech. 11.9.

51. A.B. Ehrlich, *Mikrâ Ki-Pheschutô* (repr.: New York: Ktav, 1969), vol. 1, 367 (Hebrew).

52. Cannibalism in times of siege is described in biblical historiography (e.g., 2 Kgs 6.26-30) as well as in Neo-Assyrian annals (for references, see Eph'al, *Siege*, p. 61 n. 68). The Babylonian 'siege documents' describe the sale of one's children for the sake of purchasing food, but not cannibalism; see, e.g., A.L. Oppenheim, '"Siege Documents" from Nippur', *Iraq* 17 (1955), 69–89; G. Frame, 'A Siege Document from Babylon Dating to 649 B.C.', *JCS* 51 (1999), 101–106. Most historians and commentators recognize a historical reality behind the literary references to cannibalism; see Miodovnik, 'Motif of Famine', 87–104.

53. Dobbs-Allsopp, 'Tragedy', 38; cf. Renkema, *Lamentations*, 271. Gitay indicates that the image of starving children lends the poem universal poignancy; Y. Gitay, 'The Poetics of National Disaster: The Rhetorical Presentation of Lamentations', in *idem* (ed.), *Literary Responses to the Holocaust 1945–1995* (San Francisco: International Scholars, 1998), 1–11 (6).

54. Johnson, 'Form and Message', 69.

55. For the nexus between divine wrath and collective ('corporate') punishment in biblical texts, see J.S. Kaminsky, *Corporate Responsibility in the Hebrew Bible* (JSOTSup, 196; Sheffield: Sheffield Academic Press, 1995), 55–66.

56. Gottwald, 'Key to the Theology', 58.

represented by the verb עלל, 'to perpetrate' (1.12, 22; 2.20),[57] and the children by the homophonous noun עוֹלֵל.[58]

The idea that YHWH'S punishment of Judah is way out of proportion is expressed as well in 4.6, where the penalty imposed on the Judeans is suggested to be even greater than that of the most sinful city of all time, that of Sodom.[59] Sodom, after all, was overturned in an instant while Jerusalem had to suffer a protracted siege (cf. 4.9) during which, we may remind ourselves, nice women were driven to cook their children for food.

In general one can say that the images of God in Lamentations portray the deity in a rather unflattering light. The manifold means of destruction by which a raging warrior god afflicts his own people are common both to the biblical Lamentations and to the Sumerian laments.[60] In both the devastation is understood to be the act of a tempestuous god. But in the Sumerian laments the human enemies who actually carry out the will of the gods – primarily that of the warring storm-god Enlil – are specifically called by name: Gutians, Subarians, Elamites, Amorites.[61] In Lamentations the human perpetrators – the Babylonians – are never named.[62] It is only YHWH who is described as the soldier drawing his bow and training it on his own city (2.4-5; 3.12-13).[63]

---

57. For the strongly negative connotation of this verb, see, e.g., Judg. 19.25; 1 Sam. 31:4; cf. Linafelt, *Surviving Lamentations*, 57. Linafelt's inclusion of Job 16.15 is, however, erroneous; there we have a Hebraized form of the Aramaic verb meaning 'to cause to enter' in the phrase 'to sink the horn into the ground'; cf., e.g., M.H. Pope, *Job* (AB; Garden City, NY: Doubleday, 3rd edn, 1973), 124; A. Hakham, *Job* (Da'at Miqra'; Jerusalem: Mossad Ha-Rav Kook, 1984), 129 (Hebrew).

58. Cf., e.g., Renkema, *Lamentations*, 319; Pham, *Mourning*, 144–45; Dobbs-Allsopp, *Lamentations*, 99.

59. Cf., e.g., Gottwald, 'Theology of Doom', 65–66; Hillers, *Lamentations*, 147–48; Renkema, *Lamentations*, 508–11.

60. See esp. Dobbs-Allsopp, *Weep, O Daughter of Zion*, 55–65.

61. See, e.g., Lamentation over the Destruction of Ur, line 244 (trans. S.N. Kramer; *ANET*, 455–63 [460]); Eridu Lament (n. 29 above), kirugu 1, line 21; kirugu 4, line 10; Uruk Lament (n. 29 above), kirugu 4, ll. 11, 20; Lamentation over Sumer and Ur (n. 29 above), ll. 33, 75, 146, 166, 172, 230, 254, 256–57, 261, 276, 401, 488–91; cf. also the Curse of Agade (n. 33 above), ll. 152–57.

62. Landy's notion, that at the time of Lamentations' composition, mention of Babylon would have been too sensitive politically, is, from the perspective of rhetorical meaning, irrelevant – and also perhaps historically incorrect. As Dobbs-Allsopp has shown, the language of Lamentations is from the mid-to-late sixth century BCE, perhaps even as late as the early Persian period, when Babylon had been overrun by Persia. F. Landy, 'Lamentations', in R. Alter and F. Kermode (eds.), *The Literary Guide to the Bible* (Cambridge, MA: Harvard University Press, 1987), 329–34 (333); F.W. Dobbs-Allsopp, 'Linguistic Evidence for the Date of Lamentations', *JANESCU* 26 (1998), 1–36. Gerstenberger (*Psalms and Lamentations*, 473) attributes the lack of historical detail in Lamentations to its presumed liturgical function. This argument holds no water, however, because the Sumerian laments, in which one finds historical references, were almost certainly the accompaniment to rituals of temple restoration; see, e.g., T. Jacobsen, Review of *Lamentation over the Destruction of Ur* by S.N. Kramer, *AJSL* 58 (1941), 219–24; M.E. Cohen, *The Canonical Lamentations of Ancient Mesopotamia* (2 vols.; Potomac, MD: Capital Decisions Limited, 1988), I, 38–39.

63. Cf. H. Fredriksson, *Jahwe als Krieger: Studien zum alttestamentlichen Gottesbild* (Lund:

In fact, the violent images of the attacking deity attain a fierceness and intensity in Lamentations that go beyond its Sumerian counterparts. The depiction of YHWH as a bear lying in ambush, as a lion ready to pounce on its prey (3.10), is anticipated by the prophets (see immediately below) but is more vicious than any image of Enlil one can find in the Sumerian laments. (Enlil is most commonly described as a raging storm.)[64] The prophetic literature presents two alternative ways of depicting the divine onslaught. In Hos. 13.7-8, God himself is compared to a fierce animal on the attack.[65] In Amos 5.18-20 the bear, lion, and snake are not similes referring to Yhwh himself but rather relate by indirection to the Day of the Lord – a day sometime in the future on which all the withheld punishments that the people have deserved for a long period of years will be released.[66] In Lamentations, the more severe approach is taken, as the lion and bear are theriomorphic images of the Lord himself.

In Lamentations God is characterized overall as both relentless and pitiless.[67] There are two vague references in ch. 3 to divine compassion not having been spent (vv. 22, 32), but they are effectively undermined in the same chapter by the accusation: 'You have not forgiven' (אחה לא סלחת) in v. 42.[68] The phrase holding that God 'has shown no mercy' (לא חמל) runs like a refrain through chs. 2 (vv. 2, 17, 21) and 3 (v. 43). Indeed, the syntagm verb + לא יחמול occurs elsewhere three times in the book of Job (6.10; 16.13; 27.22), in another biblical text where the deity's dark side is contemplated.

The utter lack of compassion ascribed by Lamentations to the God of Jerusalem contrasts sharply with the situation in most of the Sumerian laments. In Lamentations one is hard pressed to zero in on the brief clusters of compassion that may be found in ch. 3.[69] In the Sumerian texts we encounter great bursts of divine pathos,

---

C.W.K. Gleerup, 1945), esp. 92–105; Gottwald, 'Theology of Doom', 73–74; Dobbs-Allsopp, *Lamentations*, 30, 79–80, 83–84, who also observes that 'metaphors for God other than the warrior metaphor are almost completely lacking' (30).

64. In a generically related Akkadian text, the Erra Poem, tablet IV, where the destruction of Babylon is described and its god Marduk laments, the ravaging god Erra is depicted as having a 'lion-like aspect'; L. Cagni, *The Poem of Erra* (Sources from the Ancient Near East, 1/3; Malibu: Undena, 1977), 48 (line 21).

65. Cf., e.g., Renkema, *Lamentations*, 365. See also Hos. 5.14; Isa. 31.4; 38.13; Jer. 25.30.

66. Cf., e.g, F.C. Fensham, 'A Possible Origin of the Concept of the Day of the Lord', *Biblical Essays: Die Oud Testamentiese Werkgemeenskap in Suid Afrika* (Potchefstroom: Rege-Pers Beperk, 1966), 90–97; S.M. Paul, *Amos* (Hermeneia; Minneapolis: Fortress Press, 1991), 182–84. The reference to the Day of Yhwh's Wrath in Lam. 1.12; 2.22 clearly relates to the past; e.g., Y. Hoffmann, 'The Day of the Lord as a Concept and a Term in the Prophetic Literature', *ZAW* 93 (1981), 37–50 (48 with n. 33); Renkema, *Lamentations*, 102–104. For the release of a man-eating lion in Neo-Assyrian treaty curses, see, e.g., Parpola and Watanabe, *Neo-Assyrian Treaties*, 27, ll. 6–7; 49, ll. 467–68.

67. Cf. Gottwald, 'Theology of Doom', 76. Gottwald acknowledges that the martial imagery in Lamentations 'has a demonic coloration'; 'Theology of Doom', 85; cf. 88–89.

68. Cf. Joyce, 'Lamentations and the Grief Process', 305–306.

69. Heschel ('Meaning and Mystery', 292–96), in building a case for a monolithic and altogether benign view of divine wrath in the Bible, points selectively to these passages.

as a god, or more often a goddess, weeps over the destruction that they see.[70] In the Eridu Lament, for example, 'Father Enki stayed outside his city as (if it were) an alien city; he wept bitter tears'.[71] The typically compassionate goddess, Ningal, is described more elaborately:

> Mother Ningal, like an enemy, stands outside her city;
> The woman bitterly laments over her ravaged house,
> The princess bitterly laments over her ravaged shrine (of) Ur.[72]

In the Bible YHWH has the potential for compassionate tears;[73] but in Lamentations he does not shed any.

The intolerability of the God of Judah ravaging his land with neither tears nor remorse is poignantly reflected later in the rabbinic midrash on Lamentations. There we find several passages in which God is presented crying over the fate of his city and people. Here is one brief example:

> The Holy One Blessed Be He said to the Ministering Angels:
> 'Come and let us see, I and you, what the enemy is doing to my House!'
>
> The Holy One Blessed Be He and the Ministering Angels, and Jeremiah out in front of him, immediately went off. As soon as he saw the Holy Temple, he said: 'This must be my House and this my Resting Place, where the enemy has entered and done as he wishes'.
>
> At that moment the Holy One Blessed Be He began weeping and said: 'Woe is me for my House! My children, where are you? My priests, where are you? My friends, where are you? What can I do for you? I gave you warning, but you did not repent!...'[74]

---

70. See S.N. Kramer, 'BM 98396: A Sumerian Prototype of the *Mater-Dolorosa*', *Eretz-Israel* 16 (Orlinsky Volume; 1982), 141*–46*; *idem*, 'The Weeping Goddess: Sumerian Prototypes of the *Mater Dolorosa*', *BA* 46.2 (Spring 1983), 69–80; Dobbs-Allsopp, *Weep, O Daughter of Zion*, 75–90.

71. Eridu Lament (n. 29 above), kirugu 1, ll. 11–13; cf., e.g., Lamentation over Sumer and Ur (n. 29 above), ll. 340–42, 360–63; Nippur Lament (n. 29 above), line 90.

72. J. Klein, 'Lamentation over Ur', in W.W. Hallo and K.L. Younger, Jr (eds.), *The Context of Scripture 1: Canonical Compositions from the Biblical World* (Leiden: E.J. Brill, 1997), 537, ll. 254–56. The weeping of goddesses is nearly ubiquitous in Mesopotamian laments.

73. See, e.g., J. J. M. Roberts, 'The Motif of the Weeping God in Jeremiah and its Background in the Laments of the Ancient Near East', *Old Testament Essays* 5 (1992), 361–74; K.M. O'Connor, 'The Tears of God: Divine Character in Jeremiah 2:9', in T. Linafelt and T.K. Beal (eds.), *God in the Fray: A Tribute to Walter Brueggemann* (Minneapolis, Fortress, 1998), 172–85.

74. *Lam. Rabbah*, Petiḥta 24 (ed. S. Buber, 25); cf. also, e.g., ibid., 24–25, 28; parashah 1 (ed. S. Buber, 78–79). In *Lam. Rabbah* 1.24 the midrash places Isa. 22.4 in the mouth of the deity, ascribing to God the guise of a female mourner. See also Lk. 19.41, where (the masculine) Jesus plays the role of the weeping god(dess). For the weeping Jewish deity and his background in the ancient Near Eastern lamentations tradition, see, e.g., D. Stern, *Parables in Midrash* (Cambridge, MA: Harvard University Press, 1991), 124–30. For literary discussion of several of the pertinent midrashim, see also: G. Hasan-Rokem, *The Web of Life: Folklore and Midrash in Rabbinic Literature* (trans. B. Stein; Stanford: Stanford University Press, 2000). There are also references to

One way to remedy the divine wrath is to make an appeal to God in prayer.[75] Compare, for example, Solomon's prayer in 1 Kings 8, where in a variety of possible scenarios an appeal to God is envisioned, and in each and every case the Lord listens to and responds favorably to the prayer. The Psalter is replete with communal and personal petitions.[76] In Lamentations, beside an occasional call to prayer (e.g., 2.18-19), the charge is leveled at God that he will not listen to prayer (3.8-9, 44, 55-56).[77] In the Sumerian laments, by contrast, even an angry Enlil will heed the people's outcry, show compassion, and repair the broken relations.[78]

Many biblical psalms of lament or complaint include some praise for the deity being addressed.[79] Most of the Sumerian laments conclude with praise for a god, and sometimes the destroying god.[80] In Lamentations, there is shockingly little praise for YHWH. The only example is the single verse, 5.19: 'You, O YHWH, sit (as king) forever; your throne is everlasting'[81] – which is ironically juxtaposed with the conventional description of God's earthly seat, Mt Zion, overrun with jackals (5.18).[82]

In conclusion, it may be remarked that the theology of Lamentations, with its steely descriptions of the wrath of God and its strident yet sometimes subtle evocations of the wrath at God, with its swings and its tensions, is a direct conse-

God lamenting in the Dead Sea texts 4Q439 (*DJD* XX [1999], pp. 335–41) + 4Q469 (*DJD* XXVI [2000], 433–38; references courtesy E. Qimron).

75. Cf., e.g., Considine, 'Theme of Divine Wrath', 141–43.

76. Ferris, *Genre*; W.C. Bouzard, Jr, *We Have Heard with Our Ears, O God: Sources of the Communal Lament in the Psalms* (SBLDS, 159; Atlanta: Scholars Press, 1997); Emmendörffer, *Der ferne Gott*; K. Schaefer, *Psalms* (Berit Olam: Studies in Hebrew Narrative & Poetry; Collegeville, MN: Liturgical Press, 2001), xxv–xxxviii; C. Mandolfo, *God in the Dock: Dialogic Tension in the Psalms of Lament* (JSOTSup, 357; Sheffield: Sheffield Academic Press, 2002).

77. For a god refusing to hear prayer as a curse, see, e.g.: 'may the gods Aššur, Marduk, Adad, Sîn, (and) Šamaš not…listen to his prayers…'; A.K. Grayson, *Assyrian Rulers of the Early First Millennium BC, II (858–745 BC)* (Royal Inscriptions of Mesopotamia, Assyrian Periods, 3; Toronto: University of Toronto Press, 1996), 240, ll. 15–17 (Shalmaneser IV). The related motifs of divine 'forgetting' and 'rejection' are more common in Lamentations, occurring in chs. 2, 3, and 5; cf. S.E. Balentine, *The Hidden God: The Hiding of the Face of God in the Old Testament* (Oxford: Oxford University Press, 1983), 136–51. As is well known, God does not speak in Lamentations, but I am not sure that we can justifiably speak of God's 'silence', as some commentators do, without really knowing that a divine response to the complaints can be reasonably (generically) expected.

78. See, e.g., Lamentation over Sumer and Ur (n. 29 above), kirugu 11; Nippur Lament (n. 29 above), kirugus 4, 6, 8, 12; in kirugu 12 of the Uruk Lament (n. 29 above), and in kirugu 7 of the Eridu Lament (n. 29 above), it is suggested that An and Enlil will respond to supplication.

79. E.g., Pss. 25.8-10; 28.6-8; for the communal laments, see, e.g., Ferris, *Genre*, 135.

80. So Lamentation over Ur (Nanna); Uruk Lament (An and Enlil); Nippur Lament (Enlil and the king); so also Curse of Agade (n. 33 above; Inanna); and see the communal lament, 'O Angry Sea', where the perpetrator of devastation, Enlil, is repeatedly praised (stanzas 6, 8, 16); see R. Kutscher, *Oh Angry Sea (a-ab-ba hu-luh-ha): The History of a Sumerian Congregational Lament* (Yale Near Eastern Researches, 6; New Haven and London: Yale University Press, 1975), 146, 147, 151.

81. Cf., e.g., Ferris, *Genre*, 146.

82. Cf., e.g., Jer. 10.22; Lamentation over Ur , line 269; Curse of Agade, ll. 256–57.

quence of monotheism. The God who destroys the city and the God who ordinarily defends and protects it are one and the same. At what point does a just punishment cross the boundary into excess? The book of Lamentations as a whole is equivocal. But the overwhelming number of passages shake an angry finger at the deity. The pain is insufferable, and it is God who has inflicted that pain. At the point that it is believed that God has gone too far, God's justice ceases to be just. There is no happy ending in Lamentations – barely a glimmer of hope.[83] The hope will have to be that God will at some time exhibit a more proper justice.

83.   Contrast, e.g., Weiss and Krašovec (see nn. 2–3 above). Cf., e.g., Joyce, 'Lamentations and the Grief Process', pp. 305–307; O'Connor, *Lamentations*, 1071; Dobbs-Allsopp, *Lamentations*, 148–49; Berlin, *Lamentations*, 30. For hope as a feature of ch. 3 in particular, see, e.g., Dobbs-Allsopp, *Lamentations*, 116–19.

EVIL AND ITS SYMBOLS IN PSALMS 14; 53; 36; 12

Osnat Singer

I

In the book of Psalms, as in the other biblical books, the wicked person (רשע) is the opposite of the righteous (צדיק).[1] In the absolute sense, צדיק is first and foremost a term used primarily in Wisdom and Psalms literature as a positive characteristic of a person deserving of God's beneficence.[2] The צדיק is clean, pure, innocent, hates bribery and oppression, is merciful to the poor, etc. He is also the poor, humble, innocent person, that is, the victim of the wicked.

A kind of definition of the righteous appears in Ezek. 18.5-9, describing what the righteous person does and does not do: he is not guilty of idolatry, does not defile his neighbor's wife or approach a menstruant woman, does not wrong anyone, does not steal, withholds his hand from injustice, returns a pledge, feeds the hungry, covers the naked, and judges righteously between man and his fellow. In general: 'he walks in my statutes and has kept my ordinances, to deal truly'. A similar list, including only commandments between man and his fellow, appears in Psalm 15, but there the word 'righteous' is not explicitly used. Compare also Ps. 24.3-4 and Isa. 33.14-15.

In these three passages the author makes ascending to or dwelling in the house or mountain of the Lord conditional upon the fulfillment of ethical commandments, such as having clean hands and a pure heart, refraining from swearing deceitfully, honoring those that fear the Lord, not taking bribes or interest. These three sources

---

1.   Evils are mentioned in the great majority of the psalms. A detailed discussion on this issue is not possible here. In the first part of the article we shall have to confine ourselves to some remarks on a few of the basic themes and problems concerning the subject – evil and its symbols in the book of Psalms. The main part of the article will be dedicated to an analysis of Ps. 14 and its parallel Ps. 53; Ps. 36; and Ps. 12. *Inter alia*, we shall examine the motif of the wicked person who lives, in practice, as an atheist (who says: 'there is no God').

2.   The nature and destiny of the righteous and the wicked are discussed in detail, primarily in Wisdom literature, which elaborates at length upon the virtues of the righteous man that bring him happiness and success, as opposed to the negative traits of the wicked, that lead to failure and shame. The two concepts of צדיק and רשע, throughout the biblical literature generally, have a legal-ethical connotation, rather than a religious-ritualistic one. See Y. Kaufmann, *The History of the Religion of Israel from its Beginnings to the End of the Second Temple Period* (Jerusalem and Tel Aviv: The Bialik Institute and Dvir, 1976), II, 576, 696–99 (Hebrew).

The primary connotation of the term צדיק is 'upright', 'honest', 'correct', 'innocent', whether it is used in connection with a person or God, or even as an abstract noun. In those texts that are outside of the realm of Wisdom literature, the root צדק is usually accompanied by the root ישר.

each begin with a rhetorical question: 'Who shall ascend the hill of the Lord?' (Ps. 24); 'Who shall sojourn in thy tent?' (Ps. 15); 'Who among us can dwell with the devouring fire?' (Isa. 33.14). Hence, many scholars have attempted to see these words as bearing the impression of ceremonies of entrance into the Temple, and have even referred to them as 'entrance liturgies'.[3] In this view, ceremonies were conducted in which the priest asked the one coming to the Temple whether he had fulfilled the condition of entrance into the Temple. It should be noted that inscriptions containing restrictions upon entrance into the Temple by one who is not pure and clean of hands appear in the ancient Greek and Hellenistic world, but we have not found there any record of a priest who stands and examines those entering, as the researchers assumed there was in Israel.[4]

The book of Proverbs contains about thirty verses referring to the nature of the righteous. For example,

> The good man regards the rights of the poor, the bad man does not understand knowledge (29.7);
> But the righteous gives and withholds not (21.26).

It is clear from all this that the righteous man is the one who fulfills the commandments of the Lord in general, and particularly those that involve avoiding causing harm to others.

The method most commonly used in the Bible to indicate the essence of the righteous is the negative analogy (i.e, the צדיק is the opposite of the רשע). More than anywhere else this approach is epitomized by Psalm 1, whose main point is the categorical statement that the righteous and the wicked are two diametrically opposed poles in every possible respect, and that it is impossible to err in their identification.[5]

רשע connotes one who is an evildoer and sinner; the wicked person is the one who violates law and ethics: he swindles, seeks bribes, (murders), oppresses the poor, perverts judgement, commits adultery. He is proud, denies God and His providence, and relies upon his own wealth and power. The poor, the orphan, and the widow are his victims. A kind of definition of the evil is given, for example, in Ps. 50.16-20,[6] in several verses of Psalm 37, and elsewhere. In Ps. 50.16-20 God

3.   See: S. Mowinckel, *The Psalms in Israel's Worship* (trans. D.R. Ap-Thomas; Oxford: Blackwell, 1962), I, 178–81.

4.   See: M. Weinfeld, 'Instructions for Temple Visitors in the Bible and in Ancient Egypt', in S.Groll (ed.), *Egyptological Studies* (Scripta Hierosolymitana, 28; Jerusalem: Magnes Press, 1982), 224–50. For the protection of the holy city against sinners and evildoers, see: M. Weinfeld, *Justice and Righteousness in Israel and the Nations: Equality and Freedom in Ancient Israel in Light of Social Justice in the Ancient Near East* (Jerusalem: Magnes Press, 1985), 57–60 (Hebrew).

5.   For Ps. 1, see: M. Buber, 'Right and Wrong: An Interpretation of Some Psalms', *in Darko shel Mikra* (Jerusalem: The Bialik Institute, 1978), 139–62 (139–43) (Hebrew); M. Weiss, *Scriptures in their Own Light: Collected Essays* (Jerusalem: The Bialik Institute, 1987), 111–34 (Hebrew); Y. Hoffman, *Blemished Perfection: The Book of Job in its Context* (Jerusalem: The Bialik Institute, 1995), 239–40 (Hebrew).

6.   See: B. Schwartz, 'Psalm 50, its Subject, Form and Place', in *Shnaton – An Annual for Biblical and Ancient Near Eastern Studies*, III (1978–79), 77–106 (Hebrew).

chastises the hypocritical sinner who performs ethical transgressions, while 'reciting' God's statutes and taking His covenant upon his lips. The allusion to the Ten Commandments is clear: the sins mentioned are theft (18a), adultery (18b), and lying speech or slandering his brother (v. 19), corresponding to the seventh, eighth, and ninth commandments (Exod. 20.14-16 'You shall not commit adultery…you shall not steal…you shall not bear false witness against your neighbor').[7] It therefore seems to follow that v. 16, by the words 'my statutes' and 'my covenant', also refers specifically to the Ten Commandments. (It is worth taking note of the description of God's appearance in the opening of the psalm. The two parts of the psalm constitute a single and unified literary unit, whose subject is God's admonition for violating the Ten Commandments. This rebuke is articulated, among another things, by means of a clear verbal allusion to the Ten Commandments themselves.) The evil person here is the hypocrite, who learns, and possibly even teaches, the words of his God, yet nevertheless violates them.

There are those cases in which the wicked appears in the eyes of the believer in the figure of a rebel, who maliciously defies the word of God (Ps. 139.21-22):

> O YHWH, should I not hate those who hate You,
> not despise those who despise You
> With an uncontrolled hatred I hate them,
> They are enemies to me.

According to Ps. 58.4-6, the wicked are evil from birth, without any hope of change. The poet compares them to serpents with poisonous venom, who cannot be overcome by means of charm and magic. The lying judges mentioned in the psalm are compared to deaf adders, who shut their ears from hearing the cry of the oppressed. In vv. 7-10, God is called upon to take revenge against the wicked. At this point the poet turns the image of the wicked as serpents to images comparing them to wild beasts – that is, lions. But further on he returns to the previous image, and compares his rival, whose fangs have been removed and is powerless, to a snail (which dissolves into slime), thereby completing the picture.

As a rule, the evildoer is depicted in the Psalter in very strong colors, similar to those found in the biblical books generally. He is arrogant, proud and insolent; confident in himself and in his wealth (73.6-8; 10.2; 17.10; 36.12; 59.13; 75.6); speaks of the righteous with arrogance and contempt (31.19); plots iniquity and wrongdoing and speaks falsehood (38.13; 4.3; 5.7). He is without truth, and even when he speaks peace, there is evil in his heart (28.3). The rules of ethics and social decency are beyond him (50.17), and he exploits the weak: the widow, the stranger, and the orphan (94.6). The wicked person's main concern is with accumulating wealth or the evil desire to cause harm to his neighbor and to gain benefit from evil. The wicked person is a man of blood and violence (5.7; 9.13; 26.9 etc.). He loves oppression, robbery, and bribery (7.17 etc.). He is treacherous, rejoices at the misfortune of others (5.10; 12.3-4 etc.), testifies falsely (27.12;

---

7. See: M. Weinfeld, 'The Uniqueness of the Decalogue and its Place in Jewish Tradition', in B.Z. Segal (ed.), *The Ten Commandments As Reflected in Tradition and Literature Throughout the Ages* (Jerusalem: Magnes Press, 1985), 1–34, esp. 17–21 (Hebrew).

35.11), borrows and does not return (37.21). He performs evil rather than good, and hates for no reason (7.5 etc.). The wicked person associates with other worthless characters like himself in order to carry out crimes or for his own benefit (26.4-5 etc.). The wicked hates the righteous man and holds him in contempt, lies in wait for him, sets a trap for him (10.8-9; 17.9; 37.32 etc.).[8] The wicked person imagines in his foolish arrogance that there is neither judge nor judgement – that is, he denies the reality of Divine providence. In the final analysis, the Divine recompense will be carried out: The righteous inherits the earth, while the end of the wicked is to be cut off.[9]

8.   H.J. Kraus, *Theology of the Psalms* (trans. K.Crim; Minneapolis: Augsburg, 1986), 130–31 indicates three metaphors in the book of Psalms that illustrate the cruel and gruesome attacks of the wicked upon the righteous: (a) The wicked are likened to a hostile army, that attacks the helpless and surrounds them with overwhelming forces (Pss. 55.19; 59.2-4, etc.); (b) The enemies of godly individuals are compared with hunters or fishermen, who seek their prey (Pss. 9.16-17; 10.8-10; 140.5-6). [As for an interpretation of Ps. 140, see: M. Greenberg, 'Psalm 140', *Eretz Israel* 14 (1978), 88–99 (Hebrew)]; (c) The wicked are depicted as wild, ravenous animals, having sharp teeth for tearing the flesh of their victims (Ps. 3.8).

The persecution of the righteous by the wicked is one of the fixed subjects in the book of Psalms, but there is nothing here to suggest that this refers to the religious-political conflicts of the late Second Temple period, as has been claimed by scholars in the past.

9.   M. Weiss, *The Bible from Within: The Method of Total Interpretation* (Jerusalem: Magnes Press, 1984), 248–51 has identified a stylistic peculiarity that recurs a number of times in biblical poetry in comparable passages that contrast the fate of the wicked to that of the righteous. These verses lack the usual parallelism that characterizes biblical poetic style. Speaking of the righteous, the sentence is active, whereas the statements about the wicked are generally passive, or else the predicate is an intransitive verb. In the sentences which speak of the wicked, the subject is always 'the wicked' or their actions; in the statements about the righteous, 'the righteous' or their actions are the object, while the subject is always God. For example:

(a) 'For the Lord knows the way of the righteous
<contrast> But the way of the wicked perishes' (Ps. 1.6).
(b) 'Let lying lips be stilled
<contrast> How abundant is Your good, that You have in
store for those who fear You, that You did for those who
take refuge in You. You hide them, … You shelter them…'
(Ps. 31.19-21).
(c) 'Many are the misfortunes of the righteous, but the Lord will save him
<contrast> Misfortune will kill the wicked' (Ps. 34.20, 22).
(d) 'For the arms of the wicked shall be broken
<contrast> But the Lord is the support of the righteous' (Ps. 37.17).
(e) 'And transgressors shall be utterly destroyed; the future
of the wicked shall be cut off
<contrast> And the deliverance of the righteous is from the
Lord… The Lord helps them and rescues them' (Ps. 37.38-40).
(f) 'He will watch over the feet of His faithful ones
<contrast> But the wicked shall be put to silence in darkness' (1 Sam. 2.9).

According to Weiss, the strange parallelism is not merely a literary embellishment, or a means of avoiding monotony. The absence of formal parallelism marks an absence of parallelism of content.

The Problem of Recompense

There are several striking points of which one ought to take note. (1) The worshipers/poets in the psalms literature are never the wicked. True, the psalms occasionally cite the evildoer, but this is only as a means of creating dramatic tension in the psalm and concretizing the nature of the evildoer. (2) On the other hand, the worshipers/poets never explicitly describe themselves as 'righteous'. Their righteousness is only obliquely alluded to, in general statements or in petitioner's prayers for the end of the evildoers. (3) Some of the psalms raise the issue of recompense directly, while in others one can only detect an awareness of the problem of recompense between the lines. In any event, in all of them the faith in an ethical world order, in the constant realization of the law of recompense, is in practice predominant. (All of the psalms affirm God's righteousness without questioning it.) (4a) Among those psalms raising the problem of retribution, there are those that present only one side of the coin: namely, the success of the evildoer (thus, for example, in Ps. 73).[10]

Others present both sides of the coin of the problem of recompense – the success of the wicked and the suffering of the righteous (thus, for example, in Ps. 10). In no psalm is the problem of the suffering of the righteous presented by itself, but always alongside the other side of the problem, that of the reward or success of the wicked. (4b) The evildoer plots against the righteous, and at times is even successful, but this is only seemingly so and temporarily (Pss. 9.19; 37.1, 2, 7, 9, 35-38; 62.13; 73.19; 75.9; 92.8). In the end, the Divine judgement is carried out; in the final analysis, the righteous will be justified in his quarrel with the evildoer. The foolish person does not understand that the success of the wicked and the suffering of the righteous are but temporary (Pss. 92.19; 73.22; and cf. 28.5).[11]

We shall now examine several outstanding psalms that relate to the problem of evil, that places itself outside God's domain (i.e., considers itself to be strong enough in its own power).

For example, in Ps. 1.6 the two cola speak in different languages, one in the language of the righteous and the other in the language of the wicked. There is, therefore, no parallelism. The righteous experiences the presence and providence of God in every aspect of his life. He feels that God is the subject of his life: God acts, leads, directs, and man can only be the object of this divine activity. The wicked man, in contrast, does not perceive the discerning eye and the guiding hand of God; in his view, he acts independently, and any evil that befalls him, he believes, happens of its own accord.

10. See: Buber, 'Right and Wrong', 149–57; Kraus, *Theology of the Psalms*, 168–75; J.C. McCann, *Psalm 73: An Interpretation Emphasizing Rhetorical and Canonical Criticism* (PhD dissertation, Duke University, 1985; Ann Arbor: University Microfilms International, 1991); Hoffman, *Blemished Perfection*, 237–38.

11. It should be noted that some of the psalms, both those relating to individuals and national ones, refer to the enemies by the term 'the wicked' or its synonyms, while others refrain from doing so. Thus, for example, in Ps. 10 the wicked are portrayed as personally pursuing the praying individual; that is, in these and other psalms the speakers see themselves as victims of the wicked. In other cases the authors only complain about being persecuted, without identifying their pursuers as 'wicked'. Such is the case in Ps. 13 and elsewhere.

II
Psalms 14 and 53

In Psalm 14 the poet focuses his complaint on the corruption of values and the large number of evildoers in society. The description of evil and corruption, expressed in sharp language, does not refer to the enemies of Israel, as thought by several commentators, but to those within the people itself who deny Divine Providence, who as a result of their heresy do not fear to perform crimes and iniquity. On the contrary, their behavior becomes corrupt and abominable (v. 1 + v. 3). They take advantage of the weak strata of society (they eat them, as one devours bread), and those who suffer from their provocations are described in contrast as 'the generation of the righteous' that places its refuge in God. As against the declaration by the fool that 'there is no God' (v. 1), the author emphasizes His existence, and that He looks down upon and observes human beings and their actions (v. 2). The conclusion reached by God after examining the people is a harsh one: 'they have all gone astray, they are all alike corrupt'. And the poet returns to the conclusion made in v. 1: 'there is none that does good'. The lack of 'those that do good' is absolute – there is none among the people 'that does good, no, not one'. Now the poet turns to express astonishment at the evildoers: their reactions display an utter lack of understanding. Do they not know that God will not tolerate their actions? Yet they continue to perform their evil acts: they 'eat' the people as a person eats bread (this is an accepted metaphor for oppression; cf. Isa. 9.11: 'Aramaeans from the east and Philistines from the west, and they have swallowed Israel in one mouthful' and Mic. 2.1-2; 3.1-3), and in so doing have performed an act which is inexcusable; they have not sought God, nor called upon Him. According to v. 5 (which as extant is very difficult), the wicked are seized with terror, because God is with the generation of the righteous and protects them. In v. 6, which is likewise difficult, the poet tells the wicked: You, who take counsel among yourselves and lay plots against the poor, should be ashamed of yourselves, for God is the refuge of the poor (compare Hos. 10.6, 'Israel shall be ashamed of his counsel'). The closing verse of the prayer (v. 7), which anticipates the gathering of the exiles and the deliverance of Israel in its own land, is not part of the original work but was added, evidently as the result of a mistaken interpretation of v. 4:

> Have they no knowledge, all the evildoers
> who eat up my people as they eat bread,
> and do not call upon the Lord?

In fact, the phrase 'who eat up my people as they eat bread' is intended as an accusation against the foolish people who oppress and pain their poor brethren, and whom the author of the psalm no longer includes among his compatriots.[12]

It should be noted that quite a few of the concluding verses of psalms, including three doxologies, are additions of a national character. By the 'conclusions' and the 'doxologies', we refer to the chapter endings, and to the blessings that appear at the

---

12. See: Buber, 'Right and Wrong', 146–48.

end of the first four collections ('books') of Psalms. These do not constitute part of the body of the psalms and, like the headings, were added at a later stage. The following is a list of the secondary conclusions and doxologies that have a national character: Pss. 3.9; 25.22; 28.9; 29.11; 34.23; 51.20-21; 68.35-36; 69.36-37; 106.47; 125.5c; 128.6b (and 133 according to the Psalms Scroll from Qumran, 11QPs^a).

In Psalm 25, which is arranged in an alphabetical acrostic at the beginning of the verses, there is a decisive proof of the secondary nature of its ending verse: namely, that it deviates from the alphabetical rubric. From this, and from the conclusion of Psalm 34, which likewise has an acrostic structure, we can draw an analogy to the secondary nature of the other conclusions. Psalm 25 is considered as a personal petitionary prayer, being spoken by a person who fears the Lord, who follows His ways and strives for closeness to Him. Among the requests that he presents before God, one should mention his request for deliverance from his troubles and from his enemies (vv. 16-20); it is possible that in its wake the prayer for all of Israel (for redemption from all its troubles – v. 22) was attached at the end of the psalm. The secondary nature of its conclusion (which is, incidentally, strikingly similar to the conclusion of Ps. 130.8 – 'And He will redeem Israel from all his iniquities') is indicated by the name 'Israel', which is not at all mentioned in the body of the chapter, and possibly also the name 'Elohim' rather than the name YHWH, used therein generally speaking.

There is reason to suspect that the main purpose for adding these national conclusions was to prepare the prayers to which they were added (which are generally speaking individual psalms) for use in public liturgy. It may be that some of the psalms to which these conclusions were added were interpreted or expounded by those who made the additions as national psalms. The addition of the conclusions was generally performed in relation to linguistic allusions and in parallel (whether contrasting or complementary) to matters that appear in the body of the works.

Finally, it would seem that the national conclusions were added during the Second Temple period, no later than the fourth century BCE, in light of the fact that Psalm 106, with its concluding doxology (v. 48), is quoted in 1 Chronicles 16. (The date of the book of Chronicles is widely accepted as the fourth century BCE.)

That Psalm 14 refers to groups within the people, and is not concerned with the relation of Israel as such to the nations that oppress it, may be inferred from the use of the term נָבָל ('fool') in v. 1. This term is used as a designation for the wicked and for those who are arrogant towards God, a term that is not intended in the Bible to refer specifically to idolaters.[13]

One may arrive at a similar conclusion from the phrase 'the children of men' (בְּנֵי אָדָם) in v. 2, which serves as a general designation for a group of people, and is not intended to exclude Israel. The same is valid for Psalm 12, which is similar in contents to Psalm 14, and from which there is no ending or other reference bearing a national character.

Psalm 53 is the double of Psalm 14, but there are several differences between them:

---

13. See: Buber, 'Right and Wrong', 147.

(1) In Psalm 53, which is included in the group of Elohistic chapters (Pss. 42–83), the name Elohim is used consistently, whereas in Psalm 14 the name Yhwh is most frequently used.

(2) Another difference may be seen in the headings or titles of the chapter. It is superfluous to mention that these two differences derive from different approaches to the editing of the collections of psalms within the Psalter, as well as, evidently, from the different functions played in the ritual by Psalms 14 and 53.

(3) One substantial difference, which lends a different character to these two chapters, emerges in light of a comparison of Ps. 53.6 to 14.5-6:

> There they shall be in great terror,
> for God is with the generation of the righteous.
> You would confound the plans of the poor,
> but the Lord is his refuge (Ps. 14.5-6).
> There they are, in great terror,
> in terror such as has not been!
> For God has scattered the bones of him who camps against you;
> you will be put to shame, for God has rejected them (Ps. 53.6).

Many scholars think that Ps. 53.6 refers to the downfall of Sennacherib's army on the outskirts of Jerusalem, as told in 2 Kgs 19.35.[14] According to this view, the sense of v. 6 is: the fear of those who were besieged in Jerusalem has suddenly passed because of the miracle performed by God, smashing the enemy that camped around (i.e., laid siege to) the city, and scattering their bones. It is clear that this reference to a concrete historical incident – whether it was added to the original psalm at a later stage, as thought by most of the commentators, or whether it was part of the original psalm, as held by a minority – lends a national dimension to Psalm 53. If this explanation is in fact correct, then Psalm 53 is to be classified as a national psalm, and the terms נ בל ('fool'), פֹעֲלֵי אָוֶן ('those who work evil') and אֹכְלֵי עַמִּי ('those who eat up my people') are to be understood as referring to national enemies.[15] We therefore have here an interesting example in which the term רְשָׁעִ ם, 'wicked', is used to refer both to internal enemies within the people (Ps. 14) and to national enemies (Ps. 53). But even according to this line of interpretation, it would appear that the concluding phrase of the chapter is secondary (i.e., not an integral part of its subject matter), expressing as it does the hopes of the exiles for redemption and national rebirth, whereas the body of the chapter reflects an actual historical event that has already occurred. The reason for mentioning this act of deliverance is to teach a lesson to the listeners, to show that there is law and justice in the world: that is, that God exercises His Providence over human beings and does not allow the heretics who deny His existence to destroy and to do abominable iniquity. The proof of this is that He takes vengeance against those who plot against Him and His people.

In fact, it is difficult to arrive at any definite conclusion as to whether Psalm 53 is later than Psalm 14 and dependent upon it, whether Psalm 14 is later and is based

---

14.   Rashi interprets the word חֹנָךְ as 'those that camp against you, Jerusalem'. See also A.F. Kirkpatrick, *The Book of Psalms* (Cambridge: Cambridge University Press, 1951).

15.   See: M.E. Tate, *Psalms 51–100* (WBC, 20; Waco, TX: Word Books, 1990), 41–43.

upon Psalm 53, or whether there was an earlier common source from which both extant versions are derived. It is worth noting in this connection that the word פוּר, 'scatter', in 53.6 is parallel to the consonantal framework of the word בְּדוּר in Ps. 14.5, that is semantically equivalent to the Aramaic בדר. One should further note that the word חֹנָךְ ('who encamps against you') in Ps. 53.6 is in the form of a stop in the second person possessive, which is the form usually used in Rabbinic Hebrew.[16]

The Wicked Person's Denial of God / Challenge to the Belief in God as the Supreme and Transcendent Being Who Determines What Happens in the World

One of the characteristics of the wicked in the Psalms is their denial of Divine Providence. There are some among them who mockingly say, 'How can God know?' (Ps. 73.11); they think in their heart that 'There is no God' (Ps. 10.4); 'He will never see it' (v. 11); and who arrogantly declare, 'who is our master?' (Ps. 12.5). They do not wish to know the ways of God and refuse to serve Him (cf. Job 21.14-15).[17]

The 'heretical' passages in the book of Psalms are generally interpreted as if the wicked and the fool are stating that God does not look upon the world or involve Himself in human affairs. The approach that God does not act providentially in the world is repeated in the Bible in various ways.

Zephaniah, who prophesied at the time of Josiah, attacks those who adhere to this view: 'And it will be at that time, that I will search Jerusalem with a lamp, and I will punish those who are at ease, who are thickening upon their lees, those who say in their hearts, YHWH does neither good nor bad' (Zeph. 1.12).

In Psalm 73 the wicked and those that are at ease argue: 'How would God know? Is there knowledge with the Most High?' (v. 11).

It is possible that these arrogant heretics reached their conclusion because they did not find any indication of God's participation in the ongoing course of events. In any event, it is reasonable to assume that this is not intended as a denial of God's reality, and if they nevertheless deny His existence, it may be that their spiritual path was similar to that of modern-day atheists, who see no need for God, since the world is conducted properly without Him.

16. The differences between these two psalms are not such as to support the claim that textual corruptions have taken place in Ps. 53.6 or 14.5-6, as is maintained by some commentators. See, for example, E.J. Kissane, *The Book of Psalms: Translated from a Critically Revised Hebrew Text with a Commentary* (Dublin: Browne and Nolan, 1964); C.A. Briggs and E.G. Briggs, *A Critical and Exegetical Commentary on the Book of Psalms* (ICC; Edinburgh: T. & T. Clark, 1906–1907), I, 111. Kissane goes so far as to attempt to reconstruct the original version on the basis of these two psalms. 'There they are in great terror, in terror such as has not been! For God has scattered them; their impious counsel (עֲצַת חֹנָךְ; this is the reading reflected in LXX to Ps 53:6) will be put to shame, for God has rejected them.' According to A. Weiser, *The Psalms: A Commentary* (trans. H. Hartwell; OTL; London: SCM Press, 1962), 164, the original text is better preserved in Ps. 14.

17. Job protests against injustice; he refuses to forgo his own truth but, as harsh and difficult as his words are, and as difficult is God's answer, the author does not cross the boundary between the believer who is troubled by doubts and the wicked who are proud of their heresy.

And indeed, this is implied by the criticism directed against them by the believing author of Psalm 14: When God looks down from heaven in order to see if there are any persons that act wisely among the human beings, He finds tyrants lacking in faith who have no knowledge, and therefore 'eat up my people as they eat bread'. However, the author says further on, on these people fell terror, but they have no wisdom. They are unable to understand the meaning of their own experiences that disturb their rest.

In both Psalm 14 and in other psalms, which we shall examine below, the authors discern a strong tendency of humanity towards evil, and recognize the fact that the fear of God is the main force preventing people from sinking into iniquity. It helps a person to control his evil impulse. There is a certain degree of kindness in man, that is important for the existence of society; but only fear of God can cultivate it. Man's spirit lowers itself in total humility before God, as in the words of Micah:

> It has been told thee, O man, what is good. Yea, what does YHWH seek from thee, but to do justice and to love kindness and to walk humbly with thy God (Mic. 6.8; cf. Jer. 17.9-10).

When human beings see themselves in truth and honesty as subject to God and view themselves in God's light, their attitude towards other people, their fellows, also changes, since they know that all human beings as such are the creations of God.

Human society as a whole is made up of human beings, each one of whom is precious to God, from which it follows that each person is precious to his fellow. On the other hand, denial of God leads to the outbreak of the fundamental evil within man and its dangerous development. According to Psalm 14, human society as a whole is filled with corruption; it sinks under the weight of evil:

> They have all gone astray, they are all alike corrupt; there is none that does good, no, not one (Ps. 14.3; cf. Jer. 9.3).

And indeed, we anticipate that God will punish this corrupt society, will defeat it, and establish a new world order – yet this fails to happen. And here is the surprise to the reader.

III
Psalm 36

This psalm is divided into two parts. The first part (vv. 2-5) is a didactic poem that depicts the characteristics of evil, the dark personality traits of the wicked man. It describes his motivations, his actions, his path. No mention is made here of the fate of the evildoer. In these verses we sense the process of the strengthening of evil, from thought to deeds. The metaphorical use of the organs of the body: heart, eyes, mouth, feet (alluded to in the verb יתיצב) concretizes the manner of subjugation to transgression.

Verse 3: the wicked person's eyes are closed; he cannot see properly and is tempted to sin.

Verse 4: He has nevertheless not yet done any evil.

Verse 5: At this stage he begins to plot mischief which he subsequently carries out.

By the end of the process, his natural feeling of disgust at evil disappears. The wicked person is completely subjugated to his evil impulses.

The second part, vv. 6-13, is a hymn that concludes with a petition. Verses 6-10 consist of a song of praise to God for His righteousness and steadfast love, together with a description of the happiness of those that cling to Him; that is, the attributes or qualities of God and their manifestation in the living world, and the lot of the righteous.

The ending of the second part, vv. 11-12, contains a prayer for the lot of the righteous in general, and of the author of the psalm in particular. In v. 13 we again return to the wicked, this time, however, not to their deeds, but to their destiny.

In terms of subject matter, there is no symmetry between the two parts of the psalm. To complement the description of the acts of the wicked people, we do not find a description of the deeds of the righteous, but rather one of God's qualities and their expression – that is, the second part is problematic in relation to the first part.

Consequently, there are those scholars who claim that this psalm is a combination of two poems, which were originally separate from one another.[18] Nevertheless, it seems that this is a single work, whose two parts are organically connected with one another.[19] The difference between them is not the result of separate origins, but is an expression of diverse approaches to their common subject: namely, the inner world of the wicked and that of the righteous. While we are told what the wicked does, concerning the righteous we are told what he receives. The world of the righteous is illustrated by his destiny, while that of the wicked is illustrated by his motivations and way. These two orbs are understood by the author as two worlds existing on different planes, and not as two conflicting worlds existing on the same realm. It is this approach that creates the asymmetry between the two halves of the psalm.

In Psalm 36 the wicked person is swept up further and further into his sin, until he no longer spurns wickedness. This process of being caught up by evil begins with a denial of God, and continues and intensifies with constant thoughts of wickedness, in the sense of the verse, 'every imagination of the thoughts of his heart was only evil continually' (Gen. 6.5), until 'he spurns not evil' (Ps. 36.5). He begins with deceitful words. In his speech he still takes consideration of the good and tries to seem like a good person. But within himself he has ceased to under-

18. For example, B. Duhm, *Die Psalmen erklart* (KHAT, 14; Tübingen: J.C.B. Mohr, 2nd edn, 1922); H. Schmidt, *Die Psalmen* (HAT, 15; Tübingen: J.C.B. Mohr, 1934), 67–69.

19. Among the scholars who argue that this is a single work: Kirkpatrick, *The Book of Psalms*, 183–87; H.J. Kraus, *Psalms 1–59, 60–150: A Commentary* (trans. H.C. Oswald; Minneapolis: Augsburg–Fortress, 1988–89); Weiss, *Scriptures in their own Light*, 174–81.

stand or to do wisely, albeit he has not yet reached the stage of actively performing evil. In the next stage he plots mischief at night, and thereafter 'sets himself in a way that is not good'. The first stanza thus portrays the process by which evil gains domination over a person, in which the basic evil present within man breaks forth and becomes strengthened until 'he spurns not evil'. That is: the natural sense implanted within man to feel contempt for evil disappears and no longer exists.

The basic view underlying the first stanza is that evil is constantly lying in wait for man ('sin is couching at the door' – Gen. 4.7), and that the evil man stumbles on it and fails to control it, because 'there is no fear of God before his eyes'. For him, there is no Divine judgement present in the world. (The absence of fear of God is the counsel of the evil urge, of transgression, that the evil person is seduced to believe, as if it were a statement from God.)

The poet expresses well the moral decline of the wicked person, from thoughts of iniquity to performing terrible deeds in actuality, through the use of a semantic field that encompasses the organs of the body: the heart = thought; the eyes = vision (v. 3, 'for he flatters himself in his own eyes that his iniquity cannot be found out and hated', is reminiscent of Ps. 35.19, 'those wink the eye who hate me without cause'); the mouth = speech; and, by way of allusion, the feet = actions in practice ('he sets himself in a way'). The merismus of 'foot' and 'hand' in v. 12 returns us to the first stanza, as does the concluding phrase regarding the lot of the wicked who lies prostrate, in contrast to his former standing erect in v. 5. (It is worth noting that in the second part, vv. 6-11, the word חַסְדְּךָ, 'thy steadfast love', functions as a key word.)

In the opening words of the psalm, 'Transgression speaks to the wicked', the author mocks the wicked person, who thinks that he is free of the fear of God. In fact, the wicked person, who throws off the yoke of God, is unconsciously enslaved to another 'god', namely, transgression. The expression נְאֻם, 'speaks to', is generally used in the Bible to signify the revelation of God's word to the prophet. When the author of Psalm 36 uses this expression, he intends to say that the revelation experienced by the wicked is that of transgression. This voice of transgression guides him, just as God's voice guides the prophet.

After the poet has described the wicked, and the way of transgression that is his path, he turns without transition to God, and counterpoises the good qualities of God, that fill the entire world, against the wicked person. God's deliverance ensures a portion to all those who are called – man and beast. That is, as opposed to the wicked person, for whom there is no fear of God, the righteous person feels the goodness of God wherever he turns. The second half of the psalm, which is a hymn of praise concerning God's goodly qualities, thus indirectly illustrates the world of the righteous. In the eyes of the righteous the main thing in the world is God – not God's essence, but rather His qualities. The poet enumerates four qualities or attributes of God: 'steadfast love' (which serves as a leitmotif throughout the second half of the psalm), 'faithfulness', 'righteousness', and 'judgements'. All of these qualities assure the proper and harmonious existence of the world. 'Steadfast love' indicates that attitude which is beyond the strict letter of the law; אָמוּן בּוֹ with regard to God means faithfulness; 'righteousness' and 'judgements', in the present context, refer to activities of deliverance to assure the proper existence of the order of the world. That which emanates from God's qualities to every living thing simply by virtue of its being alive is 'saving', while that which emanates from the Divine qualities only to those human beings who desire them and act on their behalf is called 'taking refuge in the shadow of His wings'. The righteous places God's ways before him and attempts to walk in them.

At the conclusion of his testimony about God's steadfast love, the poet adds himself to those who have seen the light of the Lord. But in the subsequent prayer, he adds a separate prayer for others and for himself. For others he asks for 'steadfast love' and 'salvation' in a general way, while for himself he makes a concrete request to be saved from the oppression of the wicked. Or, perhaps, this ought to be understood as a prayer that his portion not be with that of the wicked, that he not fall into the depths of transgression, and that God help him so that the wicked will be unable to move him from his attachment to the godly way.

IV

Psalm 12

This psalm is a complaint regarding the low moral level of the generation, the lack of human kindness, the domination of lies, flattery, and hypocrisy; the casting aside of all ethical norms to the point of the utterance of the provocative 'who is our master?' (The human society is contaminated by lies. People do not speak what they genuinely think, but are in the habit of speaking with a smooth tongue.)

The structure of the psalm can be seen in the contrasting contentual parallelism (truth and lies), and, structurally, in its chiastic form.[20]

	Verse		Stanza	
PART I	2		I	A
	3, 4		II, III	B
	5		IV	C
PART II	6		V	C'
	7		VI	B'
	8-9		VII	A'

THE CONSTRUCTION OF PSALM 12 (DIAGRAM)

Notes to the Diagram:
Part I (vv. 1-5) describes the falsehood that dominates mankind (the generation that is enslaved to falsehood).
Part II (vv. 6-9) depicts the divine truth.
The first stanza (I) parallels the last (VII) in that in both the author appeals to God directly and describes the hostile environment, which lacks faith and uprightness. The two stanzas end with the same words: בנ י אדם.

20. A.L. Strauss, *Studies in Literature* (Jerusalem: The Bialik Institute, 1970), 89–94 (Hebrew), points out that the two parts of the psalm are parallel in sense and content, and chiasmic in form and in structure.

Stanzas II and III parallel stanza VI in a parallel of contrast: falsehood and hypocrisy in contrast to the pure words of God.

[Verses 2 and 9 contain a description of the surrounding reality, of lack of faithfulness and honesty in the society of that generation.

Verses 3-4 are concerned with the smooth tongues of the people, while v. 7 expresses the pure words of the Lord. In v. 6 God arises to defend the oppressed. Here is the sole instance of an explicitly dynamic style.

Verse 8 is a prayer that God shall protect the poor and the humble (pious and men of faith) from that generation, which has been dominated by falsehood, all of whose acts are falsehood and violence.]

The contrasting parallelism is particularly pronounced in the center of the poem. In vv. 5-6 (stanzas IV, V) those who pretend to be masters over their lips are contrasted with God's coming to the aid of those who are persecuted by them (the despoiled). Here, both protagonists, God and the wicked, are quoted directly, thereby creating a sort of dramatic confrontation in the transition between the two halves of the poem, [21] i.e., in v. 5 the poet refers to the 'tongue that makes great boasts' of the lying men. They encourage themselves with boasts and arrogant speech to the extent of throwing off every yoke, declaring, 'Who is our master?'[22] By the very 'arising' of the Lord (v. 6), the answer is given to the question 'who is our master?', but this voice does not explicitly answer the question. (And perhaps it is in response to the cry, 'Who is our master?' [v. 5] that we are given the answer 'Do thou, O Lord...' [v. 8]).[23]

Thus, in content and structure, in the choice of the words, and in the positioning of the latter, falsehood and truth are in opposition.

According to Strauss, [24] the subject of the psalm is 'true speech', as opposed to lying speech. And indeed, the opening words, repeated throughout the psalm, create a semantic field whose subject is speech (שפת חלקות ;אמרה ;דבר; אמור; לשון: flattering lips; say; speak; says; tongue). But v. 6 reveals what had been concealed until now: the social oppression, that lies at the root of the lies and

---

21. Strauss remarks: 'The two voices meet in a dramatic collision on the border of the two parts of the poem. To present this clash and still retain the chiasmic structure of the poem even at this turn, the poet put the narrative background of the sayings ("who have said"..."saith the Lord") before the first saying at the beginning of the fourth stanza, and in the middle of the second saying. "Who have said...saith the Lord". In this way there is no break between the two voices heard in the middle of the poem.'

22. The question asked here arrogantly, 'who is our master?', is in fact a rhetorical one. Those who asked it thought that there was no answer (i.e., that they have no master). But the emergence here of God's voice does, in fact, provide the answer, in a dramatic and unexpected manner.

23. Only in vv. 2 and 8 does the author address God directly in the second person. The appeal to God in the opening of the psalm takes the imperative form – that of a request; while in the conclusion it is in the future tense – expressing confidence. In v. 7 the author switches to the third person in speaking about God: he distances himself from Him after previously (v. 2) speaking with Him face to face. It should be noted that only in the verses describing the flattering lips and quoting from them (vv. 3, 5) is God's name not used, unlike the other phrases, in each of which the Divine name appears – a linguistic hint that the men of the flattering lips are people who have forgotten God.

24. See n. 20 and Buber, 'Right and Wrong', 143–46.

hypocrisy and from which they derive. Until v. 5 we have heard of lies and hypocrisy, but in God's words in v. 6 we hear of the despoiling of the poor and the groans of the needy, a subject which – like the voice of God speaking – suddenly breaks into the middle of the poem. The idea expressed here indirectly (v. 6) is that: at the basis of the lies and hypocrisy are hidden the interests of those who oppress their fellows.

God does not engage in debate with the flattering lips, but places against the imaginary reality of their words the true and terrible reality of the oppression of the poor; by doing so He automatically gives the lie to their speech. At the end of the poem the author again returns to the miserable reality, of which he also speaks at the end of the first stanza after calling upon God; while in v. 8 the future salvation is depicted. But it seems that the poet feels an obligation to remain faithful to the reality of the present, ending by describing the wicked people who surround him. He complains about the large number of wicked, who are everywhere. As opposed to the call in the opening of the psalm, with its complaint about the lack of pious and faithful people, the last stanza ends by seeing evil in all its power and on every side. Even though the poet's confidence in salvation is not shaken, it seems that this confidence is in constant danger from the arrogance of the evildoers who surround him.[25]

---

25. 'As vileness is exalted among the sons of men' (v. 9) is a difficult phrase. Some interpret כרום in the sense of 'when they will be uplifted, raised up'. זוללות comes from the word זול, cheapness or vulgarity, the opposite of יקר; that is, that vileness and lowness are uplifted and dominate among men. Others correct the reading to כרו מזימות לבני אדם.

THE EVIL ONES AND THE GODLESS:
A PROBLEM OF IDENTITY IN BIBLICAL WISDOM

Henning Graf Reventlow

As is well known, the paradigmatic figures in biblical wisdom are the righteous on one side and the evil on the other. The contrast between both types forms the basic dualistic structure of the group of sayings of a seemingly ethic character that are typical of a broad layer in the book of Proverbs. Because they are so conspicuous, placed in a central position at the beginning of the oldest collection of sentences in Proverbs 10–14+17 (whereas in 15–16 + 18–20 the diction changes to a looser structure), the discussion about the identity of biblical wisdom has often focused on the meaning of these two terms and their synonyms. According to a near-consensus in scholarly opinion, if one understands their significance and the background of their meaning, one will be able to comprehend the character of biblical wisdom itself.

The long-enduring discussion about the question from which ideological background biblical wisdom develops its arguments has not yet reached a final solution. In the history of research two main standpoints can be observed. Both at first sight seem to have some convincing arguments on their side.

1. The defenders of the first opinion regard original wisdom as a secular phenomenon, formulated in the circle of the wise to guide their pupils on how to cope as easily as possible with the manifold problems they will encounter on their way through life. Unquestionably a certain number of sentences contains such advice free of any moral attitude intending nothing more than to give useful practical hints.[1] A second group comprises sentences based on the principle of what Klaus Koch called 'deed-consequence connection'.[2] The well-known verse Prov. 26.27, which Koch quotes in an impressive list of similar sentences:[3] 'Whoever digs a pit

---

1.   This position stresses the sentences containing instructions on how to behave in typical situations members of the educated upper class may meet with, for instance at the royal court. Cf. William McKane, *Prophets and Wise Men* (SBT, 44; London: SCM Press, 1965), part 1, 15–62. For his later views cf. his commentary *Proverbs* (OTL; London: SCM Press, 1970), esp. p. 415.

2.   Formulated first in his famous essay 'Gibt es ein Vergeltungsdogma im Alten Testament?', *ZTK* 52 (1955), 1–42 = reprinted in *Um das Prinzip der Vergeltung in Religion und Recht des Alten Testaments* (WdF, 12; Darmstadt: Wissenschaftliche Buchgesellschaft, 1972), 130–80 = *Spuren des hebräischen Denkens: Gesammelte Aufsätze*, 1 (ed. B. Janowski and M. Krause; Neukirchen–Vluyn: Neukirchener Verlag, 1991), 65–103. ET: 'Is there a Doctrine of Retribution in the Old Testament?', in J.L. Crenshaw (ed.), *Theodicy in the Old Testament* (Issues in Theology and Religion, 4; Philadelphia: Fortress Press; London: SPCK, 1983), 57–87.

3.   *ZTK* 52, 2–3.

will fall into it/and a stone will come back on the one who starts it rolling' is a good example for an automatism, which includes the results of an action in the action itself without any form of intervention from outside. If we take this and similar sentences verbatim, they leave no room for a hidden engagement of God behind the scene. Therefore, Koch's results were frequently taken as the final proof that Israelite wisdom should be regarded as originally a secular phenomenon. The weakness of Koch's position, however, seems to lie in the far-reaching consequences he drew from his so far correct observations. He believed to have detected a dominant principle not only for early wisdom, but also for other parts of the Old Testament, including also parallels in the literature of the ancient Near East. What he actually found, however, was just one of the sub-structures in a certain layer of wisdom literature, but not a system that could be regarded as being decisive for the whole.

The crucial debate begins where sentences of a moral colouring are in view. Where terms occur characterizing a person as righteous or its opposite, we can be sure that ethical viewpoints are involved. But what is the basis of this ethics? Is it also an inner-worldly phenomenon? Can it be regarded as self-contained? Is it – to use a philosophical classification – a form of eudaemonistic ethics?

2. The alternative position is connected with the late standpoint of Gerhard von Rad in his book *Weisheit in Israel*,[4] translated into English as *Wisdom in Israel*.[5] Deviating from his earlier position, in which he left to wisdom only a position at random in the whole building of Old Testament theology, he now observed its theological weight, though he also regarded the theological orientation of the wise as a comparatively late development.[6] Because he passed away in the following year, we do not know how he would have revised the scheme of his *Theology of the Old Testament*, if confronted with the demand of a new edition.

3. Certainly the sentences in which the righteous (צדיקים) and the evil ones (רשעים), or more or less synonymous terms for both groups, occur in antithetical parallelism, or where only one of these opposite types is depicted, at a hasty look betray a religious aspect. That the terms, however, cannot be classified as profane in our sense, several important contributions to the discussion in the second half of the last century have shown. I just refer to the most important book in my view, Hans Heinrich Schmid's *Gerechtigkeit als Weltordnung*[7] Schmid convincingly explained that the idea of righteousness is an expression of a worldview spread through the ancient Near East from Egypt to Mesopotamia. According to this belief the world is arranged in an encompassing order (in Egypt: *ma'at*; Hebrew צדק/צדקה), comprising nature, justice, wisdom, war, cult, kingdom. Because this order is inherent in the world, in polytheistic thinking it is a binding rule also in the realm of the gods.[8] One cannot deny that this ideology is a

4.   Neukirchen–Vluyn: Neukirchener Verlag, 1970.
5.   London: SCM Press, 1972.
6.   Cf. Chapter 2.
7.   BHT, 40. Tübingen: Mohr Siebeck, 1968.
8.   Cf. Jan Assmann, *Ma'at. Gerechtigkeit und Unsterblichkeit im Alten Ägypten* (Munich: Beck, 1990).

form of religious view, though in an anonymous context without a specific rela-tion to a personal God.

What Schmid remarked on the relevance of the positive term 'justice' can be applied to its negative counterpart 'injustice', to indicate the plain negation, which in biblical Hebrew is represented by different terms, רשע and some equivalents. Thus רשע denotes a person who does not behave in conformity with the world-order, but lives a life in opposition to it, be it willingly or because lacking an adequate understanding of it (the אֱוִיל, 'fool'). In the view of the wise the deficit of insight is as detrimental as bad intentions and criminal acts, because wisdom as the way to understanding the world-order needs intellectual capacity and knowl-edge to be gained by learning from the wise teachers. For our way of thinking this combination of religious reverence and intellectual training seems to be self-contradictory, but it is characteristic for a primitive, but sophisticated form of theology. So far, the biblical view of evil in the proverbs does not seem to differ from the standards of the surrounding ancient Near East. The international charac-ter of wisdom stamps the whole argumentation, not to say pedagogic intention of the formulations. The antithetic structure of the sentences is adapted to learning by memory and oral tradition. The רשע and his destiny are described in contrast to acts and fate of the righteous.

As is well known, parts of the book of Proverbs (in chs. 22–23) are so similar sometimes in the exact wording to the wisdom-collection of Amen-em-ope that their direct dependence on Egyptian Wisdom-traditions appears more than likely. Sometimes rather concrete and plastic details of the wrong or stupid behaviour of the רשע or אֱוִיל are displayed, according to the practical and pedagogic inten-tions of wisdom. But the general background is everywhere the same: The רשע or אֱוִיל acts against the existing order and therefore has to expect a bad fate. Probably we are right in accepting the judgement that there once existed a just practically oriented form of wisdom. In my opinion it already included thinking in deed–consequence connections. Then we can observe that the older forms of argumentation were at this stage of the development not totally abandoned, but supplemented by the more recently overtaken thinking in the horizon of the world-order of righteousness. This method of handling different layers of tradi-tion is no speciality of wisdom, but can be observed in other parts of the Old Testament.

4. In the next stage the wisdom traditions changed their tendency decisively, when sentences were inserted at certain places into the context which express the belief that Israel's personal God has a decisive role to play in the life of the just and the evil(doer). Such proverbs can be found for instance in Prov. 16.9: 'The heart of man plans his way, but Yahweh orders his steps', or Prov. 21.31: 'The horse is made ready for the day of battle, but the victory belongs to Yahweh'. The impor-tance of these sentences for the context has long been controversial. The answer seems to depend on the basic question how to judge the literary character of the collection of Proverbs as a whole. The opinion that the present collection is an accumulation of single sayings without a visible plan or order[9] – an impression one

9.   Udo Skladny, *Die ältesten Spruchsammlungen in Israel.* (Göttingen: Vandenhoeck &

gains when trying to read the chapters in context – leads to the conclusion that these 'Yahweh-sayings' have been inserted in the form of glosses. Thus, R.B.Y. Scott[10] observed that often such sayings are found in the immediate neighbourhood of sayings they seem to correct or supplement. As an example he quotes Prov. 18.10: 'The name of Yahweh is a strong tower into which the righteous man may run and be inaccessible', which seems to correct the following: 'A rich man's wealth is his strong city, like an inaccessible wall so he supposes' (18.11). An important progress, however, seems to be reached for the understanding of the composition of the central parts of the book by the recent dissertation of Andreas Scherer.[11] He was able to show that the order of the sentences in their final context is the result of a precise planning by redactors, including also the position of the Yahweh-sayings at prominent places in the collection. In Scherer's opinion, the combination of didactic interest and Yahweh-religion, visible in the juxtaposition of sayings expressing the one and the other aspect,[12] characterizes the intentions of these redactors. If Scherer is right in putting the date of this redaction – because of the prominent role of the sayings dealing with the king in the composition – into the pre-exilic period, this would mean that the 'Yahwization' of wisdom would have happened in a comparatively early period.

5. It is of special interest to follow the development into its ensuing stages. For our purpose it seems worthwhile to check the history of the book of Proverbs in its main translations.

To begin with, let us have a look on the text of the Septuagint of Proverbs. In the context of our symposium, we will in the following focus our examination on the terms for the evil ones, the negative side of the antithetic parallelism used by the wise for describing the opposite human characters.

The first observation that strikes us, when we open the *Concordance to the Septuagint* by E. Hatch and H.A. Redpath,[13] is that רשׁע very often is translated by ἀσεβής.[14] One would expect as the more exact equivalent the term κακός, but this

Ruprecht, 1962), who reckoned with four older collections. Refuting this opinion, William McKane declares 'that there is, for the most part, no context in the sentence literature and that the individual wisdom sentence is a complete entity' (*Proverbs*, 10, cf. 413). Cf. also Otto Plöger, *Sprüche Salomos* (BKAT, 17; Neukirchen–Vluyn: Neukirchener Verlag, 1984), 122: 'Die aus Einzelaussagen bestehenden Verse lassen keinen durchlaufenden thematischen Zusammenhang erkennen' ['The verses, consisting in single utterances, do not render visible a covering thematic connection'].

10. 'Wise and Foolish, Righteous and Wicked', in *Studies in the Religion of Ancient Israel* (VTSup, 23; Leiden: E.J. Brill, 1972), 146–65 (162).

11. *Das weise Wort und seine Wirkung: Eine Untersuchung zur Komposition und Redaktion von Proverbia 10,1-22, 16* (WMANT, 83; Neukirchen–Vluyn: Neukirchener Verlag, 1999).

12. Scherer mentions Prov. 10.3; 11.1; 12.2; 14.2; 15.3; 17.3; 19.3; 21.31: *Das weise Wort,* 336 n. 7.

13. *Concordance to the Septuagint and the Other Greek Versions of the Old Testament* (2 vols.; Oxford: Clarendon Press, 1897; reprinted Graz: Akademische Druck- und Verlagsanstalt, 1954).

14. Prov. 2.22; 3.2, 33, 35; 4.14, 19; 9.7; 10.3, 6, 7, 11, 16, 20, 24, 25, 27, 28, 30, 32; 11.(4), 8, 10, 18, 2, 31; 12.5, 6, 7, 10, 12, 21, 26; 13.5, 9, 25; 14.11, 19, 32; 15.6, 8, 9, 28, 29; 16.5; 17.23; 18.3, 5; 19.28; 20.26; 21.4, 7, 10, 12 (2×), 27, 29; 24.15, 16, 20, 39 (= Hebr. 24); 25.5, 26; 28.1, 12, 28; 29.2, 7, 16.

adjective did not suit for the purpose because it means the quality of a thing, a deed etc., not of an acting person. κακός is never used as the translation of רשע. Only once do we meet in Proverbs the word κακοῦργος, as an equivalent for the Hebrew פּעל אוֹן in Prov. 21.15. The use of the term ἀσεβής in the place of רשע indicates an important shift in the understanding of the term. The etymology of the verb leads back to the verb σέβειν/σέβεσθαι, meaning 'venerate a deity', also in a cultic sense. Undoubtedly the Septuagint translators were guided by the impression that the book of Proverbs in its final text intended to characterize the רשעים as impious people, not just κακοῦργους, 'evildoers', to be condemned according to purely moral measures. But whereas the redactors of the Hebrew version left the original wording unaltered – the usual way of redactional activity – the translators were forced to search for the fitting equivalent in Greek and chose terms of a religious flavour according to their own world-view. This observation suits well what we know about the piety of Hellenistic Judaism in the whole and the Septuagint in particular. It is remarkable that, though in recent years a higher degree of attention dedicated to the theology of the Septuagint can be observed, no special inquiry into the terminology of the central passages of the book of Proverbs in the Septuagint version seems to have been undertaken.[15]

6. Secondly we observe in the Septuagint, when we peruse Hatch/Redpath's *Concordance*, an obvious tendency of homogenization, a method well known for the period. Besides the central word for the wicked רשע the Septuagint translates also other terms, which in the Hebrew originals differ distinctly in their semantics from the basic term רשע, with ἀσεβής. In Prov. 1.7 the reason is obvious: This is one of the Yahweh-sayings, placed at the beginning of their instructions by the wise in the first part of the book, which, as is well known, differs in form and contents from the following chapters and mostly is regarded as comparatively later. Already in the Hebrew original, 1.7a begins with the formulation: יראת יהוה ראשית דעת. The translators knew about the religious sense of this expression, when they quite correctly translated the first two words verbatim with φόβος θεοῦ. Thereafter they added two stichs in the middle of the sentence, which do not occur in the Hebrew text.[16] The fourth line is without doubt the translation of v.7b in Hebrew, and here the translators render the Hebrew אוילים with ἀσεβείς. They are doing this under the precondition that the whole sentence has a religious meaning, and therefore neglect the special sense of אויל in the original context.

There are other instances of such levelling in the Septuagint of Proverbs. The term כסיל, typical for wisdom language[17] and as such, as it seems, possessing also originally a double nuance of meaning: 'stupid' and (religiously) 'insolent', sometimes is rendered with ἀσεβής. Thus, twice in the first chapter of Proverbs:

---

15. The recent monograph of Johann Cook, *The Septuagint of Proverbs: Jewish and/or Hellenistic Proverbs?* (VTSup, 69;. Leiden: E.J. Brill, 1997), restricts the exegesis to chs. 1–9 and the different order of Prov. 31 in the Septuagint. The excursus 'Semantic Study of Specific Lexemes' (pp. 335–42) is mainly interested in *hapax legomena*, but not in terms of central theological importance.

16. For the discussion cf. Cook, *Septuagint*, 57–63.

17. 40× in Proverbs.

1.22, 32. Prov. 1.22 is especially worth noting, as the original sense of the stichos 22c[18] in the rest of the formulation is carefully preserved: ἀσεβεῖς γενόμενοι ἐμίσησαν αἴσθησιν - in the Hebrew original: יְשׂנאו דעת. The translators seem to know that a lack of knowledge is involved, but from the two aspects comprised in the term כסיל they choose the religious one, in this way adapting the text to their main interests. The Greek version in Prov. 13.19 confirms the impression that for the Hellenistic translators the intellectual aspect is a basic component of piety, whereas the Hebrew original contains two stichs which appear to most commentators rather unconnected: 'A desire realized is sweet to the soul/but it is an abomination for fools to turn from evil', the Septuagint alters in both semistichs the sense το ἐπιθυμίαι εὐσεβῶν ἡδύνουσιν ψυχὴν, ἔργα δὲ ἀσεβῶν μακρὰν ἀπὸ γνώσεως, 'The desires of the pious give pleasure to the soul/but the works of the godless are far from knowledge.' The tendency of the whole proverb has been shifted to the contrast between the pious and the godless: whereas v. 19a in the Hebrew original expressed a common experience free of any ideology, the translators introduced the antinomy between the εὐσεβεῖς and the ἀσεβεῖς into both hemistichs. The Hebrew original gave a handle to this procedure by commenting on v. 19a by v. 19b. We are entitled to presume that the whole verse in the Hebrew version still belongs to one of the earlier stages in the development of the text belonging to a 'secular' form of wisdom. The ancient wise intended to say that stupid boldness will destroy the pleasure one can enjoy when one's desires are fulfilled. For the translators, stupid boldness means nothing else but a lack of piety. Therefore it was quite natural for them to adapt the whole proverb to this sense.

Occasionally also rarer words are pressed into the scheme. In Prov. 11.9a the term חנף is used, an expression not easy to define. The root seems to mean 'hypocrite',[19] but this can be understood also in an inner-human sense as the behaviour of a person who deceives his fellow-Israelites about his real feelings. The object confirms this: the רע whom the חנף ruins by his mouth, which means by slander. The closer context in v. 9b shows that the word is chosen as a variation of the common רשע, because in the antithetic parallel stich the צדיקם are mentioned. צדיק and רשע, the usual pair, appear above in v. 8, and in plural form below in v. 10. The following vv. 11-13 dwell upon the topic 'slanderous gossip',[20] which explains the variation in v. 9a, where the theme begins. This is an additional proof that the context lacks the later religious aspect. It belongs, we can conclude from the antithetic pair צדיק and רשע, to the phase in which the thinking in the world-order was ruling. We have remarked already that this is true of the whole context. By the way it should be observed that the translators kept the original צדקים, rendering the term by δίκαιοι, whereas the corresponding term ἄδικοι is rare. The reason is easy to detect: the word kept its juridical connotation also in the translation. Where it is

18. V. 22 forms a tristichon.

19. Cf. *HALAT* (Leiden: E.J. Brill, 3rd edn, 1967–96), s. v. Also most commentators render the word in this way. Scherer, *Das weise Wort*, 72, does not explain why he translates 'Ruchloser'.

20. In vv. 10-11 the Septuagint contracts two proverbs into one, without disturbing the sense too much.

used, in most cases the situation directly (the unjust witness[21]) or indirectly (his instrument, the tongue[22]) is the court and the role of the wrong witness is spoken about.

Once in Proverbs (13.22) also the word חטא is rendered by the Septuagint as ἀσεβής (plur.). The participle, 6x in Proverbs,[23] is a comparatively rare term in early wisdom, perhaps because of its cultic connotations, which belong mainly to the priestly sphere. There is, however, also a profane sense, visibly in Prov. 8.36, where personified wisdom speaks. Here חטא as a transitive verb with wisdom as object can be translated by 'missing me'. The Septuagint translators rendered the term with ἁμαρτάνοντες, 'sinned against me'. Also in this case they applied the pious sense of their time to the ancient text.

One sentence in the Hebrew text seems to me especially illuminating in connection with the intention of the Greek translators. In the Hebrew text Prov. 21.30 belongs to the frame by which the Yahwistic redactors commented on the ancient wisdom tradition in view of their own belief in the incomparable might of Israel's god.[24] The sense seems to depend on how we interpret the words לנגד יהוה: 'There is no wisdom, no counsel, no understanding, no policy *against Yahweh.*' This is no condemnation of wisdom as such, but the redactors wanted to point to the limits of wisdom in the presence of God. The translators read the text otherwise: No wisdom *with* the Lord? A blasphemy! Therefore in a similar way as the Masoretes by their תקוני סופרים in the Hebrew text they altered completely the sense. We now read: οὐκ ἔστιν σοφία, οὐκ ἔστιν ἀνδρεία, οὐκ ἔστιν βουλὴ πρὸς τὸν ἀσεβῆ: 'There is no wisdom, no counsel, no understanding, no policy with the impious.' The deep sense of the original has been changed to a commonplace utterance, pious but banal.

7. One observation has to be added to what we have observed regarding the translation principles of the Septuagint so far. We can be happy that the Greek translators were not consistent in using everywhere the same equivalents for the Hebrew words in revising the text of the book of Proverbs. Thus the diversity of expressions in the original was much better preserved. This can be easily shown when we proceed the other way round and start with Hebrew terms. Where the stereotyped alternative between the צדיק and the רשע does not appear, but more diversified expressions, in many cases the Septuagint introduced an equivalent to the original. For example in Prov. 10.14 the translation is a sort of interpretation of the term עויל out of the context: the semistich 'Wise men store up[25] (or: "hide") knowledge' – the Septuagint translates κρύψουσιν αἴσθησιν – is opposed to 'The mouth of the fool (brings) ruin near'.[26] In the Septuagint, אויל is rendered by προπετής, 'rash' – a man who carries his heart on his tongue without seeing what will result from his rashness. Or in Prov. 11.29: 'He who does his household injury

---

21. Prov. 6.19; 12.17, 19; 14.5.
22. Prov. 4.24; 6.17; 12.19; (13.5); 15.26.
23. Prov. 8.36; 11.31; 13.22; 14.21; 19.2; 20.2.
24. On the passage cf. recently Scherer, *Das weise Wort*, 322–23.
25. McKane's translation, *Proverbs*, 225.
26. Cf. NRSV.

inherits wind'[27] תעבד או יל לחכם לב 'and a fool becomes slave to a wise man'. Here the Septuagint preserves the sense and even invents a word play: δουλεύσει δὲ ἄφρων φρώνιμῳ. As these examples show, the translators had a good feeling for the consequences of a lack of insight and carefulness. Therefore the sentences speaking about the mischief of a fool found an open ear with them. They knew to distinguish between a lack of cleverness and people of evil character, but disapproved of both.

8. The impact of the Septuagint on the history of biblical interpretation is important mainly for the Christian churches. The Jews rather early abandoned the Septuagint as Holy Scripture. The reasons are uncertain and debated, but the fact cannot be denied. Already in the New Testament, where the Old Testament is quoted, in most cases the Septuagint is used. This includes the term ἀσεβής, occurring seven times.[28] The Septuagint was handed down exclusively through the churches. We can distinguish between a static and a creative development. Static remained the tradition of the Greek text in the Eastern churches. In the Byzantine Empire, Greek remained the official language until the end of the state and also after the conquest of Constantinople (1453 CE). The Greek Ecumenical Patriarch kept his ecclesiastical authority even after the fall of the empire, and through the centuries the Christian population of Greek culture did not need another translation. I quote Athan Delicostopoulos from the University of Athens: 'The Greek nation has the rare privilege of having as its mother tongue the language of the New Testament as well as of the Septuagint (LXX). The Lord and the Apostles and the consensus ecclesiae throughout the centuries verified the validity of the Septuagint.'[29] This utterance is typical of the bold but static belief of the Eastern churches in the Bible, concomitant to the standstill of Orthodox theology after the first millennium, in which the reformist movements of the Occident never gained a foothold. In our connection we can therefore also leave to the specialists the history of the translations of the Bible into Slavonic and other languages of eastern and south-eastern Europe and neighbouring countries, wherever the influence of the Orthodox Church prevailed.[30] For the churches in the West – to which in the course of time also the transatlantic continent was added – the impact of the Septuagint on daughter-translations was decisive. Rather early the demand for a Bible in the official language of the Western Empire, Latin, arose, presumably first in North Africa. But this Old Latin translation, preserved just in fragments, was superseded by the so-called Vulgate, which finally received the rank of the official version in the Roman Catholic Church at the Council of Trent in the sixteenth century. Though not being the only author, Jerome (ca. 331–420) can be regarded as the person mainly responsible for this eminent project. Jerome was proud of his Hebrew,

---

27. McKane's translation, *Proverbs*, 228.

28. Rom. 4.5; 5.6; 1 Tim. 1.9; 1 Pet. 4.18. Cf. also ἀσέβεια, Rom 1.18; 11.16; 2 Tim. 2.16; Tit. 2.12; Jude 15, 18. ἀσεβεῖν, 2. Pet. 2.6; Jude 15.

29. A. Delicostopoulos, 'Major Greek Translations of the Bible', in J. Krašovec (ed.), *Interpretation of the Bible. Interpretation der Bibel. Interprétation de la Bible. Interpretacija Svetega Pisma* (Lubljana: Slovenska adademija znanosti in umetnosti; Sheffield: Sheffield Academic Press, 1998), 297–316 (297).

30. The comprehensive volume mentioned in the previous note gives complete information.

which he had learned, living in Bethlehem for decades, from a Jewish teacher, and he translated the Bible from the Hebrew original (*hebraica veritas*) into Latin. Though this included a sharp criticism of the Septuagint, there is no doubt that the translation besides the use on the Greek translations of Aquila and especially Symmachus was heavily dependent also on the Septuagint, parts of which Jerome (from the hexaplaric version) had translated earlier.[31] This can easily be checked when we compare the text of the Vulgate with respective passages of the Septuagint. It is also relevant for the Vulgate translation[32] of the term רשע. For instance in Proverbs 10ff. we find *impii* for רשעים, whereas צדיקם is rendered by *iusti*.

This translation also has found its way into the daughter-translations of the Vulgate. The most famous instance is Luther's German translation of the Old Testament,[33] which he based upon the Hebrew original, using however also the help of the Vulgate, the text of which was familiar to him since his youth.[34] For us, it is important to observe that Luther renders רשעים always by 'Gottlose',[35] צדיקם by 'Gerechte'.[36] This is exactly the usage of the Vulgate, which goes back to the Septuagint. Because Luther's translation became the standard version for German Protestantism,[37] was cited even by Roman Catholic controversialists[38] and was also influential in other languages,[39] the impact of this rendering cannot be undervalued. The positive counterpart, the term 'just', has mostly been preserved – though the exact meaning also has often been lost from sight – but the original sense of רשע has been nearly totally lost. The only exception in the sixteenth century I could detect was the *Geneva Bible* of 1560,[40] which translates רשע by 'wicked'.

31.   For an overview cf. Pierre-Maurice Bogaert, 'Versions, ancient (Latin)', *ABD* 6, 799–803.

32.   We used the edition *Biblia sacra iuxta vulgatam versionem*, recensuit Robertus Weber OSB. Editio tertia emendata quam paravit Bonifatius Fischer OSB (Stuttgart: Deutsche Bibelgesellschaft, 1983).

33.   The last edition published during Luther's lifetime is easy to obtain as reprint: *Biblia: das ist: Die gantze Heilige Schrifft: Deudsch. Auffs new zugericht* (Wittenberg: Hans Lufft, 1545). Reprint ed. Hans Volz (Munich: Rogner & Bernhard = Berlin: Deutsche Buchgemeinschaft, no year [1973]).

34.   Cf. H. Volz, 'Einleitung' in Luther, *Biblia*, 62*.

35.   Cf. Prov. 10.3, 6, 7, 11 etc.

36.   Herbert Schmid, '«Gottlose» und Gottlosigkeit im Alten Testament', *Judaica* 33 (1977), 75–85, 127–35, dealt with the problem of the word in German Bible translations starting his article with Luther's translation in its decisive influence for the German language also in the use of this term.

37.   Already in Luther's lifetime the use became popular among his followers. The decisive role of the reformer for the creation of a High German standard language is a well-known fact. It includes the use of the word 'gottlos'.

38.   Cf. Volz, 'Einleitung', in Luther, *Biblia*, 131*–33*.

39.   This is true for instance for the Coverdale Bible of 1535 (the author was Myles Coverdale, 1488–1569). Coverdale, unable to read Greek and Hebrew, worked from the Vulgate text, but also used other versions, among which presumably was Luther's translation. Cf. Jack P. Lewis, art. 'Versions, English (pre-1960)', *ABD* 6, 816–29 (820).

40.   The product of the 'Marian Exiles' who left England for Geneva and other places on the Continent during the reign of the Roman Catholic Queen Mary (1553–58) and the bloody persecution of the Protestants in her country. Cf. the facsimile edition (Madison, Milwaukee: University of Wisconsin Press, 1969).

Among modern translations the *New Revised Standard Version* does the same. But the *Zurich Bible*, the official version of the Swiss German Reformed Church since 1931 and also used by many as a more readable and presumably more exact equivalent of the original text, even goes a step further. It translates צדיק as 'der Fromme' ('the pious') and רשע as 'der Gottlose' ('the godless'). Herbert Schmid states that Luther himself did not mean the 'godless' were not believing in a God. In an overview over the whole Old Testament he shows that theoretical atheism would have been anachronistic in the Bible. Thereby he intends to refute the popular misunderstanding going exactly in this direction.

9. We conclude with the summary that the understanding of the terms רשע and צדיק has suffered a progressive shift into a more and more pious accentuation. This reinterpretation began in the successive redactions of the collection of Hebrew Proverbs itself: step by step they moved from a profane form, in which the proverbs intended nothing more than to preserve everyday experiences in memorable verses, showing among other observations a 'deed–consequence connection', to a religious accentuation. First the 'world-order' of צדקה/צדק becomes the frame, in which human deeds and fate as צדקים and רשעים are classified. A more recent, but also comparatively early redaction introduces the impact of Yahweh-belief. This movement is continued and intensified by the translators of the Septuagint, who replace the רשעים by the ἀσεβεῖς. Jerome in his Vulgate did not reproduce the original sense of the Hebrew word but the Greek expression in rendering the term by *impii*. This decision influenced the modern translations into the vernacular, beginning with Luther's famous German Bible and later on.

Whoever tries to gain a deeper understanding of the intentions of biblical wisdom should know about this development. The result of our investigations is also relevant in the actual discussion about 'canonical exegesis', which focuses its interest upon the final form of the biblical text.[41] We are reminded that in order to detect the depth of a text, the exegete has to dig into the earlier layers which are hidden below the surface of the final form. The development of earlier periods left its traces in the text, and to overlook them closes our eyes before important aspects, which are meaningful also for an adequate understanding of its theological contents.

41. As known, this approach is, above all, connected with the name of Brevard S. Childs, cf. especially *Introduction to the Old Testament as Scripture* (Philadelphia: Fortress Press; London: SCM Press, 1979); *Old Testament Theology in a Canonical Context* (London: SCM Press, 1985); *Biblical Theology of the Old and New Testaments* (London: SCM Press, 1992). On Childs and the canonical approach: Paul R Noble, *The Canonical Approach: A Critical Reconstruction of the Hermeneutics of Brevard S. Childs* (Biblical Interpretation Series, 16; Leiden: E.J. Brill, 1995); John Barton, 'Canon and Old Testament Interpretation', in Edward Ball (ed.), *In Search of True Wisdom: Essays in Old Testament Interpretation in Honour of Ronald E. Clements* (JSOTSup, 300; Sheffield: Sheffield Academic Press, 1999), 37–52.

THE DEVIL IN THE REVELATION OF ST JOHN

Klaus Wengst

1. *The Certainty in John's Speaking of the Devil*

The seer John, the author of Revelation, seems to be certain of the devil. In the last book of the New Testament the devil is a person who acts quite on his own, but who is acted upon as well. In the message to the church of Smyrna John announces, 'Indeed the devil is about to throw some of you into prison' (2.10). In the following message sent to Pergamum he talks about the devil twice. 'I know… where you dwell, where Satan's throne is.' At the end of the verse he mentions the faithful martyr Antipas 'who was killed among you, where Satan dwells' (2.13). So John uses the Greek word διάβολος on the one hand, and on the other hand the Hebrew word שׂטן which has been transcribed into Greek and made the Greek word σατανᾶς. The Septuagint already renders שׂטן into διάβολος. John is conscious of the fact that διάβολος is a translation of שׂטן. That can be proved by the fact that he enumerates a whole string of terms in 12.9 and 20.2 and only connects these two with an 'and'. In 12.9 he refers to this figure as the 'great dragon' and then continues, 'that serpent of old, called the Devil and Satan, who deceives the whole world'. After mentioning the dragon in 20.2 he adds in a similar way, 'that serpent of old, who is the Devil and Satan'.

The vision in 12.7-12 tells about a war in heaven between Michael and his angels on the one hand and 'the dragon' and his angels on the other hand. According to v. 9 the result of that war is that he is cast out of heaven, 'he was cast to the earth and his angels were cast out with him'. That leads to a woe to earth and sea, 'for the devil has come down to you, having great wrath, because he knows that he has a short time' (v. 12). According to the vision of the millennium an angel, who had come from heaven, 'laid hold of the dragon, that serpent of old, who is the Devil and Satan and bound him for a thousand years' (20.2). At the end of these thousand years 'Satan will be released from his prison' to wage war with the help of collected armies, 'and fire came down from God out of heaven and devoured them' (vv. 7-9). 'And the devil, who deceived them was cast into the lake of fire and brimstone…' (v. 10). Those are the verses in which John speaks of the devil as of a person who acts and who is acted upon. How is it possible that he is that certain of the devil?

2. *Speaking of the Devil from Experience*

The fact that John is obviously certain of the devil is mainly based on the biblical-Jewish tradition which he takes for granted. It is in this tradition that Satan develops from a prosecutor in the heavenly council-meeting (Job) to an adversary who surely remains subordinated to God but who represents what is hostile to God and men. But neither this tradition nor John talks of him apart from concrete experience. What experiences can be seen in the verses in which John speaks of the devil?

If 2.10 says that the devil will cast some members of the church of Smyrna into prison, these events normally cannot be perceived as the work of the devil. What can be perceived – if what is expected to happen (perhaps it has already happened) – may be the following: members of the church are reported by men outside the church for withdrawing from public life which means being enemies of the existing order and therefore being politically disloyal. The municipal authorities arrest the reported persons, and keep them in prison up to the next date of a hearing in Smyrna because the Roman governor is responsible for political things like these in the province. Thus, they are men who act. This raises the question why John makes the devil a subject and lets him be the one who acts. I will not answer it for the moment.

The same correlation may be seen in the message to Pergamum (2.13). Somebody is mentioned there by name – a certain Antipas – who was killed as Jesus Christ's martyr. We may imagine this procedure to be analogous to that one Pliny later describes in his letter about Christians addressed to Trajan – a procedure which he naturally obeys though according to himself he has not been involved in any trials against Christians yet. So we can say that that procedure must have been a common one: one who confessed to be a Christian even after having been asked three times and in spite of being threatened with death penalty, or one who denied being a Christian but refused to curse Christ and to express religious and political loyalty in front of idols and the bust of the emperor was executed at once. Before and after that the text talks about the 'throne of Satan' in Pergamum and about Satan's dwelling there. With this the text is likely to allude to the temple of *Divus Augustus* and *Dea Roma* as the oldest and most famous centre of emperor worship in the province of Asia. So we get a hint already here that for John the Roman power takes the figure of the devil. After all it should be recorded that the experience of being threatened with death by a political power which makes itself an idol makes him speak of the devil.

The combination of ch. 12 and ch. 13 and the description of the beast out of the sea in 13.1-3 shows that John connects Rome with the devil very closely. According to ch. 12 the dragon, who is given further names and expressions in v. 9, was cast out of heaven to the earth. The consequence of that was a woe to earth and sea (v. 12). According to v. 17 the dragon gets ready to make war against those 'who keep the commandments of God and have the testimony of Jesus Christ'. In v. 18 John says that he, John himself, stood on the sand of the seashore. In ch. 13 he then sees a beast, a terrible monster, rising out of the sea. In a way there is a change from the dragon to the beast. The dragon's war takes place in what the beast will do.

With the description of the beast John takes up Daniel 7. Four wild beasts, which symbolize four successive empires, are described there. The fact that John combines the four animals in Daniel into one monster lets us assume that he wants to mark the empire of his days, the Roman one. This assumption is based on the fact that in a way the legend of *Nero redivivus* can be seen in the description of one of the seven heads of the beast in 13.3.

Chapter 17 clearly shows that John means Rome by that beast and that his experience is defined by the Roman power. In that vision we again encounter the beast of the beginning of ch. 13; a woman equipped with luxury, who is called a 'whore', is sitting on him. The name 'Babylon the Great' which is written on her forehead is explicitly called a 'mystery', which means it is a code name. Only Rome could be called by the code name 'Babylon' and only among Jews and actually only after the Jewish Roman war from 66 to 70 CE. Rome had destroyed the Second Temple as Babylon had done it to the first. In the interpretation of the Jewish tradition God had pronounced judgement on Babylon in the meantime. A result of this is a correspondence between what happened to Babylon and what will happen to Rome. God will surely pronounce judgement on Rome as he did on Babylon. It is not astonishing that not only the beast but the woman riding on him as well symbolizes Rome. To say it just as a thesis: they express different aspects of the Roman power – the beast stands for irresistible military force and the woman for exploiting economic power. We can grasp this reference to Rome in 17.9b. It says, 'The seven heads are seven mountains on which the woman sits.' The allusion to Rome with its seven hills cannot be overlooked here.

So that is the experience which can be seen behind John's speaking of the devil. He experiences the Roman power as extraordinarily oppressive, violent and exploiting, even as deadly. It is the perception of the blood which has actually been shed that corresponds to the vision of the streaming blood in ch. 14, which covers the whole earth 'up to the horses' bridles' (v. 20). In 6.9-10 John hears the cry for justice of those 'who had been slain for the word of God and for the testimony which they held'. In 20.4 he sees 'those who had been beheaded for their witness to Jesus and for the word of God'. In 17.6 he sees Rome 'drunk with the blood of the saints and with the blood of the martyrs of Jesus'. In 18.24 he hears an angel say that 'in her was found the blood of prophets and saints, and of all that were slain in the earth'. That is the last reason for the judgement on Rome. John recognizes 'the abundance of her luxury' (18.3), which makes the products of the provinces be transported into the luxuriant capital (18.12-14). That is his experience. Is it so depressing that he can only characterize it as caused by the devil? Would that not be an expression of powerlessness, that you are not able to organize and structure the world you live in? Or can there be a certain intention in his speaking of the devil in reference to Rome?

3. *The Intention in John's Speaking of the Devil*

Why does John make Rome the devil? Why does he transform his experience of being extremely oppressed by the Roman power into visions of the devil? What is that for? And what is the relation between such a way of speaking of the devil and speaking of God? The images in John's visions are no free associations. They are fed not only by his experienced reality but by reading his Jewish Bible and further tradition. John reads the Bible and discovers in it the experienced reality of his own present. For him the Bible becomes a framework for perceiving reality. At the same time it offers him means of expression for describing reality. It does not let him be alone with that reality which has been experienced as devilish, but opens the dimension of God. It is the Bible which brings in God and with this a perspective on how to limit and overcome the evil. Neither does John actually reflect upon the evil nor does he speculate about the devil as such. He finds himself in a bad and extremely oppressive reality. The only question of interest is how to handle that reality. John's visions are a particular way to do that.

The vision of the war in heaven in 12.7-12, where the dragon is defeated and cast onto the earth, is John's way to settle the objective structures of power. The dragon has already been defeated. There is a superior place where he has no business being. He does not have a place in heaven any longer; it is only God's kingdom (v. 8). Being already defeated, the dragon wages his last, but already lost battle on earth even if this is experienced painfully enough by the persons concerned. With this vision John raises the discussion between his churches and the Roman power to a higher level on which the position of power has already been decided to the disadvantage of that party which seems to be dominant and invincible. It is fighting a lost cause. Deadly violence, which is living in the past, has no future. Its time is limited. Demonstrating the dimension of God, John introduces a perspective, which leads out of this obstructive situation. That makes him and his people bear the situation, contradict, and resist. The proclamation of the victory which was already been gained in heaven (v. 10) does not lead John to a triumphant attitude nor an illusionary view on reality – a dreamy skipping of bad reality – either. This may only just be mentioned as far as ch. 12 is concerned. The churches John writes his messages to are to recognize their own situation in the situation of the woman who was threatened and persecuted by the dragon and then rescued into the desert and miraculously kept alive. The churches John addresses do not live in the desert but in the towns of the province of Asia. But in the middle of the towns they are in the desert nevertheless, the desert as a place of oppression and protection at the same time. John regards the outskirts and not the centre as the appropriate place for the church in a world dominated by violence and lies, in a world where idolatry is practised.

The intention John pursues in his visions by the condemnation of the power of Rome, which has been experienced as oppressive, we can realize in a subtly differentiated way in the transition from ch. 12 to ch. 13, namely in the above-mentioned change from the devil to the beast out of the sea. The four wild beasts of Daniel 7, which symbolize four successive empires, are combined in one monster. We can describe in three ways what is intended. At first we are confronted with masking and camouflage. The one who does not know the Bible and the tradition which is coming from it, that is to say the one who is uninitiated, thinks the Apocalypse to be abstruse and therefore politically harmless. It clearly shows that the Apocalypse is underground literature for initiated persons. Second and third, it is this description which leads the initiated persons to the 'revelation of power' in a twofold sense. On the one hand we are shown what the power of Rome actually looks like from the victims' point of view: behind the mask which has been pulled down, the claim to rule in a humane way, you can see the grimace of a horrible beast. Combining the four beasts in Daniel 7 in a single one John expresses that all the dreadful things, which have existed in empires up to now, reached their peak in Rome's violent and exploiting power. On the other hand we are shown to whom the power actually belongs and at the same time that the power of the beast is not unlimited. John's readers and listeners know quite well that the four beasts of Daniel 7 are not totally on top. They know that this vision is followed by that of God as the true sovereign; and they know by that the vision of the Son of Man and the hope of a really humane government.

This aspect of the 'revelation of power', which means that God is the true sovereign, is presented in ch. 13 in a curiously contradictory way. On the one hand v. 2 says: 'The dragon gave him [the beast who has just risen out of the sea] his power, his throne and great authority' (cf. v. 4). On the other hand v. 5 and v. 7 say four times that he 'was given' to do what he does. Using the passive here the author must think of God as the logical subject. That can be seen as well in v. 5b, which says: '...and he was given authority to continue for 42 months'. The 42 months (cf. 11.2) as well as the 1260 days in 11.3 and 12.6 correspond to the three and a half years and by that to the 'time and times and half a time' of 12.14. Three and a half is half of seven, the number which represents perfection and completeness. So you can say that 'three and a half' stands for incompleteness and imperfection. Consequently Rome's power is limited to these '42 months'. God has caused that limitation; the 'eternal Rome' naturally does not want it. Apart from the statement that the dragon, the devil, has given power to Rome there is another one, which says that God has given it to him. John does not try to achieve a logical balance between these two statements. You could only have freedom from logical contradiction beyond price. If John only said that the dragon had given power to the beast, he would literally let the devil have the world. If he only said that God had given the beast power, he would theologically justify a devilish reality. As he wants neither to let the devil have the world, nor to justify a bad world theologically he has no other choice but to accept contradiction. How should he, in view of the experiences he gained, in view of the bloody power of Rome he himself experienced, record his belief in God as creator and Lord in another way than in a contradiction? The logical contradiction is nothing else but the consequence of the fact that God himself participates in a contradictory reality, suffers from it and contradicts, and thus lets the contradiction exist. This way of speaking seems to be dualistic and contradictory but makes us realize at the same time that God has not achieved his goal yet. That is why John speaks of the coming God.

4. *Speaking of the Devil for the Sake of God*

We might put it paradoxically: John speaks of the devil because he wants to speak of God. He speaks of God as the coming God, because he does not want to come to terms with injustice and violence, poverty and misery, and with the tears which must be shed because of grief and rage. God has not achieved his goal yet. But being the coming God he does not let despair have those who put their trust in him. John's view corresponds to the understanding of monotheism in the Bible and in its interpretation. The monotheism of the Bible is not a theoretical one, which could be put into dogmas, but a dynamic one. God himself is still on his way to being the only one. He wants to act in a reality, which has been experienced as contradictory. The Hebrew Bible expresses that very clearly in Zech. 14.9: 'And the Lord shall be King over all the earth. In that day it shall be – the Lord is one, and His name one.' The rabbinical interpretation of this text combines this text with the שמע ישראל in Deut. 6.4: 'The Lord is our God: over us. The Lord is one: over all who come into the world. The Lord is our God: in this time. The Lord is one: for the coming time. And thus the Scriptures say: And the Lord shall be King over all the earth. In that day it shall be – the Lord is one and His name one' (*Sif Dev* §31). According to another passage the statement of Zech. 14.9 will only then become effective when not only all the nations but the entire earth worship God (*MTeh* 66). Another passage infers from Ps. 97.1 'that there will be no joy in the world as long as the rule of Edom (= Rome) is established and that neither the name is perfect nor the throne.' 'But when the Holy One, blessed be He, will establish his kingdom during the fourth exile [namely that under Roman rule] it is held to be valid: The Lord will be one and His name one' (*MTeh* 97.1). Without reference to Zech. 14.9 the same ideas are expressed in an interpretation of Exod. 15.11:

> 'Who is like You, O Lord, among the gods?' (Exodus 15.11) When the Israelites saw that Pharaoh and his army had perished that the rule of the Egyptians had come to an end and that judgement had been carried out on their idolatry, they opened their mouths and said altogether: Who is like You, O Lord, among the gods? And not only the Israelites sang a song but all the nations as well. When they heard that Pharaoh and Egypt had perished in the sea, that the rule of the Egyptians had come to an end and that judgement had been carried out on their idolatry, they refused their own idolatry, opened their mouths, blessed the Highest and said: Who is like You, O Lord, among the gods? And so you will see that all the nations of the world will refuse idolatry in future. For it is said: O Lord, my strength and my fortress, my refuge in the day of affliction, the Gentiles shall come to You from the end of the earth and say: Surely our fathers have inherited lies, worthlessness and unprofitable things. Will a man make gods for himself? (Jer 16.19-10). And the scriptures say: In that day a man will cast away his idols of silver and his idols of gold which they made, each for himself to worship (Is 2.20) And it says: To go into the clefts of the rocks (Is 2.21) And what is written after that? But the idols he shall utterly abolish (Is 2.18)' (*MekhY Beshallach* [Shira] 8).

As the salvation by the Red Sea is archetypal of the final salvation, the hope for what will take place in the last days – the nations of the world refuse idolatry – is already re-projected onto the events by the Red Sea. Thus, it is already shown here in a symbolic way. With the disappearance of idolatry God's will will gain acceptance and his being the only one will only then achieve its goal.

The clearest correspondence with this can be found in Paul's statements in 1 Cor. 15.20-28 in the New Testament. He says that the final aim of Jesus Christ's work is that all that is hostile to God, is finally removed and that the world in all its fields is obviously assigned to God. 'Now when all things are made subject to Him [God], then the Son Himself will also be subject to Him who put all things under Him, that God may be all in all' (1 Cor. 15.28). According to this paragraph Jesus' resurrection from the dead aims at a kingdom of God over all human beings and all powers, which is unlimited and total. The work of Jesus Christ will be completed when there does not exist any field of the creation which is not assigned to God, and when idolatry is not practised any longer.

This view characterizes John's Apocalypse as well. God's unvarnished presence and shining lightness, which assign everything and everybody to God, will only exist at the end in the vision of the New Jerusalem. This goal had been described negatively before, namely that the devil 'should deceive the nations no more' (20.3). 12.9 had already characterized him as the one 'who deceives the whole world'. Deceiving the nations is a recurrent motive (20.8, 10; cf. 13.14; 18.23; 19.20). It results from the overwhelming impression of irresistible military force. That is why 13.3b,4 says: 'And all the world marvelled and followed the beast. So they worshipped the dragon that gave authority to the beast and they worshipped the beast, saying, who is like the beast? Who is able to make war with him?' The question, who is like the beast, is the reversal of the question 'Who is like you, O Lord, among the gods?' in Exod. 15.11. But here it is addressed to God. The following temptation is a result of the shining light of the extremely rich capital (18.23); the 'abundance of luxury' (18.3) captivates all people. Presenting the adoration of power and the surrender to the fascination of luxury as idolatry John clearly shows how much the coming God and his being the only one is the topic of his book.

Part II

RELIGIOUS HISTORY AND JUDAISM

EVIL IN THE WORLD OF RELIGIONS

Hans-Peter Hasenfratz
(translated by Henning Graf Reventlow)

1. 'Unde malum et quare' – 'From where comes Evil and why does it come?' According to the church father Tertullian this question fascinates the Gnostics and the philosophers. We can add: it intrigues all religions. The ultimate reason for Evil is equivalent to the ultimate reason for the Good: How can a reason for the existence of Good be given, if Evil co-exists? If in the following arguments occasionally just the Evil is spoken about, the Good is included as correlation or antagonistic principle. In none of the religious systems to be treated, however, is Evil the supreme principle. We interview traditional societies, cultures with polytheistic, antagonistic, and trans-moral systems and monotheistic religions.

2. The term '*traditional societies*' means 'communities of camps and villages in hunting, gathering and primitive planting, agrarian and herding-nomadic cultures', the corporate life of which is regulated by fixed oral tradition ('memory-culture' in contrast to the 'literary cultures'). Their world-view is mainly structured according to the so-called 'dual two-sphere-system'.[1] With a traditional society cosmos is always the village it inhabits, including the usable surrounding district (plantations, places for gathering, hunting, pasturing and the connecting ways between them). In this internal en-dosphere, which every group regards as navel of the world, the creating power of the divine moulder (the 'High Divinity' of the respective ethnic group) had found its densest and most perfect expression. Outside this cosmic centre it had relaxed. Much had remained uncompleted: it was bar-ren desert, exuberantly growing wilds, stony rocky districts, marshy and deceptive fens, populated by demonic mongrels, curious beasts not to be hunted, 'barbaric' people with 'crazy' customs, the language and manners of whom one could not understand. Really no 'human beings', whom a creating deity might have left so to say in a 'rough state' as punishment for some offence. This a-cosmic exosphere encompasses the cosmic centre of common life as the 'beyond', chaotic, fatal anti-world. But also this centre was not perfect, as the respective world-moulders also here were lacking the needed circumspection. Why, for instance, are human beings naked and in need of clothes? Originally they possessed a coat, but the cattle did not.

---

1. K. Müller, *Schamanismus* (Munich: C.H. Beck, 1997), 11, note.

Because the cattle nourish human beings, the gods thought it advisable to supply them with the coat of the human beings against rain, frost and heat. Therefore they 'skinned man and put his coat on the cow'. The human beings they presented with clothes. Thus an (old-Indian) myth. Even if the endospherical world – contrasted with the anti-world outside – is 'the best of all worlds', it is susceptible to disturbances. Night and winter move the borders between chaos and cosmos, anti-world and world periodically far into the endosphere, close to the settlements and thresholds of the lodgings. At any time chaos, for example bad weather or sudden attack of barbarian 'semi-humans', can irrupt into the realm of cosmos. The infectious anti-nature of the anti-world outside is so strong that if anyone goes astray while gathering or hunting in it and returns *after* a certain time, that person is no more recognized by his group as a man, one of them, but is killed as a monster. The relations inside the group and 'in the world' are stamped by sympathy and reciprocity: what happens to one member, happens to all; a gift obliges to a return gift, a service to a return service. By behaving against the norm, which rends this texture of relations to pieces – as envy, harmful magic, break of tradition – chaos, so to speak, bursts in the centre of the cosmic realm of life and can manifest itself as illness, failure of crops, or death. Individuals who are morally deviant of the own group therefore are pushed out of the community to the extraneous anti-world. They suffer 'social death' alive. Barbarian inhabitants of the exospherical outer realm are principally enemies. They are rather shunned than killed, in order not to get into contact with them. Where contact is vital (exchange of goods), it is narrowly restricted and severely ritualized. Members of another group can, if at all, be integrated into the community just by marriage (exogamy) or a ritual of adoption. This is one of the few possibilities of outer relations. Wives, if originating (by exogamy) from a foreign group, are already therefore always 'suspected of chaos'. Additionally their gender is regarded as 'unclean' by menstruation, childbirth, confinement, all of them considered and suspected as illness. Discontinuity, interruption, standstill in the cosmic flow of life (which includes, *inter alia*, each form of the loss of blood) are experienced and dreaded as eventual gaps for the irruption of disorder, of chaos, and have to be bridged by an adequate 'ritual expense'. The traditional forms are thereby meticulously observed. Breaks in continuity are also eclipses of sun and moon, the solstice in winter, and especially the phases of passage in the course of life: birth, puberty, wedding, death. Every death of a member of the group means diminution of the common potential of life, a break in the sympathetic connection of life, chaos in the midst of cosmos. Collective rites of passage secure for the dead person a passage free of disturbance to the beyond while staying at the same time in the lap of the community. Simultaneously they revitalize the group left behind and thereby make good the loss of vitality caused by the death. If the rites of passage did not take place, the dead person would not find his way into the beyond. He would become the victim of the a-cosmic sphere of power of the outside and would take revenge as 'a-cosmic dead' against the living. In traditional societies Good and Evil are *social-local phenomena*. All Evil originates in the chaotic *outer world* , even where it bursts open in the cosmic internal world. Every Good happens alone and only in the internal world. The precondition therefore, for this to happen, is that the endospherical processes of interaction of sympathy and reciprocity pass off in continuity and without friction under exact preservation of the tradition.

We devoted so much space here to the concept of the two spheres, because it has 'endured' intact all social changes and religious superstructures. Even in our period of immense streams of migration it revives without any restriction: everything 'strange' 'from outside' is potentially evil to it. In situations of social-political crises it penetrates all securing-systems of a culture and usurps the unrestrained autocracy. 'Ethnic cleansing' is its banner, genocide its bloody work. 'Clash of civilizations' is its future in a 'global world' without a common minimal consensus, in which one civilization regards itself as good alone and 'the Middle Kingdom' and the others as 'godless' or 'the realm of Evil'. One can admire it in the plan of a medieval or early modern town, which at many places still stamps the panorama of our towns, materialized in architecture. Cosmos reaches as far as the range of power of the town. The cosmic navel is occupied with church and town hall. The houses of patricians and guilds surround it closely. In a wider circle we find the houses of the citizens qualified for the guilds. Further away from the centre the simpler citizens are living. Along the walls of the town lodge the members of the despised occupations, the 'dishonest people' (millers, linen-weavers, barbers, whores, hangmen etc.), likewise in the new town and outside the wall. Here also newcomers, strangers, vagrant people and other 'shady mob' have permanently or temporarily settled. The surrounding region is according to the political situation either dominion and subject territory of the town: still cosmos – or enemy's country: already chaos. There abroad was the abode of the so-called outlawed (people who were banished from the community) and of capital criminals wanted and sentenced in their absence. As belonging to the exospherical realm of chaos their life ranked as nothing. As fugitives and wanderers they have to avoid the (cosmic) realm of peace of the cities.

3.   Where neighbouring traditional societies fuse into bigger sociological units (for whatever reasons), where conquests or infiltration by foreign cultures broke traditions open, where closed camp or village communities got into the reach of the power of expanding settlements or municipal cultures, there the world of the gods reflects the more complex social relations, cultural stratification and hierarchic structures. Evil cannot any more be fixed locally as outer-worldly and Good as inner-worldly. Both are experienced as inner-worldly as 'structurally Evil' and structurally Good: as force that produces suppression, but also as power that under altered social conditions renders right possible and enforces it. Elaborate *polytheistic* systems distribute consequently inner-worldly Evil and outer-worldly Chaotic between different divine powers, as we shall see.

4. Ancient Egyptian texts[2] tell about the two unequal divine brothers *Osiris* and *Seth*. Osiris liberated the human beings from their life full of want and from wild animals. He taught them to adore the gods, gave them laws and introduced the culture of wine and agriculture. He becomes their first king, is the 'primeval king' as such. Totally different is his brother Seth: he is the lord of the barren, deadly desert, lord of metals, of power, god of the storm, the 'red god' of aggressiveness and fury. Seth kills and cuts his brother Osiris into pieces. But Osiris, already dead, begets a son Horus. (This is a myth about the sowing of corn, resting of the vegetation in the soil, new germination.) Horus, grown up amid dangers, draws Seth before a tribunal of gods. This tribunal appoints Osiris as king of the dead and Horus – as successor to his father – as king of the living. But Seth actually is not condemned to death for his murder. He is delegated to the sun-bark of the king of the gods, Re, in order to secure its daily course over the sky and nightly through the underworld. This secures the existence of the cosmic order. Because the sun-bark on its course is attacked again and again by the chaos serpent Apophis, who threatens to destroy it and its crew and thereby the whole world, Seth, posted at the bow of the bark, thrusts again and again his enormous spear into the serpent's throat and reddens by its blood the sky in the evening and in the morning. Thus the regeneration of the sun in the netherworld and its function as daily giving life to the creatures are secured. For the Egyptian the cosmic and social, human and divine order consists in not acknowledging Evil as inner-worldly force, at best subordinating it as power to justice, in order to guarantee this order against the un-worldly chaos. Evil as such is not the will of God. In a coffin-inscription (CT 1130, ca. 2000 BCE) the 'universal lord' (Re) speaks to his creatures: 'I created everybody like his equal and did not order to commit sins (*isfet*). Their hearts (*ibūen*) are the ones who act against my word.'

5. Where in traditional societies the Cosmic and the A-Cosmic (see above, 2) are explained by the exclusive actions of *two* antipodal *divinities*, as usual in the Siberian era, antagonistic religions arise.[3] Two antagonistic systems have become scripture religions with far-reaching cultural impacts: Zoroastriansm and Manichaeism. Both are the fruit of the 'Iranian attitude of mind'.[4] The monotheistic scripture religions (Judaism, Christianity, Islam) owe to the first the popular-religious figure of the Devil as antagonist of God. To the second Christianity owes a large amount of hostility to body and world, but also a certain critical distance from this world and its structures.

2. Cf. H. Brunner, 'Seth und Apophis – Gegengötter im ägyptischen Pantheon?', *Saeculum* 34 (1983), 226–34.

3. In this case we prefer the term 'antagonistic'. 'Dual' or 'dualistic' only refers to the *number* of the opposite subjects involved, but nothing about their mutual *relationship*.

4. The origin of the Iranians, one must know, was in Siberia, about the southern Ural, before parts of them started into the direction of the highlands of Iran. Cf. H.-P. Hasenfratz, 'Iran: Antagonismus als Universalprinzip', *Saeculum* 34 (1983), 235–47.

6.   In the second millennium BCE an audition was experienced by an offering-priest (*zaotar*) of an Iranian tribe at the southern base of the Ural 'in a dream-sleep', which has to be counted among the great revelations of the religions of all times. The priest is called *Zarathushtra*; what happened to him is handed down in the holy scriptures of his community, in the Avesta (Y.30). He therefore seems to be the first documented prophet of religious history. To the prophet two primeval divine 'spiritual beings' (*mainyu*) reveal themselves, 'twins', the two basic principles of being: the Better in thoughts, word and deed, 'the holiest spirit' Ahura Mazda (the 'Wise Lord') and the 'Evil Spirit' (Angra Mainyu). These two principles now mark off their respective territories of action against one another. The Holiest Spirit, who keeps to truth (*asha*), orders for himself life and good actions; Angra Mainyu, who keeps to untruth (*drug*: 'deceit'), the non-life and bad actions. All beings have to 'choose' between these two basic principles. The righteous people and forces around the Holiest Spirit choose life, the unjust people and demons around the Evil Spirit choose non-life. Thereby, however, also their future fate is destined: Angra Mainyu and his demonic and human followers finally (in the 'last battle') fall prey to non-life, to death, the final annihilation, which they have chosen for themselves. Whoever keeps, by acting (speaking, thinking) rightly, to Ahura Mazda (and the forces around him), harvests everlasting life. The closeness to early Jewish apocalypticism is evident: here the 'public prosecutor' of the Old Testament (שָׂטָן) has become, under Iranian impact,[5] God's antagonist, as 'prince of the world'. The devil, because actually incompatible with a strict monotheism – but for an 'explanation' of Evil in the world and for a 'moral discharge' of God utterly 'practical' – in the official creeds of the three monotheistic scripture religions (Judaism, Christianity, Islam) never played a role (though even theologians believed and still believe in his existence).

7.   In cultures that know any kind of dichotomy of reality in material and immaterial, matter and spirit, corporeal and psychical, a latent inclination to a devaluation of the material-corporeal conferred with the immaterial, spiritual, psychical can be observed.[6] Where pessimism becomes the basic mood of social strata or societies – social conditions can play a role – latent feelings can become virulent. Mānī, an Iranian founder of religion in the realm of the Sassanides, himself of noble Iranian (Parthian) extraction, developed the dichotomy to a religious antagonism. Matter, substance, body are evil and creations of the 'King of Darkness', 'immaterial' spiritual-psychical phenomena belong to the good realm of light of the 'Father of Greatness'. In living creatures and of course in humans light and darkness are mixed. Psychical-spiritual sparks are imprisoned and bound in corporeal matter. Redemption consists first in the knowledge (*Gnosis*) of this fact, secondly in the 'minimizing of all life relations' (prohibition of prostitution

5.   For nearly 200 years Judah was a province of the Persian empire and praised the Persians as 'redeemers' out of the Babylonian exile.

6.   In the Occident for instance in Platonism, later in Neo-Platonism.

and sexual intercourse, of killing and meat diet, of theft and personal possessions) in order to liberate the light-soul out of the dark prison of the material body. Manichaeism has fundamentally called the self-understanding of the Christian church in the Occident into question. It reacted with the bloody extermination of the Manichaean doctrine.[7] The 'right answer' upon the Manichaean doctrine cannot be given, because antagonistic religious models (as the Iranian of Zarathustra and Mani) are the only ones capable to reply in a stringent logic upon the origin of Evil (and Good) in the world, presumed one accepts their religious axiomatic. To complete one has to add that in other (Gnostic) systems evil can be thought of as 'apostasy' (gradual dissociation) from Good and increasing materialization (in proportion to a growing distance). The lack of a sufficient explanation how this degradation could happen, these models partake with monotheism (see below, 9).

8. For religious systems of Indian origin,[8] which can be finally deduced from the philosophy of the Upanishads, the real Evil is (similar to the Gnosis, see above, 7) the lack of knowledge (*avidyā*): not to know about the identity of the single soul (*ātmā*) with the (impersonal) divine original ground of all being (*brahma*) in Hinduism, not to know about the illusionary character of human personality (*pudgala*) in Buddhism. Evil and Good in the ban of not knowing can according to the law of retaliation causality (*karma*) 'just' lead to a worse or better rebirth and deteriorate or improve the conditions for the acquisition of the redeeming knowledge (*vidyā*).[9] For the knowing, however, who has discarded false identifications and illusions of the own identity, caused by desire (*kāma*) and thirst of life (*tṛṣṇā*) (in Buddhism also personified as *Māra*: corrupter, tempter, the Evil one), for this person Good and Evil have become irrelevant. 'This one is not overwhelmed, whether he therefore (because he was in the body) did the Evil or did the Good. But he overwhelms both. Him does not burn what he did or did not.' Thus an Upanishad text (BU 4,4,22). Similarly the Buddhist Dhammapada in the 'chapter on love'. The way of the knowing takes its course in this system 'beyond Good and Evil' on *trans-moral* fields. As way *to* knowledge religion had for the knowing at best a 'propedeutic value'. He does not need it any more.

9. It is 'the misery of *monotheism*' – now we are carrying on what we started in the beginning – being forced to justify evil in the world and, if it projects the problem on God himself, to justify this God (theodicy). How can God cause evil – because nothing happens 'without him', if he is almighty, unless it must be put on his account – because as '*summum bonum*' he cannot be evil? Muslim and Christian theology present here the same 'solution': God is involved in the *material* (physical, biological) aspect of every

---

7. Finally by the devastating crusades against Catharism in the thirteenth century and later by the Papal inquisition.

8. Cf. H.-P. Hasenfratz, *Der indische Weg* (Freiburg i. Br.: Herder, 1994).

9. A woman has few chances in this connection: in Hinduism she has to be reborn as Brahmin, in Buddhism as monk in any case as male.

action (e.g. in the gravitation and the muscle-movement of a fist falling down). But in the evil that might be caused by the action – knocking down a person in order to rob him – in the *formal* happening of the same action, he does not take part. This the acting (or not preventing) *person* has to credit to himself (arab. *iktisāb*). He is personally exclusively responsible for it before God.[10] The reformed theologian Karl Barth chose another solution: Evil, sin, the devil possess an own existence – the 'Nothingness' (*das 'Nichtige'*).[11] The Nothingness is the totality of all that God has not elected, does not want. Only what God wants (the Good, salvation) exists. But exactly the 'No' of God to what he does not want, bestows to it a 'peculiar reality'.[12] The Nothingness is not simply nothing. Just in connection with God's electing acts it does 'exist' – as what God rejects. Thus Barth succeeds in granting Evil as not wanted by God a reality without 'charging' it to God and without diminishing God's power (and benevolence) – because all that God wants exists! Barth's doctrine of the Nothingness thus proves to be the last consequence of the reformed doctrine of predestination.

10. H.-P. Hasenfratz, 'Das Menschenbild des Islam', *Spectrum Iran* 12 (1999), 47–55 (49).

11. Cf. C. Frey, *Die Theologie Karl Barths: Eine Einführung* (Waltrop: Hartmut Spenner [Frankfurt a. M.: Athenäum] 1994), 200–204.

12. K. Barth, *Kirchliche Dogmatik* II/1 (Zollikon–Zürich: Evangelischer Verlag, 1940), 625.

EVIL AND ITS SYMBOLS IN THE QUMRAN SCROLLS

Bilha Nitzan

I

The existence of evil, in its variegated aspects, is an important philosophical and religious issue, as evil has implications with regard to human life, nature, and religious faith in Divine Providence. The existence of evil presents a particularly difficult religious issue for monotheism, in which God is the exclusive Creator of the world and the exclusive God, as in Judaism. The existence of evil, which spoils nature and human life, can blemish the belief in the unity and integrity of God, and in those cases in which evil is exempt from God's responsibility, may even lead to heretical ideas of polytheism. Hence, the issue of the origin of evil is dealt with by the Bible and post-biblical literature, including Jewish apocalyptic writings and the Qumran scrolls.

The Bible and post-biblical literature bear clear signs of the confrontation of Judaism with other religions and cultures regarding the issue of the existence and origin of evil. In the Bible this issue occurs in relation to the Ugaritic and Accadian myths of the primordial monsters of the sea that symbolize primordial entities, and are therefore regarded as primordial evil (see Gen. 1.21; Isa. 27.1; 51.9; Job 26.12-13.[1] In post-biblical literature, such as the apocalyptic books and the Qumran scrolls, there are signs of conflict with Persian and Hellenistic myths with which Judaism came into contact during the Second Temple period regarding the origins of evil, its types, and its symbols.

Collins, who investigated the traditions concerning the origins of evil that influenced Qumran literature, traces the traditions about this issue in the Jewish apocalyptic literature,[2] demonstrating that the Qumran scrolls contain traces of varied traditions concerning the origin of evil and its characteristics. These include the tradition of primordial sin relating to the Fall of the Watchers (see CD 2.17-21), as claimed by Sacchi;[3] the tradition of the angel משטמה and his spirits that tempted people to go astray (*Jub.* 10, etc.; cf. 1QM 13.11-12; 4Q510-511; 4Q286 7 ii 2-3); the Persian dualism of good and evil (1QS 3.15–4.26; 4QAmram, etc.); and the

---

1. See U. Cassuto, 'Serpent in Paradise', EB (Jerusalem: The Bialik Institute, 1968), V, 823–25 (Hebrew).

2. J.J. Collins, 'The Origin of Evil in Apocalyptic Literature and the Dead Sea Scrolls', in J.A. Emerton (ed.), *Congress Volume Paris 1992* (VTSup, 61; Leiden: E.J. Brill, 1995), 25–38.

3. P. Sacchi argues for the influence of this tradition in many apocalyptic and Qumran compositions (*Jewish Apocalyptic and its History* [Sheffield: Sheffield Academic Press, 1996]). See also F. García Martínez, 'Encore l'Apocalyptique', *JSJ* 17 (1987), 231.

Danielic idea of the evil kingdoms and the Son of God (cf. 4Q246, 11QMelch). However, the possible influence of Persian dualism concerning 'evil', as symbolized by darkness, and 'good', as symbolized by light, is the most prominent idea to have emerged in the study of the issue of evil in the Qumran scrolls. This possibility has been discussed in terms of its origins,[4] typology,[5] and the historical and literary secondary editorial works in the Qumran scrolls.[6]

One of the noticeable literary characteristics in most appearances of evil in the Qumran scrolls – whether abstract, angelic, or human – is the use of symbolism in this context. The symbols for evil may reveal its literary origins, the significance attributed to evil in the philosophical outlook of the authors of the Qumran scrolls, and the social, religious, and national relationship between the Qumran community and contemporary Jewish and Gentile circles. To this end, it is necessary, first and foremost, to discover the symbols of evil in the Qumran scrolls and to investigate their origins and significance.

II

Attestation to a debate in the Second Temple period regarding the principles of the providence of God over the entirety of existence is provided by Josephus in his historical report concerning the three main philosophical circles among Judaism since the Hasmonean period (*War* 2.162-63; *Ant.* 13.171-73; 18.13, 18). Among these three groups, the Essenes attribute everything, that is, good and evil, to Fate and to God; the Pharisees, although attributing everything to Fate and to God, hold that the choice of acting rightly or otherwise rests, for the most part, with men. This means that, according to the Pharisaic view, ethical decision is consigned to the free choice of men. According to Josephus, the Sadducees do not believe in Fate or God's providence, but attribute all choices to men. Josephus's information concerning the philosophical view of the Essenes, who relate all of existence to Fate and to God, is attested in many Qumran texts. The main text dealing with this issue is the instruction of the משכיל (sage) in the *Rule Scroll* (1QS 3.13–4.26). Here we read:

> From the God of Knowledge comes all that is and shall be. Before ever they existed He established their whole design, and when, as ordained for them, they

4.   See especially S. Shaked, 'Qumran and Iran: Further Consideration', *Israel Oriental Studies* 2 (1972), 433–46; D. Winston, 'The Iranian Component in the Bible, Apocrypha, and Qumran', *History and Religion* 5 (1965), 183–216.

5.   See especially J.H. Charlesworth, 'A Critical Comparison of the Dualism in 1QS 3.13–4.26 and the "Dualism" Contained in the Gospel of John', in *idem* (ed.), *John and Qumran*, (London: Geoffrey Chapman, 1971), 76–106; J.G. Gammie, 'Sapiential and Ethical Dualism in Jewish Wisdom and Apocalyptic Literature', *JBL* 93 (1974), 356–85; D. Dimant, 'Dualism in Qumran: New Perspective', in J.H. Charlesworth (ed.), *Caves of Enlightenment* (North Richland Hills: Bibal Press, 1998), 55–73.

6.   See especially J. Duhaime, 'Dualistic Reworking in the Scrolls from Qumran', *CBQ* 49 (1987), 32–56; J. Frei, 'Different Patterns of Dualistic Thought in the Qumran Library: Reflections on their Background and History', in M. Bernstein *et al.* (eds.), *Legal Texts and Legal Issues* (STDJ, 23; Leiden: E.J. Brill, 1997), 275–335.

come into being, it is in accord with His glorious design that they accomplish their task without change… He has created man to govern the world, and has appointed for him two spirits in which to walk until the time of His visitation: the spirits of truth and falsehood… (cf. 1QH[a] 6.1-12= Sukenik ed. 14.11-12).[7]

This text stresses the monotheistic-deterministic view that 'all that is and shall be', including the ethical behavior of men, is related to the providence of God the Creator. From the sequel to this text it becomes clear that the main issue disturbing its author is the existence of evil, from which all of mankind suffers, even those people whose fate is to be righteous (see esp. 1QS 3.21-24). This problem does not lessen the author's faith in the unity and wholeness of God, but leads him to detail how God the Creator rules over good and evil, regarding the fate of individuals and mankind as a whole during history and the End of Days.[8] For this purpose, the משכיל utilizes a modified dualistic outlook. 'Truth' is symbolized by light, and 'evil', by darkness (1QS 3.19, 25-26), with the משכיל claiming that the Creator gave the dominions of good and evil to two angels.

> All the children of light are ruled by the Prince of Light and walk in the ways of light, but all the children of darkness are ruled by the Prince of Darkness and walk in the ways of darkness (1QS 3.20-21).

Such a process of creation, in which dominion over the variegated works of the created world was given to different angels, is apparent in such apocalyptic writings as *Jub.* 2.2; 1 *En.* 6.7-8; 60.17-22; 82.11-20, and is explained in the *Thanksgiving Scroll* from Qumran (1QH[a] 9.10-20 = Suk. 1.10-20). According to these writings there is fundamentally one law for all of creation, for the realms of nature and of humanity. This principle posits that all the cosmological realms are dominated by angelic princes, appointed by God the Creator.[9] This principle confines all the realms of creation to fixed courses, thereby protecting all of creation from any disturbance.[10]

The cosmological and ethical aspects of the symbols of light and darkness are known in the theological system of Persian dualism. Scholars have described this source as follows. I cite Collins.[11]

> In the Gathas, the oldest part of the Avesta, which are generally considered to be the work of Zoroaster himself, humanity and even the supreme God has to choose between two Spirits, one of whom is holy and the other a destroyer. The two

---

7. G. Vermes (trans.), *The Dead Sea Scrolls in English* (Sheffield: JSOT Press, 3rd edn, 1987), 64–65.

8. The rational continuation of the subjects dealt with in 1QS 3.13–4.26 leads Frei to suspend Duhaime's assumption of relating the dualistic idea in this text to a secondary edition. See above, n. 6.

9. According to Dan. 10.20-21; 12.1, this principle also includes the variegated nations, each one of which is dominated by a nominated angelic prince.

10. The idea of the law of God that keeps the creation from destruction is stated in Jer. 5.22; Ps. 104.4-9; Job 37.7-11. In the biblical writings, however, this idea is not explained from the cosmological aspect of angelic domination over the realms of earth, as in the apocalyptic writings. The theological caution from polytheism prevents such an explanation.

11. Collins, 'Origin of Evil', 32.

Spirits are the twin children of Ahura Mazda, the Wise Lord,[12] although later the holy Spirit is identified with Ahura Mazda, and the Spirit of destruction is primordial.[13] These Spirits are associated with light and darkness from an early time, as evidenced by Plutarch, who cites Theopomphus (circa 300 BCE) as his source.[14]

Light and darkness as symbols of good and evil appear in such biblical writings as Isa. 5.20 and Amos 5.18-20, which are untouched by any Persian influence. However, in Isa. 45.7 we find an echo of a theological debate with the Persian dualistic doctrine. The Jewish monotheistic doctrine 'I form light and create darkness, I make peace and create woe, I the Lord create all these things' is a clear polemic against the Persian dualistic doctrine that these two entities are related to two different deities, Ahura Mazda and Ahariman. In Qumranic doctrine God creates the spirits of truth and evil rather than begetting them, but the ethical significance of the two spirits, the Spirit of Light as the spirit of truth, and the Spirit of Darkness as the spirit of falsehood, may be influenced by Persian dualism. In Zoroastrian doctrine the spirit of truth is one of the spirits against which Ahura Mazda, the creator of the world, acts. The 'truth' is the central axis in which Ahura Mazda does battle against his opponent, the evil spirit, Angra Mainyu, 'He who is of the Lie'.[15] This dualistic division is also evident among human beings, who are either 'men of truth' or 'men of deceit', the split between them being deep and fateful.[16] Such a division between human beings is also apparent in the instruction of the משכיל in the *Community Rule*, where the Sons of Light are defined as 'sons of righteousness' or 'sons of truth' and the Sons of Darkness are described as 'sons of evil' (1QS 3.20-22, 4.5-6). A similar doctrine appears in some of the pseudepigraphic writings, such as *1 En.* 41.8; 108.11; *Testament of Levi* 19.1; *Testament of Naphtali* 2.7; *Testament of Joseph* 20.2; *Testament of Asher* 5.2-3.[17] In the *Rule Scroll,* the virtue held by the 'sons of truth' consists in 'all the paths of true righteousness' (1QS 4.2), whereas the 'sons of evil' hold the vices of 'wickedness and lie', 'falseness and deceit', and perform 'works of falseness' (1QS 4.9, 23). In other writings from Qumran, the two rival authorities are the 'Teacher of Righteousness' with the 'men of truth' (e.g. 1QpHab 5.10; 7.4, 10) – that is, the members of the Qumran community – as against the 'Man of Deceit' with 'the seekers after smooth' (e.g., 1QpHab 5.11; 10.9; CD 1.14-15; 4QpNah 3-4 i 2; ii 2; iii 6-7; 4QpIsa^c 23 ii 10) – that is, the Pharisees. Although all these appellations are based upon biblical sources,[18] the influence of Persian dualism is nevertheless apparent.

---

12.   R.C. Zaehner, *Dawn and Twilight of Zoroastrianism* (London: Weidenfeld and Nicholson; New York: Putnam, 1961 [2nd edn, 1975]), 50–51.

13.   This development is attested as early as the fourth century BCE by Eudemus of Rhodes, a pupil of Aristole. See P.J. Kobelski, *Melchizedek and Melchires* (CBQMS, 10; Washington DC: The Catholic Biblical Association of America, 1981), 92.

14.   Plutarch, *Isis and Osiris*, 46–47.

15.   Yasna 30.3-6; 32.3-5.

16.   See S. Shaked, 'Persia', EB (Jerusalem, 1972), VI, 609 (Hebrew); Collins, 'Origin of Evil', 33.

17.   See J. Licht, *The Rule Scroll* (Jerusalem: The Bialik Institute, 1965), 92–93 (Hebrew).

18.   See the scholarly exegesis of these Qumran writings.

Jews came into contact with the Persians from the end of the sixth century BCE; it is generally agreed that the Zoroastrian religion was established at the beginning of that century. The exposure of Jews to this doctrine is apparent in religious terminology and ethical values, and in the giving of Jewish characteristics to Persian values and terminology.[19]

The oldest Qumran text to mention the doctrine of the two rival spirits ruling human beings, symbolized by light and darkness, is *4QAmram* (= *4QTestament of Amram*), written in Aramaic. Milik, on the basis of paleographic data, suggested the first half of the second century BCE as the date for the copy of *4QAmram*[b].[20] Hence this text may be attributed to pre-Essene authorship and tradition.[21] In the vision of Amram, the appearance of the Prince of Darkness and his ways are described as following:[22]

> terrif[yi]ng, [like an a]sp, [and] his cl[oak] was of colored dyes, and it was very dark…and his face was indeed that of a viper… (frg. 1.13-14).

He has three names: the one that is preserved is Melchiresa[c], the other two being possibly Belial and Prince of Darkness (frg. 2.3').

> His ways are dark and all his work is da[r]k, and in darkness he… He rules over all the dark (frg. 2.4'-5').

In *4QAmram*[c] the end of the sons of darkness, who are ruled by the Prince of Darkness, is described as following:

> [all the sons] of darkness will be darkened…the sons of darkness will be cut out …for all stupidity and wicke[dness are dark]ened…all the sons of da[rk, to darkness, to death] and to destruction (ll. 10-14).

These are all described in contrast to the names, ways, and end of the Prince of Light and the sons of light. The main difference between this text and the instruction given by the משכיל in the *Rule Scroll* is that God is not mentioned in the extant text of *4QAmram*. Thus the text seems to be a totally dualistic one, which does not deal with the religious-philosophical issue of the existence of evil under the providence of God. In other words, the influence of the Persian doctrine here seems stronger than in the *Rule Scroll*. The symbols of wickedness are apparent here, not only by means of darkness, but also in the appearance of an asp and the dyed cloaks of the Prince of Darkness. We shall deal with these symbols later.

The use of the primary *symbols of light and darkness* to indicate the dualistic entities is apparent in the texts of Qumran, not only in the ethical aspect, but from other aspects as well, such as the calendrical-cultic, physiognomic, historical, and magical, as demonstrated by Devorah Dimant.[23] In terms of the calendrical and cultic aspect, Dimant claims that light and darkness symbolize good days and bad

---

19. See above, n. 4.
20. J.T.Milik, '4Q Visions de 'Amram et une citation d'Origine', *RB* 79 (1972), 77–97.
21. Kobelski, *Melchizedek*, 25.
22. The English translation follows that of Kobelski, *Melchizedek*, 26–35.
23. Dimant, 'Dualism in Qumran'.

days in the *Calendrical Document A* (4Q320)[24] and the *Calendrical Document B* (4Q321).[25] She writes:

> These texts give two rosters. Document A (4Q320) gives the monthly dates of the lowest and highest points of the lunar brightness, which corresponds to the middle and the beginning of the lunar months. The other roster of 4Q321 enumerates the first day in every solar month together with the date of the annual festivals, which fall on longer days and bright nights, and specifies the term of the priestly course in which each festival falls.[26]

She cites the editors of this text, Talmon and Knohl: 'The moon is portrayed as a source of the dark days of evil. In contrast, the sun is seen as the fountainhead of holy and blessed days.'[27]

Another aspect in which light and darkness are used by the Qumran scrolls for symbolic purposes is the *physiognomic* one, written in a Hebrew cryptic text, 4Q186, named by its first editor 'a horoscope'.[28] This text describes the physical qualities of persons born under particular zodiac signs in terms of light and darkness. The terms 'house of light' and 'pit of darkness' are attributed to a physical part of the human's body symbolizing a given person's ratio of virtues or vices. Thus, such a horoscope was possibly used for making a decision about the place of a person in the hierarchy of the Community members,[29] or about the characteristics of candidates.[30]

Light and darkness also symbolize the opposing entities in magical incantations from Qumran, particularly the text of 11QPsAp[a], attributed to David.[31] This text

24. Partly published by J.T. Milik, 'Le travail d'édition des manuscrits du Désert de Juda', *Volume de Congrès Strasbourg 1956* (VTSup 4, 1957), 25.

25. Published by S. Talmon and I. Knohl, 'A Calendrical Scroll from a Qumran Cave: Mishmarot Ba, 4Q321', in D.P. Wright *et al.* (eds.), *Pomegranates and Golden Bells: Studies in Biblical, Jewish and Near Eastern Ritual, Law, and Literature in Honor of Jacob Milgrom* (Winona Lake, IN: Eisenbrauns, 1995), 276–302.

26. Dimant, 'Dualism in Qumran', 61–62. However, the synchronical dimension of the lots of the sunlight and that of the darkness of the moonlight during the first month, as mentioned in the daily blessings of 4Q503, serve first and foremost a calendrical-liturgical purpose. This technique is possibly intended to fix the exact time of the daily blessing of each day, and has nothing to do with ethical or calendrical symbols of light and darkness. In this scroll all the liturgical recitations are blessings of God and of Israel. There are no signs of good or bad days in these blessings, such as those mentioned in 4Q320 and 4Q321. Thus, light and darkness should not be considered here from a dualistic aspect, as claimed by Dimant (p. 65). See B. Nitzan, *Qumran Prayer and Religious Poetry* (STDJ, 12; Leiden: E.J. Brill, 1994), 49–59, 69–71; D.K. Falk, *Daily, Sabbath, and Festival Prayers in the Dead Sea Scrolls* (STDJ, 27; Leiden: E.J. Brill, 1998), 29–57; J.M. Baumgarten, '4Q503 (Daily Prayers) and the Lunar Calendar', *RevQ* 12 (1987), 399–407.

27. Talmon and Knohl, 'A Calendrical Scroll', 299.

28. See P.S. Alexander, 'Physiognomy, Initiation, and Rank in the Qumran Community', in P. Schäfer (ed.), *Geschichte-Traditions-Reflexion: Festschrift für Martin Hengel zum 70. Geburstag* (Tübingen: Mohr–Siebeck, 1996), I, 385.

29. Dimant, 'Dualism in Qumran', 62–63.

30. See I. Gruenwald, 'Further Jewish Physiognomic and Chiromantic Fragments', *Tarbiz* 40 (1971), 301–319 (Hebrew).

31. See the publications of J. van der Ploeg, 'Le Psaume XCI dans une recension de Qumran', *RB* 72 (1965), 210–17; *idem*, 'Un petit rouleau de Psaumes apocryphes (11QPsAp[a])', in G. Jeremias *et al.* (eds.), *Tradition und Glaube. Das Frühe Christentum in seiner Umwelt. Festgabe für K.G.*

includes Psalm 91, used in Jewish tradition as an incantation, and four apocryphal psalms. In the latter the sorcerer calls upon the demon:

> You are darkness and not light... Yhwh will [shut] you [in the] deepest She[ol, he will shut] the two bronze gates [through which] no light [penetrates]. [On you there shall] not [shine the light of the] sun, which [rises upon the] just man [to illuminate his face] (col. 5.7-11).[32]

In col. 4.7-12 the sorcerer again mentions the deepest Sheol, which he identifies with the darkened abyss in which the demon will be imprisoned for ever, where he will rule over his demonic hosts. This invocation is based on a pre-Qumranic apocalyptic tradition mentioned in *1 En.* 10.11-13, and in *Jub.* 10.1-11, mentioned in the Qumran scrolls in 1QM 13.11-12 and in 1QS 3.21-24. In these writings, God creates the evil demonic angel to rule the realm of evil until the eschatological time when the evil forces will be destroyed.[33] The tradition concerning the eschatological punishment of the forces of evil is also mentioned in *4QAmram*[c], ll. 11-14, and in the Qumran curses of the evil realm. In these texts the evil leader, the Prince of Darkness, is also known as מלכי ־ רשע and בל י על (see 4Q280 2;[34] 4Q286 7 ii; 4Q287 6;[35] 1QS 2.4-9; 1QM 13.1-6). In 1QM 13 and in 11QPsAp[a] col. 2.4 he is also named משטמה, as in the *Book of Jubilees*. I shall deal with these names later. The tradition about God's permission of demonic activity during the present period until the eschatological destruction of demons is a central motif in the magical *Songs of the Sage* (4Q510-511)[36] and in 4Q444,[37] albeit the symbolism of darkness is not mentioned in the extant text of these scrolls.

Kuhn (Göttingen: Vandenhoeck & Ruprecht, 1971), 128–39; E. Puech, '11QPsAp[a]: Un ritual d'exorcismes. Essai de reconstruction', *RevQ* 14 (1990), 377–408; F. García-Martínez and E.T.C. Tigchelaar (eds.), '11.11.Q Apocryphal Psalms', Qumran Cave 11.II (DJD, 23; Oxford: Clarendon Press, 1998), 181–205.

32. The English translation follows that of F. García Martínez and W.G.E. Watson, *The Dead Sea Scrolls Translated* (Leiden: E.J. Brill, 1994), 377.

33. A similar notion is found in the sapiential text of *4QMysteries* (= *The Book of Mysteries*) concerning the eschatological end of evil. The sign of this end is depicted as shutting the 'begotten of unrighteousness' (מולדי עולה) when 'wickedness is removed from before righteousness as darkness is removed from before light...and all the adherents of the mysteries of transgression/[Belial] will be no more' (1Q27 1 i 5-8 = 4Q299 1.05-08 = 4Q300 3.1-6). The English translation follows that of L.H. Schiffman, '299. 4QMysteris', in T. Elgvin *et al.* (eds.), *Qumran Cave 4.XV: Sapiential Texts, Part 1* (DJD, 20; Oxford: Clarendon Press, 1997), 36. For the sapiential outlook on evil, see Frei, 'Different Patterns of Dualistic Thought', 275–335.

34. J.T. Milik, 'Milki-sedeq et Milki-resa` dans les anciens écrits juifs et chrétiens', *JJS* 23 (1972), 95–144 (127–29); Kobelski, *Melchizedek*, 37–38; B. Nitzan, '280. 4QCurses', *Qumran Cave 4.XX, Poetical and Liturgical Texts. Part 2* (DJD, 29; Oxford: Clarendon Press, 1999), 1–8.

35. Milik, 'Milki-sedeq', 130–35; Kobelski, *Melchizedek*, 43–48; B. Nitzan, '286. 4QBerakhot[a], in E. Eshel *et al.* (eds.), *Qumran Cave 4.VI: Poetical and Liturgical Texts, Part 1* (DJD, 11; Oxford: Clarendon Press, 1998), 27–30; *idem*, '287. 4QBerakhot[b], in E. Eshel *et al.* (eds.), *Qumran Cave 4.VI*, 57–58. In 4Q287 frg. 7, line 1, the preserved word מהתשכיהמה ('their darkness') refers, possibly, to the darkness of the pit in which the demons will be punished. See Nitzan, '287. 4QBerakhot[b], 58.

36. See Nitzan, *Qumran Prayer and Religious Poetry*, 227–72.

37. E. Chazon, '444. 4QIncantation', in E. Chazon *et al.*, *Qumran Cave 4.XX* (DJD, 29; Oxford: Clarendon Press, 1999), 367–78.

All the aforementioned texts from Qumran demonstrate the monistic philosophical doctrine of the *Rule Scroll*, in which evil is a cosmological realm under the providence of God the Creator, and its variegated entities, activities, and times of activity and destruction are predestined by God. We may also suggest how light and darkness were accepted as symbols of the entities of 'good' and 'evil' in Jewish writings. According to the biblical religious-philosophical doctrine of creation *ex nihilo*, light and darkness are integrative realms of creation. Thanks to their nature, these cosmological realms became symbols of ethics, and of the calendrical, physiognomic, magical, and historical phenomena by which the created world acts. Thus the notion of God's providence over creation encompasses the entirety of all the phenomena of the world. The historical aspect of this religious-philosophical conception will be dealt with later.

III

The names given to the Spirit of Darkness, such as מלכי ־ רשע ,בל י על, and משטמה, are also symbolic, as is its appearance as an asp or a viper and its cloaks of colored dyes. The symbolism of these names and appearances may refer to pre-Qumranic traditions, either biblical or other.

$$\text{מלכי ־ רשע} = \text{משטמה} = \text{בל י על}$$

In the Bible, the term בל י על is an adjective, not a proper noun. It is attributed to wicked persons (cf. Deut. 13.14; Judg. 19.22; 1 Sam. 30.22; 2 Sam. 20.1; Nah. 1.11, 2.1,[38] etc.), or to wicked things or thoughts (Deut. 15.9; Nah. 1.11; Pss. 41.9; 101.3) in the sense of 'worthlessness'. In 2 Sam. 22.5 (= Ps. 18.5), the metaphor 'rivers of *belial*' is parallel to 'waves of death'. Thus בל י על here means 'destruction,' or something which causes death.[39] In the pseudepigraphic *Testaments of the Twelve Patriarchs*, בל י על is one of the names of the devil who sends his spirits to tempt people to evil ways (*T.Dan.* 1.7; *T.Benj.* 6.1; 7.1).[40] In the *Book of Jubilees*, the Devil, whose spirits tempt human beings to go astray towards evil ways and thereby cause them punishment, is called משטמה (10.1-10),[41] possibly in the sense

---

38. See Peter von der Osten-Sacken, *Gott und Belial* (Göttingen: Vandenhoeck & Ruprecht, 1968), 72–78. He deals with the possibility that the term 'belial' in Nah. 2.1 was the origin for the notion concerning the eschatological war against Belial as a private entity in 1QM 1.4.

39. See F. Brown, S.R. Driver and C.H. Briggs, *A Hebrew and English Lexicon of the Old Testament* (Oxford: Clarendon Press, 1906 [1951]), 116. According to A. Hacham's commentary on Ps 18.5, 'belial' in the sense of 'one who does not go up', בל ־ י על, is one of the names of the angel of death. According to this meaning, the metaphor 'belial rivers' symbolizes water that serves the angel Belial, the angel of death (*Sefer Tehillim* [Jerusalem: Mosad Harav Kook, 7th edn, 1990; Hebrew]). This comment may refer to an ancient tradition, mentioned also in the Qumran scrolls. Cf. 1QH^a 3.28-29; 5.39; 6.21-24 (Sukenik ed.). See also. N. Tur-Sinai, 'Belial', EB (Jerusalem, 1965), II, 132–33 (Hebrew).

40. See J. Licht, 'Satan', EB (Jerusalem, 1982), VIII, 281–82 (Hebrew). Licht also mentions this notion in *T.Sim.* 2.7; 3.1; *T.Naph.* 8.6; *T.Gad* 4.7, although the name of the devil Belial is not written there explicitly.

41. Licht, 'Satan', 281. Licht mentions *Jub.* 11.4-5, 11; 17.16; 48.2, 9-12, for the events in which משטמה tempts persons to act with evil.

of enmity or maliciousness. In the Qumran scrolls these two names of the devil are conflated, as in 1QM 13.10-12:

> You created Belial for the pit,
> the angel Mastemah (= the angel of enmity);
> his [dom]ain is darkness,
> his counsel is for evil and wickedness.
> All the spirits of his lot
> angels of destruction
> walk in the laws of darkness,
> towards them goes his only desire.[42]

The combination of these two traditions is also apparent in the curse of Belial recorded in 1QM 13.4 (cf. 4Q186 7 ii 2): ‏ארור בליעל במחשבת משטמה‎ ('Accursed be Belial in his malicious plan').[43]

In the *Rule Scroll* the tradition of the temptation of the sons of light is related to the angel of darkness who leads the realm of ‏משטמה‎ (1QS 3.21-24). This is another way in which the term ‏משטמה‎ is associated with the tradition of the angelic origin of evil. In *Jubilees* 10 the spirits or the realm of ‏משטמה‎ originate in the tradition of the Watchers. Their appellation there is ‏רוחות ממזרים‎ ('bastard spirits'), related to the contaminated intercourse of the Watchers with women. In the Qumranic *Songs of the Sage* (4Q510-511), these are the demonic spirits that tempt the sons of light to go astray, causing them punishments (4Q510 1.5-8; 4Q511 10.1-6).[44] However, the term ‏בליעל‎ is mentioned in 4Q511 18 ii 5, concerning evil speaking, and ‏[משטמ[‎ (possibly ‏[מ[שטמ[ה]‎) is mentioned in 4Q511 frg. 152.3, but the text there is fragmentary. Demonic spirits sent by ‏בליעל‎ are also mentioned in CD 5.17-19, related to the tradition about the danger encountered by Moses when he returned to Egypt (Exod. 4.24; cf. *Jub.* 48.2-3),[45] and to a member of the Community who speaks apostasy (CD 12.2-3 = 4Q271 5 i 18).

Another name given to the devil in the Qumran scrolls is ‏מלכי־רשע‎: This name is mentioned in *4QAmram* 2.3', and in the curses found in 4Q280 2.2, which are partly parallel to the curses of ‏בליעל‎ and his lot in 1QM 13.4-5 and 4Q286 7 ii 2, 11-12, and partly to the curses of the lot of ‏בליעל‎ in 1QS 2.5-9.[46] This is thus another parallel name of the devil. Kobelski argues that the name ‏מלכי־רשע‎ is evidently derived in opposition to ‏מלכי־צדק‎, who appears in 11QMelch as the leader of the forces of good.[47]

IV

A notion common to all these writings is the restriction of the realm of ‏בליעל‎ to a limited period: ‏יומי ממשלת בליעל‎ ('the days of Belial dominion': 1QS 2.19;

---

42. For the English translation, see García Martínez and Watson, *Dead Sea Scrolls Translated*, 108.

43. García Martínez and Watson, *Dead Sea Scrolls Translated*, 107.

44. See Nitzan, *Qumran Prayer and Religious Poetry*, 227-72.

45. According to *Jub.* 48.2-3, ‏משטמה‎ was responsible for this danger.

46. See Nitzan, '280. 4QCurses', 2-4.

47. Kobelski, *Melchizedek*, 33.

cf. 1QS 3.23; *1 En.* 16.1; 4Q510 1.6-7; 4Q511 10.3; 35.8). In the *Damascus Document* it is written: בכל השנים האלה יהיה בליעל משולח בישראל ('and during these years Belial will be sent against Israel'; CD 4.12-13). This refers to the years predetermined by God for the realm of Belial. During those years Belial traps Israel in three 'nets': fornication, wealth, and defilement of the Temple (CD 4.15-18). The transgressions involved in these 'nets', according to the halakhic perception of the Qumran community, are detailed in CD 4.20–5.13, while the ways of preventing them by the members of the Qumran community, who are considered to be righteous, is detailed in CD 6.11–7.11. All these writings demonstrate the *deterministic historical perception* of the Qumran doctrine, in which the entity of 'evil', in its variegated phenomena during history, is predetermined by God, as is its final eschatological destruction.

The doctrine concerning the restriction of the dominion of evil to a limited period may have been influenced by the Zoroastrian perception, in which history is divided into predetermined epochs, symbolizing the struggle between justice and evil, until the final destruction of the latter.[48] The influence of this doctrine is apparent both in pre-Qumranic apocalyptic writings and in the Qumran scrolls. Note, for example, the visions of four different metals in Daniel 2, and of four different beasts of prey in Daniel 7, symbolizing four historical evil kingdoms that will rule the world until their dominion is reversed by the establishment by God of the kingdom of justice.[49] In *1 Enoch* 85–90 there is a vision of a struggle between black animals and white animals, symbolizing in its final section an apocalypse of seventy periods divided into four epochs of evil. According to this apocalypse, the dominion of the evil kingdoms will continue until the first signs of the victory of the white animals, symbolizing the establishment of the messianic epoch of justice. Another apocalypse, appearing in *1 En.* 93.1-10 and 91.12-17, consists of ten historical weekly epochs of struggle between justice and evil, from the creation of humanity until the final eschatological destruction of evil human and angelic forces. In these Jewish apocalyptic writings, the different periods are related to biblical and post-biblical history, as they are in a Qumranic apocalyptic text, *The Ages of Creation* (4Q180-181), which mentions seventy periods of biblical and possibly post-biblical history.[50] The *pre-determined perception of history* held by the Qumran community appears in 1QpHab 7.13-14: כול קיצי אל יבואו לתכונם כאשר חקק להם ברז י ערמתו ('all the ages of God will come at the right time,

48. See B. Uffenheimer, *The Visions of Zechariah* (Jerusalem: Kiryat Sepher, 1961), 168–69 (Hebrew); Dimant, 'Dualism at Qumran', 68–69, and the bibliography, n. 37.

49. The symbols of four different metals for four historical epochs are known in the Zoroastrian doctrine as the 'tree of the world' of four branches made of four different metals: gold, silver, copper and ironed soil. The ancient origin for this symbolic scheme of historical epochs is known since the eighth century BCE in the writings of Hesiod, but its influence on Jewish apocalyptic writings from the third and second centuries BCE is probably Persian. See Uffenheimer, *Visions of Zechariah*, 168–69.

50. This text was published by J.M. Allegro in *Qumran Cave 4.I* (DJD, 5; Oxford: Clarendon Press, 1968), 77–80, and reconstructed by Milik, 'Milki-sedeq', 109–19; and D. Dimant, 'The Pesher on the Periods', *IOS* 9 (1979), 77–102.

as he established for them in the mysteries of his prudence').[51] See on this notion the sapiential texts using the term קצי עולם (4Q417 1 i 7) or קצי עד (4Q416 1.14; 4Q418 2.6). It seems that in the Qumran writings, the historical periods are mostly not symbolized, but rather defined according to their quality. As demonstrated above, this literary phenomenon is apparent in such terms as קץ הרשעה (*passim*), referring to the period of wickedness, or a term referring to the evil angelic prince who dominated the bad time: יומי ממשלת בליעל (see above). Terms related to periods of the history of Israel are קץ חרון ('period of wrath,' 4Q266 2 i 3; CD 1.5 = 4Q266 2 i 10) or קצי חרון ('periods of wrath', 4Q266 11.19 = 4Q270 7 ii 13; 4Q268 1.5),[52] and קץ חרבן הארץ ('age of devastation of the land',[53] CD 5.20), related to the period of the destruction of the First Temple and the Judean kingdom and the exile of its Jewish inhabitants. The term קץ משפט נחרצה ('ordained time of Judgement', 4Q369 1 i 4) is related to the eschatological judgement of wickedness.[54] In a parabiblical narrative text (4Q462), historical periods are symbolized by light and darkness, where it is written in the context of biblical history עבר [ן]קץ החושך וקץ האור בא ('[passed is the per]iod of darkness and the period of the light is coming', frg. 1.10).[55] Definitions of good periods are קץ שלום ('period of peace', 4Q215 1 ii 5;[56] 4Q418c line 9[57]) and קץ האמ[ת] ('epoch of tru[th]', 4Q416 1.13).[58]

V

The Appearance of the Prince of Evil

According to *4QAmram* 2.13-14, the appearance of the Prince of Evil as an asp or a viper is terrifying, while its colored cloaks are not explained. The allusions related to the asp and viper and its colored cloaks were evidently clear to the author of this text

51. For the English translation, see García Martínez and Watson, *Dead Sea Scrolls Translated*, 200. For the conception of predetermined epochs of history, see J. Licht, 'Time and Eschatology in the Apocalyptic Literature and the Dead Sea Scrolls', *JJS* 16 (1965), 177–82; B. Nitzan, 'Apocalyptic Historiosophy in Qumran Literature: Its Origins and Perspectives in the Legacy of Jacob Licht', in G. Brin and B. Nitzan (eds.), *Fifty Years of Dead Sea Scrolls Research: Studies in Memory of Jaacob Licht* (Jerusalem: Yad Ben-Zvi, 2001), 37–56 (Hebrew).

52. For the English translation, see J.M. Baumgarten, *Qumran Cave 4.XIII: The Damascus Document (4Q266-273)* (DJD, 18; Oxford: Clarendon Press, 1996).

53. For the English translation, see García Martínez and Watson, *Dead Sea Scrolls Translated*, 36.

54. See H. Attridge and J. Strugnell, '369. 4QPrayer of Enosh', *Qumran Cave 4.VIII: Parabiblical Texts, Part 1* (DJD, 13; Oxford: Clarendon Press, 1994), 353–56.

55. See M. Smith, '462. 4QNarrative C', in M. Broshi *et al.* (eds.), *Qumran Cave 4.XIV: Parabiblical Texts, Part 2* (DJD, 19; Oxford: Clarendon Press, 1995), 195–208.

56. B.Z. Wacholder and M.G. Abegg, *A Preliminary Edition of the Unpublished Dead Sea Scrolls* (Washington, DC: BAS, 1995), III, 7; = 4Q215a 1ii6, in E. Chazon and M. Stone, '4Q215a. 4Q Time of Righteousness in: P. Alexander *et al.* (eds), *Qumran Cave 4.XXVI: Cryptic Texts and Miscellanea, Part 1.* (DJD, 36; Oxford: Clarendon Press, 2000), 179.

57. J. Strugnell *et al.* (eds.), *Qumran Cave 4.XXIV: Sapiential Texts, Part 2* (DJD, 34; Oxford: Clarendon Press, 1999), 501–503.

58. Strugnell, *Qumran Cave 4.XXIV*, 81–83.

and to the readers of his time. According to biblical and post-biblical literature, these visions dismay because they symbolize cruelty, death, falsehood, and temptation.

In other Qumran writings the viper and the asp are not themselves described, but rather the danger of their venom. In the *Thanksgiving Scroll* the acts of the opponents of the author are depicted by means of metaphors of the poisoned bite of serpents, as following:

> They plot evil in their heart,
> [men of] Belial have opened a lying tongue,
> like vipers' venom which stretches for periods,
> and like (serpents) which creep in the dust
> so do they let fly [their poisonous] darts
> serpent's venom, against there is no charm.
> They have become incurable pain,
> a wasting disease in the innards of your servant,
> which makes [the spirit] stagger
> and makes an end of strength.
> (1QH^a 13.26-29; Suk. 5.26-29)[59]

This description of the venom of the serpents refers to that of the enemies of Israel in Deut. 32.33; cf. Ps. 58.4-5, where the speech of liars is symbolized by the venom of serpents.[60] In another reference to Deut. 32.33 found in the *Damascus Document*, the serpents symbolize the kings of the peoples, while the serpents' venom symbolizes the cruelty of the king of Greece (CD 8.9-12 = 19.22-24). In a poetical description of the last burst of evil in the *Thanksgiving Scroll*, evil itself and the spirits of evil are symbolized by the venom of serpents (1QH^a 11.12, 18 = Suk. 3.12, 18). It therefore seems clear that the terrifying appearance of asp and viper given to the Prince of Darkness is based on a known tradition. Cassuto has claimed that the tradition concerning the serpent as a symbol of evil and falsehood already appears in the biblical narrative about the serpent that tempted Eve to violate God's commandment (Gen. 3).[61] Biblical writings identify the primordial monsters of Ugaritic and Accadian myth with serpents (cf. Isa. 27.1; 59.1; Job 26.12-13) and, according to Ps. 40.5, these monsters symbolize falsehood.[62] Nevertheless, Cassuto notes that the author of the Genesis narrative does not identify the serpent that tempted Eve as one of the monsters that rose from the sea, but rather as one of the animals that God had created on the earth. The serpent was chosen by the author to tempt Eve because this animal traditionally symbolized evil and falsehood. Cassuto has also claimed that the use of the primordial serpent as the symbol of the devil, as it appears in Rabbinic homilies,[63] is a late discourse concerning the context of

---

59. The English translation follows partly García Martínez and Watson, *Dead Sea Scrolls Translated*, 338, and partly Vermes, *Dead Sea Scrolls in English*, 180. For comments on this poetical description, see J. Licht, *The Thanksgiving Scroll* (Jerusalem: The Bialik Institute, 1957), 105–106 (Hebrew).

60. See also Isa. 59.5, where the ways of the wicked, and their falsehood, are symbolized by serpents.

61. U. Cassuto, 'Nahash', EB (Jerusalem, 1968), V, 823–24 (Hebrew).

62. See N. Sarna, 'Rahab', EB (Jerusalem, 1976), VII, 328–29 (Hebrew).

63. See: *Pirkey Derabi Eliezer* (Warsaw, 1852), ch. 13, 31/2.

Genesis 3. Nevertheless, the tradition symbolizing falsehood and cruelty by means of the serpent is ancient. The aforementioned Qumran scrolls demonstrate that, already during the Second Temple period, the serpent symbolized the devil and his false ways.

The cloaks of colored dyes with which the Prince of Darkness appears in the vision of Amram seems to symbolize temptation. Note the tradition mentioned in *1 En.* 8.1 concerning 'Azazel, the leader of the Watchers, who taught the women to prepare coloring tinctures and alchemy by which they could prepare colored cloaks. These and other works of preparing adornments and coloring the eyebrows are used for temptation, as explained in a medieval midrash about Semihaza and 'Azazel.[64]

In a text from Qumran (4Q184) about the strange woman, who symbolizes wickedness, it is written:

> ...her clothes [...]
> Her garments are the shades of twilight,
> and her adornments are touched with corruption...
> Her eyes glance keenly hither and thither,
> and she wantonly raises her eyelids
> to seek out a righteous man and lead him astray,
> and a perfect man to make him stumble (ll. 4-5, 14-15).[65]

Although this text does not describe the appearance of the woman's cloaks and eyes,[66] but rather her acts of temptation, this text alludes to the same tradition of the symbols of evil.

In Conclusion

We have dealt with the religious-philosophical issue of the existence of evil and the explanations of this issue in the Qumran scrolls. From our investigation it becomes clear that evil in its variegated aspects is depicted in the Qumran scrolls by means of symbols. Most of the symbols of evil and falsehood are of 'darkness', as opposed to the 'light' that symbolizes good and justice; of serpents, because of their dangerous venom; and of symbolic names for the angelic and demonic leaders of evil. The Qumran writings did not invent these symbols, but used traditional symbols of evil known from the Bible and the apocalyptic writings, in which the symbols of the serpents are influenced by Ugaritic and Accadian traditions, while those of light and darkness are influenced by Zoroastrian dualism.

The concept of the embodiment of evil in angels and demons has apocalyptic origins. The embodying of human and cosmological phenomena in angelic entities, and the explanation of such phenomena by symbols, are characteristic of apocalyptic literature. The symbolic technique uses known elements, and those that awake

---

64. See Milik, '4Q Visions de 'Amram', 81; Kobelski, *Melchizedek*, 30 n. 9.

65. For the English translation, see Allegro, *Qumran Cave 4.I*, 65.

66. The eyes of the Prince of Darkness are mentioned in *4QAmram* 2.15, but the text is fragmentary, and it is not clear how these were described.

emotions of fear or religious admiration, to explain religious notions.[67] The coherent use of symbolism facilitates the explanation of typical events throughout sequential periods, and among different nations, religions, and cultures. Thus apocalyptic writings, including the Qumran writings, could borrow Zoroastrian and other symbols, imparting to them Jewish characteristics and ideology for the religious-philosophic contest with polytheistic ideologies that spread in the Persian and Hellenistic periods.

67.   See M. Eliade, *Patterns in Comparative Religion* (Lincoln, NE and London: University of Nebraska, 1996; originally published: New York: Sheed & Ward, 1958), 9, 32–33, 39, 111.

THE CONCEPT OF EVIL AND ITS
SANCTIFICATION IN KABBALISTIC THOUGHT

Yoram Jacobson

The essential relation between Stern Judgment (ד י ן) and Evil, which is also a substantial one, is axiomatic in Kabbalistic thought, and its expressions are too numerous to even count.[1] Gershom Scholem defined and elucidated this relationship in his paper on the subject of evil[2] (particularly with regard to dicta and ideas whose sources are in early Kabbalah). Isaiah Tishby also devoted several comprehensive studies to this subject,[3] and later scholars added several important new aspects to their discussions.[4]

I wish to add here several new aspects to these discussions. I shall begin specifically with a late source, namely, the beginning of *Derush Heftzibah* by R. Joseph ibn Tabul,[5] one of the major disciples of R. Isaac Luria of Safed. Already in the opening section we encounter a surprise, in that Ibn Tabul interprets the phrase in Gen. 1.2, תהו ובהו ('formless and void'), as referring to the Infinite (*Ein Sof*). That is, the 'formless and void' designates a situation in which things – including

---

1.   In the present context I will not relate to the issue of man's status as a factor isolating a given force within the harmonic integration of divine reality, uprooting it from the unity of holiness and giving it – through the process of its actualization – a separate status as a demonic entity. This question is admittedly a highly interesting one. However, even if all Kabbalistic sources were to agree that the actual reality of evil depends entirely upon human action, they could not avoid the assumption that its root *in potentia* lies in God Himself, and hence could not avoid a discussion of its metaphysical nature. I wish to devote the following discussion to the question of the nature of evil, as it flows from that root.

2.   G. Scholem, 'Sitra Ahra: Good and Evil in the Kabbalah', in *Pirqei Yesod beHavanat haKabbalah uSemaleha* (trans. J. Ben-Shlomo; Jerusalem, 1981), 187–212 [ET: *On the Mystical Shape of the Godhead: Basic Concepts in the Kabbalah* (trans. J. Chipman; New York, 1991), 56–87]. Cf. his *Major Trends in Jewish Mysticism* (New York, 1961), 235–39.

3.   I. Tishby, *Mishnat haZohar* (Jerusalem, 1957), I, 285–377 [ET: *The Wisdom of the Zohar* (trans. D. Goldstein; 3 vols.; Oxford, 1989), II, 447–546]; *idem*, *Torat haRa' vehaQelippah beKabbalat haAri* (Jerusalem, 1963).

4.   See below in the course of my discussion. It is worth mentioning here the article by J. Dan, 'Samael, Lilith and the Concept of Evil in Early Kabbala', *AJSReview* 5 (1980), 17–40. Dan discusses there the source of evil according to R. Eleazar of Worms and especially according to R. Isaac Hacohen, attributing it to God's will and His intention to benefit His creatures, and presenting the myth of evil as expressing messianic Kabbalistic apocalypse. He does not, however, discuss the substantial root of evil – namely, its origin in the divine essence.

5.   This text was first printed at the beginning of R. Mas'ud haCohen elHaddad, *Simhat Cohen* (Jerusalem, 1921).

the emanated entities, which are the manifested aspect of the Godhead – have not yet come into existence in their specificity, as distinct, explicit, and delimited beings. This term thus refers to an amorphous, pre-creation reality, in which contours have not yet burst forth from a primordial point which has not yet appeared, and the boundaries shaping reality have not yet been drawn. Everything is still incorporated within the Infinite, in whose depths there is no differentiation, and nothing can be recognized in itself, within clear, distinct and separate boundaries. This situation is likewise expressed in Ibn Tabul's interpretation for the verse, 'He is one and His name is one',[6] according to which this dictum refers to the integration of God's name within His essence. This integration signifies *ipso facto* the absolute unity of the Infinite, in which there is neither revelation, distinction and differentiation, nor measure and size. God's name is the supreme principle of all the worlds, and the hidden root of their divine pre-existence.

What does this mean? In and by itself, a thing does not require a name, and it has no name. The name indicates the manifestation of a given thing to the other, and is thus the aspect of its movement from hiddenness and concealment towards manifestation. The name is the metaphysical principle of revelation, namely of the distinct being, defined within its own boundaries, as it springs up from within the Infinite in its initial root. Moreover, a name signifies connection and relationship between one differentiated thing and another, thus being the aspect in which the thing is revealed and known.

For our purposes, these statements are only of interest in terms of their theological and theosophic significance regarding God. All other beings that exist apart from Him are involved in dynamic interaction with one another, whereas God is so to speak beyond it: His transcendent being is immersed in His infinite recesses, beyond name or manifestation. This interaction is the very nature of all creatures, and their names – which embody this interaction – express their essence, the essence found in their interrelations or, if you like, the essence of the very fact of their being immersed in systems of relationships. According to the law of reality their essence is characterized by manifold, multifaceted relations on the cosmic chessboard, and these are revealed through the multitude of their names. Thus, the name involves an element of revelation, which is *ipso facto* an element of דין, of Stern Judgment or Rigor, which imposes boundaries and limitations and shapes frameworks. In the beginning that precedes all beginnings, before there was any movement, when God was immersed in the recesses of His infinity, the name was integrated within His essence, and דין was incorporated within the unity of pure

---

6.   See *Zohar Hadash* (Jerusalem, 1978), *Bereshit* (*Midrash haNe'elam*), 2b; and cf. *Zohar* I, 29a; R. Hayyim Vital, *Sha'ar Ma'amarei Razal* (Jerusalem, 1988), *Masekhet Shabbat*, 9. The expression interpreted by Ibn Tabul appears in various forms: in the Bible (Zech. 14.9); in Rabbinic literature (*Yalqut Shim'oni*, *Devarim* 6, §835); in the *Siddur* (in the Shabbat afternoon prayer; in R. Shlomo Alkabetz's well-known liturgical poem for Kabbalat Shabbat, *Lekha Dodi*). In *Pirqei deRabbi Eliezer* (ch. 3), the statement appears: 'Before the world was created there were the Holy One blessed be He and His Great Name alone.' When quoted by Lurianic Kabbalists, this formula was often altered to 'there was He and His Name alone', and is quoted thus as the formula of *Pirqei deRabbi Eliezer*.

רחמים (Compassion). No revelation had yet occurred, and no boundary line had yet been drawn to fashion the cosmos and its manifestations.

> His name is called the worlds within which He is embodied… And all the worlds were incorporated within Him. Namely, naught was recognizable but He, may He be blessed, whose name indicates some little bit of manifestation, which is the aspect of דין; but in its entirety His substance was רחמים, and all was a total unity, and all was *Ein Sof* [the Infinite], may He be blessed.[7]

דין was indeed swallowed up and unrecognizable, like a mote of dust in infinite waters – but it nevertheless existed in its hidden state, for were this not so, we would posit a fault in the absolute unity of God, that incorporates all opposites:

> For if you do not say that the root of Judgment was there [i.e., incorporated in unrecognizable fashion in the depths of the Infinite], then there would be imperfection, Heaven forbid, in His essence, may He be blessed. For He is not called whole in the quintessence of wholeness, unless He is not lacking in any thing [i.e., including His contradiction or opposite].[8]

God incorporates within Himself His other; His own Name that is hidden within His inwardness. And when He calls Himself by His Name, which is the supreme metaphysical principle of everything that exists apart from Him and is other than Him,[9] He thereby reveals the root of דין in the depth of His hiddenness, and causes the movement of manifestation, and finally establishes the beginning point, from which the boundary line is drawn. And when that same metaphysical boundary is drawn, there appears that which is not God, and the Other is separated from Him. This is the first manifestation of evil. The divine name is a revelation and a boundary. As such, it is the root of דין, and also the root of evil.

This latter statement requires some elaboration. חסד (Grace or Mercy) indicates infinite flow and abundance, without limit or condition, given to all, both those who are needy and those who are not needy. By contrast, דין signifies giving in proper measure, 'as is deserving', no more and no less. Because, unlike חסד, it is conducted on the basis of exact, firm, fixed and therefore also strict criteria – in other words, by law and rigor, for it is impossible that it be conducted otherwise – דין involves acts of judgement and punishment, even, as is sometimes required, to the point of catastrophe and destruction. There follows from this the well-known Kabbalistic conclusion, that the power of evil is included within the essence of דין, and the demons lurk within its depths. Once Stern Judgment acts with all its uncompromising strength, and there is no one to stand against it to quiet its fury and to calm down the tempestuous anger aroused within it – this being its most striking quality and the manifestation of its very essence: its constant striving to

---

7. *Derush Heftzibah*, 1a.
8. *Derush Heftzibah*, 1b.
9. On the name as the process of God's breaking through and His revelation from the depths of His Infinity, see Scholem, *Major Trends*, 215–17 (including a brief and incomplete discussion of the mystical meaning of the pronouns); *idem*, *Pirqei Yesod*, 39–47; Tishby, *Mishnat haZohar*, I, 154–55 (English: I, 293–95). The idea is usually presented in relation to the mystical concept of the Torah.

realize itself, to be strengthened within its own realm and to manifest itself with all its concentrated power, which is naught but fury and uncompromising firmness (as opposed to the tender, amorphous and limitless nature of חסד, that flows, expands and gives itself as far as possible, to all and to whoever is ready to absorb it) – its appearance is that of a destructive force, bringing harsh disaster upon the world. The flaming fury of דין expressses its strength, aggressiveness and lack of patience towards whoever exists next to its domain. דין does not know the constructive way of moderation, which leads to compromise and encounter, which in its deepest meaning signifies the unity of opposites. It is only with regard to דין that one can say 'Let [it] split the mountain.'[10] The Sages already observed and taught that the world cannot exist upon the basis of Stern Judgment alone,[11] and ordered that it be invoked only in moderation.

All this implies that, in the echoes of its conflagration and explosions, דין sheds a certain waste matter, its own waste, which is nothing but the power of evil in the cosmos. The concentrated manifestation of דין hence implies the appearance of evil, while its 'sweetening' signifies the reintegration of evil and its return to the divine unity, which had been disturbed. In terms of their theoretical context, and over and beyond the usual mythical form of their presentation, the significance of these ideas needs to be clarified according to the understanding of דין as the principle of limiting boundary within the divine being.

As is well known, דין is that power that defines boundaries and fixes quantities and measures, even within the divine world. The emergence of 'the dark flame' (*botzina deqardinuta*) within the depths of the supernal brilliance that encompasses the Infinite is interpreted throughout the whole Kabbalistic tradition as the appearance of the power of Stern Judgment, which is the measuring rod by whose means the Sefirot are initially depicted.[12] The power of דין shapes the contours and framework of reality or, in the usual terminology of the teachers of Kabbalah, it creates its vessels. דין is the boundary line of reality and the defining force of all its phenomena. As such, it is constantly tempted to trespass these boundaries. If it deviates from the integration of the harmonic totality of the divine forces, and is strengthened beyond its proper measure – namely, that measure which God has established for it – it will be exposed with all the destructive power that lies within it. This danger of violating and crossing boundaries applies uniquely to דין, for it alone possesses the power of intensification and concentrated manifestation, which cannot be stopped. By contrast, חסד (Mercy or Grace) embodies the amorphous tenderness of infinite life, which as such lacks the will of concentrated revelation or the desire of forceful, penetrating and destructive self-aggrandizement. Kabbalists thus have had good reason to portray *Ein Sof* as the substance of 'simple' חסד (in

10. *b. Yebamot* 92a.
11. *Gen. Rab.* 12, 15.
12. See Tishby, *Mishnat haZohar*, I, 137–38, 163 (English: I, 276, 309). Scholem's English translation of the famous passage from *Zohar* I, 15a appears in *Major Trends*, 218–19. Lurianic Kabbalah also identifies *botzina deqardinuta* with דין and its limiting and measuring power. See R. Hayyim Vital, *Mevo She'arim* (Jerusalem, 1988), 2–3; *idem*, *'Etz Hayyim* (Jerusalem, 1988), 28; *idem, Sha'ar Ma'amarei Rashbi* (Jerusalem, 1988), 61.

the sense in which this term was used in the Middle Ages) and as total Compassion (רחמים), and Ibn Tabul was justified in speaking of the ingathering and concentration of the roots of דין in one place. It is regarding them alone that such concentration can exist, and it is necessitated by their very nature. According to its essence, חסד embodies harmonious integration, the sweetening of the bitter powers of judgement and the incorporation of opposites, the negation of boundaries, division and controversy, and the endless flow of divine life, while דין by nature entails the disturbance of harmony and the strengthening of its particular and autonomous standing, distinct from and opposed to the other forces of the cosmos. As a boundary line, דין lies at the root of all division and controversy, quarrel and conflict.

The intensification of דין beyond the appropriate limit set forth for it in the divine balanced plan of the cosmos and its transgression of its own boundary is tantamount to its emergence as evil, the waste matter of דין. This 'waste matter' is nothing other than דין itself – in its distortion and falsification: דין that has transgressed its proper boundary, דין that is deviant or deviating, דין that is not in its right place. These things have already been explained, at least in their main outlines, in the above-mentioned study by Scholem. I only wish to complement them here by emphasizing the relationship of Evil to the essence of דין and its inherent nature; namely, its natural tendency to cross its own boundaries, to burn in its unlimited lust and impulsiveness and to become intensified through demonic, unrestrained outbursts of destructive anger.

But these same things may also be formulated somewhat differently.

The appearance of evil – certainly in its potential existence – is a necessary outcome of God's will to reveal Himself. Revelation implies a boundary line, by whose means and within whose limits alone it occurs. This line *ipso facto* implies division and dispute, controversy and argument. By its very nature the boundary line inevitably implies the appearance of the opposing forces of חסד and דין, which as the fundamental opposites within the Divine and in the cosmos as a whole are the roots of good and evil. We may conclude from this that, when God wishes to reveal Himself, or to uncover from the depths of His being the boundary line – by whose means alone and through its action His Sefirot are depicted and His attributes appear as the dynamic image of the Godhead – it is impossible for Him to be revealed save through His own opposites, namely the opposites of good and evil, which are the necessary result of His leaving the recesses of His infinity to manifest Himself and appear within the world of boundary and measure.

We may conclude from the above that evil is everything that is separate and distinct unto itself, everything that has been uprooted or that has removed itself from the harmonic integration of the world of holiness and the realm of unity, that has acquired for itself separate existence and bastioned itself within its own private space. It is everything that strengthens itself within its own boundaries that seeks only for itself, that wishes to absorb and incorporate everything else within itself, everything that only follows its own impulses. All these aspects appear repeatedly in the Kabbalistic and Hasidic sources as the most explicit characteristics of the realm of impurity or of the shells (*qelipot*), which is conceived as the metaphysical principle of separation and division, dispute and argument (on every plane of existence: the theosophic, cosmic, historical and psychological). Unlike holiness, which is always unity, and the plenitude of whose vitality flows and extends to all, the Shell always divides, separates and cuts off, interrupting the constant and continuous flow of divine life, sowing loss and death wherever it appears. It is not for naught that death is one of the most salient symbols of demonic reality. In this context, death signifies the surrounding and outstretched hand of the power of evil, that snatches up life (which is divine by its very nature) so as to swallow it up, until it nourishes and strengthens itself. Death is no more than a passing deviation in the ongoing flow of divine life: life that has been snatched and uprooted from its place, and is distorted and falsified in its improper place. Death is no more than a mutation of divine life.

The very essence of Evil's separation and separative power implies also its barrenness: by separating itself from the harmonious world of holiness, the fruitful and fructifying encounter does not take place within the *Qelipa*, and evil appears as a reality without offspring.[13] The nature of evil as chaos thereby becomes clear: evil is chaotic in the sense that everything is incorporated and assimilated within it, and every expression of individuation is erased in its depths. No fruitful encounter can exist within it, nor can a sequence of offspring, which develops successively in the world of holiness and its unfolding, appear. Everything is swallowed up and halted, disappearing in evil's thick darkness.

Evil is everything that is not in its proper place – whether it fell or dropped from its place, or whether it endeavored to hold fast and rule in a place that is not its own. One must therefore relate to evil as a reality of exile, which is repeatedly connected in a profound way with the idea of God's revelation. When God sets forth to reveal Himself, or to uncover His own personal dimension from within His Infinitude, the aspect of the reflective 'I' within Him, He is so to speak exiled within Himself, or from Himself. It is only thus that He is able to hew out from within His essence that which is destined to be revealed from within Himself as the Other, the 'Other' within Himself, which will ultimately be manifested as the 'Other Side' that stands against Him. Through the revelation of God – that is, through the revelation of the 'Other' that is incorporated within Himself (the aspect of the name, as explained above) – the appearance of evil is unavoidable. Lurianic Kabbalah refined this idea with a profoundly dialectic understanding, but the early Kabbalah already explained this subject according to the various aspects of its doctrine of emanation.[14]

---

13. On evil as barren, see Scholem, *Pirqei Yesod*, 202 (English: *On the Mystical Shape of the Godhead*, 75–76); cf. Tishby, *Mishnat haZohar*, I, 341, 348 (English: *The Wisdom of the Zohar*, II, 509, 517). On barrenness in relation to the powers of destruction, cf. A. Farber-Ginat, '"The Shell Precedes the Fruit" – On the Origin of Metaphysical Evil in Early Kabbalistic Thought' [Hebrew], *Eshel Be'er Sheva* 4 (1996), 118–42 (136). Y. Liebes relates to the blemish of the unmarried state of the Kings of Edom, 'The Kabbalistic Myth of Orpheus' [Hebrew], in M. Idel, Z. Harvey and E. Schweid (eds.), *Shlomo Pines Jubilee Volume* (Jerusalem, 1988), I, 425–59 (456–57).

14. The issue of the place of evil in the cosmos and its source in the Godhead is discussed by J. Dan, '"No Evil Descends from Heaven"', in B.D. Cooperman (ed.), *Jewish Thought in the*

The appearance of evil is indeed unavoidable; but the Kabbalah knows the great secret – man's ultimate goal – of its return and restoration to its original place.

The *Zohar* presents us with an exciting theory concerning the confrontation with evil, based upon the idea of man's entrance into the garden of impurity. This entrance is the opposite of the well-known entry into the *Pardes* in the Tannaitic tradition[15] and in the descriptions of the Kabbalists. Gershom Scholem[16] and Isaiah Tishby[17] already pointed at this idea, but did not fully expound its significance, as we shall see below. The theory depends upon the great figures of Adam and Noah, on the one hand, and those of the patriarchs (and righteous men) of the people of Israel, on the other. The former two failed in the challenge, while the latter executed it successfully, paving the way for succeeding generations.

To what are we referring here?

According to the *Zohar*, it is desirable for a person who follows the path of (Kabbalistic) truth, intended to lead him upwards towards holiness, the path of ascent and perfection, to also have a certain experience of evil. He must descend or leave his own place, enter into the gates of evil and deliberately establish contact with it, know it and contemplate its systems and powers, be exposed to its temptations and have his desires awakened. At the same time he must not become attached to it or be drawn towards its temptations, but withstand the trials of its incitements and once more ascend from within its dark depths, strengthened, refined and purified. 'It is thus fitting that a person know good and know evil and return himself to the good.'[18]

The retreat of the *Sabba* (the 'Grandfather'; hero of one of the sections of the *Zohar*) to the desert, to the place of impure powers, so as to engage in Torah specifically there, is explained in light of the need to overcome evil in its own place, specifically. In the words of the *Zohar*:

> Words [and conducts] of Torah do not 'sit' [i.e., are not clarified and do not acquire meaning] except there, for there is no light but that which comes out of darkness… And there is no service of the Holy One blessed be He but from within the darkness, and there is no good save through and out of evil. And when a

Sixteenth Century (Cambridge, MA, 1983), 89–105. This paper deals primarily with R. Moses Cordovero's exposition of this issue, against which he presents – unconvincingly, in my opinion – the Lurianic model. Dan's discussion is not clear enough concerning two separate points: (a) the substantial source of evil in the divine being, or, to put it differently, the source of its unavoidable emergence from within its recesses. According to Cordovero, too, evil descends from heaven – is there any thing whose source is not there? – but there it is still good, and its evil aspect only becomes manifested once it descends and during the process of its devolution. Likewise, Lurianic Kabbalah does not attribute the source of active evil to the Divine; (b) the dialectical dimension involved in the return of evil to the good, that is alluded to even in Cordovero's *Tomer Devorah*. To the discussion of this dialectical dimension the rest of my paper is devoted.

15. *b. Haggiga* 14b.

16. G. Scholem, *Shabbetai Zevi vehaTenu'ah haShabbeta'it biYemei Hayyav* (Tel Aviv, 1988), II, 691 (ET: *Sabbatai Sevi: The Mystical Messiah 1626–76*, Princeton, 1973, 806).

17. Tishby, *Mishnat haZohar*, I, 295; II, 673–74 (English: *The Wisdom of the Zohar*, II, 457–58; III, 1421–22).

18. *Zohar* II, 34a; we shall return to this dictum below.

person enters upon the evil path and then abandons it – then the Holy One blessed be He ascends in His glory. Hence the perfection of all is in [integrating] good and evil together, and to thereafter ascend in the good, and there is no good except for that which comes from and out of evil.[19]

True perfection, both in the Godhead and in the cosmos as a whole, is that in which good and evil are integrated with one another: as they originate and split from one root, they should be returned to their dialectic unity by man's worship. There is a certain resemblance between the behavior described here and that of the path of repentance, but the formula used in this passage – as in others to be discussed here – indicates that we are not dealing here with the penitent, but with a person who, because of his elevated level of righteousness, is prepared to undergo the trials of evil and even to be inflamed by its desires, albeit without falling into the trap of sin. In this state God ascends in His glory and becomes known through the power of His rule, since by means of his undoubted ethical conduct man comes to His aid, rejects His enemy the evil, subdues and defeats it in His presence, and at the height of his spiritual ascent even annexes evil and incorporates it in the camp of holiness.

In the light of these ideas we may now examine the failures of Adam and of Noah. Indeed, their descent 'in order to know all that is beneath'[20] ended in a tragic result. Adam was drawn by the temptation of demonic forces, followed the serpent, was caught in its net, adhered to its improper desires, and allowed the serpent to take hold of him.[21] In so doing he deviated from the path of faith that signifies the divine world which is complete in its integrated opposites and its Central Line; slipped away from the realm of the Tree of Life, whose entire being is one of integration, unity and stability, and fell into the realm of changes, that is, that of the Tree of Knowledge of Good and Evil.[22] Adam thus descended and did not ascend, entered into the garden of impurity, and failed to leave it whole. A similar thing happened to Noah, who is attached to his predecessor Adam through a clear relationship: Noah wanted to be tested in the same sin in which Adam stumbled, thereby expressing his own status as one who was destined to correct the transgression of Adam:

When Noah set out to be tested in that same sin in which Adam had been tested – not to be attached to it, but [only] to know [it] and to correct the world – he was unable to do so. [Why was he unsuccessful? Because] he squeezed grapes[23] so as to be tested in that vineyard. Once he got to that place, 'he became drunk and was uncovered' [Gen. 9.21], and he had no strength to stand up, and thus 'he was uncovered' – he discovered [and opened up] a crack in the world that had been

19. *Zohar* II, 184a; cf. Tishby, *Mishnat haZohar*, I, 295, 366; II, 674 (English: *The Wisdom of the Zohar*, II, 457, 534; III, 1422).

20. *Zohar* I, 52a.

21. *Zohar* I, 52a.

22. See *Zohar* I, 221a-b; and cf. Y. Jacobson, 'The Final Redemption from the Viewpoint of Adam according to Italian Sages during the Renaissance' [Hebrew], *Da'at* 11 (1983), 71.

23. The 'squeezing of the grapes' is well known as the sin of Eve; see *Gen. Rab.* 19.5; 15.7; *Lev. Rab.* 12.1; *Num. Rab.* 10.2. *Pirqei deRabbi Eliezer*, ch. 23, draws a connection between Adam's sin involving wine and that of Noah. A similar connection appears in *b. Sanh.* 70a-b.

closed. 'Within his tent' (בְּתוֹךְ אָהֳלֹה) [ibid.] – it is written with a [final] h [in contradistinction to the correct reading]. And for that reason it is written, 'Do not approach the gate of her house' [Prov. 5.8].[24] 'Within his tent' – [the tent] of that vineyard.[25]

The 'crack' (an allusion to a sexual sin) which had been closed during the initial period of Noah's righteousness, but which he uncovered and opened up, is simultaneously 'the gate of her house' and 'her tent' (according to the written form). All these signify the seductiveness and the seductions of Lilith, the faithless woman of the world of impurity.[26]

The nature of the wine mentioned is explained further on in reference to the sin of Nadab and Abihu, the sons of Aaron:

> Certainly they drank from that same wine, as it is written: 'and they brought before the Lord strange fire' [Lev 10.1]. It is written here 'strange fire', and it is written there, 'to protect you from a strange woman' [Prov. 7.5]. And it is all one thing.[27]

The wine in which Adam, Eve and Noah stumbled thus signifies the harlotry of the impure Lilith. Further on another motif appears: before he sinned with the bitter wine, Noah was 'righteous' in the secret of the בְּרִית, which signifies according to the Kabbalistic symbolism both the holy covenant and the male sexual organ. By the fulfillment of the covenant, which symbolically means the erection of the male organ, Noah came to the ark,[28] the Holy Shekhinah, the divine female, to unite with her. But once he was overcome by his drunkenness and the flame of his lust (Ham) was aroused to the extent that he abandoned holiness to turn to the harlotries of the Other Side, he was castrated[29] and no longer possessed the 'strength to stand up'.

Further on in this passage, the *Zohar* explains the secret of the Land of Israel being given initially to Canaan, as well as the reason for Bath-Sheba being the wife of Uriah the Hittite before she became David's wife. The dialectic of the revelation of the good from within evil, and of the light that bursts forth from the depths of darkness, appears to us now as a comprehensive principle in the cosmos as a whole: be it on the metaphysical plane, on the historical level, or in the process of inner perfection of the individual (which has automatically cosmic and theosophic significance). The complete good that also incorporates evil can only be manifested through prior experience of its urges and temptations.

Unlike Adam and Noah, the patriarchs carried out this dangerous practice successfully, as expressed in their leaving the Holy Land to go to alien lands, to the

---

24. This alludes to the tempting woman who is described in the previous verses as having 'strange lips' and whose 'legs descend to death'. These descriptions are interpreted by the Kabbalah as referring to the impure female.

25. *Zohar* I, 73a-b. The *Midrash* already refers to the difference between the reading and the writing of the phrase, and interprets it as 'in the tent of his wife' (*Gen. Rab.* 36.4).

26. A marvelous description of this faithless woman, whom Jacob shall also visit in the future, evidently as an expression of the same 'ritual', appears in *Zohar* I, 148a-b (*Sitrei Torah*).

27. *Zohar* I, 73b.

28. *Zohar* I, 59b, on Gen. 6.18.

29. See *b. Sanh.* 70a; *Pirqei deRabbi Eliezer*, ch. 23.

realms dominated by the Shells, and their return-ascent thereto. Concerning Abraham, the *Zohar* says the following:

> Rabbi Shimon said: Come and see, all this is the secret of wisdom, and it alludes here to the wisdom and the lower levels, for Abraham descended to their depths [i.e., of the lower levels] and knew them, but did not become attached to them, and returned to his Master. And he was not seduced by them as was Adam, who when he reached that level was tempted by the Serpent and caused death to the world, nor was he tempted like Noah, who when he descended and reached that level, what is written? 'And he drank of the wine and became drunk, and was uncovered within his tent' [Gen. 9.21]... But concerning Abraham what is written? 'And Abram ascended from Egypt' [Gen. 13.1], [meaning] that he went up and did not go down, and returned to his place.[30]

Unlike Adam, who became entrapped in the pleasures of the Evil Urge and forgot whatever knowledge of the Divine he had succeeded in attaining while he still clung to the wisdom of the supernal levels, Abraham did not stumble: in his descent to evil, he did not follow his improper desires, but returned, together with Sarah his wife:[31] 'And he ascended to his first [and original] level...and he entered in peace and came out in peace.' The same held true for his son Isaac and for all the righteous, upon whom God imposes the difficult task of raising up their heads and adorning their glory in this world and the world to come.[32] This purifying and refining experience is emphatically presented regarding Jacob. Due to the importance of this passage and its many interwoven motifs, I shall quote it *in extenso*:

> Jacob entered in this beginning [i.e., the beginning of his mystical journey] into faith. Once he attached himself to this faith, he needed to be tested in the same place where his fathers had been tested, who entered in peace and came out in peace. Adam entered and was not careful and was tempted by her... Noah entered and was not careful and was tempted by her... Abraham entered and came out, as it is written: 'and Abram descended to Egypt' [Gen. 12.10]; and it is written, 'and Abram ascended from Egypt' [Gen. 13.1]. Isaac entered and came out, as it is written: 'And Isaac went to Abimelekh king of Philistines to Gerar'[Gen. 26.1], and it is written, 'and he went up from there to Beer-Sheba' [Gen. 26.23]. Jacob, once he entered in faith, needed to bring in a gift to that side,[33] because he who is saved from there is the beloved and chosen one of the Holy One blessed be He. What is written? 'And Jacob went out from Beer-Sheba' [Gen. 28.10] – the mystery of the secret of faith. 'And he went to Haran' [ibid.] – the side of the wife of harlotry... The fool who approaches her, she takes hold of him by force and kisses him and pours for him the dreggy wine, which is the asps' bitter poison.

---

30. *Zohar* I, 83a. A translation of this passage appears in Tishby, *Mishnat haZohar*, I, 295 (English: 457). The 'lower levels' (*madregot shelemata, madregot tahtonot*; see *Zohar* I, 74a) or simply 'levels' (*madregot*; see *Zohar* I, 83b) indicate the forces of the *Sitra Ahra*.

31. On the contrast between Eve and Sarah, see *Zohar* I, 122b.

32. *Zohar* I, 140b; the phrase is based upon the famous expression in *b. Hag.* 14b and 15b. But whereas the aggadah deals with entering the divine realm, the *Zohar* is dealing here with an opposite entry, into the gates of impurity. Cf. *Zohar* I, 83b.

33. Tishby ignored this important motif in its context; see *Mishnat haZohar*, II, 674 (English: *The Wisdom of the Zohar*, III, 1422). We shall return to it below.

Once he drinks – he goes astray after her... Jacob descended to her and went to her place, as it is said 'and he went to Haran', and saw all the structure of [her] house, and was saved from her. This thing was bad in the eyes of her male partner, Samael, and he went down to wage war with him [Jacob], and could not defeat him... Then he was delivered from all, and gained perfection, and ascended to a level of wholeness... and became the central pillar.[34]

This passage implies, first of all, that a person can only acquire his true spiritual level by means of tests and trials. He needs to leave or descend from his place in order to return to it, and only thus, once he has acquired it by his efforts to stand up against the temptations of evil and overcome them, does it truly become his own place. But what is the nature of this place? This place is 'a level of wholeness', 'the central pillar' – in other words, the central line that was revealed and embodied in Jacob, the unity of the opposites of חסד and ד י ן, of Mercy and Stern Judgment, within the divine structure, or, if you prefer, good and evil within the entire being. True good is not good alone, taken as the opposite of evil, but the dialectical integration of good and evil. Man's experiences and trials – in Egypt, in Gerar, in Haran, in the encounter with the faithless woman, in the flaming lust of intensified carnality – are a process of purification and refining. When evil is purified and refined – that is, when it joins good and is incorporated within it, or, in other words, when there takes place the process of transformation and sublimation – then the divine unity includes its opposites, and holiness is elevated in its glory and is perfected in all its wholeness.

G. Scholem[35] and I. Tishby[36] pointed at the similarity of this idea to the moods of Sabbatianism. Indeed, Nathan of Gaza makes extensive use of the *Zohar* passages discussed here. But a more comprehensive understanding of this requires that we also take note of the relation between the idea discussed here and the Hasidic thought, in which evil is seen as the distortion and falsification of good, and in which the solution to the riddle of its existence and its ultimate goal lies in restoring it to the good, by turning it around, uplifting and sanctifying it.

We need to decipher the meaning of another motif found in the above passage. What is the meaning of the phrase, 'a gift to that side', that Jacob needed to offer in order to free himself from the temptations of Lilith? It seems to me that the *Zohar* is referring here to the very act of Jacob going to her! Only when a person goes to the evil, when he experiences the intensity of its lusts, and when he does not deny its divine source, can he be freed from it. This very act of going is thus considered as giving a portion to the Other Side! One who separates himself from evil and pushes it away grants it a special place, assisting it to build for itself a fortress of frightening and threatening power.

An interesting expression of this concept appears in the *Zohar*'s approach to the destiny of Job, whose conduct and its results are repeatedly discussed in the Kab-

---

34. *Zohar* I, 147b–148b (*Sitrei Torah*).

35. Scholem, *Shabbetai Zevi*, II, 691; cf. *idem*, *Mehqarim uMeqorot leToldot haShabbeta'ut veGilguleha* (Jerusalem, 1974), 63–64, 248–49, 270–71.

36. Tishby, *Mishnat haZohar*, II, 674, n. 68 (English: *The Wisdom of the Zohar*, III, 1455, n. 125).

balistic tradition (from the *Zohar* on) to illustrate the daring idea of giving a portion to the Other Side. According to the well-known interpretation, Job's sin consisted in his offering burnt-offerings alone, thereby indicating his deepest wish to be connected with the realm of holiness alone. By his refusal to give a portion to evil, to acknowledge it and to act so as to appease it, to satisfy and bribe it, he aroused its anger: evil thereby took hold of him with intense wrath and did to him what it did. Although the notion of the pacification of evil, as a minimal degree of serving Satan, carries a rather mythic-dualistic character, there nevertheless emerges from it a certain principle that may also be formulated on a theoretical level: namely, that the calming and pacification of evil involve its subjugation and even its temporary negation. The very essence of evil lies in its strength, in its self-identity and independence, whether this is achieved by breaking away from the Divine with all its power of separation and setting up a kingdom unto itself, or whether this is attained by its breaking through into the Divine to grasp some of its holy vitality. By allotting it a certain portion, man thwarts its plots and weakens its power to cause harm. Evil that is at peace with good is no longer evil. According to one formula, God delivered Job to the powers of evil so as to distract them, through their enthusiasm of being engaged with him, so that the path toward holy unity would be free at this moment.[37] The following passage contains a deep understanding of Job's error and is distinguished in its sharp and clear formulation:

> He never gave it[38] a portion, as it is written: 'and he offered burnt-offerings like the number of them all' [Job 1.5]. A burnt-offering ascends higher and higher, and [Job] did not give any portion to the Other Side, for had he given it a portion, it would have been unable to harm him thereafter, and everything it took – it took from its own. And if you ask: Why did the Holy One blessed be He harm Job? Rather [the answer is,] that had he [Job] given it a portion, it [the force of evil] would have cleared the way and turned away from the Temple, and the Side of Holiness would have ascended ever higher and higher. But he did not do so, and for that reason the Holy One blessed be He called [him] to account. Come and see: Just as he [Job] separated himself [from evil] and did not integrate good and evil, so did He [God] judge him by the same coin: He gave him good, and thereafter evil, and thereafter returned him to good; for it is thus fitting that a person know good and know evil, and return himself to good – and this is the secret of faith.[39]

In this passage, the contrast between Jacob and his forebears on the one hand and Job on the other, is revealed in its fullness. Jacob was elevated to the status of

---

37. On Job, see Tishby, *Mishnat haZohar*, I, 291–92 (English: *The Wisdom of the Zohar*, II, 453–54).

38. The Other Side.

39. *Zohar* II, 34a. The end of this passage is quoted above, near n. 18. Concerning Job, who was constantly only 'turning away from evil' (Job 1.1), and refused to give pleasure to the powers of evil through his sacrifices, see *Zohar* II, 181a-b. In the Sabbatian tradition, Job's status was changed once Nathan of Gaza portrayed him as the prototype of the Messiah. See Scholem, *Major Trends*, 296, 298. In the passage quoted there by Scholem, the aspect of 'turning away from evil' is no longer identified with the one who avoids *ab initio* any contact with evil, but rather with the one who establishes contacts with the shells and leaves them. See *idem*, *Shabbetai Zevi*, I, 104–105, 249–50 (English: *Sabbatai Sevi: The Mystical Messiah*, 130–32, 318–19).

'the central pillar', because he integrated good and evil together. This integration is the secret of faith and lies at the depths of Kabbalistic cognition and experience. It was regarding this selfsame matter that Job sinned or erred (thereby bringing about a serious mishap – to both himself and to the cosmos): by refusing to give a portion to evil, he withdrew from it completely, connecting himself to and seeking to know only good alone. By so doing he separated good and evil from one another, rather than integrating them into a dialectical totality! For this reason there happened what did: harsh disasters befell him, and the separated evil, strengthened in its autonomous being, fell to his lot. Thus, it is precisely the person who turns away from evil who causes it to visit him.

What happened to Job may be interpreted in one of two different ways: (a) as an 'external' event, that is the arousing of the fury of evil due to Job's ignoring it and showing contempt for it; (b) as an 'inner' event, in which Job, by separating himself from evil, gave it greater power and made it more significant in his life.

What then is required in such a situation in terms of a person's path and his religious-ethical behavior? One might answer: to enter into the garden of impurity. By knowledge of evil the *Zohar* does not mean the actual performance of sin; for the doing of evil means that a person 'makes' and builds it up. Rather, the discussed knowledge means: drawing close to it and experiencing its urges through contact with it. This may be viewed as a kind of giving a portion to the Other Side. But this practice is of course intended to overcome evil: by drawing close to it, a person arouses within evil a fool's joy over the spoils that are about to fall into its net. But then, at the decisive moment, the person stands up against evil, taunts it and says: You have erred, your efforts are in vain, and your joy is for naught – thereby defeating it and leaving it empty and powerless, allowing God to ascend in His glory. Man can only attain the true meaning of existence by knowing both good and evil and by understanding their overall unity, which is alone the complete good. Only by contact with evil and the awakening of its lusts and urges can a person harness the evil awakened in him, which is the psychological embodiment and manifestation of metaphysical evil, defeat it and restore it to holiness, of which evil is merely a distortion and falsification. Holiness means unity, and man is called upon to establish it as his ultimate goal through the integration of its opposites: that is, by combining and integrating evil within it as well – in its elevation, correction, and transformation to good.[40]

Several scattered elucidations of the above-mentioned nature of evil appear in R. Joseph Gikatilla's *Sha'arei Orah*.[41] Gikatilla associates evil with ר י ן,[42] but does not elaborate upon the essential connection between them. Although he does not answer the question as to why evil develops specifically from the aspect of

40. See D.H. Freedman, 'Man as the Subject of the Theogony in the Lurianic Cabala' (Dissertation, University College London, 2001;supervision A. Rapoport-Albert). Her brief discussion of the descent to Egypt as symbolizing the knowledge of evil and the contact with it (23-25) is part of a more comprehensive chapter dealing with the question of the harmonious encounter between the forces of חסד and ר י ן, the male and the female, in the Kabbalistic outlook.

41. J. Ben-Shlomo (ed.) (2 vols.; Jerusalem, 1971).

42. *Sha'arei Orah,* I, 82.

דין, there does emerge from his discussions the distinction between דין that is included within the unitary system of the Divine, in which its activity serves for good and is in accordance with its goals – even if troubles and pains are incorporated therein – and excessive and deviating דין, which acts outside the boundaries of the realm of holiness, and whose activity is a sore evil:

> Know that the Name called אדני – according to that which is drawn towards it, whether from within or without, so is its name called, whether for good or for evil... And this is the secret of the Tree of Knowledge of Good and Evil... If the drawing down is from the side of דין – there is a side that is called good, even though it is from the side of דין, if it is from the side of דין of the inner camps... But if it is from the side of דין of the external forces...this is an evil matter, [that comes] from the side of the external forces that are outside of the line.[43]

Gikatilla thus acknowledges the negative activity of deviant דין, and the very possibility of its manifestation as such. He says similar things when discussing the term 'good' with reference to the *Sefirah* of *Yesod*. Good exists in the descent of Divine abundance – even an abundance of דין – into the tenth *Sefirah* of *Malkhut* via the Central Line. If the source of this abundance is *Yesod*, 'all comes via the path of pure good, and evil never acts in that thing, but only for the welfare of that which is blemished... and it is all for the good'. The assumption is that, through the manifestation of the divine world in the unity of its opposites, and its harmonious activity intended to benefit and sustain, there will be no destruction, and evil will not be established. 'No evil thing descends from heaven'[44] – that is, from the Central Line,[45] from the source of unity and the root of innerness. But when this unity is disturbed, and the channel of abundance from *Yesod* is blocked, and the emptied *Malkhut* draws down to itself various forces to refill it, then evil forces, that crouch down 'outside of the barriers of the Sefirot...all around', are drawn to and flow to it, and through it they 'descend' and spread about in the world to destroy it.[46] Good – not only in its mythic context and in its meaning as the phallic element within the Divinity, but also as an ethical principle within human existence and in the cosmos as a whole – signifies the fertility in both the material and the spiritual realms and the unity that spreads about to encompass all. Therefore, 'in anything in which there is division and separation, good does not exist, for good only comes to bring peace and to connect all things'.[47] Good is the principle of the Central Line, the unity of opposites, the holy and fructifying union,[48] while evil is all that which is uprooted from this unity and destroys it and pushed itself inside it, to disturb it.

43. *Sha'arei Orah*, I, 91.
44. *Gen. Rab.* 51.5.
45. The secret of שמים (heaven), i.e., the *Sefirah of* תפארת, which constitutes the balancing and stabilizing center according to Kabbalistic symbolism.
46. *Sha'arei Orah*, 101–102, 135.
47. *Sha'arei Orah*, 122. 'Peace' is a well-known Kabbalistic symbol for the fertile encounter of opposites, including the male and the female.
48. *Sha'arei Orah*, 123.

An exciting description of the invasion of the holy unity by evil, which deviates from its own place and penetrates into a place that is not its own, appears in the fifth chapter of *Sha'arei Orah*, devoted to explaining the status of the *Sefirah* of תפארת, the center of the manifest divine forces. Gikatilla describes being as arranged in a series of concentric circles. In the center is the Tetragrammaton, that signifies the divine being in its fullness and abundance, being the power of creation and constituting complete holiness. Around the holy name of YHWH are arranged the other holy names – those 'that must not be erased' – which are 'attached' to it[49] and connected with it, being its manifestations and appearances. The angelic princes of the nations attach themselves in turn to these names. The outer circle consists of the attributes 'which may be erased'. These attributes 'are drawn to the holy names'[50] and describe them, and to them the nations themselves are attached. Gikatilla describes the names and their attributes as garments or wings for the holy name of YHWH.[51] Together, these concentric circles constitute the proper structure of being, when all of them reside in their proper place, for only in their proper place does there exist the functionality meant to be manifested by them, and the all-encompassing divine unity can thus be realized. This functionality is intended to reveal the greatness of God and the glory of His kingdom within the spaces and circles and different stages of His developing world, and to thereby connect them by their fructifying unity with the root of the divine existence:

> God may He be blessed arranged the supernal systems and the form of the Chariot through the secret of the seventy princes, in which His kingdom is seen in its great highness and elevation. And the princes are like servants who stand outside the king's house and are ready to perform His wills, and through the multitude of princes and attendants and servants there is seen the greatness of the king and his dominion… Therefore, all the seventy princes who stand outside of the inner row, all of them are as if testimony to the great kingship of the name YHWH, blessed be He, and all of them are connected [with each other] according to the secret of the form of man.[52]

> They are [fulfilling] a great need in the [world of the] Chariot, and they are a great honor to the Name [of God].[53]

The concentric circles thus signify the divine unity of being, whose all existing phenomena turn their eyes to its center, to be sustained by its flowing vitality. This unity is revealed specifically through the multitude of layers of reality, all of which are integrated therein in a broad spectrum of expanding holiness. But when, due to the sins of Israel, the princes push themselves in between the name יהוה and *Keneset Yisrael*, the holy *Shekhinah*, the proper order is distorted, and everything is

49. *Sha'arei Orah*, 199.

50. *Sha'arei Orah*, 199.

51. *Sha'arei Orah*, 204, and many other passages.

52. *Sha'arei Orah*, 208.

53. *Sha'arei Orah*, 214; cf. 218, and also what appears in *Sod haNahash uMishpato* in Scholem, *Pirqei Yesod* 205. (English: *On the Mystical Shape of the Godhead*, 79–80).

uprooted from its place: the unity fails to take place, and the blessing that initially flowed to the *Shekhinah*, when the world still existed in its proper structure, is spilt out upon the princes and the lands of their nations.[54] The external invading forces that now appear in their improper place, forcing themselves into the center, which is not theirs, become dividing and interrupting shells[55] – and thus evil is revealed. As opposed to this serious confusion and distortion of the existing divine order, redemption signifies the return of things to their proper place.[56]

Concerning this matter Gershom Scholem writes that the discussed approach, which he presents on the basis of the tractate known as *Sod haNahash uMishpato* by R. Joseph Gikatilla, 'is opposed to the doctrine of left-handed emanation that is separated from holiness'.[57] I cannot accept his statement, that 'these two motifs are in principle not subject to unification'.[58] There is a contradiction between them only in the sense that, according to Gikatilla, the appearance of the serpent in the Garden of Eden signifies the breakthrough of evil into holiness, whereas according to the doctrine of the left-handed emanation and its developments, evil expresses the breakthrough of the demonic forces included within holiness from the divine world out of it, embodying fall and destruction. But the contradiction is diminished in light of the understanding that, in both conceptual systems, evil indicates that which is deviant and uprooted from its place, and in a place not its own it attempts to gain a foothold for itself, to build its fortress, and to strengthen itself beyond God's will and balanced plans. Either way, whether from within or without, it threatens holiness and upsets its harmonious order. Its departure from holiness (in the doctrine of the left-handed emanation, in which the question of its precise origin is not at all important for this discussion) is none other than an opportunity to acquire power and daring for itself – since only outside of this order is such strengthening possible – until it can return and burst into holiness, attacking and invading it aggressively and ruthlessly.

Similarly, R. Meir ibn Gabbai, represented by Scholem as one in whose work the two motifs mentioned appear in tandem,[59] dealt very little with the nature and origins of evil, even though in various passages he refers to its realization as dependent – as does Gikatilla – upon Adam's sin. In any event, it is clear that evil indicates an order that has been upset, and a structure that has been destroyed, when 'those who were within came out, and those who were outside came in'.[60] Evil signifies confusion and lack of order, 'without a correctly established structure' (*tikkun habinyan*).[61] Only the proper order, the establishment of being in the

54. *Sha'arei Orah*, I, 211.
55. *Sha'arei Orah*, I, 212.
56. *Sha'arei Orah*, I, 214.
57. *Pirqei Yesod*, 206 (English: *On the Mystical Shape of the Godhead*, 80–81).
58. *Pirqei Yesod*, 206.
59. *Pirqei Yesod*, 206, despite his stating their principled contradiction.
60. *'Avodat haQodesh* (2 vols.; Jerusalem, 1992): *Heleq ha'Avodah*, ch. 38, 179.
61. *Heleq ha'Avodah*, ch. 38, p. 179, *Heleq Sitrei Torah*, ch. 5, p. 424. Ibn Gabbai explains further on that *tikkun habinyan*, 'the correction of the structure', is none other than the manifestation of the form from the chaotic being and within it. This form is, by its very nature, a perfection

image of man, achieved by the process of separation for the sake of integration – that is, the distinct and separate manifestation of all phenomena in the positive functionality that unites them – allows for existence and continuity. In the same chapter Ibn Gabbai interprets the first of God's ten creative utterances ('In the beginning God created...') that indicates the primordial totality in which 'everything was concealed [and unrecognizable]...in the air that was not apprehended', and all existed 'surreptitiously [and silently]'. He further explains that, from its very inception – already in the hidden motion alluded to in the above passage – the process of emanation was intended to nullify the primeval chaotic confusion, to remove the dross and to put it 'in its proper place'.[62] This confusion relates to the primeval divine situation in which no differentiation had yet occurred: 'Prior to the manifestation of the Supernal Glory...all things were concealed and united in the hidden and not yet unfolded thought', and 'the powers of light and darkness and good and evil and all the opposites there were mixed together, like silver and dross that are mixed together, and all was in one source from which came all the opposites'.

In light of the unity and uniqueness of the divine source, one can well understand Ibn Gabbai's statement, that evil is 'only for the perfection of the good and its strengthening and sustaining. We can thus conclude that all was hewn from one source.' The process of emanation was intended to cause and establish the separation until 'each one was fixed in its suitable place, light and good in its place, and darkness and evil in its place'.[63] This is the reality of redemption. There are also places in which Ibn Gabbai uses the formula of separation to characterize the reality of *tikkun*: since the Tree of Knowledge signifies 'good and evil connected together in confusion', Adam was warned not to eat of it 'until it will be entirely good', integrated within 'the unity of the Tree of Life', while evil 'will be separated and pushed away to its place, which is the place of chaos, and then the tree will be entirely good'. At that time evil will be destroyed and vanish like smoke.[64] There are also places where Ibn Gabbai speaks of the transformation of evil into good, which is the highest conceivable level: when the Messiah completes 'the intention of creation and returns the crown of truth and unity to its original state [an allusion to the Kabbalistic sexual unity]', 'he will restore that side, which until that time was the "Other", beneath the wings of the *Shekhinah*, and it will no longer be called "Other", for the evil that is in the Tree of Knowledge will be transformed to good and will be entirely good ... and then the oneness will be a complete'.[65]

The reconciliation of these two formulae – that involving the rejection and destruction of evil, as opposed to its transformation to good – requires further

whose deep meaning is the secret of unity: the fertile and fructifying integration of male and female as the fundamental principle of the cosmos as a whole.

62. *'Avodat haQodesh, Heleq Sitrei Torah*, ch. 5, 423; and cf. ch. 4, 421.

63. *'Avodat haQodesh, Heleq Sitrei Torah* ch. 35, p. 523. God's glory – in both senses: the mystical structure of the Sefirot, and the strength of His rule and greatness – is only revealed by His power of separation, which is the power of freedom and redemption above and below.

64. *'Avodat haQodesh, Heleq Sitrei Torah*, ch. 13, 448.

65. *'Avodat haQodesh, Heleq Sitrei Torah*, ch. 14, 451–52. And cf. *Heleq haYihud*, ch. 19, 44.

examination, but it seems to me that, in terms of Ibn Gabbai's approach, the latter formula is the main one. It is clear, in any event, that the task of *yihud*, which lies at the heart of his outstanding book, one of the most important systematic works of Kabbalah prior to the monumental oeuvre of R. Moses Cordovero, repeatedly refers to the establishment of the complete and harmonious structure of the divine world and the fixing of each thing in its place.

One of the sharpest and most interesting discussions dealing with the nature of evil and depicting it as a deviant being, uprooted from its place, appears in *Minhat Yehudah*, R. Judah Hayyat's extensive, important and influential commentary on the book *Ma'arekhet haElohut*. In his commentary to the ninth chapter of that book, entitled *Sha'ar haHarisah* ('The Gate of Destruction'), the main subject of which is the sin of cutting off the shoots, performed time and again along history, Hayyat says the following:

> Before the sin [Adam] was entirely holy, and the serpent also was [good and would have remained] good, had he not changed his place. And for that reason the Shells are called 'the Tree of Knowledge of Good and Evil', for when they are in their place they are good, and when they change their place they become evil, for each one must 'return to his place in peace' [Exod. 18.23].[66]

In terms of human existence, the deviating departure of the Shell from its place is expressed in the strengthening of 'the [sexual] lust that comes from the side of the serpent' until 'intercourse has become profane'. The inflamed passion of the sexual urge bursts through and moves beyond the limits initially established by God, who placed the urge within man in a functional context, 'for the propagation of the species alone'. Thus, 'it was fitting that man should not become inflamed by it' except within that context, as a reflection, manifestation and embodiment of the divine fertility on earth as well, rather than for the satisfaction of his lust and the attaining of his carnal pleasure.[67]

---

66. *Ma'arekhet haElohut* (Mantua, 1558), 120b.

67. *Ma'arekhet haElohut*, 120b, and cf. Hayyat's discussion, 115b. I wish to call attention to the unusual formulation in which R. Judah Hayyat speaks of the prohibition of incest, that was only imposed upon Adam after he had distorted and corrupted his image, and has ever since appeared on the stage of history as an anthropologic mutation, in the wake of his crucial sin. Adam's sin was a sexual one (as already noted by the Sages in one of their well-known sayings on this subject – *b. Sanh.* 38b) and involved arousing bodily pleasure. 'The use of the organs of reproduction' was initially intended to be like the use of 'the hands and feet, in which [man] does not find any pleasure'. The formulation indicates the functional nature of this 'use', which was only intended for reproduction or, as we saw above, for the propagation of the species alone. In the wake of the sin, and as the sour fruit of the distortion caused thereby, the propagation of the species, which as the embodiment of the divine fecundity is portrayed and should be considered as a sublime and holy goal, was transformed into carnal and pleasurable sexuality. Since lust, which originates from the serpent, is that which now drives man to attain his sexuality and enjoy it; or, to put it differently, since man's sexual organ, which had initially been 'the sign of the holy covenant' 'the righteous in the land' (Eccl. 7.20), and the foundation of its existence (following the well-known phrase from Prov. 10.25, that is repeatedly and consistently interpreted throughout the course of the Kabbalistic tradition, as referring to the male – symbolized by the righteous, the sustaining foundation [יסוד], and the ברית, which is both the covenant and the male organ – and the female – symbolized by the land – in the Godhead and the cosmos as a whole), has become 'a serpent' in its

R. Judah Hayyat makes some important statements regarding this matter in an earlier passage in his commentary to the ninth chapter of *Ma'arekhet haElohut*:

> When the point of emanation appeared, there emanated from it those shells that preceded [being], and their existence was from the side of the deficiency that is attached to the newly produced thing, as it newly produced after not having been actual or manifest, and as it is in need of and dependent upon its cause. And therefore they [i.e., the shells] preceded, for they came from the side of the absence, and absence precedes being ... And all the Chariots that are within are also without, and had they not changed their place they would have been good, for 'He did not create it for chaos, but for inhabitation did He form it' [Isa. 45.18].

Thus, even the lust that originated from them was only intended for the inhabitation of the world.[68]

Two points are worthy of notice here: (a) the definition of the nature of evil as that which has changed and moved away from its proper place; (b) the identification of evil as embodying the negative aspect of that which has been newly produced, which until then did not exist in actuality, and whose actual existence was absent. This may refer to that same aspect, by which being strives to once again be swallowed up and assimilated in its source without recognition, disappearing within the infinity of the Divine, in which its limits and contours are totally erased. R. Judah Hayyat connects the aspect of the absence that precedes being to the Kings of Edom, the forces of destruction and chaos that preceded the building of the well-structured world; and also to the shell that guards its fruit; and to the body, that encompasses the soul as a garment. These two latter aspects clearly emphasize the significance of evil when in its proper place and context.

lustfulness and sexual appetite, man is now required to exercise great care in its 'use', lest he causes the penetration of the serpent (who is in any event involved in the sexual act, since lust derives from it) to interfere between the supernal brother and sister, תפארת and מלכות. Initially, before man's organ was transformed into a serpent, incest of close relatives was not prohibited to him. Now, because of the status of the serpent, who 'enters...within' (as a result and expression of the distortion which occurred in the world after the primordial sin), one should not 'use' the 'sign of the holy covenant' but 'on Sabbath nights, so as not to make the holy profane', to mix good and evil, and to cause the presence of evil in a place that is not its. At these times intercourse is holy and performed 'with the power' of the 'sign of the covenant', rather than the power of the Serpent, which symbolizes the improper sexual appetite, for 'the week days, surrounded by the shells come to an end on the Sabbath day'. In brief: since the time of Adam's sin, 'coition has become profane ... and the serpent has entered within' as the source of the sexual lust, and the demons are ready to force themselves into 'a realm that is not theirs' – and therefore all the sexual prohibitions are in force regarding man; *Ma'arekhet haElohut*, 119b–120a.

68. *Ma'arekhet haElohut*, 115b. R. Judah Hayyat differentiates between two aspects in the manifestation of the sexual urge: the heart of stone and the heart of flesh (based on Ezek. 11.19). Unlike stone, which 'once a part of it is hot, all of it is hot', flesh 'does not become hot except that side that reaches [and touches] the fire'. The heart of stone thus symbolizes the overwhelming arousal of the urge, which in its inappropriate strengthening beyond God's initial intention is evil, whereas the heart of flesh, which mankind will eventually possess as at the beginning, before he sinned, signifies the controlled, functional arousal, which as such – and also according to its ultimate goal – is holy (*Ma'arekhet haElohut*, 120b). This arousal of the heart of flesh is the sexual drive which originates from the external chariots, or shells, which when in their proper place contribute to the inhabitation of the world.

The above identification also includes the aspect of dependence: the existence of evil is not autonomous, but contingent and dependent. When its existence is newly produced from the state of being absent, 'after not having been actual', it is 'in need of and dependent upon its cause'. At the same time, its status as the necessary outcome of the process of production, that originates in absence, or in the still potential, not actualized existence (for if this were not the case, it would be pointless to speak about new production, which implies *ipso facto* the absence that precedes it necessarily), is clear. When the reality of a thing is newly produced, its aspect of absence is also necessarily manifested and realized in the existence of the Shell, characterized both by its preceding manifestation and by its being external. The conclusion is clear: when man brings about the confusion of the cosmic order and the malfunctioning of its systems – that is, when he causes the inner forces to be uprooted from their place and the external demonic powers forced within – he strengthens the aspect of absence in the cosmos (the powers that sow destruction and desolation), and turns the inhabited world to 'chaos without a path', to chaotic reality.[69]

R. Judah Hayyat's discussion, which is partially based upon the other printed commentary of *Ma'arekhet haElohut* known as *Paz*,[70] in elucidating Adam's sin, is extremely interesting for the presentation and understanding of the relation between the myth of Eve's rebellion and the appearance of evil as the sour fruit of 'cutting off' and separating. The subject is an extremely important one, deserving a comprehensive study in its own right. But in this framework I shall limit myself to a few comments related to the subject of the present paper. The myth of the matriarchal rebellion is presented by the author of *Ma'arekhet haElohut* himself when he points out Eve's emphatic activism. She 'went very deeply into that sin, because she sought to augment her strength above that of her husband in the lowly world'.[71] According to the commentators on that work, Eve intended by her rebellion to express her female essence, which is the essence of דין, as opposed to the nature of רחמים (Compassion), which is male in its essence. Moreover: the contrast is also

69. See A. Farber-Ginat, '"The Shell Precedes the Fruit"', 118–42. On p. 125 Farber-Ginat refers to the above-cited passage from Ibn Gabbai. She presents two models for the understanding of evil: according to the former, evil came into being by the very process of cosmic differentiation, when דין strives to crystallize in distinct individual frameworks; according to the second, evil signifies and embodies an anti-cosmic will to return to the origin, to be absorbed therein and to be entirely assimilated. Regarding this distinction, that is already found in the discussions of scholars such as Scholem and Tishby (both explicitly and implicitly), it seems important to me to add the dialectical logic that connects the two models. Extreme individualization involves separation, division and dismemberment, particularistic strengthening, conflict and dispute and fierce war – absolute chaos. For that reason, the holy union is of such decisive importance in Kabbalistic thought: it leaves distinctive beings (such as חסד and דין, male and female) as they are, but seeks to connect them together in the constructive realization of the functionality unique to each of them. M. Idel, '"The Evil Thought" of God' [Hebrew], *Tarbiz* 49 (1989), 356–64, also deals with the source of evil in the thought of God and its preceding the emanation of good, but he does not relate to the essence of evil and its relation to the root of Nyd.

70. See E. Gottleib (ed.), *Mehqarim beSifrut haKabbalah* (Jerusalem, 1976), 357–69.

71. *Ma'arekhet haElohut*, 115a.

between lust, that originates in the forces of דין, and the intellective nature of רחמים. Compassion is intellective in its being simple, without the aspect of contraction and limitation, clear, transparent and without the dregs of דין.

The pairs of conflict represented are thus:

Female	Male
דין (Stern Judgment)	רחמים (Compassion)
Man's carnal being	The spirituality of the supernal angels
Lust	Intellectuality
Disintegrative force of division	Integrativeness of human spiritual existence

The following is R. Judah Hayyat's description (copied from the commentary of *Paz*, with minor changes, some of which I shall note):

> Upon seeing that Adam was created in the supernal image [*Paz*: 'in the image of the supernal angels'; the change is significant, as Hayyat's formulation alludes to the reflection of the Sefirotic system within man] and that he was entirely intellective, like the higher angels, who are angels of compassion, she thought, that she would not have any [*Paz*: the word 'any' is absent] dominion, as the forces of דין [*Paz*: 'the created forces'] would not perform their activity, and from them lust is manifested. Therefore she 'squeezed grapes' – she separated [*Paz* adds here: 'the *yod*'] and gave [*Paz*: 'placed'] [as] the head of the foxes [*Paz* adds here: 'according to the secret of *yod* with *kaf*, and she separated the *yod* from the *tet*], and then there acted [*Paz*: 'will act'] the powers – and this is a complete 'cutting off.'[72]

We may conclude from this passage that Eve, who wished, as we said, 'to augment her strength above that of her husband in the lowly world', needed to be strengthened as a separate female entity; namely, to separate the Sefirah of *Malkhut*, the supreme female principle, and to reveal it as separate and distinct unto itself. Prior to the sin, Adam was immersed in his intellectuality and spirituality, which mean also the total, harmonious integration of all of his forces and desires. In this holy integration, or if you prefer: in this integration, which is holy by virtue of its very integration, which is among the distinctive signs of the realm of holiness and its order, Adam's urge existed without transcending its boundary or crossing its limit, as conceived by God and according to His will. Its manifestation was functional and in accordance with its goal, which had been fixed by God's will and His great wisdom. Following the sin, in which the female principle became a distinct entity, and Eve was separated from Adam unto herself, the forces of matter and of lust, which originate from the aspect of her separate existence, were manifested, and she enjoyed dominion and self-expression. But this dominion was one of destruction and loss, because it expresses the destructive element in the Divine, the element of separation and disintegration. At this point, the connection between the female and evil can be clearly understood in the light of separating, cutting off and uprooting: femaleness in its aspect of Stern Judg-

72. *Ma'arekhet haElohut*, 115a.

ment, is an entity that strives to strengthen itself within its own domain and seeks an autonomous expression. This is opposed to the initial situation, in which she was incorporated within the intellective unity of Compassion, the dominant principle in man who was created 'in the supernal image'. This image, that is none other than the sefirotic system, embodies the unitary structure of the divine world, which has alone, through the unity of opposites embodied therein, the power of existence. This destructive element finds interesting expression in the understanding of the relationship between the feminine and the demonic. The feminine appears in Kabbalistic sources as a transformative element, a transitional point between one world and the other, a kind of liminal phase between one level and the next that devolves from it: it receives the abundance from above and gives it to that which is below. But when the female ceases to act according to this transformative functionality, but seeks to demand and take all for itself, halting the flow within itself without transferring it to those that long for it – that is, by separating itself, by dint of the separative ן ׳ ד within itself, from the flow of integration and the order of devolution, and lifting itself up through its own autonomy – it violates the unity, cuts off the flow of vitality, disrupts the process of God's self-manifestation in His flowing fertility (all these are the explicit signs of evil), and appears as a 'shell': the female is transformed into the demonic, and evil is manifested by forcing itself into the holy unity and separating itself therefrom.[73]

In the myth of the feminine uprising, there is exposed an extremely interesting aspect of the concept of evil as embodying and expressing all that was cut off and separated from the source of holiness. In one passage Hayyat says:

> The intention of the Holy One blessed be He was that man should be on earth like an angel of God, [and] that he would not incline to evil while exercising his free will, but would be one in his parts, turning towards the true One.[74] And for this reason He told him that he should eat of the Tree of Life that indicates this, in order to keep him away from evil and death and changes. And so long as he acts in this manner down below, he shall arouse unity above as well, and the shells will be submissive, and each one will go to his place in peace.[75]

Man was thus destined to establish the harmonious integration of his different parts[76] and to adhere to 'the true One', who signifies the integration of the opposites of חסד and ד ׳ ן, good and evil.

Hayyat states his concept about this subject even more clearly in another passage, interpreting the verse, 'Behold, man has become like one of us, to know good and evil' (Gen. 3.22):

---

73. It is obvious that the discussed ideas are none but the Kabbalistic mythical interpretation of the biblical story about Eve, who was initially included within Adam (as his rib), and thereafter was separated from him and given a distinct existence.

74. And not to evil, which is a departure from unity, duality and changes, distortion of life and death.

75. *Ma'arekhet haElohut*, 116a.

76. 'Shell and soul'; *Ma'arekhet haElohut*, 116a. The 'shell' (קל ׳ פה) in this context is the human body, as is also indicated by the verse quoted from Job at the end of the previous page of *Ma'arekhet haElohut*.

Man became like one [combined] of his parts [*mehalaqav*].[77] For even though there are two parts within him – good and evil, which are the soul and the body – before he sinned it was as if there was only one part, for the soul overcame the body, and this was in order to connect the supernal good and evil, which are רחמים and דין. And this was the intention of the creation of man. But once he sinned he strengthened the power of lust, and drew down to the Crown [i.e., *Malkhut* or the *Shekhinah*] the quality of גבורה, from which derives the urge, and this he did by separating the good from her.[78]

The feminine was thus left isolated and disconnected. The question of the identity of the sinner – was it Adam who 'cut off' the shoots or perhaps Eve, who went deeply into the sin which she initiated with great intensity? – is of secondary significance here. For our purposes, the importance lies in the fact that the female aspect – being from the source of דין – is that, that tends to fortify itself and to be strengthened within its separate boundaries, to be cut off and manifested as the actual embodiment of evil. The process of correction and the struggle against evil are thus involved in the rescuing of the divine feminine from its isolation, in raising the *Shekhinah* from the dung heaps of impurity, and bringing her to her wedding canopy. The joy of her wedding unification is thus the celebration of the integration of good and evil together.

Appendix: Some Comments on the Idea of Holiness

My intention in the following remarks is to deepen the understanding of the Infinite as 'chaos'. By doing so I hope to propose a new perspective on the concept of holiness in the Kabbalah, particularly in Lurianic Kabbalah.

The description of the Infinite as 'chaos' indicates, as we have already stated, its chaotic being: everything is included therein in absolute concealment, absorbed in its depths and assimilated without distinction in its recesses, without any process taking place. Nothing comes into being. And if any movement does occur there, it is infinite and without purpose: the 'static motion' of an amorphous mass moving about within itself. In this sense one might say that the chaotic indicates an inward motion, one that vanishes in the darkness, in which everything is obscured and disappears in the infinite unity, a motion that fades away in the silence of the absolute. The opposite of this opaque and impervious motion exists in the movement that bursts forth outwards to be revealed, the movement of the flow of life, which goes on in a constant renewal, the movement of the *holy union*, in which the abundant fertility of God is manifested (which according to my understanding is the most important motif in all of Kabbalistic mythic thought) or, in the terminology of Lurianic Kabbalah, the movement of *Beirur*.

By this term, which has several aspects, I refer here to the process of constructive shaping, and not necessarily to the separation and elimination of waste mate-

---

77. That is, like one who was combined and integrated from different and opposed parts.

78. *Ma'arekhet haElohut*, 122a-b. 'Good' here as both the masculine principle and the flow of holiness and vitality which, when halted, evil dominates. The two meanings are, of course, identical in their inner sense.

rial (although both meanings are closely interconnected).[79] *Beirur*, as exemplified by various civilizational activities of man (like that of the baker, in which the seed of the grain is separated from its shell and chaff; that of the tailor, who 'separates' the shape of the garment from the woven cloth spread before him; or that of the goldsmith, who fashions the form of the vessel from the raw matter at hand), involves the manifestation of constructive functionality from the undifferentiated nature of chaos (or from corporeal matter. Matter is chaotic in the sense that form is incorporated and assimilated within it. I cannot relate here to the original Aristotelian position, but only to its development in later Jewish sources such as the writings of the Maharal of Prague, in whose view matter signifies a destructive metaphysical principle[80]).

Since *Beirur* signifies the manifestation of holiness that had been lost in the captivity of the 'shells' and of corporeity, there is implied here a new and exciting meaning of the concept of holiness. The holy is not only the numinous, the transcendent, or – as in the usual definition found in many Jewish sources – the separate from all kinds of cosmic existence and the totally different. One might say almost the opposite: *the holy is the functional*, that which is incorporated in a constructive manner within the course of life and participates in the rhythm of its coming into being and its fertile uninterrupted flow. In this understanding there is embodied, in my view, the most important aspect of the concept of holiness in the Kabbalah; because the most important, and the most common motif in the Kabbalistic sources is, as I have already noted, that of the holy union – that is, the manifestation of divine life in its abundant fertility.

This fertile manifestation does not exist in the divine world alone, but in the cosmic worlds, as well as, of course, in the world of man, since all manifestations of life are manifestations of divine life. Hence God expects and demands that the same principle will be revealed on all levels of existence: constructive holiness, which is none other than constructive functionality.[81] This subject is related to the idea of order, because order means functional encounter. Order is achieved, first of all, by the separation of various elements (such as the male and the female), after having initially been incorporated in an unrecognizable manner in the chaotic and non-distinctive being. In their separation from one another the unique functionality of each of them is manifested – the male, as the principle of giving, and the female as the principle of receptivity, that absorbs and receives. Only thus can a functional encounter between them be achieved, and this precisely is what order means. Order is thus an encounter, an encounter means union which generates offspring. The divine movement is one of functional manifestation, in which the opposites are

79.   As I demonstrated in my paper on the female figure in Lurianic Kabbalah, Y. Jacobson, 'The Aspect of the Feminine in Lurianic Kabbalah', in P. Schäfer and J. Dan (eds.), *Gershom Scholem's Major Trends in Jewish Mysticism, 50 Years After* (Tübingen, 1993), 241–43.

80.   See Y. Jacobson, 'The Image of God, as the Source of Man's Evil according to the Maharal of Prague' [Hebrew], *Da'at 19* (1987), esp. 112–15, 122–23.

81.   Regarding the labors of בֵּרוּר, see R. Hayyim Vital, *Sha'ar haMizvot* (Jerusalem, 1988), *Behar*, 60–61; *'Eqev*, 96, and other passages in the same section – in relation to the mystical meaning of eating. Cf. Vital, *Sefer Ta'amei haMizvot* (published together with *Sefer Liqqutei Torah*; Jerusalem, 1988), 199; *Sha'ar haKavvanot* (Jerusalem, 1988), 134.

hewn out of the infinite chaos (gradually: first הכמה and ב ׳ נ ה, then חסד and ד ׳ ׳ ן), and there occurs a process of functionalization, in which each of the distinct powers is manifested in its unique function, until the decisive encounter between them (תפארת) takes place. The conclusion is clear: offspring can only come into being in a world ruled by order; in chaos there is not and cannot be offspring. And when man acts so as to manifest holiness (*Beirur*) even in his mundane, profane activities, he reveals the divine order within the cosmos, and realizes the constructive functionality among all its distinct parts. The disclosure and realization of this fundamental principle of existence are none other than the sanctification of reality and the ascent to that same level in which the vital processes of existence attain their divine actualized meaning fully and completely.

In the first chapter of his book, *On Sanctity*,[82] Joseph Dan draws an important distinction – also methodologically interesting – between the meanings of the concept of holiness in Judaism (and Islam), on the one hand, and in Christianity, on the other. It is regrettable that his important discussion, that may be seen as a kind of a concluding study in his manifold references to his predecessors, was not accompanied by an analysis of the positive contents of this concept and its multiple meanings. I do, however, agree with his basic thesis. Judaism in general – and the mystical, Kabbalistic-Hasidic aspect of its development, in particular – considers all the levels of existence as the all-embracing extension of holiness. But this holiness is generally represented only as potential holiness, so that in its absence or concealment the seeds of evil are sown, and impurity – as its distortion and falsification – spreads and grows stronger, covering and darkening the world with its heavy shadow. In this context a crucial importance is ascribed to the decisive imperative – to sanctify reality even in its profane and impure realms and to reveal the Divine also within them.

---

82. J. Dan, *'Al haQedusha* (Jerusalem, 1997), 11–30.

Part III

SYSTEMATIC QUESTIONS

Augustine and Luther on Evil

Dietmar Wyrwa

It goes without saying that the voices of Augustine and Luther, as the most important in western, Latin-speaking, Christian history cannot go unheard and surely do not need elaborate explanation. Concerning Augustine I shall have to concentrate on very few elementary issues that will be no more than a prelude to the main part, which is concerned in greater detail with Luther.

I

Augustine

Let me begin with Augustine and a review of the biographical circumstances[1] under which the question of Evil became a crucial and decisive question for his whole life. Deeply moved by the reading of Cicero's *Hortensius*, a protreptic appeal for a philosophical life, the 19-year-old Augustine experienced a philosophical conversion that led to a complete change of his whole being. The direction of his will was orientated anew towards that freshly revealed dimension of the spirit that is wisdom.[2] At the same time, though, he developed a dualistic attitude which, within days,[3] led him straight into the arms of the Manicheans. His newly woken aspirations towards wisdom had put aside the trivial hopes of a career and public reputation that the young ongoing orator had cherished. Inside of him the questions about the great mysteries of the world kept vexing him. Augustine himself states that it was predominantly the matter of Evil – *unde malum?* – that made him join the Manicheans[4] where he was then to be an auditor for nine years.[5] However, the Manichean system of religion with its absolute duality of two antagonistic eternal principles, the battle between good and evil, was undoubtedly not really able to give satisfactory answers to the restless desire in his mind to master the great

---

1. See H. Chadwick, *Augustine* (Oxford: Oxford University Press, 1986), 1–29.

2. Aurelius Augustinus, *Confessiones* (ed. L. Verheijen; CChrSL, 27; Tournhout: Brepols, 1981), III, 4, 7–8. For cross-references to the so-called 'first confessions', in *De beata vita* 1, 4 (ed. J. Doignon; *De beata vita. La vie heureuse* [Bibliothèque Augustinienne 4/1; Paris: Desclée de Brouwer, 1986], 54–58, 135–40), cf. P. Courcelle, *Recherches sur les confessions de Saint Augustin* (Paris: de Boccard, 1968), 269–90.

3. Aurelius Augustinus, *De duabus animabus* (ed. J. Zycha; CSEL, 25/1; Vienna: Hölder-Pichler-Tempsky, 1891), 1, 1.

4. *Conf.* III 6, 10. 7, 12.

5. *Conf.* IV 1, 1.

questions. On the contrary, increasingly it left him feeling deeply torn. Only years later did he receive intellectual guidance in this desperate situation. A friend in Milan lent him a couple of Neoplatonic books, in Latin translation, that he devoured.[6] They opened up an understanding of the spiritually structured unity of reality in its entirety and, in particular, an understanding of how the mean and the evil are an integral part of this reality, that is how Evil is realized as the removal or corruption of Good – *privatio boni.*[7]

Augustine had found a fixed constituent of his view of the world, and I could stop here in my depiction of Augustine's inner development, which will find its final stage only with his conversion, or, if you like, his discovery of the concept of divine grace. Following his scriptural encounter with Paul the Apostle,[8] the dramatic nature of his conversion results in a merging of his intellectually acquired ideas to the life experience of the creatively renewing faith.

Later on, the intensive study of Paul that became the breakthrough for the doctrine of divine grace[9] was to lead one step further and generally helped his going beyond the mainly philosophical framework of his thinking. There can be no doubt, however, that Augustine, through his life and work, held on to the Neoplatonic ideas, namely to regard Evil as a defect or violation of Good.

The concept of *privatio boni* plays a pivotal role in the literary battle against the Manicheans[10] and it naturally plays a main role in his autobiography, the *Confessions*. It is one stone in the mighty framework of his doctrine of the two *civitates,*[11] and Augustine did not hesitate to make it known in his parish in Hippo Regius.[12] It also ranks prominently in his *Enchiridion,*[13] the late summary of his doctrine. And still at the end of his life, in his controversy with Julian, he returns to his basic insight.[14]

---

6. *Conf.* VII 9, 13.
7. *Conf.* VII 11, 17–16, 22.
8. *Conf.* VII 21, 27.
9. Aurelius Augustinus, *De diversis quaestionibus ad Simplicianum* (ed. A. Mutzenbecher; CChrSL, 44; Turnhout: Brepols, 1970), I, II, 1–22 (concerning the exegesis of Paul's Epistle to the Romans 9.10-29); R. Lorenz, 'Das vierte bis sechste Jahrhundert', in K.D. Schmidt and E. Wolf (eds.), *Die Kirche in ihrer Geschichte 1*, C1 (Göttingen: Vandenhoeck & Ruprecht, 1970), 60, rightly stated: 'diese Seiten haben weltgeschichtliche Bedeutung' ['These pages are important for world history'].
10. Aurelius Augustinus, *De moribus ecclesiae catholicae et de moribus Manichaeorum* (ed. J.B. Bauer; CSEL, 90; Vienna: Hölder-Pichler-Tempsky, 1992), II, II, 2–VIII, 11; *idem, De natura boni* (ed. J. Zycha; CSEL, 25/2; Vienna: Hölder-Pichler-Tempsky, 1892); *idem, Contra epistulam Manichaei* (ed. R. Jolivet and M. Jourjon; Bibliothèque Augustinienne, 17; Paris: Desclée de Brouwer, 1961), XXV, 27.28, XXXIII 36–XL 48.
11. Aurelius Augustinus, *De civitate Dei* (ed. B. Dombart and A. Kalb; CChrSL, 47, 48; Turnhout: Brepols, 1955), XII, 1–8.
12. Aurelius Augustinus, *Sermones* (ed. J.-P. Migne; PL, 38; Paris, 1845), 96, V, 5; 182 III.V, 5; 214, 3; *idem, Enarrationes in Psalmos* (ed. E. Dekkers and J. Fraipont; CChrSL, 39.40; Turnhout: Brepols, 1956), LXVIII s.I 5; CXLI 18.
13. Aurelius Augustinus, *Enchiridion ad Laurentium de fide et spe et caritate* (ed. E. Evans; CChrSL, 46; Turnhout: Brepols, 1969), III, 11–16.
14. Aurelius Augustinus, *Contra secundam Juliani responsionem imperfectum Opus* (ed. J.-P. Migne; PL, 45; Paris, 1865), III, 206; V 44; VI 16.

The main venture of my article will be to outline as precisely as possible the concept of *privatio boni*, fully developed from the mid 390s onwards.[15] I shall attempt this in seven short propositions.

1. Augustine's theory of Evil as *privatio boni* is based on the concept of God's creation, without which it cannot be understood. One has to start with the trinitarian God, the *summa essentia*, the *summum bonum*, the Creator who summoned everything into being out of nothing. The nature of the creation is a God-given one, that he made in a hierachical, yet diverse, order so that everything is in its entirety.[16] And because it was made out of nothingness it is a changeable nature, made to keep its order in dependence on God. As such, everything that is is good – and this is not just a tautology but means that every being, every creation, is made according to God's creation plan and has its very own size and form and is at peace with itself.[17] This monistic view of the order of creation has no space for a being that could be contrary to the greatest One, because everything was made by Him – except nothingness.[18]

---

15. The book of G.R. Evans, *Augustine on Evil* (Cambridge: Cambridge University Press, 1982) intends to show the development of Augustine's reflexions on evil in all its perplexity from a biographical point of view, stressing two decisive intellectual stages, the encounter with the Manichean religious system and the Pelagian controversy. It covers indeed the wide range of aspects Augustine associated with it. Little, however, is said about his central concept of 'privatio boni' he shaped by means of what he had read in the Neoplatonic books (yet see pp. 34–36). In consequence G.R. Evans holds that in Augustine's view evil was nothing – what is not exactly the position of Augustine (in spite of *Soliloquia* I 1, 2) – and that he regarded evil as irrelevant, insignificant, trivial or even as ineffably ridiculous – what he clearly did not. Still of value are the older studies of G. Philips, 'La raison d'être du mal d'après St Augustin' (Louvain Dissertation, University Grégorienne de Rome, 1927) and R. Jolivet, *La problème du mal d'après St Augustin* (Paris: Beauchesne, 1936). Cf. also D.A. Cress, 'Augustine's Privation Account of Evil. A Defense', *Augustinian Studies* 20 (1989), 109–28, who strikingly discusses misunderstandings underlying modern criticism against Augustine's theory. Just recently the book of Chr. Schäfer, *Unde malum. Die Frage nach dem Bösen bei Plotin, Augustinus und Dionysius* (Würzburg: Königshausen & Neumann, 2002) has been published.

16. *Ench.* III 9-10: '...bonitatem credere creatoris qui est deus unus et verus, nullamque esse naturam quae non aut ipse sit aut ab ipso: eumque esse trinitatem... Ab hac summe et aequaliter et immutabiliter bona trinitate creata sunt omnia, nec summe nec aequaliter nec immutabiliter bona, sed tamen bona etiam singula: simul vero universa valde bona, quia ex omnibus consistit universitatis admirabilis pulchritudo.' *De civ. Dei* XII 2: 'Cum enim Deus summa essentia sit, hoc est summe sit, et ideo inmutabilis sit: rebus, quas ex nihilo creavit, esse dedit, sed non summe esse, sicut est ipse; et aliis dedit esse amplius, aliis minus, atque ita naturas essentiarum gradibus ordinavit...'; cf. *De civ. Dei* XI 16.

17. *De civ. Dei* XII 5: 'Naturae igitur omnes, quoniam sunt et ideo habent modum suum, speciem suam et quandam secum pacem suam, profecto bonae sunt; et cum ibi sunt, ubi esse per naturae ordinem debent, quantum acceperunt, suum esse custodiunt'; Wis. 11.21: '*sed omnia mensura et numero et pondere disposuisti*', concerning the physical-mathematical structure of God's creation, plays a considerable role in Augustine's cosmological conception, cf. *De civ. Dei* XI 30; XII 19, *Ench.* IX 30; XXXI 118.

18. *De civ. Dei* XII 2: 'ac per hoc ei naturae, quae summe est, qua faciente sunt quaecumque sunt, contraria natura non est, nisi quae non est. Ei quippe, quod est, non esse contrarium est. Et propterea Deo, id est summae essentiae et auctori omnium qualiumque essentiarum, essentia nulla contraria est.'

2. What follows from the above is: Evil is not a substance.[19] That could only be if there was a being or principle opposed to God, which is impossible.

3. If Evil itself is not a substance there has to be an essence which it can affect.[20] This essence must necessarily be good, though changeable. Where Evil emerges it is the annihilation, distortion and degradation of nature in its entirety, and it takes away the Goodness from it – hence *privatio boni* – but without reducing it to nothingness.[21] If nothingness were the result of this process, there would be no nature, and neither would there be Evil that could corrupt nature. This means, somewhat paradoxically,[22] that Evil can only be what is Good – good in nature, evil in its corrupt state.[23] Consequently, the Devil, in spite of his profoundly evil disposition, must still possess traces of a good nature and peace that God allows him to exist at all.[24]

4. Evil manifests itself through the ill-disposed will, in the intentional averting from God. Augustine defines the situation very accurately: the bad turning of the will does not tend towards Evil – for what could that be? – but in a bad way in an act of vanity and self-love where the will turns away from the highest good and descends down low, and thus breaks apart the order of nature designed by God.[25]

---

19. *Conf.* VII, 12, 18: 'malumque illud, quod quaerebam unde esset, non est substantia'; *Conf.* VII 16, 22; *Ench.* III 11: 'non enim ulla substantia…'; *De mor. eccl.* II IV, 6: 'malum…non enim secundum essentiam, sed secundum privationem verissime dicitur'; *Contra epist. Man.* XXXIII 36: 'quaesivimus, quid esset malum, neque hoc naturam, sed contra naturam esse cognovimus'.

20. *De civ. Dei* XXII 1: 'quae (sc. mala) omnino nulla essent, nisi natura mutabilis, quamvis bona et a summo Deo atque incommutabili bono, qui bona omnia condidit, instituta, peccando ea sibi ipsa fecisset; quo etiam peccato suo teste convincitur bonam conditam se esse naturam; nisi enim magnum et ipsa, licet non aequale Conditori, bonum esset, profecto deserti Dei tamquam luminis sui malum eius esse non posset'; *De civ. Dei* XI 17: 'Quia sine dubio, ubi est vitium malitiae, natura non vitiata praecessit.'

21. *De civ. Dei* XII 5: 'ita ut nec tanta corruptio, quanta usque ad interitum naturas mutabiles mortalesque perducit, sic faciat non esse quod erat'.

22. *Ench.* IV 13: 'res mira…dici videatur absurde'.

23. *De civ. Dei* XII 3: 'isto modo dici potest, vitium esse nec in summo posse bono nec nisi in aliquo bono. Sola ergo bona alicubi esse possunt, sola mala nusquam; quoniam naturae etiam illae, quae ex malae voluntatis initio vitiatae sunt, in quantum vitiosae sunt, malae sunt, in quantum autem naturae sunt, bonae sunt.' *De civ. Dei* XIV 11: 'bona tamen sine malis esse possint, sicut Deus ipse verus et summus…mala vero sine bonis esse non possint, quoniam naturae, in quibus sunt, in quantum naturae sunt, utique bonae sunt'.

24. *De civ. Dei* XI 17: 'Quapropter etiam voluntas mala grande testimonium est naturae bonae…diabolus institutione illius (sc. Dei) bonus, voluntate sua malus'; *De civ. Dei* XIX 13: 'Quapropter est natura, in qua nullum malum est vel etiam in qua nullum esse malum potest; esse autem natura, in qua nullum bonum sit, non potest. Proinde nec ipsius diaboli natura, in quantum natura est, malum est; sed perversitas eam malam facit.' *De civ. Dei* XXII 24: 'Neque enim damnando aut totum abstulit quod dederat, alioquin nec esset omnino; aut eam removit a sua potestate, etiam cum diabolo poenaliter subdidit, cum nec ipsum diabolum a suo alienarit imperio; quando quidem, ut ipsius quo que diaboli natura subsistat, ille facit qui summe est et facit esse quidquid aliquo modo est.' Aurelius Augustinus, *Tractatus in Iohannis Evangelium* (ed. M.-F. Berrouard; Bibliothèque Augustinienne, 72; Paris: Desclée de Brouwer, 1977), XXVII, 10. *Contra sec. Juliani resp. imperfectum Opus* VI 16.

25. *De civ. Dei* XII 8: 'Deficitur (sc. mala voluntas) enim non ad mala, sed male, id est non ad

Furthermore, he explains, there is no actual cause for the will to turn away from God and become Evil, there is no *causa efficiens*.[26] Attempting to find such a cause would be like trying to see the darkness or hear the silence: we can sense them only deficiently. Likewise there is a *causa deficiens* for the will, but no *causa efficiens*. This means that the will makes itself evil for no reason by falling off from God. Augustine thinks of the fallen angels and Adam and Eve, for the rest of humanity was already born with this defect.

5. At this point we should take a brief look at Neoplatonism. Neoplatonism was the decisive inspiration for Augustine. We shall direct our attention to Plotinus[27] in particular as his theories differ considerably from Augustine's. Plotinus demands us to go further than to explain Evil as a reversed expression of the will, a derived spiritual defect. One had to get close to the primary defect, but this, he argues, was not simply a flawed disposition of the soul but something exterior: it was *matter*. The lowest and weakest emanation of the One, close to nothingness, and as such in the true sense of the meaning *privatio boni*. When any part of the material world hosts matter, or directs itself from afar towards matter, as the unsound part of the soul does, this would be a derived defect in a second or further degree.[28] We can see that Augustine does not follow Plotinus's theory to this last stage. He stops at the point of the derived defect, the spiritual defect of the ill-disposed will. In consequence, Evil in flora, fauna and the inanimate nature, is not affected according to Augustine's theory of *privatio boni*, because it does not result from a reversed will. With regard to the goodness of God's order of creation generally, Augustine tends to neutralize it after Stoic patterns.[29]

6. However, it would be wrong to accuse Augustine of underestimating the effects of Evil. Indeed, his pessimism about sin is hard to beat. The descent of the free will as an act of vanity and self-love, has damaged the good nature of humanness and severely lessened the quality of being – therefore *privatio boni*. The

malas naturas, sed ideo male, quia contra ordinem naturarum ab eo quod summe est ad id quod minus est.'

26. *De civ. Dei* XII 7: 'Nemo igitur quaerat efficientem causam malae voluntatis; non enim est efficiens sed deficiens, quia nec illa effectio sed defectio. Deficere namque ab eo, quod summe est, ad id, quod minus est, hoc est incipere habere voluntatem malam.' For the following comparison (as well in *De civ. Dei* XXII 1) see Plotinus, *Enneades* (ed. P. Henry; Oxford: Clarendon Press, 1964), I, 8 (51), 4, 30ff.; I 8 (51), 9, 19ff.

27. Especially relevant are two treatises: Plotinus, *Enn.* II 4 (12) (περὶ τῶν δύο ὑλῶν) and *Enn.* I 8 (51) (πόθεν τὰ κακά), though the doctrine occurs throughout his works, e.g. *Enn.* III 6 (26), 11, 24–36; VI 7 (38), 28, 7ff. Cf. A.H. Armstrong, 'Plotinus', in A.H. Armstrong (ed.), *The Cambridge History of Later Greek and Early Medieval Philosophy* (Cambridge: Cambridge University Press, 1970), 193–268, esp. 256f., and the more detailed discussion by K. Alt, *Weltflucht und Weltbejahung: Zur Frage des Dualismus bei Plutarch, Numenios, Plotin* (Abhandlung der Akademie der Wissenschaften und der Literatur. Geistes- und Sozialwissenschaftliche Klasse 1993, 8; Stuttgart: Franz Steiner Verlag, 1993), 55–81, 112–21.

28. Cf. Plotinus, *Enn.* I 8 (51), 8, 37–44; 11, 1–18; 14, 49–54. I cannot enter the question here, whether Porphyrius in his lost works should have anticipated Augustine's solution.

29. *De civ. Dei* XII 4: 'Ceterum vitia pecorum et arborum aliarumque rerum mutabilium atque mortalium vel intellectu vel sensu vel vita omnino carentium, quibus eorum dissolubilis natura corrumpitur, damnabilia putare ridiculum est.'

immediate effect of original sin is the long line of misery that man is burdened with: the loss of free will, moral ignorance, a desire for things harmful; failure and pain, fear and lust, and last but not least death.[30] As descendants of Adam and Eve, contaminated from their roots and caught up in a web of sin, punishment and death, the whole human race stands under God's wrath. The physical ills of the extra-human nature that punish mankind for original sin have also to be taken into account here.

In spite of this, human nature as God's creation stays essentially good, although degenerated. This is evident in the God-given benefactions of propagation and subsistence of the species in form, kind and unity of its members, as well as reason. The list could be continued. It would be illuminating in this context to read three chapters from *De civitate Dei*,[31] where, over the span of 11 pages, Augustine weighs the miseries of human life against the natural benefactions of the Creator, including the interesting question of why we learn with such difficulty and forget with such ease. The rule of thumb is: *malum, quod a parente trahitur, et bonum, quod a creante tribuitur* – Evil derives from the parents, Goodness is given by God.[32]

7. One last point concerns the question of God's attitude to original sin. Augustine explains: God foresaw the first sin and let it happen. But he also knew how to make use of Evil by fitting it in a good order, according to its predestination, either with the just punishment of everlasting damnation or with merciful salvation. God cannot be blamed for this, and nobody can justifiably complain.[33]

30. *Ench.* VIII 23ff.: 'rerum quae ad nos pertinent bonarum causam non esse nisi bonitatem dei, malarum vero ab immutabili bono deficientem boni mutabilis voluntatem, prius angeli hominis postea. Hoc primum est creaturae rationalis malum, id est prima privatio boni. Deinde iam etiam nolentibus subintravit ignorantia rerum agendarum et concupiscentia noxiarum, quibus comites subinferuntur error et dolor, quae duo mala quando imminentia sentiuntur, ea fugitantis animi motus vocatur metus. Porro animus cum adipiscitur concupita, quamvis perniciosa et inania, quoniam id errore non sentit, vel delectatione morbida vincitur vel vana etiam laetitia ventilatur [the well-known four Stoic passions according to Plato, *Phaedo* 83b, *Republic* IV 429d, *Theaet.* 156b]. Ex his morborum non ubertatis sed indigentiae tanquam fontibus omnis miseria naturae rationalis emanat... Sed homo habet et poenam propriam, qua etiam corporis morte punitus est.'

31. *De civ. Dei* XXII 22-24.

32. *De civ. Dei* XXII 24.

33. *De civ. Dei* XII 23: 'Nec ignorabat Deus hominem peccaturum et morti iam obnoxium morituros propagaturum eoque progressuros peccandi inmanitate mortales... Sed praevidebat etiam gratia sua populum piorum in adoptionem vocandum.' *De civ. Dei* XVII 11: 'et quos liberandos non esse praescivit, ad utilitatem liberandorum et comparationem duarum inter se a contrario civitatum non utique vane in totius rationalis creaturae pulcherrima atque iustissima ordinatione constituit'. *De civ. Dei* XXI 12: 'ita dispertiatur genus humanum, ut in quibusdam demonstretur quid valeat misericors gratia, in ceteris quid iusta vindicta. Neque enim utrumque demonstraretur in omnibus, quia, si omnes remanerent in poenis iustae damnationis, in nullo appareret misericors gratia; rursus si omnes a tenebris transferrentur in lucem, in nullo appareret veritas ultionis.' *De civ. Dei* XXII 1: 'qui (sc. deus), cum praesciret angelos quosdam per elationem...tanti boni desertores futuros, non eis ademit hanc potestatem (sc. liberum arbitrium), potentius et melius esse iudicans etiam de malis bene facere quam mala esse non sinere...quem (sc. hominem) similiter cum praevaricatione legis Dei per Dei desertionem peccaturum esse praesciret, nec illi ademit liberi arbitrii potestatem, simul praevidens, quid boni de malo eius esset ipse facturus'. *Ench.*

At last, even the doctrine of predestination, itself not free of tribulations, leads towards reflections that serve the theodicy. I have to finish with my short account of Augustine at this point and proceed with the main part.

II
Luther

I shall start once more with a review of the biographical background. As is well known, the question: *unde malum?* did not have the same crucial, all-important meaning for Luther as it did for Augustine. When Luther went through ordeals of challenges and despondency in his monastic life it was the anxiety about his sinful conscience before the wrath of the judging God that tormented him, and not the relatively abstract question about Evil. Being severely challenged, even after the liberating breakthrough concerning his certainty about justice of faith, Luther experienced Evil of a very particular kind. In those challenges he saw the personified Evil at work – the Devil, Satan, Lucifer or whatever one may call him.[34] As a consequence Luther made frequent and drastic mention of him, as his contemporaries did not fail to notice.[35] Interestingly, a certain tendency seems to develop in Luther's speeches about the Devil. The greatest occurrence of Devil images is not to be found in the young Luther. Only gradually do frequent allusions occur along with more substantial images and beginnings of a very individual concept of the Devil, until they reach a climax in 1535.[36] The after-dinner speeches are a case apart in this matter. Luther's talk of the Devil is apparently not a relic of the late mediaeval worldview that was gradually disappearing. Apart from the usual elements, the following issues move increasingly into focus. They are: the Devil as censurer and denouncer of consciences, as falsifier and suppressor of the Gospel, and as destroyer of God's array of earthly creation. These are the central issues that provide an underlying dialectic antithetical scheme for the theological

XXIV 95f.: 'Non ergo fit aliquid nisi omnipotens fieri velit, vel sinendo ut fiat vel ipse faciendo. Nec dubitandum est deum facere bene etiam sinendo fieri quaecumque fiunt male. Non enim hoc nisi iusto iudicio sinit, et profecto bonum est omne quod iustum est.' *Ench.* XXVI 100: 'impleret ipse (sc. deus) quod voluit, bene utens et malis tanquam summe bonus, ad eorum damnationem quos iuste praedestinavit ad poenam, et ad eorum salutem quos benigne praedestinavit ad gratiam …ut miro et ineffabili modo non fiat praeter eius voluntatem quod etiam contra eius fit voluntatem, quia non fieret si non sineret, nec utique nolens sinit sed volens [a remarkable statement!]; nec sineret bonus fieri male, nisi omnipotens et de malo facere possit bene'. *Ench.* XXVIII 104.

34.   Cf. from this specific point of view the biography by H.A. Oberman, *Luther: Man between God and Devil* (New Haven: Yale University Press, 1989). Special studies are H.-M. Barth, *Der Teufel und Jesus Christus in der Theologie Martin Luthers* (FKDG, 19; Göttingen: Vandenhoeck & Ruprecht, 1969), G. Ebeling, *Lutherstudien* (Vol. 2. Disputatio de homine. Part 3. Die theologische Definition des Menschen: Kommentar zu These 20–40; Tübingen: Mohr, 1989), 208–271 and H.-Chr. Knuth, 'Zwischen Gott und Teufel – Martin Luther über den Menschen', *Luther* 64 (1993), 10–23.

35.   Martin Luther, *Vom Abendmahl Christi, Bekenntnis* (WA 26; Weimar: Böhlau, 1909), 241–509, 401, 3f., 402, 18ff.

36.   H.-M. Barth, 'Zur inneren Entwicklung von Luthers Teufelsglauben', *KD* 13 (1967), 201–11.

outlining of the doctrine of the word of God. This will have to be taken into account.

My following comments will deal predominantly with Luther's tract *De servo arbitrio* from 1525.[37] It is the book in which Luther passionately argues with Erasmus about the question of the free will. Within the development of the discussion about the Devil, the tract occupies a mature although not quite finished position. Above all it is the piece of writing in which Luther discusses the topic of Evil more profoundly than ever before or after in his life, and it is incidently the only tract apart from his catechisms that he later found worth preserving.[38] I will now give a concise profile in five subsections.

1. The world is a battlefield where God and Devil collide and lead a most fierce war against each other. Luther has an endless supply of ways to describe this irreconcilable struggle of global, even cosmic dimension which goes along with tumult and chaos. Devil, world and sin belong to a kind of triad[39] here that mark the satanic front line on the evil side: the realm of darkness stands against the light, and the realm of light against darkness.[40]

---

37. Martin Luther, *De servo arbitrio (1525)* (WA 18; Weimar: Böhlau, 1908), 551–787. Less historically orientated but expounding the theological position is the emphasis of the commentary by H.J. Iwand in Martin Luther, *Daß der freie Wille nichts sei: Antwort D. Martin Luthers an Erasmus von Rotterdam*, in Martin Luther, *Ausgewählte Werke* (ed. H.H. Borcherdt and G. Merz; Ergänzungsreihe 1, 3; Aufl. Kaiser: Munich, 1975). The word-index (WA 66, Lateinisches Sachregister; Weimar: Böhlau, 1995), s.v. 'malus' 365-70, is an indispensable help, and a complete survey of Luther's word-usage is now available since the first volume of the German word-index is published recently (WA 69, Deutsches Sachregister; Weimar: Böhlau, 2001), s.v. 'böse', 417–29. Among the numerous studies about Luther's treatise, which as a rule do not deal with the problem of Evil specifically, I only want to mention M. Doerne, 'Gottes Ehre am gebundenen Willen. Evangelische Grundlagen und theologische Spitzensätze in De servo arbitrio', *Luther – Jahrbuch* 20 (Weimar: Böhlau, 1938), 45–92, and Th. Reinhuber, *Kämpfender Glaube: Studien zu Luthers Bekenntnis am Ende von De servo arbitrio* (Berlin and New York: de Gruyter, 2000), where the problem of Evil is taken into consideration.

38. Martin Luther, *Brief Nr. 3162, Luther an Wolfgang Capito in Straßburg 9. Juli 1537* (WABR 8; Weimar: Böhlau, 1938), 99, 5–8.

39. Cf. the references given by J. Meyer, *Historischer Kommentar zu Luthers kleinem Katechismus* (Gütersloh: Bertelsmann, 1929), 100–101.

40. *De serv. arb.* (WA 18), 743, 32–35: 'Quodsi a regno et spiritu Dei alienum est, necessario sequi, quod sub regno et spiritu Satanae sit, cum non sit medium regnum inter regnum Dei et regnum Satanae, mutuo sibi et perpetuo pugnantia' (WA 18), 627, 34–38: 'Ita implacabili discordia verbum Dei et traditiones hominum pugnant, non aliter atque Deus ipse et Satan sibi invicem adversantur et alter alterius opera dissolvit et dogmata subruit, tanquam si duo reges alter alterius regnum populetur. Qui non est mecum, ait Christus, contra me est' [Mt. 12.30]; (WA 18), 658, 13–16; 659, 6f.: 'Quid enim est universum genus humanum, extra spiritum nisi regnum Diaboli …confusum chaos tenebrarum?' (WA 18), 782, 21–23: 'Scriptura ubique Christum per contentionem et antithesin praedicat…ut quicquid sine Christi spiritu fuerit, hoc Satanae impietati, errori, tenebris, peccato, morti et irae Dei subiiciat'; Martin Luther, *Predigten des Jahres 1537* (WA 23, Weimar: Böhlau, 1901), 716, 33–37: 'Weiter folget, das auch der Teufel nichts wider uns schaffen kann, denn durch Christum sind wir von des Teufels gewalt und Reich erloeset, welchs ein Reich der finsternis, irthums, der sunde und des todes ist, weil Er uns in sein Reich versetzt hat, das ein Reich des liechts, rechten verstands, der gerechtigkeit und des lebens ist.'

At this point a glance at Augustine suggests itself. Augustine juxtaposes two *civitates*, *civitas Dei* and *civitas diaboli*, and he points out that the decisive distinction was the issue of the *will*: one led by good will, one led by bad will. This opposition, though, did not concern the essence or nature of either, for hierarchically-teleologically ordered according to their natural category, they are, after all, God's good creation.[41] Luther left no space for this kind of differentiation and its ontological aspect. It never occurred to him that even Evil could be resident in the essentially good creation. Probably owing to his nominalist background, the basis of ontology which would have been able to balance out this very dualistic image of a battle between God and Satan is completely out of his sight, or rather, it has evaporated.

It is interesting in this context that Luther did not accept the citation of the line that concludes the first account of the Creation, Gen. 1.31 'and behold, it was very good'. This, claims Luther, was said before the Fall of mankind, and what is more, and this is his more pungent challenge, it was a judgement from God's perspective, which is utterly incommensurable with human dimensions (including of course ontology).[42]

Just how close Luther came to the borderline of the theologically bearable can be seen in his adoption of Paul's word of 'the God of this world' (2 Cor. 4.4). The explosive potential of this passage was already in the air when Marcion in the early Church made it the focal point of his doctrine of two Gods, a heretical opposition between the God of the Old Testament, the just creator and judge, and the God of the New Testament, the benevolent saviour and father of Jesus Christ.[43] Another proof of the importance of the passage is the fact that we find it in Augustine's works, where it is cited five times exclusively in the anti-Manichean works as one that is a stronghold of Manichean belief.[44] Luther may not have known about this,

---

41.　*De civ. Dei* XI 33: 'has duas societates angelicas inter se dispares atque contrarias, unam et natura bonam et voluntate rectam, aliam vero natura bonam, sed voluntate perversam'; *De civ. Dei* XXII 1.

42.　*De serv. arb.* (WA 18), 708, 19–709, 4: 'Altera caussa, quod ea, quae fecit Deus, sunt valde bona… [Gen. 1.13]. Primo dicimus, quod hoc dictum est ante lapsum hominis, ubi quae Deus fecerat, erant valde bona. Sed mox sequitur tertio capite, quomodo sit homo factus malus, desertus a Deo ac sibi relictus… Secundo dicitur: si de operibus Dei post lapsum intelligi voles, Erant valde bona, Observabis hoc dici non de nobis, sed de Deo. Non enim dicit: Vidit homo, quae fecerat Deus, et erant valde bona. Multa videntur Deo et sunt bona valde, quae nobis videntur et sunt pessima … Igitur quomodo sint bona coram Deo, quae nobis mala sunt, solus Deus novit et ii qui oculis Dei vident, id est qui spiritum habent. Sed tam acuta disputatione nondum opus est.'

43.　Irenaeus, *Adversus Haereses*, III 7, 1 (ed. A. Rousseau and L. Doutreleau; SC, 211; Du Cerf: Paris, 1974), IV 29, 1 (ed. A. Rousseau, B. Hemmerdinger, L. Doutreleau and CH. Mercier; SC, 100; Du Cerf: Paris/Lyon, 1965). Tertullian, *Adversus Marcionem* (ed. E. Evans; Oxford: Oxford University Press, 1972), V 11, 9–12. 17, 9. While Irenaeus does not explicitly name his opponents here (cf. *Adv. Haer.* III 4, 3), it is Tertullian who allows the ascription because he launches his attacks in the same matter against Marcion.

44.　Aurelius Augustinus, *Contra Faustum* (ed. J. Zycha; CSEL, 25/1; Vienna: Tempski, 1891), XXI 1f.2f.9; *idem, Contra Felicem* (ed. J. Zycha; CSEL, 25/2; Vienna: Tempski, 1892), II 2; *idem, Contra adversarium legis et prophetarum* (ed. K.-D. Daur; CChrSL, 49; Turnhout: Brepols, 1985), II 7, 29.

as far as we can tell, but he knew what he said: 'The world and its God cannot and do not want to endure the word of the true Lord. The true Lord wants not to be and cannot be silent. What can the struggle of these two (!) gods bring about, if not global chaos.'[45] After this quotation the dualism seems complete.[46]

2. Mankind is no mere neutral spectator in this battle; we are directly involved; the battle is fought for the sake of us. Mankind itself, static and bound in its will, is already on the one side or the other.[47] Mankind's inescapable involvement is best described with Luther's brief and recognizable simile of a human as a horse, ridden either by God or Satan, which he used against Erasmus.[48] The multilayered image itself was already well known in the ecclesiastical tradition and its propagation was interestingly enough mainly driven by a pseudo-Augustinian tract of a semi-

45. *De serv. arb.* (WA 18), 626, 22–24: 'Mundus et Deus eius verbum Dei veri ferre non potest nec vult, Deus verus tacere nec vult nec potest; quid iam illis duobus Diis bellantibus nisi tumultus fieret in toto mundo?' (WA 18) 628, 5–11. Cf. (WA 18) 627, 32–38; 782, 30–33: 'Sciunt (inquam) duo esse regna in mundo mutuo pugnantissima, in altero Satanam regnare, qui ob id princeps mundi [Jn 12.31] a Christo et Deus huius saeculi [2 Cor. 4.4] a Paulo dicitur, qui cunctos tenet captivos ad voluntatem suam, qui non sunt Christi spiritu ab eo rapti'; Martin Luther, *Wider die Antinomer (1539)* (WA 50; Weimar: Böhlau, 1914), 473, 34–40: 'Aber der Teuffel ist herr inn der welt, und ich habe es selbs nie koennen gleuben, das der Teuffel solt Herr und Gott der welt sein, bis ichs nu mals zimlich erfaren, das es auch ein artickel des glaubens sey: Princeps mundi, Deus huius seculi, Es bleibet aber (Gott lob) wol ungegleubt bey den menschen kindern, und ich selbs auch schwechlich gleube, Denn einem jglichem gefellet seine weise wol, Und hoffen alle, das der Teuffel sey jenseid dem Meer, Und Gott sey inn unser tasschen.'

46. Small wonder therefore, that Luther had to defend himself against reproaches of Manichaeism now and then. Martin Luther, *Tischreden Nr. 5194* (WAT 5; Weimar: Böhlau, 1919), 4, 19–21: 'Si Diabolus ex se malus est? – Tum Doctor: Bene dictum est esse duo principia, sed Manichei in hoc errant, quod dicunt ea principia esse aeterna. Sed alterum incepit cum Diabolo.' Martin Luther, *Enarratio Psalmi XC* (1532/33) (WA 30, 3; Weimar: Böhlau, 1930), 516, 25–517, 18.

47. *De serv. arb.* (WA 18), 670, 1–9: 'Deinde hoc merum figmentum Dialecticum est, quod in homine sit medium et purum velle... Sic potius res habet, ut Christus ait: Qui non est mecum, contra me est [Lk. 11.23]. Quia si Deus in nobis est, Satan abest, et non nisi velle bonum adest. Si Deus abest, Satan adest, nec nisi velle malum in nobis est. Nec Deus nec Satan merum et purum velle sinunt in nobis.'

48. *De serv. arb.* (WA 18), 635, 7–22: 'Summa, si sub Deo huius saeculi sumus, sine opere et spiritu Dei veri, captivi tenemur ad ipsius voluntatem, ut Paulus ad Timotheon dicit, ut non possimus velle, nisi quod ipse velit [2 Tim. 2.26]... Si autem fortior superveniat et illo victo nos rapiat in spolium suum, rursus per spiritum eius servi et captivi sumus... Sic humana voluntas in medio posita est, ceu iumentum, si insederit Deus, vult et vadit, quo vult Deus... [according to Ps. 73.22f.]. Si insederit Satan, vult et vadit, quo vult Satan, nec est in eius arbitrio ad utrum sessorem currere aut eum quaerere, sed ipsi sessores certant ob ipsum obtinendum et possidendum' (WA 18), 750, 5–15. Martin Luther, *Predigten des Jahres 1524* (WA 15; Weimar: Böhlau, 1899), 714, 28–32: 'Sed nos scimus non esse medium: aut deus aut diabolus. Si spiritum Christi non habes, es sub regno diaboli. Per hoc sequitur, ut sis eciam obnoxius ei, ut non habeas liberum arbitrium. Impellit te, ut fureris; scortaris, et facis libere. Tu es der hengst, diabolus te equitat. Aut sub diabolo es aut spiritu sancto.' Martin Luther, *Predigten des Jahres 1537* (WA 45; Weimar: Böhlau, 1911), 405, 24–28: 'Der Sathan Ist der Hellisch Reutter, Davon die Poeten gesagt haben: Er Reittet die Arme Seel und gewißen, Wie sein pferdt und fuehret sie, wue er hin will, von einer Sunde Zu der andern. Hie dem Teuffel zw weren ist nymmand mechtig denn Christus allein.'

Pelagian kind,[49] but only with Luther did the image gain its full impact as a fully fledged theological comment. In the context of the outlined 'dualistic' antagonism between God and Devil it aims to demonstrate how humanity in its will is worked by forces that leave it helpless and passive. The ridden animal stands for human will and thus for its whole physical existence: when God is the rider the will moves towards Good, when it is Satan the will moves towards Evil. Mankind itself has no freedom to decide who rides his will. It is God and Satan who battle over it in the attempt to rule it. Whoever wins, wins humans' will.[50]

Luther allows for a so-called 'psychological freedom' to act with regard to earthly matters and possessions such as money, food, drink etc., things that are below human themselves, but all of this does not change the fact that humanity is entirely dependent in all matters that are above it. Luther remains consistent and does not forget to point out that this so-called psychological freedom to act is only able to sin or respectively that it is also steered by God's free will.[51]

To come back to the comparison with the horse: one should think the image is designed in an infra-lapsarian way and this is surely quite right for the time being. That the human will is limited is, in our context, a statement that presupposes the fall of humanity and the inevitability of original sin. However, this does not ask the question where Sin or Evil come from, let alone give an answer to it. The Devil in

---

49.   Cf. Pseud. Augustinus, *Hypomnesticon* (ed. J.-P. Migne; PL, 45; Paris, 1865), III 11, 20: 'Recte namque arbitror comparari liberum arbitrium jumento, unde et dictum est, *Velut jumentum factus sum apud te* (Psal. LXXII, 23): gratiam vero sessori. Quia sicut jumentum animal vivacissimum, ut dometur ad opus homini necessarium, de armento vagum apprehenditur, et incipit per curam domantis se ad ejus proficere voluntatem: ita et liberum arbitrium, quod vulneratum vivit in homine, gratia Dei apprehenditur de armento et luxuriae saeculi, in quo pastore diabolo vagabatur per incongruas voluptates.' The semi-Pelagian character of the simile in the *Hypomnesticon* is clearly to be seen in its synergism. The ridden horse stands for man's free will which has to cooperate with the rider i.e. with God's grace. Satan is not a rider at all but the bad herdsman. For the history of the simile in the scholastic tradition cf. H.J. McSorley, *Luthers Lehre vom unfreien Willen: Nach seiner Hauptschrift De servo arbitrio im Lichte der biblischen und kirchlichen Tradition* (BÖT, 1; Munich: Hueber, 1967), 309–313, and H. Bornkamm, *Martin Luther in der Mitte seines Lebens: Das Jahrzehnt zwischen dem Wormser und dem Augsburger Reichstag* (Göttingen: Vandenhoeck & Ruprecht, 1979), 381f. n. 73f.

50.   Though McSorley criticizes Luther's position from a Tridentine-catholic point of view, historically he has rightly pointed out Luther's own intention when using the simile of the riding animal (McSorley, *Luthers Lehre*, 311).

51.   *De serv. arb.* (WA 18), 638, 4–11: 'Quod si omnino vocem eam omittere nolumus, quod esset tutissimum et religiosissimum, bona fide tamen eatenus uti doceamus, ut homini arbitrium liberum non respectu superioris, sed tantum inferioris se rei concedatur, hoc est, ut sciat sese in suis facultatibus et possessionibus habere ius utendi, faciendi, omittendi pro libero arbitrio, licet et idipsum regatur solius Dei libero arbitrio, quocunque illi placuerit. Caeterum erga Deum, vel in rebus, quae pertinent ad salutem vel damnationem, non habet liberum arbitrium, sed captivus, subiectus et servus est vel voluntatis Dei vel voluntatis Satanae' ; (WA 18), 781, 8–13: 'Scimus, quod homo dominus est inferioribus se constitutus, in quae habet ius et liberum arbitrium… Sed hoc quaerimus, an erga Deum habeat liberum arbitrium'; (WA 18), 672, 7–20; 752, 7–11: 'Scimus liberum arbitrium natura aliquid facere, ut comedere, bibere, gignere, regere…cum tamen Lutherus donarit liberum arbitrium valere nihil nisi ad peccandum' ; (WA 18), 768, 23–26: 'In Deum peccat impius, sive edat sive bibat, aut quicquid fecerit.'

this comparison denotes no more and no less than the force of sin and evil which suppresses the human will, but he is not exposed as the origin of Evil.

Luther, indeed, does not linger over the infra-lapsarian explanation. To be exact, he says, the phrase 'free will' is an idiom that befits the majesty of God alone, for only God can do and does as He pleases,[52] while 'we have lost the meaning and matter of this glorious word' – but here he corrects himself: 'lost, no not lost, we never had it!'[53] The limitations of the will – and this goes beyond Augustine – are therefore an indication of the nature of humanity that is defined as a created receptive being, liable to God's judgement who embraces or dismisses it. Because humanity's basic situation is only determined by its relation to God, its *coram Dei*, an autonomous, independent self-reference of humanity has to be positively dismissed. Anything else would be sacrilegious. With this supralapsarian approach the impression of a dualism that arose with the image of a battle between two Gods is implicitly withdrawn. Since humans with their unfree will were only able to receive passively[54] from their maker, the question of how Evil could come into the pure primitive state of creation becomes all the more painfully pressing. I will have to take up this question once more.

3. Evil in the world is a terrible reality – as a matter of fact. One will look in vain for a comprehensive handy definition of Evil in Luther's works (which is no surprise) but he insists emphatically that Evil is not Nothingness. The following extract from Luther is usually interpreted in a way as if he tried to reject the Augustinian concept of *privatio boni*: 'This will and this nature of Satan and the fallen human, turned away from God, is not Nothing. Because neither Satan nor the godless human is nothing, nor do they have no nature or no will, although their nature is corrupt and turned away from God.'[55] Luther's criticism aims against the evaporation of Evil into Nothingness; but we should be cautious about his refer-

---

52. *De serv. arb.* (WA 18), 636, 27–32: 'Sequitur nunc, liberum arbitrium esse plane divinum nomen, nec ulli posse competere quam soli divinae maiestati. Ea enim potest et facit (sicut Psal. canit [135, 6]) Omnia quae vult in coelo et in terra. Quod si hominibus tribuitur, nihilo rectius tribuitur, quam si divinitas quoque ipsa eis tribueretur , quo sacrilegio nullum esse maius possit.'

53. *De serv. arb.* (WA 18), 637, 17–20: 'Cum ergo significationem et rem vocabuli tam gloriosi amiserimus, imo nunquam habuerimus (quod Pelagiani voluerunt et ipsi hoc vocabulo illusi), quid inane vocabulum tam pertinaciter retinemus in periculum et illusionem fidelis populi?'

54. The scholastic term *aptitudo passiva* is the keyword, how Luther describes man's relationship to God's grace. *De serv. arb.* (WA 18), 636, 16–22: 'At si vim liberi arbitrii eam diceremus, qua homo aptus est rapi spiritu et imbui gratia Dei, ut qui sit creatus ad vitam vel mortem aeternam, recte diceretur; hanc enim vim, hoc est, aptitudinem, seu ut Sophistae loquuntur dispositivam qualitatem et passivam aptitudinem et nos confitemur, quam non arboribus neque bestiis inditam esse, quis est qui nesciat? neque enim pro anseribus (ut dicitur) coelum creavit.' Cf. B. Lohse, *Luthers Theologie in ihrer historischen Entwicklung und in ihrem systematischen Zusammenhang* (Göttingen: Vandenhoeck & Ruprecht, 1995), 273.

55. *De serv. arb.* (WA 18), 709, 15–18: 'Haec igitur eorum (sc. Satan et homo lapsi) voluntas et natura sic a Deo aversa non est nihil. Neque enim Satan et impius homo nihil est aut nullam naturam aut voluntatem habent, licet corruptam et aversam naturam habeant.' H.J. Iwand represents a widespread opinion when he suggests in his commentary on this passage, that Luther wants to dissociate himself form Augustine's theory of *privatio boni* (H.J. Iwand in Martin Luther, *Ausgewählte Werke*, Ergbd. 1 [l.c.] 297f.). This is not the case.

ence. It is not the Augustinian position that Luther refers to and rejects. This should be assumed from the fact that the expression *privatio boni* is missing and that Augustine's name does not appear,[56] above all it follows almost necessarily from the fact that *natura* and *voluntas* are interchangeable, and almost synonymous, here, what is contradictory to Augustine. On the other hand the above-quoted statement reveals that for Luther Evil had its place within the godless person and this indeed is Augustinian. In the same sentence[57] he mentions that the godless in their deviating ways of self-love are bound to pervert the creaturely destination: *non possunt non quaerere quae sua sunt.* They have therefore only a distorted remainder of their nature – an expression also to be found in Augustine[58] – but this nature is still essentially the work of God.

At this point let me include a brief historical philological digression. Luther knew at least one of Augustine's central texts about the issue. In his marginal notes to the *Confessions* which he read through in 1509, he observes that in book VII 12.18, Augustine investigates what Evil is.[59] That is all he writes down. Luther does not reveal how he understood the passage. As far as I know, it is the only passage relating to the issue in which Luther evidently refers to Augustine.[60] Around one year later, in his marginal notes about passages from Petrus Lombardus from 1510/11, Luther returns to the issue of Evil[61] without mentioning Augustine and lacking any contact with Augustine's teaching – and announces the *mala* were pure

56.   In the dispute against Erasmus Luther knows Augustine completely on his side, cf. (WA 18), 640, 9: 'Augustinus...meus totus est' (WA 18), 670, 21–33.

57.   *De serv. arb.* (WA 18), 709, 12–21: 'Iam Satan et homo lapsi et deserti a Deo non possunt velle bonum, hoc est ea quae Deo placent aut quae Deus vult. Sed sunt in sua desideria conversi perpetuo, ut non possint non quaerere quae sua sunt. Haec igitur eorum voluntas et natura sic a Deo aversa non est nihil. Neque enim Satan et impius homo nihil est aut nullam naturam aut voluntatem habent, licet corruptam et aversam naturam habeant. Illud igitur reliquum quod dicimus naturae in impio et Satana ut creatura et opus Dei non est minus subiectum omnipotentiae et actioni divinae quam omnes aliae creaturae et opera Dei.'

58.   For the term *reliquum naturae* cf. Augustinus, *De civ. Dei* XIX 13: 'aliquid relinquit, ut sit qui doleat quod ademit. Et ipse dolor testimonium est boni adempti et boni relicti. Nisi enim bonum relictum esset, bonum amissum dolere non posset.' *Ench.* IV 12: 'remaneat aliquid necesse est, si adhuc natura est, unde natura sit'.

59.   Martin Luther, *Randbemerkungen zu Augustini opuscula (1509)* (WA 9; Weimar: Böhlau, 1893), 8, 1f.: Bl. CXIX: '*Et manifestatum est mihi, quam bona sunt* (= Augustinus, *Conf.* VII 12, 18): Unde invenit quid sit malum.' Cf. p. 7, 41f. Bl. CXVII: '*Sed rursus dicebam. Quis fecit me* (= Augustinus, *Conf.* VII 3, 5): Quare coactus ponere principium mali.'

60.   There are no hints in P. Courcelle, 'Luther interprète des Confessions de Saint Augustin', *RHPR* 39 (1959), 235–50, nor in H.-U. Delius, *Augustin als Quelle Luthers: Eine Material-sammlung* (Berlin: Evangelische Verlagsanstalt, 1984).

61.   Martin Luther, *Randbemerkungen zu den Sentenzen des Petrus Lombardus (1510/11)* (WA 9; Weimar: Böhlau, 1893), 56, 5–8. 13–16: '*Cognoscit ergo deus et bona et mala* (= Petrus Lombardus, *Sententia*, lib. I, dist. 36, 2.4 [PL 192, col. 620f]): Sciendum, quod mala, inquantum talia, non includuntur in hac dictione omnia, quia sunt purum nihil et privationes. Scit ergo deus mala i.e. scit ea quae sunt non bona. Et omnes sunt negative exponendae quae sunt similes orationes.' C.4 am Ende: 'Ratio est: quia peccatum non est aliquid, sed negat aliquid. Bonum enim et malum differunt sicut ens et nihil. Unde deus scit bona et mala: utpatet tantum: Scit entia et non entia: iam patet improprietas locutionis, quia quod nihil est sciri non potest.'

nothing and *privationes*, Good and Evil were equivalent to Being and not Being. At this time, Luther apparently thought of and believed in the possibility for a theory of Evil, which he later denounced in *De servo arbitrio*. I assume this theory originates in nominalism and its essence would be a removal of Evil from an ontologically preconditioned substance. The fact that in the high scholastic period the privation theory was reproduced by Aquinas[62] perfectly correctly in the basic Augustinian way could be taken as a crosscheck, although this would have to be proven by more research on the late scholastic texts.

Whichever way, it is, of course, not the case that Luther simply stated that Evil was not Nothing and did not know to describe it in detail. The opposite is true. In his explanations of the Decalogue,[63] or his sermons on catechism,[64] Luther comes up with long, sometimes endless instances of how Evil influences the whole breadth of human actions and endurance. All of it confirms word for word that Evil comes from within the godless person, the sinner.

Such incalculable variety of manifestations of Evil will occasionally be put in a concise and closely defined form by Luther – namely in the by then traditional differentiation between *malum culpae* and *malum poenae*: the Evil of sin and the Evil of punishment.[65] Thus he writes: 'The law (nota bene: it is again the law) uncovers a double Evil, an inner and outer Evil; the one is Evil we have loaded upon ourselves, sin or corruption of nature; and the other is the Evil that God puts upon us: his wrath, death and damnation.'[66] Luther's main personal interest in this ambiguous traditional differentiation of sin and punishment is to cover human misery of sin in its entirety. When all human activity and desire is determined under the eyes of a wrathful God, man becomes painfully aware of his own ines-

---

62. Thomas Aquinas, *Summa Theol.* I, Quaest. 48, art. IIIc: 'malum non est ens; bonum vero est ens; Quaest. 49, art. IIIc: 'quod omne ens, in quantum est ens, bonum est; et quod malum non est nisi in bono ut in subiecto'. Particularly instructive is Thomas's treatise *Quaestiones disputatae de malo*.

63. Martin Luther, *Eine kurze Form der zehn Gebote, eine kurze Form des Glaubens, eine kurze Form des Vaterunsers (1520)* (WA 7; Weimar: Böhlau, 1897), 204–229. The summary of man's trespassing against the law is of primary importance; (WA 7), 212, 4–7: 'In allen dißen wercken sicht man nit anders, dan eygen lieb, die das yhre sucht, nympt gott was sein ist und den menschen was derselben ist, und gibt nit noch gott noch menschen etwas von dem, das sie hatt, ißt und mag, das wol Augustinus sagt: Der anfang aller sund ist die eygene seyns selbs liebe.' Luther does not only hold original sin, i.e. self-love, responsible for the Evil as Augustine did, but also denounces it a robbery from God's glory.

64. Martin Luther, *Katechismuspredigten (1528)* (WA 30 I; Weimar: Böhlau, 1910), 2–122.

65. The distinction between *malum culpae* and *malum poenae* occurs more frequently in the early lectures on the Psalms, Martin Luther, *Dictata super Psalterium (1513–1516)* (WA 3; Weimar: Böhlau, 1885), 212, 33–36; 477, 27–478, 7; 584, 26–29. (WA 4; Weimar: Böhlaum, 1886), 63, 25f.; 243, 33–35; 253, 26–30; 411, 29–31; cf. 596, 18f; 601, 34–38. Cf. also *De serv. arb.* (WA 18), 683, 35f.

66. Martin Luther, *Rationis Latomianae confutatio (1521)* (WA 8; Weimar: Böhlau, 1889), 104, 22–24: 'Igitur duplex malum lex revelat, internum et externum: alterum, quod ipsi nobis irrogavimus, peccatum seu corruptionem naturae, alterum, quod deus irrogat, iram, mortem et maledictionem.' The whole context, (WA 8), 103, 35–105, 35, must be taken into account here.

capable fundamental corrupted state that is evil and tends towards Evil from youth onwards.[67]

It is remarkable, as mentioned earlier, that all these observations are made in the context of the preaching of the Law and the unfolding of the issue of Law in general. Evil in this context is, at times, of particular importance. This is hardly a coincidence, since what is true for sin is also true for Evil in general; according to Luther, man himself does not know about Sin or Evil.[68] It is the task of the demanding and accusing Law to point out Sin, Evil, Death, Hell and the Wrath of God.[69] Secondary and less strong, but in the same function stands the conscience which gives voice to the natural law that is inscribed into the hearts of all humans by God.[70] Personal experience when made under these omens may have contributed to Luther's views as he in particular encountered how menacingly Evil stood up against and tried to suffocate the renewed proclamation of the Gospel.[71] No power of detecting and judging Evil appropriately, however, is ascribed to human reason, which is blind, self-referential and incapable in the presence of God.[72]

67. *Rationis Latomianae confutatio* (WA 8), 104, 25–29: 'nimis tenuiter et frigide culpam et poenam sub iis vocabulis tractavimus, nescio quas relationes et imputationes fingentes. Nos crasse et plene secundum scripturam peccatum seu culpam seu internum malum universam illam corruptionem naturae vocamus, in omnibus membris, malam et ad malum pronam ab adolescentia nostra, ut Gen. vi. et viij. [Gen. 6.5 ; 8.21] scribitur.' A very different intention associated with the distinction of *malum culpae* and *malum poenae* is found in Martin Luther, *Tischreden, Nr. 3760* (WAT 3 ; Weimar: Böhlau, 1914), 595, 5–10: 'Malum est duplex: culpae et poenae; malum culpae est ipsum peccatum, malum poenae sunt ipsae afflictiones. Et haec duo sunt bene discernenda, ne impingat aliquis in locis scripturae, ut ille locus Esaiae 45.: Ego sum Deus faciens pacem et creans malum [Isa. 45.7]; item: Non erit malum in civitate, quod non faciet Dominus [Amos 3.6]. Qui loci loquuntur de malo poenae'.

68. *De serv. arb.* (WA 18), 767, 11. 14–16: 'se solo nescit, quid sit peccatum et malum... Peccatum in quo nati sumus, in quo vivimus, movemur et sumus, imo quod in nobis vivit, movet et regnat, ignoramus.'

69. *De serv. arb.* (WA 18), 766, 8. 25–28: 'Per legem (inquit [Rom. 3.20]) cognitio peccati... Is enim est fructus, id opus, id officium legis, quod ignaris et caecis lux est, sed talis lux, quae ostendat morbum, peccatum, malum, mortem, infernum, iram Dei, Sed non iuvat, nec liberat ab istis, Ostendisse contenta est.' (WA 18), 695, 2f.: 'per legem fit cognitio peccati et admonitio impotentiae nostrae'.

70. *De serv. arb.* (WA 18), 719, 33–35: 'Sicut et omnis alia lex (teste Paulo [Rom. 2.15]) in cordibus nostris scripta, tum agnoscitur, ubi recte tractatur, tum obscuratur, ubi impiis magistris vexatur et aliis opinionibus occupatur.'

71. *De serv. arb.* (WA 18), 628, 5–11: 'Quid enim malorum et antea non fecerunt impii homines, cum nullum verbum esset? imo quid boni fecerunt? An non semper mundus bello, fraude, violentia, discordia et omnibus sceleribus inundavit? ... Nunc vero venienti Evangelio imputari incipit, quod mundus malus sit, cum verius Evangelio bono elucescat, quam malus fuerit, dum sine Evangelio in tenebris suis ageret.' (WA 18), 766, 13–17: 'experientia satis declarat, quam odiat et persequatur mundus per eos, quos optimos et studiosissimos habet iustitiae et pietatis, iustitiam Dei Evangelio praedicatam et haeresim, errorem, ac pessimis aliis nominibus infamat, sua vero opera et consilia, quae vere peccatum et error sunt, pro iustitia et sapientia iactet et venditet' [here Isa. 5.20, a central text since the Heidelberger Disputation, stands in the background, as in 779, 8f.]. (WA 18), 625, 19 – 626, 34; 641, 3–17.

72. *De serv. arb.* (WA 18), 707, 22–24:'Ratio humana offenditur, quae cum in omnibus verbis et operibus Dei caeca, surda, stulta, impia et sacrilega est, hoc loco [sc. Exod. 9, 12.16], adducitur

4. It is now unavoidable to touch upon the relation between God and Evil. How did Luther see God in relation to Evil? It is not easy to confront Luther with the conventional answer that God is not the source of Evil but lets it happen. For Luther too it is essentially impossible to think of God as the effective cause and source of Evil.[73] For if this would be the case and we would declare God as the cause of Evil and ascribe to him Good and Bad alike, it would not only deconstruct our concept of God, but also discard the difference between Good and Evil. Luther clung on to this conviction throughout his life, although striving at times and with ambiguous feelings.[74] However, the other part of the sentence: that God admits Evil which was one of Augustine's cornerstones Luther would quote only very reluctantly,[75] and more often than not he changed the wording or dismissed the point altogether. It must have been sacrilegious to him that God, who is the embodiment of powerful activity, is suddenly cast in the undignified role of a mere passive spectator.[76] For God to admit Evil cannot be thought without His will and intervention: what God allows He wills and works.[77] With regard to this, Luther's position could briefly be

iudex verborum et operum Dei.' (WA 18), 784, 36–39. 785, 3–5: 'Ecce sic Deus administrat mundum istum corporalem in rebus externis, ut si rationis humanae iudicium spectes et sequaris, cogaris dicere, aut nullum esse Deum, aut iniquum esse Deum... Obsecro, an non omnium iudicio iniquissimum est, malos fortunari et bonos affligi? At ita fert cursus mundi.'

73.   Martin Luther, *Tischreden, Nr. 2026* (WAT 2; Weimar: Böhlau, 1913), 298, 21–25: 'Nos autem negamus Deum esse autorem malorum. Creaturarum enim autor est, at creaturae Dei utique bonae sunt. Qando autem sic loquimur, considerandus est terminus autor vel causa: Effective enim Deus non est causa mali, licet det impios in reprobum sensum, sed secundum id: Et dimisi eos secundum desideria cordis eorum [Ps. 81.12f.]'. Martin Luther, *De serv. arb.* (WA 18), 708, 31. 709, 30: 'ipse bonus male facere non potest'.

74.   A sentence like *De serv. arb.* (WA 18, 708, 25–34), impressively shows how Luther was struggling with aporetic problems: 'Condidit... Deus Pharaonem impium, hoc est ex impio et corrupto semine... Non igitur sequitur: Deus condidit impium, ergo non est impius... Licet enim Deus peccatum non faciat, tamen naturam peccato, subtracto spiritu, vitiatam non cessat formare et multiplicare... Ita qualis est natura, tales fiunt homines, Deo creante et formante illos ex natura tali.'

75.   *De serv. arb.* (WA 18), 710, 28ff.; Martin Luther, *Tischreden, Nr. 963* (WAT 1; Weimar: Böhlau, 1912), 488, 1; Martin Luther, *Vorrede zu Wider die gottlosen blutdürstigen Sauliten und Doegiten...ausgelegt durch D. Urbanum Regium (1541)* (WA 51; Weimar: Böhlau, 1914), 575, 8–11: 'On zweivel lesst Gott dem Teuffel solchen grossen mutwillen und jamer nicht zu, er wird viel guts zuletzt dadurch wircken, wie S. Augustinus [contra Secundam Juliani responsionem imperfectum opus V 60] spricht: "So gut ist Gott, das er kein boeses liesse geschehen, wo er nicht ein bessers daraus machen wolt"'. Martin Luther, *Predigten des Jahres 1531* (WA 34 II; Weimar: Böhlau, 1908), 60, 19f.: 'das gott allmachtig sey, ob er schon vil boses geschehen und ungestrafft lasse wegk gehen'; cf. Barth, *Der Teufel*, 197.

76.   *De serv. arb.* (WA 18), 615, 33f.: 'Voluntas enim Dei efficax est, quae impediri non potest, cum sit naturalis ipsa potentia Dei'; cf. also the context (WA 18), 615, 35 – 616, 12; (WA 18), 747, 24–27: 'quae (sc. inclinatio according to Prov. 21.1) non est res tam stertens et pigra, ut fingit Diatribe, Sed est actuosissima illa operatio Dei, quam vitare et mutare non possit, sed qua tale velle habet necessario, quale illi Deus dedit et quale rapit suo motu'; (WA 18), 750, 7–10: 'tam Deum, quam diabolum fingis longe abesse, veluti solum spectatores mutabilis illius et liberae voluntatis (sc. humanae), impulsores vero et agitatores illius servae voluntatis, mutuo bellacissimos, non credis'.

77.   *De serv. arb.* (WA 18), 747, 32f.: 'Sive sinat, sive inclinet Deus, Ipsum sinere vel inclinare

outlined thus: God is not the cause of Evil, He does not act malevolently, but He works in the domain of Evil.

The starting point and key phrase of all comments with which Luther unfolds his opinions in this matter is the term *omnipotentia Dei*. Luther's understanding of it is not an abstract concept in which God is potentially able to do a great many things that He does not – that would be nominalist – but quite directly God's actual active power that works everything in everything.[78] Thus it is not a potential 'can do', but a 'will do' that touches everything. It is the reason why He alone called creation into being and why He alone, again exclusively, sustains His creation. Any romantic notion, though, should be kept aside here. The sustenance of creation for God means a continuous compulsive effort by Him. God is the never-resting driving force in His creatures; His almightiness is the *motus*, the highly dynamic power that carries everything along, keeps it in motion, drives it, repels it and is utterly irresistible.[79]

Satan and the godless, however, are not excluded from the principles of this almighty power. As God keeps everything in motion He necessarily acts and works in them. It is not that He endows them with an evil disposition but he finds them to be evil and through His *generalis motus omnipotentiae*[80] drives them further ahead in the direction of Evil by not withholding their ability to sin. He uses the wicked like defect instruments as a rider would a limping horse or a carpenter a jagged hatchet. He uses them as deficient material, as if an artist had to make statues out of rotten wood.[81] This way the end product can only ever be rotten or bad, *movente*

---

non fit nisi volente et operante Deo'; Martin Luther, *Vorlesung über den Römerbrief (1515/1516)* (WA 56; Weimar: Böhlau, 1938), 182, 25–28: 'Quomodo enim mali esse et malum facere possent, si ipse non permitteret? Et quomodo permitteret, nisi vellet? non enim nolens hoc facit, Sed volens permittit.' Martin Luther, *Predigten über das zweite Buch Mose* (WA 16; Weimar: Böhlau, 1904), 140, 1–6; 143, 3–8.

78.   *De serv. arb.* (WA 18), 718, 28–31: 'Omnipotentiam vero Dei voco non illam potentiam, qua multa non facit quae potest, sed actualem illam, qua potenter omnia facit in omnibus, quo modo scriptura vocat eum omnipotentem.' Cf. the historical and systematical analysis by W. Maaser, *Die schöpferische Kraft des Wortes: Die Bedeutung der Rhetorik für Luthers Schöpfungs- und Ethikverständnis* (Neukirchen–Vluyn: Neukirchener, 1999), 209–33.

79.   *De serv. arb.* (WA 18), 753, 28–32: 'Hoc enim nos asserimus et contendimus, quod Deus, cum citra gratiam spiritus operatur omnia in omnibus, etiam in impiis operatur, Dum omnia, quae condidit solus, solus quoque movet, agit et rapit omnipotentiae suae motu, quem illa non possunt vitare nec mutare, sed necessario sequuntur et parent, quodlibet pro modo suae virtutis sibi a Deo datae'; (WA 18), 752, 12–14: 'sub generali omnipotentia Dei facientis, moventis, rapientis omnia necessario et infallibili cursu'; (WA 18), 711, 1: 'inquietus sit actor Deus in omnibus creaturis suis nullamque sinat feriari'.

80.   *De serv. arb.* (WA 18), 709, 21–24: 'Quando ergo Deus omnia movet et agit, necessario movet etiam et agit in Satana et impio. Agit autem in illis taliter, quales illi sunt et quales invenit, hoc est, cum illi sint aversi et mali et rapiantur motu illo divinae omnipotentiae, non nisi aversa et mala faciunt.'

81.   *De serv. arb.* (WA 18), 709, 24-28.33: 'tanquam si eques agat equum tripedem vel bi-pedem, agit quidem taliter, qualis equus est, hoc est equus male incedit. Sed quid faciat eques? equum talem simul agit cum equis sanis, illo male, istis bene, aliter non potest, nisi equus sanetur … Non aliter quam si faber securi serrata et dentata male secaret.' (WA 18), 708, 32: 'tanquam si faber ex ligno corrupto statuas faciat'.

ipso Deo. Luther concludes God does not create Evil, neither does He act in an evil way, because He as the Good One cannot act malevolently. But He acts in and through the wicked due to His *motus omnipotentiae*.[82]

The strangest element in this intellectual abstraction is undoubtedly the concept of *motus omnipotentiae*.[83] When Luther elsewhere interpreted the continuation of creation as *creatio continua* out of nothingness in the sense of a permanent direct performative speech act by God through His word,[84] he does not do so in our present tract. Both points of view, divergent already in terminology, cannot easily be brought into congruency. Philosophers know little about the first; the other must be recognised by common sense.[85] According to the former, God creates *ex nihilo*, according to the latter, he finds the wicked to be bad and propels them.[86] Luther did not make it clear how the relation between these two explanations is to be understood. Both of them can be found in his writing very early on.[87] I have the impression, although there is admittedly only a brief allusion to it, that these two explanations might be reflected in the two spheres: *intra regnum suum* – inside the reign of God – and *extra regnum suum* – outside the reign of God.[88]

Another difficult question, and one that we cannot answer here, is the specific question of where the roots to the concept of *motus omnipotentiae* lie. The concept

82. *De serv. arb.* (WA 18), 709, 28–33: 'Hic vides Deum, cum in malis et per malos operatur, mala quidem fieri, Deum tamen non posse male facere, licet mala per malos faciat, quia ipse bonus male facere non potest, malis tamen instrumentis utitur, quae raptum et motum potentiae suae non possunt evadere. Vitium ergo est in instrumentis, quae ociosa Deus esse non sinit, quod mala fiunt, movente ipso Deo.' Luther rejects the objection God created Evil in us *quasi de novo* and behaved like a wicked innkeeper (WA 18), 711, 2–6: 'In nobis, id est, per nos Deum operari mala, non culpa Dei, sed vitio nostro, qui cum simus natura mali, Deus vero bonus, nos actione sua pro natura omnipotentiae suae rapiens, aliter facere non possit, quam quod ipse bonus malo instrumento malum faciat.'

83. G. Ebeling, *Luther: Einführung in sein Denken* (Tübingen: Mohr, 1964), 306, speaks of 'die geradezu schauerliche Vorstellung, als sei Gott der Motor einer Riesenmaschine, die man selbst dann, wenn die Menschen von ihr gepackt und zu Tode geschleift werden, nicht zum Stillstand bringen kann' ('the actually gruesome idea that God should be the engine of a gigantic machine, which cannot be stopped, even when human beings are dragged along by it to death').

84. Maaser, *Die schöpferische Kraft*, has investigated this aspect in its full scope (especially 191–208). In this sense cf. Martin Luther, *Genesisvorlesung (1535–1545)* (WA 42; Weimar: Böhlau, 1911), 23, 3–7. 8ff. 17f.: 'est opus Dei creatum per verbum... Deus ista sic distinxit, gubernat et conservat...omnia talia opera sunt opera verbi, quod hic celebrat Mose: "Ipse dixit"'; (WA 42), 57, 17–20: 'Et tamen operatur Deus adhuc, si quidem semel conditam naturam non deseruit, sed gubernat et conservat virtute verbi sui.' In fact Maaser seems to neglect the differences in Luther's explanations.

85. *Genesisvorlesung* (WA 42), 23, 19–24 versus *De serv. arb.* (WA 18), 709, 10f.; 718, 15–22; 719, 22–25.

86. *Genesisvorlesung* (WA 42), 147, 8f.; 254, 6–8 versus *De serv. arb.* (WA 18), 709, 22–24.

87. On the one hand see the references by A. Beutel, *Im Anfang war das Wort: Studien zu Luthers Sprachverständnis* (Tübingen: Mohr, 1991), 107–10, on the other hand the references by E. Seeberg, *Luthers Theologie: Motive und Ideen I* (Göttingen: Vandenhoeck & Ruprecht, 1929), 159–82. Also Martin Luther, *Von den guten Werken (1520)* (WA, 7; Weimar: Böhlau, 1888), 212, 32 ff., belongs to the latter context.

88. *De serv. arb.* (WA 18), 754, 1–7.

does not really seem to be philosophical for there is no consideration of mediating second causes, neither is it Augustinian. Augustine developed his thoughts about God's sustenance of creation along the lines of the concepts of *providentia Dei* and *rationes seminales*.[89] Implicitly this aspect was part of the ontological reading insofar as it reflected the origin of all creatures from the Highest Being and at the same time their preservation within their own nature or their being through God. Let us remember, this concept made it possible for Augustine to draw a distinctive line between the being or nature of God's creatures and the corruption of their will. In Luther we look in vain for anything comparable, within the concept of *motus omnipotentiae*, he has no terminological means to convey the idea of an intrinsic goodness and dignity of the creatures God sustains. His assurance that Satan and the godless remain God's creatures, God's work, does not say much more than that they cannot escape the motus of the Almighty. In the broader context it also means that God alone reigns supremely over everything, so that any glimpse of a dualism must now expire completely.

The above-described concept of *motus omnipotentiae* explains the phenomena of Evil in an infralapsarian way. However, in two passages Luther goes beyond this and touches again on the profound problem of how Evil could enter the pure primordial state of God's creation. However, Luther remains ambiguous – he does not give an answer. At one point[90] he states that God comes upon Satan's evil disposition, but did not create it, this disposition has become evil: *deserente Deo et peccante Satana* – 'in that God left him, Satan, and in that Satan sinned' – two ablative absolutes here, that leave the logical link, essential as it would be, ambiguous. Did God leave him, because he sinned – or did Satan sin because God left him? Was God the driving force? In another passage Luther takes up the question why God let Adam fall even though He could have saved him from it.[91] In his customary use of the language this can only really mean: why did God

89. Aurelius Augustinus, *De genesi ad litteram* (ed. J. Zycha; CSEL, 28, 1; Vienna: Hölder-Pichler-Tempsky, 1884), VI 14-29; IX 32, cf. R. Williams, 'Creation', in A.D. Fitzgerald (ed.), *Augustine through the Ages: An Encyclopedia* (Grand Rapids and Cambridge: Eerdmans, 1999), 251–54.

90. *De serv. arb.* (WA 18), 711, 7–10: 'Sic Satanae voluntatem malam inveniens, non autem creans, sed deserente Deo et peccante Satana malam factam arripit operando et movet quorsum vult, licet illa voluntas mala esse non disinat hoc ipso motu Dei.' Already Lohse, *Luthers Theologie*, 268, stressed this point.

91. *De serv. arb.* (WA 18), 712, 29–32: 'Idem dicetur illis, qui quaerunt: Cur permisit Adam ruere, et cur nos omnes eodem peccato infectos condit, cum potuisset illum servare et nos aliunde vel primum purgato semine creare. Deus est, cuius voluntatis nulla est caussa nec ratio'; Martin Luther, *Tischreden, Nr. 2164b* (WAT 2), 342, 24–34: 'Cum Deus sciret hominem non permansurum in sua origine, cur creavit eum? Respondit Martinus Lutherus irridens: Ein grosser herr mus auch scheisskecheln in seinem hause haben; alias bene novit, qui sint sui. Abstineamus ab eis interrogationibus et cogitationibus absconditis, et revelatam voluntatem Dei consideremus. Sunt autem plerique, qui audito et percepto Dei verbo optarent se non scire neque percepisse, propterea quod servus voluntatem Domini sciens et non faciens multis vapulabit, ignari vero paucis. Illis respondet Paulus: Inexcusabilis es, o homo, etiamsi ignoras. Sathan in omnibus verbis et factis contrarius est Deo. Sic quilibet est impius, quia certissime obsessus est a Sathana, quamvis non corporaliter.'

want and cause Adam's fall? As indicated before, Luther only takes up this question to reject it categorically.

5. At last: If God works in and through the wicked, does He not become an accomplice of the wicked, does He not stain His own hands? How can God still be free of Evil and be called good? The obvious way around such alarming and dangerous conclusions would have been to say that God knows how to use Evil for good causes, that God's omnipotence thrusts Evil and Sin into the framework of His benevolent plans, as Augustine assured us. Such finalizing argumentation is not unfamiliar to Luther,[92] particularly since it could be linked to the eminent theological concept of divine action *sub contrario*.[93] However, in our present, otherwise wholly radical and advancing tract, he refrained from this type of explanation, except for a brief allusion,[94] and he certainly did so with good reason. He prefers to take up a point of view from which it is in principle impossible to judge God's actions in any way, a point of view that is strictly and exclusively oriented on the absolute sovereignty of God, on His unconditional and wholly free will, which is consequently out of reach for us humans to judge. The idea is that God's divineness, his being God is given by the very fact that there is no cause or reason for His will that could be held against Him as a guideline or benchmark. If this were the case and His will were liable to some law, it would no longer be the superior sublime will of God. God Himself is the one and only measure.[95] Thus we could

92. Martin Luther, *Tischreden, Nr. 566* (WAT 1; Weimar: Böhlau, 1912), 258, 34–259, 7: 'Deus omni malo bene utitur, et tamen homo et Diabolus omni bono male utuntur'; Martin Luther, *Vorlesung über Jesaja* (1527/1534) (WA 25; Weimar: Böhlau, 1902), 265, 16–21: 'Hic [Isa. 41.20] addit causam, cur Deus suos exerceat tot malis: conscientia peccati, sensu mortis, desperatione, potentia mundi, dolis Sathanae et aliis malis infinitis, nempe ut videant manum Domini haec fecisse, hoc est, ut mortificent fiduciam iusticiae propriae et sentiant se nihil esse ac desperent de sua sapientia, iusticia, potentia atque expectent et orent auxilium a Deo.'

93. *De serv. arb.* (WA 18), 633, 7–24.

94. *De serv. arb.* (WA 18), 711, 5–7: 'aliter facere non possit, quam quod ipse bonus malo instrumento malum faciat, licet hoc malo pro sua sapientia utatur bene ad gloriam suam et salutem nostram'. Cf. (WA 18), 714, 12ff.

95. *De serv. arb.* (WA 18), 712, 32–38: 'Deus est, cuius voluntatis nulla est caussa nec ratio, quae illi ceu regula et mensura praescribatur, cum nihil sit illi aequale aut superius, sed ipsa est regula omnium. Si enim esset illi aliqua regula vel mensura aut caussa aut ratio, iam nec Dei voluntas esse posset. Non enim quia sic debet vel debuit velle, ideo rectum est, quod vult. Sed contra: Quia ipse sic vult, ideo debet rectum esse, quod fit. Creaturae voluntati caussa et ratio praescribitur sed non Creatoris voluntati, nisi alium illi praefeceris creatorem.' Martin Luther, *Predigten über das zweite Buch Mose* (WA 16), 140, 23–141, 35: 'Dem Menschen ist ein mass gesetzt…da du mit Gott also auch handeln wollest, so hast du Gottes gefeilt, Denn was da mit Gott fuergenomen wird nach gesetz, mas und ziel, das trifft nicht zu… (sc. die Vernunft) machet im also eine mass, sie meinet, Gott sey wie ein Mensch, das man von Gott als von Menschen urteile… Aber Gott gibt dir gesetze und nimet von dir keins … Sondern wisse, das ers also wil haben und also gebeut, sein wille ist gesetzt uber alle gesetze … denn er ist ein unendlicher Gott und hat es macht und fug… Gott hat kein mass, gesetz oder ziel (wie gesagt) daruemb so kan er dawider nicht thun, er kan wider gesetz nicht suendigen, dieweil im keines fuergestellet, derhalben ist es gut alles was er thut. Es fleusst auch daher ein andere frage: Ob Gott zur suenden treibe? Solches machet, das ich Gott fasse in ein Rinck und Circkel oder in ein Glas, darinnen ich in wil behalten… So halt du es, wie du wilt, dennoch ists recht, was Gott thut, denn es ist sein wille nicht unrecht noch

argue with good reason that God's will is indeed beyond what we call Good and Evil. And yet this is not all. Sovereignty is not the same as despotism: what God wants is not simply a superficial absolute act He remains indifferent to. In spite of all Luther persists in his belief that God is essentially wholly good. As said in the above-quoted passage: God does not act malevolently because it is entirely contrary to His good nature.[96] For that reason, whatever occurs must be rightful and just because God wants it.[97] To wish for God to stop acting in and through the wicked was to wish for God to stop being God, or – to bring it to culmination – to wish for God to stop being good.[98] No doubt such argumentation is beyond human reason – it has to be – for God were not God, His justice, His benevolence not divine if man were able to comprehend it.[99]

All of these statements lead up to the much discussed controversial issue of the 'concealed God', that Luther himself very rarely ever touches on – and literally only twice in our present tract.[100] The issue requires a final comment. With regard to the historical roots the influence of Nicholas of Cusa has been considered[101] – after all he wrote a tract with the title *De Deo abscondito* – but there seems to be agreement that Luther's formal prerequisite is the nominalist doctrine of the *deus absolutus*, yet not simply a continuation of it but a reinterpretation used as a pungent critique.[102]

---

boese, er hat nicht mass oder gesetze, waruemb er diesen erleuchtet oder jenen verstocket. Solt ich hierin Gott messen und urteiln nach meiner vernunfft, so ist er ungerecht und hat viel mehr Suende denn der Teufel, ja er ist erschrecklicher und grewlicher denn der Teufel.'

96. *De serv. arb.* (WA 18), 709, 30: 'ipse bonus male facere non potest'.

97. *De serv. arb.* (WA 18), 712, 36f.: 'Quia ipse sic vult, ideo debet rectum esse, quod fit.'

98. *De serv. arb.* (WA 18), 712, 20–24: 'quaerat quispiam, cur Deus non cesset ab ipso motu omnipotentiae, quo voluntas impiorum movetur, ut pergat mala esse et peior fieri? Respondetur: hoc est optare, ut Deus propter impios desinat esse Deus, dum eius virtutem et actionem optas cessare, scilicet ut desinat esse bonus, ne illi fiant peiores.'

99. *De serv. arb.* (WA 18), 784, 8–13: 'donandumque est saltem non nihil divinae eius sapientiae, ut iustus esse credatur, ubi iniquus nobis esse videtur. Si enim talis esset eius iustitia, quae humano captu posset iudicari esse iusta, plane non esset divina et nihilo differret ab humana iustitia. At cum sit Deus verus et unus, deinde totus incomprehensibilis et inaccessibilis humana ratione, par est, imo neccessarium est, ut et iustitia sua sit incomprehensibilis.'

100. *De serv. arb.* (WA 18), 685, 21: 'Deus absconditus in maiestate'; (WA 18), 685, 25f.: '(sc. Diatribe) nihil distinguit inter Deum praedicatum et absconditum, hoc est, inter verbum Dei et Deum ipsum'. Synonymous expressions are: 'occulta illa et metuenda voluntas Dei' (684, 35f.; 690, 21f.); 'secretum longe reverendissimum maiestatis divinae' (684, 38f.; 689, 21); 'voluntas illa imperscrutabilis [et ignoscibilis]' (685, 29ff. 32ff.); 'secreta illa voluntas maiestatis [metuenda]' (689, 18. 28. 33; 690, 10f., 20); 'Deus non praedicatus, non revelatus, non oblatus, non cultus (685, 4f., 12); Deus in sua natura et maiestate' (685, 12–14).

101. R. Weier, *Das Thema vom verborgenen Gott von Nikolaus von Kues zu Martin Luther* (Buchreihe der Cusanus-Gesellschaft, 2; Münster: Aschendorff, 1967). Yet cf. the recension by B. Lohse, *Zeitschrift für Kirchengeschichte* (Stuttgart: W. Kohlhammer, 1968), 414–17.

102. Thus the historical result of the thorough and convincing interpretation by E. Jüngel, *Quae supra nos, nihil ad nos: Eine Kurzformel der Lehre vom verborgenen Gott – im Anschluß an Luther interpretiert* (*EvT* 32; Munich: Kaiser, 1972), 197–240. The following remarks are based on Jüngel's interpretation namely in that respect, that Luther's opposition of *Deus absconditus* and *Deus revelatus* is not to mean a dialectical relationship without which God's revelation could not be unterstood. Luther argues in a different direction.

The fixed starting point for the understanding of the issue of *deus absconditus,* respectively the opposition of *deus absconditus* and *deus revelatus* or *praedicatus,* must be that, grammatically, the expressions *absconditus* and *revelatus* are not adjectives but, as similar verbal idioms show, they are participles.[103] This means that by using such wording one does not express two qualities or facets of God that are contradictory or could be put in dialectic opposition to each other, but it is an act, a deed of God respectively. Even though there is one single divine will, God's reaction to the corrupt world is divergent. On the one hand He conceals Himself with sublime majesty,[104] wanting to remain obscure and undiscovered – which for Luther includes, above all, God's restricted salvationism and the workings of his omnipotence, that is the very spheres in which the problem of Evil becomes virulent. On the other hand God reveals Himself through His word,[105] binds Himself to His word and thus wants to be known. By revealing Himself in the the cross of Golgotha He remains in a certain sense, *sub contrario* concealed though at the same time revealed and made known through the word of the cross, God wants to share in community with us and wants us to correspond through our belief. The crucial target of this opposition – which touches on the central question of our symposium – is that Luther holds up a stop sign to our theological work and our reflections that we cannot ignore. Again and again he hammers it into his readers that we must abstain from God in His dark and awesome majesty, that we must not attempt to explore and investigate Him, because God is not our territory.[106] We have to revere and worship Him in His majesty, but this must happen only through His word which we are to turn to. Through our belief in him who came down to us as a man and was crucified can we and shall we worship God, who Himself remains concealed in the enigma of His glory.

---

103. In the present context the verbal character as participles is obvious in (WA 18), 685, 5, but the statement rules generally for Luther's vocabulary, cf. Bornkamm, *Martin Luther,* 394 n. 139.

104. *De serv. arb.* (WA 18), 685, 21–24. 27–29; 686, 8–12; 689, 33f.

105. *De serv. arb.* (WA 18), 685, 16–21; 686, 5–8; 689, 22–33.

106. *De serv. arb.* (WA 18), 684, 37–39: 'Quae voluntas non requirenda, sed cum reverentia adoranda est, ut secretum longe reverendissimum maiestatis divinae soli sibi reservatum ac nobis prohibitum'; (WA 18), 685, 5f.: 'Quatenus igitur Deus sese abscondit et ignorari a nobis vult, nihil ad nos. Hic enim vere valet illud: Quae supra nos, nihil ad nos.' (WA 18), 685, 14f.: 'Relinquendus est igitur Deus in maiestate et natura sua, sic enim nihil nos cum illo habemus agere, nec sic voluit a nobis agi cum eo.' (WA 18), 686, 1–3: 'Satis est, nosse tantum, quod sit quaedam in Deo voluntas imperscrutabilis. Quid vero, Cur et quatenus illa velit, hoc prorsus non licet quaerere, optare, curare aut tangere, sed tantum timere et adorare.' (WA 18), 689, 18f.: 'Nos dicimus...de secreta illa voluntate maiestatis non esse disputandum'; (WA 18), 690, 1f.; (WA 18), 690, 19f.: 'Puto istis verbis satis monstrari, non licere hominibus scrutari voluntatem maiestatis.' (WA 18), 695, 31–34. Martin Luther, *Genesisvorlesung* (WA 43; Weimar: Böhlau, 1912), 458, 36–459, 6: 'Esse distinguendum, quando agitur de notitia, vel potius de subiecto divinitatis. Aut enim disputandum est de Deo absc ondito, aut de Deo revelato. De Deo, quatenus non est revelatus, nulla est fides, nulla scientia et cognitio nulla. Atque ibi tenendum est, quod dicitur: Quae supra nos, nihil ad nos. Eiusmodi enim cogitationes, quae supra aut extra revelationem Dei sublimius aliquid rimantur, prorsus Diabolicae sunt, quibus nihil amplius proficitur, quam ut nos ipsos in exitium praecipitemus, quia obiiciunt obiectum impervestigabile, videlicet Deum non revelatum. Quin potius retineat Deus sua decreta et mysteria in abscondito. Non est, cur ea manifestari nobis tantopere laboremus.' Cf. Once again Martin Luther, *Tischreden, Nr. 2164b* (WAT 2), 342, 24–34.

The concept of a *deus absconditus* may be a theological borderline thought necessary to know what faith has nothing to do with, but a special theological issue, according to Luther, it is not. With special stress, Luther therefore places at the end of his essay another aspect. In the midst of all temptations and against the apparent reality of the course of this world, he argues, faith knows itself strengthened and consoled by God's promise. A solution for all these problems is at hand in a short word: 'A life after this life does exist.' In this afterlife all the darkness of divine acting will be removed, 'whereas this life is not more than the preliminary heat, better the beginning of the future life'.[107]

---

107. *De serv. arb.* (WA 18), 785, 16-19.35-39: 'Estque totius istius quaestionis insolubilis ista brevis solutio in uno verbulo, Scilicet Esse vitam post hanc vitam, in qua, quicquid hic non est punitum et remuneratum, illic punietur et remunerabitur, cum haec vita sit nihil nisi praecursus aut initium potius futurae vitae … At lumen gloriae… Deum, cuius modo est indicium incomprehensibilis iustitiae, tunc ostendet esse iustissimae et manifestissimae iustitiae, tantum ut interim id credamus, moniti et confirmati exemplo luminis gratiae, quod simile miraculum in naturali lumine implet.' Cf. Reinhuber, *Kämpfender Glaube*, 186–233.

GOOD AND EVIL IN ETHICS

Christofer Frey

1. *Introduction*

The well-known German sociologist Niklas Luhmann, an intellectual architect of one of the most complicated theoretical constructions and a promoter of an interesting but abstract general systems theory, revived Max Weber's plurality of social gods in the form of different binary codes associated with different areas of experience (*Erleben*). The code for morals is 'good-bad', the code for science 'true-false' and so on. Whereas Plato and his tradition permitted the true and the 'good' (and the beautiful also!) to coincide finally, they are in this particular modern theory structurally separated; and none of them proves a universal competence.[1] Luhmann's conception appears – compared with the Athenian type of metaphysics – strictly anti-metaphysical. But it goes far beyond the empirically oriented theorizing of modern theory. Luhmann's intellectual construction neither presupposes a sovereign point of view (as in Kurt Baier's 'moral point of view', the apparently triumphant but illusionary 'God's eye view point'[2]) nor does it permit to use the critical reflection of the 'good' to control the observer of any good or bad item or circumstance. According to Luhmann there cannot be a moral – and therefore reflective – discussion on the definition of the code of 'good' or respectively 'bad'. Every code – and especially the moral one – has a blind spot. There is no supertheory capable of evaluating the evaluation or of estimating the appraisal of good itself as 'good'.

In this anti-metaphysical theory is only one severe problem open – a question which could be called 'metaphysical' in an uncharacteristic sense: What is the perspective directing and controlling all the different codes, and who at all is able to define the realms to which the different codes apply? This question can – surely a strange case! – learn from the Bible (a significant point to be discussed later on).

Before biblical memories are introduced into the debate, it should be mentioned, that recent ethics runs into enormous difficulties when the holy Scriptures are quoted directly and therefore without any feeling of the historical distance. Christianity is not a religion of a holy book, but of a living testimony conveyed by written tradition. And a second introductory remark: Many modern Anglo-American ethi-

---

1.   Cf. N. Luhmann, 'Einführende Bemerkungen zu einer Theorie symbolisch generalisierter Kommunikationsmedien', in *idem*, *Soziologische Aufklärung*, vol. II (Opladen: Westdeutscher Verlag, 1975), 170–92.

2.   Cf. K. Baier, *The Moral Point of View* (Ithaca, NY: Cornell University Press, 1958).

cists thought that the right, not the 'good' should be the central theme in ethics, whereas philosophical antiquity preferred the 'good'.[3]

The opposite of good is, however, veiled by a problem of language: the English language uses 'bad' and 'evil', 'bad' for the antonym of a very general (even a moral) 'good', 'evil' more in the sense of wickedness, of moral corruption or of events that seem to contradict God's justice in the world or to challenge a general human sentiment of justice. In German both can be translated by 'böse', exactly as Leibniz used 'malum' for all kinds of deficiencies, evils and bad circumstances, either moral or physical.[4]

The following passages discuss

1.   the attempts to define the 'good' and the 'evil',
2.   the reflective use of 'good' (and – perhaps – of 'evil'),
3.   the impossibility of a positive–negative balance of 'good' and 'evil',
4.   the hidden axiom behind all attempts of a negative correlation of 'good' and 'evil', a kind of substitute of a 'world formula',
5.   the sources of knowledge and recognition of the 'evil' and the ambivalence of 'good'; and they aim at
6.   an understanding of sin ('optimi corruptio pessima') and
7.   a conclusion in the field of social ethics.

2. Definitions of the 'Good' and its Contradiction

The 'evil' and the morally wicked are usually defined in contrast to the 'good'. Their particular definition seems to be worked out by the negation of the definition of 'good'. But it is extremely difficult to find a sufficient definition of the 'good', and this is not a modern problem. The failure to define the 'good' (in the scope of classical philosophy) starts with Aristotle. Aristotle knew, like the comedian Aristophanes, that eating spinach could be 'good' for health and reading poems 'good' for the inner balance of the soul.[5] But what could then be the common denominator of all the different meanings of 'good'? 'Good' is, according to Aristotle, the purpose included into the basic tendency of everything that is. This – and the Platonic idea – is the starting point of the Neoplatonist and the Christian vision, that there should be one definite destination of all tendencies and processes and that the divine eschaton integrates all the minor and major 'good's of this world, if they reveal at least some 'good'. If God is intrinsically connected with this eschaton and if he is a singular god – not only in consequence of philosophical arguments, but because of the exclusiveness of Yhwh – there is no 'room' for a comparable antagonistic power representing or emitting the 'evil'. The unity of this exclusive god should be reflected in the diversity of human life,

---

3.   Cf. W.D. Ross, *The Right and the Good* (Oxford: Clarendon Press, 1930).

4.   Cf. G.W. Leibniz, 'Causa Dei asserta per justitiam ejus...', in *idem*, *Essais de Théodicée sur la bonté de Dieu, la liberté de l'homme et l'origine du mal*, vol. II (Frankfurt a. M.: Insel Verlag, 1965), 326.

5.   Cf. Aristotle, *Nicomachean Ethics* (Cambridge: Cambridge University Press, 2000), I, 1–12.

because it presupposed the unity of a natural moral and legal order, the law of nature.

How is the problem of the final good reflected in modern thought? Utilitarianism could be an obvious example: the protagonist of this approach, Jeremy Bentham, was an atheist. He acknowledged the 'good' in a large variety, but he refused to accept the authority of the one 'good' integrating all other 'goods'. 'Good' then is what people think is 'good'; this is primarily an individual affair and not a common characteristic in mankind. A generalization of the individual 'good' is hardly possible. On the conceptual level, however, the maxim, that everybody should choose his own goods in a personally organized hierarchy, could be a formal and all-embracing 'good'.[6]

Moral rules or values, implies the tradition of Hume, are not deduced from facts; what is moral is then a matter of psychology, of individual assessment and evaluation. Consequently G.E. Moore – in his *Principia Ethica* – argued that 'good' is an undefinable property, like the quality of colours (which at least could be defined by the length of waves, but their perception does not cover the aesthetical effect in the human eye).[7] The utilitarian relativity of good ignores the question of the foundation of a pluralistic sphere of goods. A grim irony may speak like Shaw: 'Do not do unto the others as you would that they should do unto you. Their tastes may not be the same… Do not love your neighbor as yourself. If you are on "good" terms with yourself, it is an impertinence, if on 'evil', an injury. The golden rule is that there are no golden rules.'[8] Although it seems to be logically odd to utilitarian thought, there must be a minimal moral foundation which permits people with different tastes and divergent moral convictions to live together. Is the common foundation of morals a theme of a renewed ethics of *natural law* or a problem of *meta-ethics*? And could meta-ethics be neutral, not exposed to the normative challenge of 'good' and 'evil'?

If 'good' cannot be defined and if 'evil' is the deficiency of (a certain amount of) 'good', the 'evil' cannot be defined either. Already ancient philosophers got into similar difficulties with the good, but were rather innocent facing the evil: Socrates was convinced that an enlightened reason should – and even could! – control the will, and consequently any moral 'evil' would result from the absence of reason, which – according to Socrates – is unthinkable. If somebody had to choose between the better and the worse, he would not choose the worse by a rational act of decision. We know that even the will of a criminal proves some evidence of a certain amount of rationality. Aristotle continued to reflect the Socratic contradiction by his own theory of the *akrasia* of the will: Being too weak to arrive at its destiny the will goes off course.[9] The 'evil' seems to him to be a kind of disorientation. The

---

6. Cf. J. Bentham, *An Introduction to the Principles of Morals and Legislation* (ed. J.H. Burns and H.L.A. Hart; rev. edn, ed. F. Rosen; Oxford: Oxford University Press, 1996 [1789]).

7. Cf. G.E. Moore, *Principia Ethica* (ed. T. Baldwin; Cambridge: Cambridge University Press, rev. edn, 1993 [1903]).

8. Cf. G.B. Shaw, 'Man and Superman. Maxims for Revolutionists', in *The Complete Prefaces of G.B. Shaw* (London: Paul Hamlyn, 1965), 188–95.

9. Aristotle, *Nicomachean Ethics*, book VII, chs. 2–4.

contradiction between the constant appeal to rationality and the loss of a certain rational capacity was never overcome in classical ancient thought.

Christian metaphysics had an analogical problem: in the Augustinian tradition 'evil' was defined as deficiency of the 'good', as the lack of a certain amount of 'good'; and this deficiency led one to fall below one's own final destination. How could a human person, created in the image of God, lose its moral capacity and enter an immoral way? Although the theory of deficiency was established among intellectual Christians and helped to avoid an ontology of evil, the popular Christian faith tended to convert the evil and its source into substantial figures. Many paintings – not only of Hieronymus Bosch – demonstrate a sensual symbolism of the evil.

3. *'Good' is Not Simply 'Good'*

The theoretical arrangement by a balanced distribution of 'good' and 'evil' obliterates the reflective capacity of 'good'. Reflection could for instance control the psychological evaluation of some action as 'good': Is the normal good even the real 'good'? Beyond all 'goods', which fulfil human desires, the true 'good' is bound to the integrity and identity of the fellow person. The Priest and the Levite in the parable of the Samaritan are not immoral in their general orientation, when they overlook the victim of robbery, but they fail to see the only goodness that is valid in the light of the commandment of love.[10]

The New Testament knows different strata of the 'good'. In Rom. 12.2 Paul uses the word 'good' like the common sense of his time did, but he encourages at the same time to reflect the 'normal' good in the light of the true will of God. The divine 'good' superimposes the everyday 'good'. 'Good' in the New Testament means always a direction, not a defined quality; and it aims at a vision of an integrated life in the new community. In Romans 14 and 1 Corinthians 12 Paul defends his main criterion, the reconciled integrity of those whose faith is endangered, because they are still afraid of pagan gods.

One of the difficulties in defining the 'good' results from the different strata of thought and life. It cannot be deduced by a 'differentia specifica' from a quality higher than 'good'. The fundamental 'good', however, can be a criterion of an everyday 'good' – 'good' evaluates 'good'.

If the good is judged by the true good, the 'evil', usually defined as the contrary to the good, must in analogy presuppose a kind of meta-criterion also. Does the 'evil' share the reflective capacity of the good? It could be 'evil' to insist on a 'good' when the 'good' is part of a strategy of moral dominion and causes danger to the autonomy of the fellow person. And it could be an 'evil' to assign the 'evil' to certain people or circumstances without being aware of one's own involvement in the 'evil' and without willingness to be penitent and remorseful. Many of the great moralists are incapable of a critical reflection of their own involvement in attempts to dominate fellow persons. Whenever moralism causes a blind spot, the

---

10. Lk. 10.25-37.

critical capacity of the social psychology should uncover the mechanisms of prejudice – for instance the attempts of projecting the 'evil' on others: America as the great Satan, the stereotype of strangers and so on.

Nietzsche was often regarded as the prophet of immorality; but we should acknowledge that he wanted to unmask moralism and to find the true life beyond 'good' and 'evil' (*Jenseits von Gut und Böse*).[11] He considered the code of 'good' and 'evil' as a special instrument of self-defence of the weak against the strong. If the will is finally liberated, it resembles a playing child in a world without the basic code of good and evil. Nietzsche hoped that he had overcome metaphysics (of good and evil), but today we doubt that he really succeeded. Was the attempt to overcome 'good' and 'evil' not in itself an 'evil'? There is a voice as distinct as the individual's will to live, and that is the challenge of the fellow person.

4. *Is the Evil Only Deficiency?*

These hints provoke the question whether the 'evil' can be regarded as the constant contradiction of the moral 'good' and vice versa. Are 'good' and 'evil' in a logical balance, because they are founded in a cosmic order of 'good' and 'evil'? Neoplatonic philosophy and Augustinian theology rely indeed on a cosmic order and a hierarchy of the 'good', which is continuously fading away from the highest to the lowest. The 'evil' is then regarded as the deficiency of 'good': the lower the stage of the cosmos, the more deficient the good of being. But deficiency cannot only signify a logical negation, it marks especially an experience, it causes suffering and is felt as a real force by all persons who suffer. The Christian practice of exhortation and even more each act of true repentance assume a kind of real power in moral evil. Persons are fighting with real evil; their tribulations are not the simple resonance of a state of deficiency without reality. 'Good' and *not*-'good' may be in a formal but contradictory symmetry, but the true 'good' and the real 'evil' are not positive or respectively negative in the sense of a metaphysical balance.

Mankind always hoped that either the cosmos or the universal history would one day confirm the preponderance of 'good'. This is particularly true of the Leibnizian solution: God created the best of all possible worlds – a rationalist's attempt to restore in his time the Old Testament wisdom of divine order and retribution.[12] As long as being in general is seen as a 'good' and as long as men have some hope for the future of this world and mankind, this seems to be a valuable cosmic hypothesis. But all ideas of a rational order in the framework of a rational cosmology already vanished in utilitarian thought: 'good' and 'evil' since then are identified on a scale which presupposes individual pleasure and pain as its ends. Utilitarian thinkers expect that a person is able to successfully strive after the fulfilment of his or her own pleasure. The end which God warranted once according to meta-

11. F. Nietzsche, 'Jenseits von Gut und Böse/Zur Genealogie der Moral', in *Sämtliche Werke: Studienausgabe*, vol. V (ed. G. Colli and M. Montinari; Munich: Deutscher Taschenbuch Verlag, 1980).

12. Cf. G.W. Leibniz, *Essais de Théodicée sur la bonté de Dieu, la liberté de l'homme et l'origine du mal* (Frankfurt a.M.: Insel Verlag, 1965).

physical systems is now assigned to a well-ordered society and its market. But does it – combined with the endeavour of individuals – really achieve the 'good' life? Utilitarian thinkers must rely on a kind of background faith expressing the idea that a well-organized society is possible and that the social 'good' – apt to fulfil individual human desire – always prevails. Any similarity to Old Testament wisdom is superficial, because – as G. von Rad remarks – the 'it was very "good"' of Genesis 1 must frequently have been proclaimed in times which did not at all confirm the goodness of the world; therefore it was a risked belief, that God could act in dark situations; it was not a more or less habitualized background conviction.[13]

5. *Tendencies to Define Evil*

The problem of a rationalization of good and evil is reflected in modern ethics. Although modern ethics tends to individualize 'good' and 'evil' and to neglect the ancient cosmic view, a latent general perspective of the world as a whole guides the methodological and material individualism. Even an adept of utilitarian ethics must put his basic trust in the possibilities of changing some aspects of the world or developing one's personal life. Persons who despair of any human future tend to flee from hopelessness to apocalypse: they take for granted that the world is corrupt and coming to its end, because the forces of evil dominate. The history of apocalyptic beliefs and their consequences are a sombre demonstration of this mechanism of thought.

The background assumptions in rationalist and in apocalyptic conceptions have been developed into a kind of world formula. The formula of the non-apocalyptic position is brilliantly systematized in Leibniz's thought: The world created by God cannot be as 'good' as God himself, unless there were two gods. Consequently the world includes a well-defined proportion of evil, the

- metaphysical evil (cosmic deficiency in comparison with divine abundance – see the Augustinian programme),
- moral evil (resulting from the free will in human monads, i.e. individual entities) and
- physical evil.[14]

These evils relate

- to the very foundations of the world,
- to spiritual beings in the world separated from the source of all being and
- to the Old Testament law of retaliation.

Apocalyptic thought marks the breakdown of these all-embracing convictions.

Modern thought may be fascinated by certain hypothetic formulas of the cosmos in physics or by a transcendental view of life as the most developed and the out-

---

13. Cf. G. von Rad, *Weisheit in Israel* (Neukirchen–Vluyn: Neukirchener Verlag, 1970), 251–52.
14. Cf. n. 4.

most complex form of reality, but it lost the former trust in an irresistible and overwhelming view of the world, which could integrate manifold cognitive and existential approaches to it as a whole. In modern theory and modern ethics the evil is no longer integrated by a supertheory, as it was in the rational metaphysics of Leibniz. As theoretical systems are no longer able to prove a cosmic balance of good and evil, poetry has become a means to indicate the problem. Lyric poetry by Baudelaire – under the heading 'fleurs du mal'[15] – reflects a civilization of steel and marble without life. Consequently the universe of life becomes an issue of esoteric approaches or of non-cognitive emotion. The human spirit creates an ideological framework of the universe without a theological basis. The guiding perspective of life changes between optimism and pessimism; both tendencies can alternate in the life span of the same person. The last alternative left to a person seems to be existential scepticism: 'Everything could be different, but there is hardly anything I can change' is a famous commonplace in an early essay by Luhmann.[16] Whoever wants to overcome this ambivalent experience of contingency could easily escape to totalitarian schemes of thought and action. Modern versions of the evil are concealed by totalitarian world-views and camouflage themselves by an alleged 'good' like the power of the Germanic race or the legitimate dominance of the working class represented by its leading committee.

6. *The Ambivalence of 'Good'*

The cosmic basis of a definition of 'good' and evil has faded. How can ethics then discriminate between both? The human conscience needs both – an inner judge, who critically reflects common values and standards, and an encouragement to continue life and work, although the world very often may be in darkness. The positive challenge of the encounter of the other person may strengthen such an encouragement.

Utilitarianism is – like some other concepts of ethics in our time – more or less convinced that men are capable of developing a kind of humane reciprocity. Moral orientation should restrict or even overcome the 'evil' and together with it many wicked desires or intentions; according to some thinkers however ethical egoism could do the same – induced by the discernment, that a widespread unrestricted egoism damages even own interests.[17] But the agreement between moral egoists may finally produce an in-group-solidarity or an unspoken contract at the basis of social life, which excludes strangers. The moral intention could change completely and be turned into the dialectical opposite and consequently into a moral evil injuring not only outsiders or outcasts, but the identity and integrity of the agent himself. The moral intellect or the moral conscience cannot attain a cosmic or a divine

15. Ch. Baudelaire, *Les fleurs du mal* (ed. J. Delabroy; Paris: Poulet-Malassis et de Broise: 1986 [1857]).

16. N. Luhmann, 'Komplexität und politische Planung', in *Politische Planung* (Opladen: Westdeutscher Verlag, 1971), 44.

17. H. Sidgwick, *The Methods of Ethics* (London: Macmillan and Company, 7th edn, 1907 [1874]).

point of view, but has to stay the course of frequently contradicting situations in this world and must learn to discriminate between a relative 'good' and a distinct moral evil (which cannot be relative). The true moral 'good' must therefore critically apply to the common assumption of a 'good', and the moral evil must even be identified in the alleged 'good', because the evil often masks itself as a 'good'.

But how is the moral 'good' or the moral 'evil' then to be defined? Kant, the philosopher, relies upon the intellectual procedure of universalization;[18] but this type of reflection should not be regarded as an equivalent to generalization, because it includes an attention to concrete circumstances, in which the fellow person lives and upon which the commandment of love insists.

7. The Consequences

According to Christian faith and ethics the good can only be assessed by God's own tendency not to remain in the glory, but to meet and help men and to be the servant of his creatures. Biblical faith does not pursue the Platonic idea of 'good'; for the biblical 'good' is a quality of a personal life encountering the personal God; it is a perspective of a life blessed by God; this particular 'good' includes the integrity of life – in a communion with fellow persons – and encourages the personal identity as a final human existence directed to the unity with God. This 'good' helps to discern the 'good' in everyday life. The moral evil must subsequently be interpreted as sin; it is an active contradiction to God's own way and the perversion of any true humane concern. This interpretation of the moral (not moralistic!) evil reveals the true evil.

The consequences are assembled in the following survey:

	In the light of the relation to God and the fellow person:	*Contradicting the relation to God and to the fellow person:*
the prima facie 'good' is	(dialectically) evaluated as penultimately 'good'[19] or	unmasked as self-justification (by analogy with this particular theological interpretation) respectively as the ideological use of the moral code;
the prima facie 'evil'	is evaluated as divine pedagogy	or as sign of false and autocratic righteousness of a person which despises or violates the existence of the fellow person.

'Good' and 'evil' are not balanced on contradicting sides; any 'good' in the finite life can only be a penultimate good, whereas the moral evil will always be morally definite.

18. Cf. the third version of the categorical imperative: 'Handle so, dass du die Menschheit, sowohl in deiner Person, als in der Person eines jeden anderen, jederzeit zugleich als Zweck, niemals bloß als Mittel brauchest' (I. Kant, *Grundlegung zur Metaphysik der Sitten*, BA 66-67). ('Act in the way, that you use humankind in yourself as well as in the other person always and at the same time as goal and never only as means.')

19. D. Bonhoeffer, *Ethik* (ed. H.E. Tödt *et al.*; Munich: Christian Kaiser 1992), 137–44.

This is a starting point to read the Bible anew. The mythological story of the snake in Genesis 3 illustrates the dialectical framework of any moral argumentation; moreover it refuses to indicate a cause of the deeply rooted moral defect in human beings. The snake offers to Eve the point of view of God – at the first glance the most outstanding 'good', which however proves to be the greatest moral and spiritual evil. In different words: the ostensibly greatest freedom turns over into the loss of all freedom.

How can the human being which lost this initial freedom differentiate between 'good' and 'evil' after the fall? According to Kierkegaard man should return to the innocence of the initial situation, exist 'transparently' in God and rely entirely on him.[20] But at the same time he has to be a responsible person; the initial unity is dissolved, man encounters other men and moral objects. The doctrinal interpretation of a person's basic situation differs not only between Judaism and Christianity, but also inside Christianity. The reformers' interpretation emphasized the paradoxical situation of man: he has lost his foundation in God and needs therefore a new fundamental address by his creator and redeemer ascribing anew the status as a child of God and reaffirming the status as God's creature. Ascription signifies the fundamental determination of man. Nobody is his own sovereign. To be a self is to exist in expectation of God's coming. This includes the true 'good', which is the criterion of all other 'good' – though not in the form of logical generalization; it includes the concrete experience of the fellow person. Generalization fails especially in ethics, but universalization includes the concrete.

8. *Moralism Missing the Force of Evil*

The ethics – at least in modern Protestantism – is confronted with a double challenge:

1. It should interpret human autonomy in the horizon of the analysed fundamental dialectics of 'good' and 'evil': the seeming 'good' of self-assertion could be the worst, because it undermines the legitimate otherness of fellow man. Even love can be extremely authoritarian. Consequently Protestant ethics should lead to a consequent critique of the kind of moralism, which neglects or even hates the possible autonomy of the fellow person and undermines its otherness. Many ecumenical appeals during the last three decades unfortunately used this strategy. Moralism can be poisoned by the strife for domination and by attempts to dictate the 'good' to the other.

2. Ethics should be attentive to the masks of evil. An example: there is a particular conservative type of thinking which focuses on the 'evil'. It profits by the dark side of reason, but can be mingled with a bewildering type of authoritarian dialectics: as man is corrupted, his chaotic attitudes must be embanked and the consequences of his sin should be regulated by a strict legal order. Society therefore needs authority and leadership. But how could leadership be immune from

20. S. Kierkegaard, 'Sygdommen til Døden', in *Samlede Værker* (ed. A.B. Drachmann *et al.*; Copenhagen: Gyldendal, 1962–64, vol. XV) = *The Sickness Unto Death* (Princeton, NJ: Princeton University Press, 1980).

the type of moral evil, which causes this kind of disorder? Anti-constitutional theories of the nineteenth century directed their hope to the God-given charisma of princes.[21] Twentieth-century conservatives went far beyond this attitude: they welcomed the 'Führer' on a similar basis of thought. And many conservative Protestants apologized for their orientation in the Third Reich by the excuse that a 'Dämonie' (demonic force) had overwhelmed them.[22]

Evil – especially in its moral connotation – cannot really be understood as a deficient modus of 'good', which – on the other side – would be the quality of the only substance in the cosmos; nor should it be substantiated as a devilish or demonic force. The demons of the German 'Dämonie' were products of the socialization and of a widespread world-view, but not estranging transempirical powers overwhelming men.

'Good' and evil have deep existential roots; both cannot be transposed into a cosmic formula or calculus. They are combined in a dialectical relation: the supposition of the outmost 'good' can be a severe moral evil affecting the life of fellow man. Unfortunately post-enlightenment philosophical ethics hardly ever acknowledged this existential dialectic. Contrary to conservative Protestant thought ethics cannot be antirational, but has to encourage a new enlightenment, which overcomes a fundamental shortcoming of the earlier enlightenment, the neglect of evil.

21. It was a convert from Judaism to Protestantism, F.J. Stahl, who favoured the regimen of princes without constitution: *Die Philosophie des Rechts* (2 vols.; Heidelberg, 2nd edn, 1845). Converts are usually conservative.

22. Especially apologists of a 'theology of orders'. Cf. W. Künneth, *Politik zwischen Dämon und Gott* (Berlin: Lutherisches Verlagshaus, 1954). (Künneth fought Nazi ideology, but was sceptical with regard to democracy.)

THE RIDDLE OF EVIL – THE AUSCHWITZ-QUESTION

Christian Link

In Dante's *Divine Comedy* the gate of hell is depicted as being inscribed above the entrance by the words: 'You, who are passing through me, let fall all hope'. Insofar as in how the mythic image of hell is figured, how evil in the midst of our world is constituted and how its effects in it are, the most comprehensive definition that can be formulated about it, is the statement: Evil is Hopelessness as such. Wherever evil comes to power, every hope dies. It is as if the future has been totally extinguished before our eyes. It is contracted to the inescapable presence of the existing reality. We are not able to get rid of it, even if we wanted. The world sticks fast in the monotone circle of its own rules; it presents itself in the light of death. Because, however, we cannot live and apparently also cannot think without hope, without the expectation that our Today could be another Tomorrow, we cannot understand evil under the conditions of our normal life. For because we know that we exist in time, all human thinking and acting is directed to the future and receives its perspective from it. Thus evil remains an insoluble riddle. We are just able to touch upon its border. This does not exclude that there are appearances of evil, in which it confronts us with evidence not veiled, from which we cannot escape. In the twentieth century the name Auschwitz represents this dark evidence.

'Auschwitz', the American rabbi Richard Rubinstein writes, 'represents something novel and materially distinct from previous Jewish misfortunes. There is…a difference between the "civilised" anti-Semitism of earlier ages and what must be called the anti-Semitism of the technological barbarians of the twentieth century.'[1] If the death of Spanish Jews during the reign of Ferdinand and Isabella still could be understood as martyrdom – as 'a matter of free decision' – this last assertion of a sense is turned upside down into absurdity, if one does not murder on behalf of a creed or any personal will, but 'under the fiction of race',[2] so to speak as 'refuse collection' of superfluous human material. The remembrance of these crimes confronts us with people in which we cannot recognize ourselves: with the *victims* of the concentration camps, on which the transformation of human beings into raw material was executed (the 'utilization' of their skin, their hairs and their golden teeth), and with the *perpetrators*, on whose lack of feeling the human category of understanding injustice regularly rebounds.

---

1. F.H. Littell and H.G. Locke, *The German Church Struggle and the Holocaust* (Detroit: Wayne State University Press, 1974), 256–68 (263).
2. H. Jonas, *Der Gottesbegriff nach Auschwitz: Eine jüdische Stimme* (Frankfurt a. M.: Suhrkamp, 1987), 13.

In order to render understandable the unimaginable that happened here, Manès Sperber reformulated the beginning of the ancient hymn *Akdamut Mellin* from the standpoint of those who escaped:

> If the firmament above us would consist of paper, all the oceans of ink, if all the trees would be pens, all inhabitants of the world be scribes, and they were writing day and night, they would not be able to describe the passions and the deaths of Israel...[3]

Immeasurable as the greatness and almighty power of the creator is the horror, through which the Jews have passed in the death camps of the Third Reich. If one tries nevertheless to understand the incomprehensible in part, one has to distinguish again these 'passions and deaths of Israel' from what they are the expression and consequence of. Only then does one encounter the *Evil* devoid of any sense, which Kant defined as the 'purposeless', because not even a divine intention is imaginable which it could serve. Already this includes – according to philosophical tradition – that we are not able to form a positive definition of it. On the other side, in 'our' century we had enough opportunities to gather some experiences related to its consequences. Hannah Arendt, who chose as her life-task to analyse these experiences, has at least indicated, with incorruptible accurateness, how we can recognize Evil the easiest: 'that we can neither punish nor forgive such offences and that they therefore transcend the realm of human affairs and the potentialities of human power, both of which they radically destroy wherever they make their appearance. Here, where the deed itself dispossesses us of all power, we can indeed only repeat with Jesus: "It were better for him that a millstone were hanged about his neck, and he cast into the sea."'[4] 'Or: it would be better he were never born – doubtless the worst one can say about a human being.'[5]

1. *Evil – a Parasitic Regulation System*

We have to renounce the attempt to understand or explain evil – be it out of the motives of selfishness, avarice and envy, or out of a resentment turning into despite and uncovered force. We have to focus upon the few that we recognize from its manifestations. Hannah Arendt hits exactly the point by stating: We can neither punish it nor forgive it, because thereby an exact boundary is drawn to all offences and all injustice, on the consequences of which human beings elsewhere might suffer. We can *punish* offences against rules and trespasses against laws, even those reaching as far as homicide and murder. For even if punishment is understood as expiation (and not as a means of re-socialization) the criminal, whatever his motives might have been, by the judgement is acknowledged as human being, capable of adapting himself to an order prohibiting the killing of other people's

---

3.   M. Sperber, *Churban oder Die unfaßbare Gewißheit* (Vienna: Europaverlag, 1979), 65.
4.   H. Arendt, *The Human Condition* (Garden City, NY: Doubleday Anchor Books, 1959), 217.
5.   Retranslation of: H. Arendt, *Vita activa oder Vom tätigen Leben* (Munich: Piper, 10th edn, 1998), 308.

life. We can punish actions, which can be interpreted as guilty deviations from a recognized norm. We can forgive the worst evil one has inflicted upon us, if it is confessed as such, as a sometimes grave offence originating in the nature of human acting itself, which creates 'new relationships within a web of relations'.[6] Forgiveness, seen under this aspect, means the acknowledgement that the offence can interrupt an order worthy to live in, but not annul it. It is 'the ability of correcting the failing' on which we are dependent, if human life shall continue and not be choked on the consequences of past deeds. Punishment and forgiveness do not repair what has happened, but they finish the succession of revenge and retaliation, which could result out of its consequences. They render possible the continuity of human acting, open it for a reorganized future.

Exactly here is the boundary marked by Hannah Arendt. Deeds that we cannot forgive and therefore as a rule cannot punish, because in it Evil is realized, are deeds behind which no future can be opened, because they annul the order-connection of life definitely. They render 'all further doings impossible', as already Schiller in a classical exactness has formulated: 'This is the curse of an evil deed that it perpetually generating must bear Evil.' Therefore we are powerless against evil. It 'transcends' the 'area of human matters', which we can influence. It established an order, better: a counter-order, which behaves repudiating and strange against the rules of human intercourse, which we instituted and acknowledged in freedom.

A comparison which one may not over-stretch, could be helpful: Can an illness be punished? Can an illness be forgiven? Both seem to be totally inadequate – first, because an illness has no subject, it hits us anonymously like a shower or a wave of heat. But what is it that disturbs our equilibrium in this case? We cannot define the phenomenon of illness (an influenza, a cancer or an endogenous depression) as deviation of an individual from the norm of health, not speak of the consequence of such a deviation.[7] Rather illness itself seems to possess or to form a norm. Otherwise it could not be explored in medical research, it could not be recognized by certain symptom-complexes – whatever their causes might be. The norm of health defines a system of rules aiming at the self-preservation of the organism. If a disturbance of the organism shall be conspicuous as illness, it must not be so grave as causing an immediate death, but neither so inconsiderable that it turns unexpectedly back into the norm of health. Rather the illness has to show 'a certain self-conservation as this illness'. 'It seems to presuppose something like a system of rules, by which it is preserved itself.'[8] Exactly here is the point of comparison. We are inclined to regard evil as without order, as chaotic, as a sometimes catastrophic irruption, as arbitrary and therefore irregular destruction of an approved order. We understand it from *what* it demolishes and destroys, that means, as its negation (*privatio boni*). But thereby we undervalue it. It manifests itself as a parasitic

---

6. Arendt, *Human Condition*, 216.
7. Cf. C.F. von Weizsäcker, 'Modelle des Gesunden und Kranken, Guten und Bösen, Wahren und Falschen', in *idem, Die Einheit der Natur* (Munich: Hanser, 1971), 320–41 (327).
8. von Weizsäcker, 'Modelle', 328.

system of rules, following its own order, an order incommensurable with the rules of a normal, healthy organism, and therefore it can neither be hit by its sanctions – punishment – nor be stopped by its resistance or even restricted. And with illness evil has also in common that it can affect – spoken metaphorically – every organ. It plays around us in innumerable masks, even in the cloth of beauty – as in the art of the Third Reich – which can fascinate us by the reflexes of narcissism. It reveals itself not just in evil deeds, force and crime, but hides itself behind civil virtues (industry, conscientiousness, obedience), in ideals, successes, and scientific achievements. It can pervade as much a rigorous sense of duty as fondness of techniques or enthusiasm for sports. Therefore the fate normally takes place unconsciously. We perceive it always too late. Finally we are confronted disconcerted by the outbreak of the evil that we ignore as much as an unknown appearance of illness.

This seems also to be the reason why we are not able to fix evil morally in any way. Moral is the order that we framed according to practical reason, directed upon human living together. Evil frames a likewise firm order according to its destructive aims. 'What meaning has the concept of murder', asks Hannah Arendt, 'when we are confronted with the mass production of corpses?',[9] executed by murderers, who are not at all acting out of 'murderous' motives, who do not even know what murder is, but are organizing the millionfold murder in a way that all persons involved are subjectively innocent. The sentence 'You shall not kill' – she remarks – 'fails regarding a population policy which systematically and like a factory gets down to eradicate the "races which are unfit for life and inferior" or the "dying classes", and this not as a single action but as a calculated one, based on permanence'.[10] If one should want to find a term for evil, at least in its outer face that became visible, one would have to say: It is the undertaking of making possible what according to our standards and norms is impossible. Under the title 'The Nothing' Karl Barth has described evil with a correct judgement of this characteristic feature of evil as 'impossible possibility'.[11] If this characterization is correct – I do not doubt it is – its consequence is a simplification that is not allowed. It declares as harmless what is not at all harmless, if one derives with Konrad Lorenz evil from roots in natural history. It is the human aggression instinct exploding because of permanent over-stress in a surrounding that became too complicated.[12] More than ever it is then impossible to declare God the author of this evil, without rendering him unbearably ambiguous: He would have to be simultaneously creator of our world and of its counter-world disfigured into absurdity.

9.   H. Arendt, *The Origins of Totalitarianism* (New York: Harcourt, Brace & World, 1951), 441.

10.   Retranslation of H. Arendt, *Elemente und Ursprünge totaler Herrschaft, Antisemitismus, Imperialismus, totale Herrschaft* (Munich and Zürich: Piper, 6th edn, 1998 [9th edn, 2003]), 912.

11.   K. Barth, *Kirchliche Dogmatik* III/3 (Zollikon–Zürich: Evangelischer Verlag, 1950), 327–425 (405).

12.   K. Lorenz, *Das sogenannte Böse* (Vienna: Borotha-Schoeler, 29th edn, 1971). Cf. p. 349: 'The natural inclinations of man are not as bad. Man is not as evil from youth, he is just not totally good enough for the demands of modern society life.'

2. The Rationality of Evil

In her book *The Origins of Totalitarianism*, especially in its two closing chapters, Hannah Arendt describes in oppressing analyses, how the impossible could be staged in Auschwitz according to a plan – with the specific rationality of evil. Let us begin with the fact that would be mentioned with right again and again in the first place: Without the technical perfectionism of the concentration camps the wholesale murder would not have been possible. Therefore Rubinstein speaks about the 'technological barbarians'. Actually this catastrophe could not happen earlier than in the twentieth century. Who started it? If one turns to this technological aspect – asking for the complex evil one cannot avoid touching upon it – the first answer is: It was not the monster without conscience, who let loose the inferno, but the conscientiousness of a research, which after years of troublesome preparations delivered its results to the ones who ordered the *experimentum mortale*. Auschwitz is also the symbol for naivety of a science, which regarded itself as free of value, because it had not learned to reflect upon the consequences of its deeds. Its ambivalence seems to be unavoidable:

> Out of natural science follows technology. Technology produces engines. Engines are misused for killing and torturing. At last the apprentice of magic is standing there and does not know *when* the evil actually started. Was this science only used in an evil way, or was it evil from the beginning? I would say: it was neutral. This was its fate. For: 'Logic gives reason to the thinking of the murderer and the Quaker'.[13]

These facts of the case, which are worth considering, can direct our attention upon two problems – in Hiroshima they became still more evident. First: the term 'perpetrator' seems to fail here. The action, which initiated the disaster, is mediated through so many intermediate steps – laboratories and administrative instances – is composed out of so many partial judgements and partial decisions, that everybody did *something*, but nobody 'it', the definite step. The responsibility can be delegated to the chemical industry, to the judgement of the situation by the SS or to the participants of the Wannsee Conference. The result is that the moral instance, which sometimes bore this name, has been methodically eliminated by a specialized accuracy. A subject of responsibility in the sense of classical ethics cannot be identified for the technical enforcement of the murders.

And now, second: the 'apprentice of magic'. In Goethe's ballad he is the involuntary hero in a scenario of terror that meanwhile had become the normal situation in our technical civilization. He is superior to us only in the aspect that he sees the danger he has caused with his own eyes and understands, that here a reason to despair is given. He cannot get rid of the spirits, whom he called, and these spirits obey him well, at the end terribly well, and start this devilish circle, which causes that the rationality of the instrument produces an irrationality not to be interrupted or at least dammed by anybody. For the 'master', who alone would be able to do it, is no more cared for. That the instruments have become independent created the new situation that made Auschwitz possible: the few who can dispose of these instruments (of 'command' cannot be spoken in earnest) possess a God-like power and use it with a fearfulness transcending all human measures. To this unlimited power corresponds on the other side a completely new, never known impotence. Günther Anders expressed it by the formulation: We are 'today mainly not "mortal" beings, but beings "to kill" '.[14] No theorist of morals would have dared to ask in earlier centuries to put into question the premise *that* human beings would and should exist. No sooner than with the technical possibility of a collective destruction this premise has become shaking. That man, as Kant formulated,[15] exists as 'end in himself': this fundament of European ethics has come off the hinges.

Nothing demonstrates this severe truth more urgently than the frequently described testimony that the inmates of the concentration camps were deprived of the last that everybody can call his own: his individual death, the sense which dying always could possess. 'The camps', remarks Hannah Arendt, 'took away the individual's own death, proving that henceforth nothing belonged to him and he belonged to no one'.[16] 'The last messengers of a dignified dying were those... who, in order to avoid being extirpated collectively, anticipated the gas by suicide.'[17] The connecting link between these assassinated was not the fate of finiteness, to which we can behave asking, mourning or also protesting, but anonymous death, annihilating them without reflection. Most of them had no individual murderer, no 'perpetrator', who could have aimed at them as person, but were, as we know, killed in gas-chambers, technical inventions that achieved the work of liquidation automatically. Evil – at this these reflections aim – changed its residence. We do not meet it any more embodied in individuals, whom we could fight against, but in the anonymous passing of functions, which these individuals have made their instruments. We meet people, who, with the indifference of machines, drove their victims, whom they were not able to perceive, into death. Or unsuspecting 'apprentices of magic', who, fascinated by the technical possibilities, could not know and did not ask, for what their inventions and experiments one day would be used. This seems to be one of the most dismaying insights of Auschwitz: the machines of death were 'operated'.

We experience this manifestation of evil, which can no more be identified individually, still today in being overtaxed in our faculties of imagination and feeling, which cannot cope with what happened there. It seems that we can extinguish the population of whole towns and districts. It is impossible to imagine the more than five million dead of the Nazi rule, to keep them present in mourning and remembrance. Already to repent for ten murdered people overtaxes us, because repen-

14. G. Anders, *Die Antiquiertheit des Menschen*. II. *Über die Zerstörung des Lebens im Zeitalter der dritten industriellen Revolution* (Munich: Beck, 1986), 405.

15. E. Kant, *Kritik der praktischen Vernunft* (1787), in Königlich Preußische Akademie der Wissenschaften, *Kant's Gesammelte Schriften*, V (Berlin: Georg Reimer, 1908), 87. Translation from: www.knuten.liu.se/~bjoch509/works/kant/cr_pract_reason.txt

16. Arendt, *Origins of Totalitarianism*, 452.

17. Anders, *Antiquiertheit*, 405.

tance cannot be extended so much that it could 'mean' even ten people. Therein we experience the disguise of evil in the mask of techniques: our feeling does not reach any more what our arms and hands effect. Its reach is too restricted to be able to catch up with Auschwitz emotionally, not to speak of 'digesting' it. We are speaking rightly about the inhumanity of the crimes perpetrated there, but just seldom we clarify to ourselves that only this can be meant: already in the conditions that rendered possible such a camp, we cannot find the measure of humanity. We are not created for the divine predicate of being almighty.

If we confer evil, as I tried to do, with a parasitic, but 'autonomous' system of rules intending to keep existing permanently an ill state, this description meets rather exactly the basic characteristics of the concentration camps that Hannah Arendt outlined as 'totalitarian' or ideological rule. Its essence is 'terror'. The extinction of the moral and juridical personality preceded the physical elimination, like a 'preparation to fit each of them equally well for the role of executioner and the role of victim'.[18] This, however, is just possible under conditions, which cause to vanish totally the space of acting, personal responsibility, and that means, the reality of *freedom*. Guilt can be spoken about just as long as we are able to act also otherwise. If, however, as we know from many reports, the prisoners were involved in the crimes of the SS by being commissioned with many functions in the administration of the camps, so that they were delivered to the insoluble conflict between sending their friends or by chance unknown people to death, the problem of guilt is destroyed. Evil manifests itself in regulations, which abolish the difference between executioner and victim, between guilty and not guilty. Appealing to *conscience* is just possible as long as a visible alternative to the apparently unavoidable constraint of conditions exists, an elbow-room of personal freedom opening an exit to better conditions. 'When a man is faced with the alternative of betraying and thus murdering his friends or of sending his wife and children, for whom he is in every sense responsible, to their death – how to decide? The alternative is no longer between good and evil, but between murder and murder.'[19] The reality of evil appears in a closed result connection that renders the decision of conscience absolutely irrelevant, because without consequences, and thereby eliminates and destroys conscience itself, the meadow of personality rooting in freedom.

It is obvious and has often been described that this *circulus vitiosus* effected the dissolution of positive right and thereby a complete deprivation of right for the people who were subjected to it. For justice, the 'statue of freedom', as one of its present protagonists (Burckhard Hirsch) formulated concerning the right of asylum and human rights with a fine pathos, is the external pillar of all opposition against arbitrariness and barbarism. It embodies a comparative permanence against the continually changing circumstances of human beings and effects thereby a likewise comparative calculability of their acts. If it is not just re-interpreted according to the motto 'Justice is, what is useful to the people', but actually re-defined, this

---

18. Arendt, *Origins of Totalitarianism*, 468.
19. Arendt, *Origins of Totalitarianism*, 452.

continuity is removed. Justice is pulled into the whirlpool of the *movement* – National Socialism understood itself as 'movement' from the beginning – which the 'national departure' with all its ideological ideas prescribes. Here, where the ancient *lex aeterna* is replaced by the new terms 'people', 'race', 'blood', 'soil', most impressively the force of this parasitic counter-order becomes visible, as which I have characterized evil. What yesterday still was justice, has become today injustice. Law – in a juridical formulation – is debased to the level of a mere decree. It has become changeable and useable, as it fits to the short-living purposes of a totalitarian use of power. Nevertheless it is executed with an inhuman 'lawfulness', for which human beings are not more than material.[20]

In this process – insofar as it can be understood and be described from its radiation at all – the core of evil becomes visible. The most terrifying observation in looking back is the abstract consequence, not interrupted by any logical argument or consideration regarding expediency, which in times of war would have been at least imaginable. It went on for all who were involved actively or passively with an evidence not to be shaken from outwards and therefore finally not to be called in question. As the reality of law turned imperceptibly to the contrary, thus the conditions, under which human beings can live even in extreme situations, changed to the unreal state of shadows in a realm of death. The loss of reality, the destruction of all sense-connections, which we use to reckon normally, more exactly: the despising and systematic devaluation of all measures that teach us to estimate 'reality' in the right way and deal with it in appropriate manner, seems to be the least visible, but most unfailing characteristic of this system of rules, by which evil undermines the normality of daily life.

Ideologies, we are told, are blind. But the blindness in this case is not caused (as during the night, in which all cows are grey) by the under-definition of reality, but, on the contrary, by its glaring over-definition. In the conviction of having found the key, by which the riddles of history can be solved and the world be lifted out of its rusted hinges, they construct their simple, but clear-cut world-view and produce – to speak again with Hannah Arendt – in this 'way over and above the senselessness of totalitarian society' some kind of 'supra-sense'[21] '…through which – in absolute and never expected consistency – every, also the most absurd action and institution receives its sense'.[22] Here is finally confirmed, what the descriptions of the vexatious roll-calls and punishment-rituals prove at any case: Not too little order, but too much, not the decay of order, but its super-elevation to a regulation that suffocates every spontaneity and thereby sets free subversive motion and renders manifest the destructive power of evil. It creates the fictitious totalitarian world, in which without regard to any historical, cultural or even natural preconditions it could be attempted to render the impossible possible: the transformation of man to an organism perfectly to be governed. Therefore 'Auschwitz' means a break of continuity to all previous history. Because wishing the impossible means causing its end, the end of any imaginable future. With the means of thinking and acting,

---

20. Arendt, *Origins of Totalitarianism*, 462.
21. Arendt, *Origins of Totalitarianism*, 457. Cf. 472–73.
22. Retranslation of Arendt, *Elemente und Ursprünge*, 939.

which history provides in its traditions. Therefore it is impossible to cope with evil, as it became manifest here.

3. *Evil – a Question to God?*

Nobody will take these considerations as an *explanation* of evil. I tried to describe evil at one of its striking aspects. Is it possible to do more? Before evil all categories fail. Nevertheless philosophy developed a lot of fall – and defection-theories for explaining this dark riddle.[23] Because, if evil is not just a deprivation of Good, but introduces itself as a reality *sui generis*, then, it is argued, it must be rendered understandable as the result of the change from an original perfection of creation to the worse. This change can have two causes: either it is the result of a fall caused by the human, which God just tolerated. Then evil would be the special property of the human, and its consequences would not affect God himself. Or evil is already posed in creation, so to speak as its negative condition and as the condition of human freedom. In this case God himself would be subjected to it and would have to suffer by and under it.

The most moving attempt at rendering the tragedy of Auschwitz before the background of the old question: *Unde malum?* a bit more understandable, Hans Jonas's essay about the 'Image of God after Auschwitz', argues on the second level.[24] For in spite of all that happened there to *keep fast* to God, not to abandon the vanishing point of Jewish identity, is only possible if – thus the thesis – this God cannot be made responsible for these 'years of Auschwitz-rage', because he suffers from it himself. Jonas recurs to elements and ideas of the Jewish Kabbala.[25] In order to produce a world outside himself and make it possible for it to develop freely, the infinite God has to restrict himself. He has to allow the final space in himself, has to take back his all-presence, limit his unlimited power, to allow nonentity (of the creation *ex nihilo*) can 'come into being' as this outer-divine space, in which the world finds its created independence. It is dismissed into its independent existence, separated from God. Thereby the fact of *estrangement* from the origin is placed, which proves to be the reason for the realization of *evil*. Already for creating the world, in order to exist as creator of the world, God has to tolerate cuts of his own being, has to subject himself to a condition, without which a creation unfolding *freely* and thereby liable to the irruption of evil would not be imaginable. Passion and melancholy of creation and its root, evil, thus do not *come from* God. They belong to the conditions, without which he would not have been able to act as creator. Their possibility is a dowry of creature freedom.

This dialectic relationship between God and his antipode – evil – does *not* come from God, however it would not be without God, and renders the riddle of evil insoluble. Jonas's reflections circulate around the divine pole: 'In order that the

23. Cf. P. Koslowski, 'Sündenfälle. Theorien der Wandelbarkeit der Welt', in *Die Wirklichkeit des Bösen* (ed. F. Hermanni and P. Koslowski; Munich: Fink, 1998), 99–132.

24. Jonas, *Gottesbegriff*, 16-17,25.

25. Cf. G. Scholem, 'Schöpfung aus dem Nichts und Selbstverschränkung Gottes', *Eranos-Jahrbuch* 25 (1956), 87–119.

world be and be for itself, God renounced his own being.' He 'emptied himself' for the benefit of his world, and this emptying has the sense to make plain, that 'God's relation to the world from the beginning of creation has been...suffering'.[26] He has given up the title of being the almighty. He is a God without power. For the crimes of Auschwitz he cannot be made responsible. Even if he had wanted, he would not have been able to stop the Evil.

I will not dwell upon the theological objections, which Jonas himself has for-mulated.[27] Obviously his God has nothing more 'to give'. He is a god without providence. One cannot pray to him, not call him, there is no help in his name. He has delegated the competence for the world to humans. More important seems to me in this connection the departure from the traditional attempts at answering the question of the origin of evil in an anthropocentric manner, by deriving it from the fall of man. Evil, one can interpret the tradition which Jonas took over, has its origin in life itself. Cruelty, force, cunning, malice, and craftiness are also to be found in the realm of animals. The forming of a parasitic system of rules that destroys the intact organism, has all sorts of models there. We humans overtook the animals only by developing the same qualities to a higher efficiency. For we are able to step out of the binding of nature. We have learned to keep our distance from nature. This is meant, when the Bible says that we have eaten from the tree of knowledge (Gen. 2.17). We can redetect evil, with which we are familiar in and by ourselves, in nature. Above all: we are able to start (what no animal is able to do) the circle of evil consciously, out of our own freedom. We have perceived that the sense of the word 'good' and 'evil' is not touched by the question of what behav-iour is more successful in the course of history. However, it becomes still more mysterious thereby, what evil *is*.

Still more it remains a riddle, how one should render its existence and efficiency to conform with the existence of God, how solve the dialectics we have described above. Must not every attempt at co-ordinating evil with the creator of the world misunderstand its damaging character and render God himself highly ambiguous? But on the other side: Can one derive its efficiency from the activity of the created beings alone without, as Jonas does, reducing God's rule to a mere passive observ-ing and permitting it? It is a walk on the ridge that theology has to begin, if it wants to enter into the problem of theodicy. Eliezer Berkovits, a modern representative of Jewish orthodoxy, speaks openly about a 'divine dilemma': 'God took a risk with mankind, and he can't escape the responsibility for men'.[28] If he respects his created freedom, he has to remove himself out of the human action sphere. If the human shall not perish by the consequences of his freedom, he has to stay in the world. Both are just imaginable if he is at the same time away and present, that means, if God *hides* his presence and restricts his power. In the shade of his

---

26. Jonas, *Gottesbegriff*, 16–17,25.

27. Cf. W. Dietrich and C. Link, *Die dunklen Seiten Gottes* (Neukirchen–Vluyn: Neukirchener Verlag, 2000), II, 114–18, 299–306.

28. Retranslation of E. Berkovitz, 'Das Verbergen Gottes', in M. Brocke and H. Jochum (eds.), *Wolkensäule und Feuerschein: Jüdische Theologie des Holocaust* (Gütersloh: Kaiser, 1993), 43–72 (65).

absence the tragedies of humankind happen, the suffering of the innocuous. The necessity of his presence establishes the hope that at the end evil will not triumph. Berkovitz sees this hope confirmed in the existence of the escaped, the continuity of Israel's history: 'No matter how often God keeps the silence we received his voice; (no matter) how godless and desolated the history may appear, we know that he is present when we, full of awe, look at our own existence.'[29] Can Christian theology say more? It will sharpen the dilemma by seeing the shade of God's absence now also fall upon the authentic witness of this God, the man Jesus, and interpreting him as judgement *on*, and this means, as a token of divine protest *against* the injustice of the world. 'In this shade', Karl Barth says, 'Israel suffered, in this shade suffers the church... The shade would not fall, if the cross of Christ would not stand in the light of his resurrection.'[30] Thereby it confirms, what Jewish theology since 'Job' knows before and with it: That one cannot explain evil, that one can talk about it at all only if one keeps to the hope that it will not have the last word. 'It has no power not given him by God.'[31]

---

29. Retranslation of Berkovitz, 'Verbergen Gottes', 72.

30. K. Barth, *Kirchliche Dogmatik* II/1 (Zollikon–Zürich: Evangelischer Verlag, 1940), 456.

31. Barth, *Kirchliche Dogmatik* III/3, 405. This seems to be the core of the dialectics mentioned above: Also the shade one can only see in the light.

EVIL: A TOPIC FOR RELIGIOUS EDUCATION?

Franz-Heinrich Beyer

1. *The Complexity of the Topic*

In the Christian tradition evil has always been a present topic: the book of Job and the search for God, the argument between Jesus and the demons, and the final victory over the devil in the Apocalypse. When the Bible speaks of the devil or demons it aims not to demonize the world but rather to de-demonize it. Where God is at work, the devils and demons are out of place. Therefore neither devils nor demons have a place in the Christian confession. Nevertheless, the topic is always present. For example, the seventh and final request in the Lord's Prayer reads: 'and deliver us from evil'. Icons of evil in medieval times as well as during and after the Reformation still show the 'fascination of evil' – although it is, in a theological sense, already overcome.

Evil has its place in the practice of the church too. A part of the baptism liturgy, for example, was and is the 'rejection of the devil', an exorcism prayer. (See Rietschel and Graff[1] who refer to the problem of exorcism in the baptism liturgy: The power and control of the devil is not only broken in the baptism – it is already broken by the salvation of Christ. Satan will not be judged, he is already judged... The question arises whether a child of Christian parents can be considered as subjected to satanic control at all.) Since the Enlightenment the discussion about the devil in theology and church has become a problem. The discussion about the devil is suspicious on a theological level, it is accepted in the sphere of piety. This becomes especially clear by a closer look at – even contemporary – Christian hymns. In his *Glaubenslehre* Friedrich Schleiermacher says: 'Die Vorstellung vom Teufel, wie sie sich unter uns ausgebildet hat, ist so haltungslos, dass man eine Überzeugung von ihrer Wahrheit niemandem zumuten kann.'[2] Schleiermacher, however, believes that a liturgical use of the image of the devil is possible. In his opinion a displacement of the devil from the Christian hymns would be irresponsible.

---

1. G. Rietschel and P. Graff, *Lehrbuch der Liturgik* (Göttingen: Vandenhoeck & Ruprecht, 1951), 583.

2. 'The image of the devil which is common amongst us is unacceptable, so that nobody really can be expected to believe in its literal truth', F. Schleiermacher, *Der christliche Glaube nach den Grundsätzen der evangelischen Kirche im Zusammenhange dargestellt von Dr Friedrich Schleiermacher* (ed. M. Redecker; Berlin: W. de Gruyter, 7th edn of the 2nd version, 1960), §44.

The pride and pathos of the Enlightenment when talking about the devil becomes especially clear in a text by Adolf von Harnack. In 1899 he writes in a letter to his daughter: 'Es könnte ja einen Teufel geben, und tiefsinnige, keineswegs auf den Kopf gefallene Leute behaupten das heute noch. Sie glauben, die innere Erfahrung von seiner Existenz gemacht zu haben; ich habe eine solche Erfahrung nicht gemacht...'[3] In the twentieth century and especially after World War II – often in much too late attempts to speak about the Shoah and Auschwitz – the talk about demons, the powers of evil and the devil was an obvious but highly dangerous explanation for some people.

The fact that a person is responsible for his or her own deeds, that he or she cannot refer to another human or even the devil as an excuse for their misdeeds, is the heritage of the Enlightenment. Due to the psychoanalytical theory of projection this has become common knowledge.

This makes the following statistical data even harder to understand: according to a poll from 1991, 15 per cent of the population of West Germany and 7 per cent of the population of East Germany believe in the devil. In the whole of Europe the percentage is 24 per cent; in the USA 64 per cent. The symbols of evil in present time are not only not absent, but highly and publicly visible in popular culture.

2. *The Presence of the Topic*

Evil and its symbols are important elements of today's culture, especially in popular culture. This is especially true for today's generation of children and adolescents. They are highly fascinated by images of the devil, demons and other personal representations of evil. Movies, videos, music, comics and computer games seem to dwell on such images. It is difficult to assess the actual amount of experience of the occult in young people.

The media and their style of news-making have to be mentioned here. There have been more than one report on ritual killings in satanic groups. In the light of such reports the question of how satanic cults can be assessed arises. The answer to this question is not an easy one, since such cults can be described as youth-cultural phenomena, experiments in taboo-breaking, or on the other hand as perverted, violent and intent on the destruction of personality, in other words as criminal. This has to be differentiated. A photo-love-story published by the magazine BRAVO[4] containing satanic elements has made clear that Satanism can be counted as a part of youth culture. Evil, especially the Devil/Satan, is a topic which is present in today's generation of children and adolescents. It is a topic of popular culture that plays an important role relating to the adolescent perception of the world.

---

3.   'There could be a devil, and profound people who are not fools claim this, even today. They believe that they have made an inner experience of its existence; I have not made such an experience...', A. von Zahn-Harnack, *Adolf von Harnack* (Berlin: Hans Bott Verlag, 1936), 285.

4.   BRAVO-magazine is a German magazine for adolescents interested in pop-culture. It is part of youth-culture and reporting on it. See http://www.bravo.de

Religious education cannot and must not ignore this topic, if it wants to refer to the *gelebte Religion*[5] of adolescents and to contribute to coping with life and orientation. Some references can illustrate that this challenge has been met with in Practical Theology, especially in religious education. One can refer to the following issues of journals of religious education: 1989 *Das Böse* (Evil); 1992 *Wohin mit dem Teufel?*;[6] 1997 *Das Böse – eine oft verdrängte Herausforderung* (Evil – an often dismissed challenge); 1999 *Geheimnisvolle Kräfte* (Mysterious powers). The article 'Teufel' (devil) in the *TRE* now for the first time contains a subchapter 'practical-theological'. Finally one can refer to research projects at other universities. 'Practical-theological Investigations of "Evil" in Popular Culture' is the title of a project at the University of Bayreuth.

3. *The Topic in Contemporary Religious Education*

In the curriculum 'Evangelische Religionslehre, Sekundarstufe II – Gymnasium, Gesamtsschule' (Protestant Religious Education, *Sekundarstufe II* – grammar-school, comprehensive school) of the state North-Rhine Westphalia, Germany, one can find the following suggestion for the topic: 'Wieso gibt es das Böse auf der Welt? Welches sind Ursachen und Erscheinungsformen in Vergangenheit und Gegenwart? – Religionen versuchen Antworten auf diese drängenden Fragen zu geben.'[7]

Before I go into detail, I want to describe the discussion of the topic in the last decades. The topic was not excluded from the curriculum in North-Rhine Westphalia in the past. It was not stressed like today, however. One could find it in the problem of theodicy, or in the question of the image of God, or in the human search for meaning within the scope of anthropology.

The book *Das Böse* (Evil) by Siegfried Vierzig, published in 1984, can be regarded as characteristic of the 1970s and 1980s. The author diagnoses fear as a common social mood in this time. Fear is the physical reaction to experiences with evil, which can appear in an individual and in a collective way. Experiences with evil are experiences that question both the physical existence and the meaning of life. Especially teenagers are concerned. They notice that the rationalization of all events in life does not guarantee and protect a good life any more. Rather rationalization changes into rendering things irrational. They notice that there are not many possibilities left to feeling emotional moments, and therefore participate in violent acts to experience emotions. The main question of the author reads as follows: How can we live with the experiences of evil as irrational (*Widersinn*), how can we process this, and how can we find new motivations for life in view of evil?[8]

---

5.   *Gelebte Religion* refers to the religious fragments adolescents collect from all the religious events and movements they encounter, experience and live and form into a patchwork.

6.   Translated literally, this title would be 'Where to put the devil?' The obvious answer is: 'Where the sun never shines!', which in this case refers to hell, of course.

7.   'Why does the evil exist in the world? What are the reasons and different forms in the past and present? Religions try to answer these important questions.'

8.   S. Vierzig, *Das Böse* (Stuttgart: W. Kohlhammer, 1984), 11.

The following passages concern methods of how to deal with evil, especially the knowledge about projections of evil in both tradition (jahwistic-history, the devil, witches) and history by means of describing certain religious, political, ethnic groups as evil (Jews, Communists, foreigners). Furthermore, some approaches in the humanities concerning the rationalizing of evil are described. Finally the author names new motivations for life in view of evil. According to Vierzig we can only be strong against the potentials of evil by declaring our solidarity with the weak and the suffering. Solidarity makes the final request '…and deliver us from evil' come true.[9]

I now want to focus on the current curriculum again: Why does evil exist in the world? What are the reasons for and different forms of evil in the past and present? Religions try to answer these important questions. One of the reasons that this theme found its place in the curriculum of 1999 is that questions and experiences of students are important from a didactic point of view. Such questions and experiences shall be intertwined with both statements concerning faith and theology and competing interpretations in other religions and philosophies in a way of argument and dialogue in the new curriculum.

The importance of the questions and experiences of students corresponds to the attention to 'ways of speaking religiously'. These can be: denominations, symbols of faith, but also literature, art, music, film, architecture, mass media and everyday speech. Such ways of speaking religiously shall be developed, interpreted and finally applied by the students by choosing appropriate methods.

Therefore our topic is of interest for two reasons:

1. The didactic conception of the curriculum with reference to the lived, or 'experienced religion' (*gelebte Religion*);

2. The presence and fascination of the topic in the context of youth-culture. This can be described as a 'way of speaking religiously'.

4. *The Horror Film as Paradigm*

In literature encounters with forms of Satanism can be described as an esoteric enjoyment. This can be applied to the Satanism of romantic and recent novels like *Rosemary's Baby* (Ira Levin, 1967) and *The Exorcist* (William Peter Blatty, 1971) as well. Both novels were filmed successfully. At the present time the medium 'film' is one of the best examples where the medial presence of evil can be described very clearly. This feeling of being overwhelmed is characteristic of films, since they have the best ability to cause it. This effect must be considered, although it should not be over-simplified.

The sociologist Alexander Schuller wrote about the renaissance of evil a few years ago in his article: 'Grässliche Hoffnung. Zur Hermeneutik des Horror-Films'.[10] Schuller refers to the Enlightenment and its consequences: in our world where paradises were invented by the human spirit and brought into existence through human hands, there should be no darkness, no sluggishness, nothing

---

9. Vierzig, *Das Böse*, 64.
10. 'Hideous hope. About the hermeneutics of horror films.'

clouded nor double-bottomed, and neither tears nor anything transcendent should exist.

All the evil dreams have returned, however. And everybody who has looked into these horrors, must ask for their meaning beyond his own shock and disappointment.

In the following I shall attempt to summarize Schuller's main theses:

1. Horror films want to familiarize with hideous and absurd things – the evil. They fascinate, because they are a strident contradiction to our reality and fulfil it at the same time.

2. The horror film continues a long tradition of illustrations of hell during medieval times and the baroque period. That horror, however, was embedded in a theology, a morale, and a cosmos where good and evil were restricted. It was a ritualized and restrained horror. In today's films evil is one-dimensional, repressing nearly everything else completely.

3. In the horror film the familiar contrast between God and good on the one hand and Devil and evil on the other hand is abolished. Evil is no longer a contrast to God; it has rather become a contrast to society.

4. There is no social placement of evil in a horror film. Evil stands in contrast to everyday life in our world.

5. The horror film is not about protest, but about salvation. The Christian claim remains in effect: The real kingdom is not of this world. Evil is the alternative – a chance. Without evil the world would become absorbed in banality. Evil brings life and motion into the rigid and dead world of civilization and normality.

6. Evil is the alternative. By the loss of transcendence, however, evil is not there, but here in our world. The horror films can be seen as attempts to recognize, name and ban the evil that we face daily. In this way evil can be seen as a new transcendence in this world.

7. Horror films often neither speak nor argue. The evil is without alternative. Reality is no longer accessible by reason, but rather by magic. Horror films demand a new, a gory faith.

8. The fragmental configurations of mostly Christian images one can recognize as a longing for a good, a planned world. It is the longing for a world where heaven and hell, God, human being and Devil, good and evil have their place. In the films, however, the fight against evil is not completely hopeless. Evil can be assigned a place, evil can be driven from this world. The fight however is never over; the one major certainty of horror films is that there is going to be a sequel.[11]

Schuller's conclusion reads as follows: The films try to find a way in a world that has become unsteady, for themselves and through themselves for us. They are a trivial contrast to the anthropological discussion in which the question arises: What

---

11. Computer games should be mentioned here, where by one's own action one can choose between good and evil and in this way strengthen the position of either good or evil in the universe of games.

can the human being be, if it can create itself?[12] How can the fascination of the evil and horror be explained? One reason for the fascination of evil and horror can be the loss of knowledge about and experience with transcendence, shock experiences and border situations in our modern society. The idea of a ruled, administrated, and planned world does not only seem to hinder a 're-enchantment'[13] of reality, but rather support it. This is consistent with the thesis of youth-sociologists that the fascination of adolescents for horror films cannot be regarded as equal to a tendency to violent behaviour. The film, for example a video cassette, is used for the constitution of a private world outside of the world of everyday life. The horror film has a special ability to transcend everyday life. The horror trip is experienced as a border-situation, which in itself is taboo in everyday life. The familiarity of adolescents with the special effects used in these films is their way of segregating from adults. For adults, the films are a useless string of blood and gore scenes. Adults do not have the appropriate decryption code to look behind the dramatization in these scenes. Instead they enjoy the excitement that lies in being able to decode the various special effects and in this way to watch the horror film with a focus mostly detached from the actual violence on the screen.[14] Youth cultural video-groups are the platform for this self-presentation of adolescents.

The phenomenon of horror films is therefore an expression of the search for meaning among adolescents, their interest in the symbols of evil as compensation for a lack of meaning in the world of everyday life and a way of creating their own life-styles.

5. Life-styles and Symbols of Evil –
Youth-sociological and Youth-cultural Aspects

Now I want to deal briefly with some results of research into youth culture:

Since the 1980s it is no longer possible to see youth culture as counter-culture to adult culture. The most important role of youth culture is no longer the building-up of a coherent belief-system, but rather something one could call 'showmanship': the ability to promote oneself by eccentric means and provoking by means of rule-breaking.

The term 'life-style' seems to be characteristic for this phenomenon. Life-styles are an expression of individuality. One does not have to choose one life-style for ever. There is no duly ordered period of affiliation. And you can combine several life-styles into one of your own.

---

12. A. Schuller, 'Gräßliche Hoffnung. Zur Hermeneutik des Horrorfilms', in A. Schuller and W.V. Rahden (eds.), *Die andere Kraft: Zur Renaissance des Bösen* (Berlin: Akademie Verlag, 1993), 341–54 (354).

13. W. Helsper, '(Neo)religiöse Orientierungen Jugendlicher in der "postmodernen Moderne", in W. Ferchhoff (ed.), 'Jugendkulturen – Faszination und Ambivalenz. Einblicke in jugendliche Lebenswelten' (Weinheim: Juventa, 1995), 66–81.

14. W. Vogelsang, V*ideocliquen. Action- und Horrorvideos als Kristallisationspunkte von jugendlichen Fangemeinschaften*, in: W. Ferchhoff (ed.), *Jugendkulturen – Faszination und Ambivalenz. Einblicke in jugendliche Lebenswelten* (Weinheim: Juventa, 1995), 120–32 (130).

Therefore it is a characteristic of their life-style orientation that adolescents are playing with styles. This means that the affiliation to a scene is no longer related to an existential pathos. Th. Ziehe remarked: 'Ich "bin" nicht mein Stil, sondern ich "bin" das Verhältnis, dass ich Stilen gegenüber gewählt habe.'[15] It is important to note that nowadays collective and individual perceptions, fantasies, fears and expressions are expressed far more aesthetically than ethically. The cognitive is replaced by the sensual, structure by experience.

In these processes the assessment of criteria changes as well. This is especially true for autonomy and individuality as points of orientation. Autonomy and individuality are not negated. They are, however, far less important nowadays than the acceptance of ambivalence.

Therefore the answers, which the *gelebte Religion* of adolescents gives to the consequences of modernization, can only be described from several different perspectives. Werner Helsper distinguishes between six kinds of (neo-) religious, occult or magical-religious engagements of young people:[16]

• Die ontologisierende Beheimatung;	• ontological residence
• der religiös-konventionelle Traditionalismus;	• conventional religious traditionalism
• der antiinstitutionelle Protest-Okkultismus;	• anti-institutional protest-occultism;
• die eigenverantwortete religiöse Transformation;	• religious transformation in one's own responsibility;
Jugendliche generieren eigene neue Welt- und Selbstbilder.	*Adolescents generate their own views of the world and themselves.*
• die okkult-religiöse Identitätssuche;	• occult-religious search for identity;
Es geht hier um Erlebnishaftigkeit, um Intensitätserfahrungen. Eine spezifische Form des Umgangs mit der anspruchsvollen Sinnstiftung in individualisierten Lebensverhältnissen.	*This concerns identity experiences – a specific kind of dealing with the demanding production of meaning in individual life.*
• die privatisierte Religions-Bricolage.	• personalized patchwork-religion.

This creates some serious challenges for religious education, of which I want to name but five:

1. As far as evil is a part of youth culture, it is also a part of the *gelebte Religion* of adolescents. These phenomena have to be observed carefully and differentiated.
2. The adolescents' attitude toward the symbols of evil is more playful or selective than existential. Religious education has to consider this when choosing evil as a subject. This way evil can be disenchanted and does not have to be exorcized.

15. 'I am not my style, but I am the relationship that I have chosen in respect to some styles.' Th. Ziehe, 'Vom vorläufigen Ende der Erregung – Die Normalität kultureller Modernisierungen hat die Jugend-Subkulturen entmächtigt', in W. Helsper (ed.), *Jugend zwischen Modernen und Postmoderne* (Opladen: Leske + Budrich, 1991), 57–73.
16. Helsper, '(Neo)religiöse Orientierungen, 66–81 (69f.).

3. The fascination of evil is a challenge to theology and religion, which feels exclusively obliged to the quest for meaning, the search for identity and salvation, and does not consider the experience of the unfathomable in religion itself.

4. What has been described for religion is also true for the adolescents' conception of God. For them God is not love, peace and justness alone, but has a 'dark side' as well. Religious education has to consider these 'dark sides of God'[17] too.

5. Considering the acceptance of ambivalence in today's adolescents a further challenge for religious education arises: Religious education has to learn the ways of thinking in terms of contrast and distinction, especially when it comes to the concept of God. But it has to be quite clear that what we call evil always includes a destructive and a constructive element. Religious education cannot entirely give up the distinction between God and evil for God can be accepted as the 'unconditional dependable ground'.

17. W. Dietrich and Chr. Link, *Die dunklen Seiten Gottes* (2 vols.; Neukirchen–Vluyn: Neukirchener Verlag, 2000).

Part IV

MODERN LITERATURE

The Question of Evil in Israeli Holocaust Fiction

Yochai Oppenheimer

Holocaust literature scholarship, which has developed in Israel during the last thirty years, has taken an interest in two interrelated issues. The first of these is concerned with different literary approaches to the Holocaust, and makes intensive use of concepts such as 'realism', 'metarealism', 'documentation', 'fiction' and 'de-automatization' to explore the differences between the first generation of Holocaust survivors who wrote about the Holocaust and the following generations. The second issue is the different treatments of Zionist ideology, including the relationship between the Holocaust and the establishment of the State of Israel, the literary representation of Holocaust survivors, and the use of the collective memory of the Holocaust in the Israeli–Palestinian conflict. Even if one cannot agree with the claim of Saul Friedlander[1] that works written before the Eichmann trial in 1961 are ideological in nature, while those written after it are not, one has to admit the existence about 1961 of a clear transformation between different and perhaps opposing ideologies. Yael Feldman has written about *Ghetto,* the well-known play by Yehoshua Sobol:

> Dichotomy unravels Sobol's technique but also exposes the limits of this 'new' representation: unable altogether to deconstruct the old oppositions, he simply inverts their markers, glorifying everything that has been traditionally marked as negative…and debunking the previously valorised values.[2]

This change has already been discussed by scholars as a change from a Zionist worldview, expressed in realistic works of a documentary nature, to a post-Zionist stance, using a meta-realistic style, and since the middle of the 1980s, also post-modernist techniques. This phenomenon is part of the changes that have occurred in the Israeli public consciousness during the last forty years, that include the removal of the subject of the Holocaust from an exclusively national framework and placing it in both private and universalist frameworks.[3] A correlative expres-

---

1.   S. Friedlander, 'Roundtable Discussion', in B Lang (ed.), *Writing and Holocaust* (New York: Holmes and Meier, 1988), 287–89 (289).

2.   Y. Feldman, 'Whose Story Is It, Anyway? Ideology and Psychology in the Representation of the Shoah in Israeli Literature', in S. Friedlander (ed.), *Probing the Limits of Representation: Nazism and Final Solution* (Cambridge, MA: Harvard University Press, 1992), 223–39 (226).

3.   See A. Raz-Krakzkin, 'Exile within Sovereignty: Towards a Critique of the "Negation of Evil" in Israeli Culture, II', *Theory and Criticism* 5 (1994), 113–32 (Hebrew); A. Shapira, 'The Holocaust: Private Memory and Collective Memory', in *eadem, New Jews Old Jews* (Tel Aviv: Am Oved, 1997), 86–103.

sion of the depth of this change can be found in the new way the Israeli educational system treats the topic of the Holocaust.[4]

The above is meant to provide background for the current discussion, which is concerned with the representation of evil in Israeli Holocaust fiction. The thesis of this paper is that the representation of evil is not dependent upon any historical periodization: it is directly influenced neither by a Zionist worldview, nor by a post-Zionist one. It contends with evil according to esthetical criteria, beyond the limits of ideology or moral perspective.

1. *Holocaust and Language*

At the start of each study of Holocaust literature, a great deal of attention is given to statements by writers and scholars regarding the linguistic difficulties involved in writing on the Holocaust. Many cite Adorno's comment that 'it is barbaric to continue to write poetry after Auschwitz'.[5] Fewer authors cite Primo Levi, who said that the expressions we use, such as 'hunger', 'fear', 'pain', 'exhaustion', and many others, are not valid in describing the experience of the concentration camps, and therefore a new language is required.[6] When Lyotard speaks of 'differend', he means a new kind of language:

> The differend is the unstable state and instant of language wherein something, which must be able to be put into phrases cannot yet be. This state includes silence, which is a negative phrase, but it also calls upon phrases which are in principle possible. This state is signalled by what one ordinarily calls a feeling: 'One cannot find the words', etc. A lot of searching must be done to find new rules for forming and linking phrases that are able to express the differend disclosed by the feeling, unless one wants this differend to be smothered right away [...]. What is at stake in a literature, in a philosophy, in a politics perhaps, is to bear witness to differends by finding Idioms for them.[7]

Lyotard has formulated the sensitivity to the fact that expressibility does not correspond with known language. However, this theoretical discussion of the representation of the Holocaust and the limits to this representation remained foreign to the literary product concerning the Holocaust in the first years after the war, when it was dominated by national and didactic needs. At any rate, in Hebrew literature before the beginning of the 1960s, we hardly see writers debating about the language or the type of narrative they should use to tell about the Holocaust. Only later did this become a central issue for them.

The 1940s and 1950s witnessed the tendency to use Jewish tradition (which David Roskies found in the Jewish responses to the pogroms of the end of the

---

4. See R. Fierer, *Agents of Holocaust Lesson* (Tel Aviv: Hakkibutz Hameuchad, 1989) (Hebrew).

5. T. Adorno, 'Commitment', in *idem, Notes to Literature, II* (trans. S.W. Nicholsen; New York: Columbia University Press, 1992), 76–94.

6. P. Levi, *The Drowned and the Saved* (New York: Summit Books, 1988).

7. J.F. Lyotard, *The Differend: Phrases in Dispute* (Minneapolis: Minnesota University Press, 1988), 13.

nineteenth century and beginning of the twentieth),[8] primarily in the poetry of Uri Zvi Greenberg. His use of the language of the Bible and prayer and that of medieval Hebrew poetry is fully connected to his view of the Holocaust as a direct continuation of the anti-Semitic pogroms of the past. The analogy which Greenberg proposed between the throwing of Abraham into the oven in Ur and the crematoria in the death camps, or between 'Haman' and 'German',[9] led to the mythicizing of the Holocaust, which in his case meant waiving any attempt to relate to its historical uniqueness. Greenberg, whose works since the beginning of the 1920s had emphasized the complete opposition of Judaism and Christianity (which he identified with absolute evil), did not need a new language to write about the Holocaust. He even pointedly expressed his opposition to the term 'Holocaust', which he felt ignored the continuity of the destruction of the Jews in the past and the present, and therefore preferred the traditional term חרבן גליות, the 'destruction of the Exiles'.

Greenberg's poetry is, from this point of view, an example of a somewhat marginal option in Israeli fiction of the 1940s and 1950s, although writers of fiction who wanted to document or tell of the heroism of Jews during the Holocaust (especially the Warsaw Ghetto revolt) emphasized the analogy between these events and examples of bravery from Jewish history, such as Samson and his battle against the Philistines, Masada, and even those who preferred to die rather than convert during the Middle Ages.[10] However, as far as the representation of evil in Israeli fiction is concerned, there is no tendency toward traditional mythicizing. Except for the rare use of standard adjectives such as 'satanic' and 'monstrous', writers used a descriptive language which is alienated and lacking a developed metaphoric system. Even when language inclines to pathetic expression, in the texts of Katzetnik for example (the pen name of Yehiel Dinur),[11] this strengthens the description of the consciousness of the hero of the story, or belongs to the interspersed remarks of the narrator, but is not seen as appropriate for a description of evil and those who engage in it.

2. *Evil and Subjectivity*

Katzetnik was the main author in Israel who was not only a survivor of the concentration camps but also made them the sole topic of his work. Other authors who

---

8.   D. Roskies, *Against Apocalypse: Responses to Catastrophe in Modern Jewish Culture* (Cambridge, MA and London: Harvard University Press, 1984).

9.   U.Z. Greenberg, *Streets of the River* (Tele Aviv and Jerusalem: Schocken Books, 1951) (Hebrew).

10.   A collection of Hebrew poetry that praises the Warsaw Ghetto revolt is to be found in Y. Zukerman and M. Basok, *The Book of the Wars of the Ghettos* (Tel Aviv: Hakkibutz Hameuchad, 1954) (Hebrew). A similar attitude is salient in fiction written on the same topic: Katzetnik, *Salamandra* (Haifa: Shikmona, 1971) (Hebrew); Y. Sened and A. Sened, *Between the Living and the Dead* (Tel Aviv: Hakkibutz Hameuchad, 1964) (Hebrew).

11.   Dan Miron has clarified the expressionist background of Katzetnik's works and his tendency to develop a grandiose and pathetic first person. See D. Miron, 'Between Ashes and Books', *Alpayim* 10 (1994), 196–224 (Hebrew).

dealt with the Holocaust almost never described the camps (such as Yehudit Hendel, Uri Orlev, Shamai Golan, and Alexander and Yonat Sened). Katzetnik coined the expression 'the other planet' as a starting point for his description of the death camps. In his short testimony at the Eichmann trial he said:

> I was there for about two years. Time there was different from what it is here on earth. Every split second ran on a different cycle of time. And the inhabitants of that planet had no names. They had neither parents nor children. They did not dress as we dress here. They were not born there nor did anyone give birth. The laws of another nature regulated even their breathing.[12]

However, this view of the death camps as another planet does not produce different writing, even though Katzetnik repeatedly argued that his works were documentary and not literary. In his first novel *Salamandra,* written in Yiddish in 1945 and translated into Hebrew, its depiction of the concentration camp is part of a chrono-logical plot, following a Jewish family from before the war to its end and the liberation of Auschwitz. Despite the informative emphasis on the daily routine of the concentration camps, this book is a novel following the consciousness of its heroes who stand out in their human environment and manage to do the unbeliev-able, whether in Auschwitz itself or in the Warsaw Ghetto. Thus, despite the mani-fested ideology of 'a different planet', this is a story centered on the autonomous subject, whose human qualities are unambiguously affirmed, no less than on the extreme historical circumstances into which he has been cast.

Adorno wrote about subjectivity in literature that 'the impossibility of portraying fascism springs from the fact that in it…subjective freedom no longer exists. Total unfreedom can be recognized, but not represented.'[13] Berl Lang added that

> Imaginative literature presupposes individuality and subjectivity in the representa-tion of its characters and their actions, and that to represent certain literary sub-jects in those terms is a falsification. This does not mean that such representations are impossible; but it does mean that the moral strain within the literary subject, and between it and the historical subject, will disclose itself in the process of representation.[14]

Adorno's question if it is possible to portray fascism in subjective terms is different from Lang's question whether it is moral, but both sharpen our ability to see that in the different periods of Israeli literature there is a clear tendency to attribute sub-jectivity or autonomy to both the representatives of the victims (not the anonymous crowd in the background, but rather the hero of the story) and some of the figures associated with evil, the causing of suffering, and murder.

The first to express the moral tension created by literary discussion of evil was the poet Natan Alterman in his discussion of the book *Between the Living and the Dead* by Alexander and Yonat Sened (1964):

---

12. T. Segev, *The Seventh Million* (Jerusalem: Keter, 1983), 3 (Hebrew).
13. T. Adorno, *Minima Moralia: Reflections from Damaged Life* (London: Verso), 144.
14. B. Lang, *Act and Idea in the Nazi Genocide* (Chicago: University of Chicago Press, 1990), 155.

> The Germans do not appear in this book. A miracle happened to the authors, who were not caught in what many are caught today throughout the world – an attempt to supposedly solve the German riddle, to delve into the hidden realms of the Nazi soul. This sort of riddle does not need to waken the desire for a solution, but instead the desire to remove it from the world. This is the only solution, which can be demanded from a Jewish person.[15]

This violent formulation expresses an unambiguous moral taboo against any attempt to examine evil and focus the lens on those who represent it.[16] However, anyone who reads Katzetnik's books will see that, although he has no special interest in deepening the understanding of the Nazi soul, he does not refrain from describing Nazi figures. At the same time, he does not tend towards demonizing evil, but rather prefers to indicate its relative human dimensions. Even the fear-inspiring figure from Auschwitz, 'the head of the camp', was accordingly sentenced 'to a life sentence as a child murderer and sexual criminal even before Hitler's rise to power. The Gestapo searched all the jails of Germany to find an appropriate figure to be head of the camp at Auschwitz.'[17] The same was true of the kapo Hans, 'a pure racial German, a criminal sentenced even before the war to eleven years in jail'.[18] The deviant nature of these criminals, who do not represent the typical German, and the connection of evil to criminality whose murderous nature does not necessarily stem from a hatred of Jews or a Nazi worldview, allow the telling of a story of evil events without reaching any conclusion about 'the Nazi soul'.

In addition, Katzetnik chooses to focus on figures or events which cannot easily be judged from a moral perspective. I do not mean only the detailed story of the art-loving Austrian doctor who admired the talent of his Jewish acquaintance to paint landscapes, hid him from the Gestapo, and when the Jew was caught and brought to Auschwitz, tried to save him from death.[19] I am referring to the many stories about devoted Nazi soldiers who are described at the very moment when compassion overcomes evil. For example, Rudolph Hess, the commander of Auschwitz, studies the row of Jews who know how to run printing presses, and who are to leave Auschwitz, 'and again studied the face of each one individually, with a fatherly look in his eyes'.[20] Seeing the hero cross the barbed-wire fence in an escape attempt, 'Robert, the most cruel of the heads of the blocks, could not contain his admiration anymore... Vatzek, the kapo of the peeling machine, swallowed

15.   N. Alterman, 'Dark Time's Eyes', in *idem, In the Circle* (Tel Aviv: Hakkibutz Hameuchad, 1975 [1964]), 87–89 (Hebrew).

16.   Alan Mintz explains in a similar way the exclusion of Nazi figures from the fiction of Appelfeld: 'To represent the figure of the enemy in the medium of narrative prose fiction, moreover, means to understand and humanise it, and this is a project which leads in its own direction and carries its own responsibilities.' A. Mintz, *Hurban: Responses to Catastrophe in Hebrew Literature* (New York: Columbia University Press, 1984), 226.

17.   Katzetnik, *Piepel* (Tel Aviv: Hakkibutz Hameuchad, 1988), 41 (Hebrew).

18.   Katzetnik, *Salamandra*, 146 (Hebrew).

19.   Katzetnik, *Salamandra*, 174–79.

20.   Katzetnik, *Piepel*, 208.

openmouthed at the unbelievable sight. For the first time since he was at Katzet he now felt the warmth of tears in his eyes.'[21] The hero of *Salamandra,* who managed to hide in the truck taking dying Muselmanner to the crematoria, was admired by the Germans: ' "After he succeeded in pulling off such a successful trick", one of them decided, "I won't send him to the crematorium. If he succeeded in cutting the hangman's rope from his neck, I won't hang him now. Let him work for the time being… Give the guy some work, he's a quick one".'[22]

3. *'The Grey Zone' versus 'The Banality of Evil'*

Primo Levi has written enlightening remarks on this topic, telling of different cases where the obviousness of evil is undermined:

> That single, immediately erased instant of pity is certainly not enough to absolve Muhsfeld [= the Nazi character]. It is enough, however, to place him too, although at its extreme boundary, within the grey band, that zone of ambiguity which radiates out from regimes based on terror and obsequiousness.[23]

Levi has called this 'the grey zone'. Just as he has described the experience of remembering verses from Dante's *Divine Comedy* while walking with his soup bowl in Auschwitz, and has given his readers a varied portrait of the concentration camp where the shades do not make the few points of light go away, he is similarly capable of undermining the one-dimensional stereotype of the 'torturers' that

> brings to mind twisted individuals, ill-born, sadists, afflicted by an original flaw. Instead, they were made of the same cloth as we, they were average human beings, averagely intelligent, averagely wicked: save the exceptions, they were not monsters, they had our faces, but they had been reared badly.[24]

The expression 'the grey zone', that is, the turning of attention to the margins of what had been seen as the center or a homogeneous experience that could easily be defined and given an unambiguous value, presents a complicated approach to human evil. I believe this expression to be more relevant to the literary approach to evil than that proposed by Hannah Arendt, 'the banality of evil'. After the Eichmann trial, she wrote that 'one cannot extract any diabolic or demonic profundity from Eichmann', as 'it was sheer thoughtlessness…that predisposed him to become one of the greatest criminals of that period'.[25] She did not find in him any interest in doing evil as a goal in itself, nor any deviation from the desire to carry out orders perfectly. The 'banality of evil' offers a social explanation for the ability to enlist the masses to perform inhuman acts, and describes the mental mechanisms necessary to this end. Arendt's work, which is not psychological in nature, claims that the ability to turn a person into someone lacking subjectivity, the power to

21. Katzetnik, *Piepel*, 223.
22. Katzetnik, *Salamandra*, 161.
23. Levi, *The Drowned and the Saved*, 58.
24. Levi, *The Drowned and the Saved*, 202.
25. H. Arendt, *Eichmann in Jerusalem: A Report on the Banality of Evil* (New York: Penguin Books, 1977 [1963]), 288–89.

think critically, and access to his human feelings and language beyond the barrier of distorted slogans, created the perfect and conscienceless killer. Banality thus means a negative definition of people as lacking 'subject', where no 'grey zone' is possible for them.

This is the reason why Eichmann seemed to Arendt to be someone who was not capable of phrasing any human, 'authentic' statement, someone who reached the peak of ridiculousness in his last words before being executed ('Long live Germany, long live Argentina, long live Austria. I will not forget them'). In addition, his testimony of how he tried to help a Jew he knew who was sent to Auschwitz, or his feeling of suffering, almost nausea, when he saw Jews being shot or gassed, are understood by Arendt as stories 'whose macabre humor easily surpasses that of any Surrealist invention',[26] or 'self-deception, lies, and stupidity'.[27] The idea of 'banality' is linked to a parodic approach to the Nazi experience, and *a priori* eliminates any complexity.

4. *The Duplicity of Nazi Evil*

One could say that the choice of a writer such as Katzetnik to place the evil of Auschwitz in 'the grey zone', despite his rhetoric of 'a different planet', indicates a principled stand in Israeli fiction to provide a complex approach to human evil and to expand as far as possible this 'grey zone'.

Katzetnik, like Primo Levi, writes literature based on documentation. Other texts that I will discuss are imaginary in nature, that is, they create different possibilities for expanding the 'grey zone' from the relatively limited scope of reality to the fantastic. Even so, it is necessary to emphasize that the latter are not lacking in unambiguous moral judgement, but rather show the growing interest in examining those human facets that are included in it, even if they are not compatible.

The clearest example of the possibility that fantastic writing could represent the internal world of the Nazi is David Grossman's novel *See Under – Love* (1986). The third part of the book describes the amazing grandfather who survived all of the attempts to kill him in the concentration camp and served Neigel, the camp commander, in a special way. He told the commander an installment of a continuing story every evening. The grandfather had been a Hebrew writer whose story about a group of children who fight against evil had been translated into German, and read and even committed to memory by Neigel when young. Now he was asked to return to and continue his story, with the Nazi taking an active part in the development of its plot. The Nazi, who enjoyed leaving his office from time to time in order to kill Jews who had arrived on the transports on their way to death, turned out to have great sensitivity and identification with the hero of the imaginary story, who was eventually killed in that same war he waged against evil. The slow undermining of the Nazi beliefs of Neigel, the entry of the story into his private life and his relations with his wife, who did not identify with Nazi culture, and his sui-

26. Arendt, *Eichmann in Jerusalem*, 50.
27. Arendt, *Eichmann in Jerusalem*, 52.

cide at the end out of identification with the victim in the story, do not overcome his murderousness, but they add another aspect to it. If a children's story can change the killer, make him recognize suffering, and reject evil, then love, the most human and universal value, is still deserving of trust. The literary fantasy that creates the meeting and dialogue between the killer and his victim exposes both the spiritual and cultural proximity between them, and especially the utopian possibility that all of Grossman's works repeatedly check in various contexts: seeing human evil as a mistake, blindness, forgetfulness, surrender to a false and lying language which does injustice primarily to the human within each person, both Jew and German. For Grossman the Nazi is not only a figure firmly anchored in history, but also a metaphor for human evil in all of its forms. In an interview, Grossman elaborated on this topic:

> [We are] not used to reading about Nazis as humans. The books that have been written from an Israeli point of view described the Nazis as some sort of monster. I wanted to examine this process, and I read a great deal of psychological research on the commanders of the camps. I took a regular, banal individual, without any special marks of identification... There will be Israelis who will ask how I dare to treat Neigel as a human being. This is exactly the approach that leads to distancing from the topic and a lack of understanding how these things develop. Look, we have this Kahana of ours and he has so many admirers. Neigel is human. A medio-cre man, a captivating figure. People have two possibilities: to be human or to be a Nazi. It is the choice of Neigel that is unforgivable.[28]

The continuity existing between good and evil, or between the human and the Nazi, and the ability to choose and to correct mistakes are at the center of this novel. The dichotomy which Grossman displays is not between two peoples (Jews/Germans) but between opposing possibilities of existence, which can be found not only in the Holocaust but also can be identified in other contexts. Just as the German may find the human side within him, everyone who lives in a nationalistic society may expose the Nazi aspect within himself.

The complexity of the figure of the camp commander may be found earlier in *Ghetto,* a play by Yehoshua Sobol (1992) describing the decimation of the Vilna Ghetto. The figures appearing in the play, and likewise the controversies that characterized the life of the ghetto and the tension between the head of the Judenrat and the underground, on the one hand, and the Zionist movement, on the other, are faithful to the historical accounts. The figure of the Nazi officer who was com-mander of the ghetto, a man who had learned Hebrew and Jewish studies in Jerusa-lem in the 1930s, is also historically accurate. However, the cultural-political stand taken by Sobol which exalts Jewish spiritual strength also uses the figure of the Nazi to praise the spirit of Judaism that is foreign to all military or political desire for power, and to draw a distinction between it and the spirit of Nazism. 'What is Yiddish: *Mittelhochdeutsch* (middle high German). When I speak and hear Yid-dish, I feel the warm and wild vitality that sparkled in my ancestors in those lost Middle Ages, before we became fossilized and got lost in the dark forest.'[29] The

---

28. Dalia Karpel, Interview with David Grossman, *Ha'ir*, 10 January 1986 (Hebrew).
29. Y. Sobol, *Ghetto* (Tel Aviv: Or Am, 1992 [1984]), 65 (Hebrew).

Hebrew-speaking Nazi is supposed to save the Jewish library after the end of the destruction of the ghetto; he is a combination of uninhibited cruelty and admiration for the Jewish spirit which is expressed in the ability of the few Jews of the ghetto to depict their lives, which are coming to a final end, in an artistic and theatrical way.

5. *The Distribution of Evil*

The attempts to make the figure of Nazi evil a complicated one that started with Katzetnik, intensified in the 1980s. The story of a Nazi who fell in love with a Jewish girl, hid her in his home, and took care of her while endangering himself,[30] or the story about the naive wife of the commander of a concentration camp who did not know anything about the extermination of Jews during the war,[31] would have been less possible previously. As was noted, however, even before the 1980s there were important literary attempts to place evil in the 'grey zone', especially by distributing it to different perpetrators. For example, books dealing with the Holocaust not only displayed the crimes of the German people toward the Jews, they also described the cruelty and inhumanity of the Jewish ghetto guards, and especially the Jewish kapos in the concentration camps. Katzetnik's portrays the cruelty of the kapo Fruchtbaum at Auschwitz as being no lesser than the evil of the Ukrainians or Germans. In addition, the emphasis on the reduction of the prisoners in the camps almost to the state of animals, the near loss of their humanity, is supposed to emphasize the different nature of the hero of the story, which the reality had not managed to destroy. However, this description also strengthens the impression that the boundary between human and inhuman evil is not stable. Just as the Germans sometimes showed compassion, their victims might easily turn into animals operating solely according to the survival instinct.

The question of the complexity of the evil figure exceeds loyalty to historical truth. It is a matter of answering an esthetic need, as the writer A.B. Yehoshua put it:

> Literature and art work amazingly well in complicated situations where the decisions between black and white are not unambiguous. Real human situations are those where the moral decisions are much more subtle. In the Holocaust there was something extremely pathetic in the confrontation between two poles. This situation created a sort of automatic identification… It is interesting that works which dealt with the conflict within each side, and not with that between them, had greater aesthetic strength, as here the decisions were much more complicated.[32]

The works of Aharon Applefeld are an example of an esthetic manner of dealing with situations, which do not allow clear moral judgement. He has devoted a large

---

30. N. Semel, 'A Trip to Two Berlins', in *eadem*, *A Hat of Glass* (Tel Aviv: Sifriat Poalim, 1988), 145–72 (Hebrew).

31. S. Liebrecht, 'Strawberry's Girl', in *eadem*, *Chinese I Talk to You* (Jerusalem: Keter, 1993), 61–82 (Hebrew).

32. A.B. Yehoshua, *The Wall and the Mountain: The Extra-Literary Reality of the Writer in Israel* (Tel Aviv: Zmora Bitan, 1989), 138 (Hebrew).

part of his works to a description of Holocaust survivors, but has chosen to avoid touching directly upon the hard core of the issue, the ghettoes and concentration camps. There are no German or Ukrainian murderers in his stories. At the same time the survivors, who flee from the Germans or hide from them, are depicted as having a mental handicap that cannot be explained outside the context of the Holocaust. In the story that opens his first book, *Smoke*,[33] he tells about three Jews who managed to escape to the forest. The oldest one and initiator of their actions kills a man and his son whom they found in the forest, in order to rob them of clothes and food. At the end of the story, after the oldest one is wounded, the other two abandon him and run off in different directions. Evil may appear in less dramatic forms, in stories where people betray each other, abandon each other, cheat, and ignore the suffering of others, without the narrator judging their actions or discussing their motives. In stories which lack a definitive closure, it is impossible to decide if the stories express identification or criticism. This decision has been placed in the hands of the reader; it is not at all self-evident within a system of values, including the ability to distinguish between right and wrong, that has been undermined.

6. *Sideshadowing and Parody*

Writing about the Holocaust from an artistic or esthetic perspective is a way of exposing aspects that are incompatible with reports and researches by historians, or with the ideology of a national school system that seeks to further the ideal of heroism and revolt in the Holocaust. A child's perspective is another suitable way to describe evil imaginatively, while paying attention to what might be seen as trivial. In 1956 the writer Uri Orlev, better known for his writing for teenagers, published a novel called *Lead Soldiers,* that was based on his experiences in Poland during the war. The narrator is a nine-year-old boy, who, together with his younger brother, is hidden by Poles until they are discovered and taken to Bergen-Belsen toward the end of the war. The childish perspective is capable of seeing the death of the family members in a legendary space where the dead continue to watch the living. It can be deeply impressed by the colors of the sunset over the deportation site, [34] and can even describe humorously the horribly thin people seen on the other side of the fence at Bergen-Belsen. The blunting of the sharp edge of the events and the creation of a correcting stratum (esthetically, fantastically) allow Orlev, among other things, to achieve a childish, fearless view of evil:

> Zofia held Yurek's arm and walked slowly forward. The burden of fear and tension closed her throat. She stood on the tips of her toes and peered past the Germans separating the people, those to life and those to death. Who are they?, she thought. What did they earlier, before the war? What did they learn in school? Do they love their girls? Zofia pressed hard on her son's hand. 'What is, Mother?' 'Nothing, my son. You're a good boy…' '*Rechts*' the soldier screamed at her. To

---

33. A. Appelfeld, *Smoke* (Jerusalem: Akhshav, 1962) (Hebrew)
34. U. Orlev, *Lead Soldiers* (Jerusalem: Keter, 1989 [1956]), 70 (Hebrew).

the right! Zofia pulled Yurek to the left. The soldier pushed her aside. 'To the right! Are you deaf, or what?' From under the rim of his iron helmet the blue eyes of a child peered at her.[35]

Michael Bernstein has called this sort of narrative 'sideshadowing'. Opposing any sort of writing (historical or literary) which focuses on the larger developments with which deterministic or teleological relationships are developed, Bernstein has proposed focusing on the range of buried possibilities in a moment of life divorced from its context, without taking the end of the process into account.

> ...sideshadowing champions the incommensurability of the concrete moment and refuses the tyranny of all synthetic master-schemes: it rejects the conviction that a particular code, law, or pattern exists, waiting to be uncovered beneath the heterogeneity of human existence. Instead of the global regularities that so many intellectual and spiritual movements claim to reveal, sideshadowing stresses the significance of random, haphazard, and inassimilable contingencies, and instead of the power of a system to uncover an otherwise unfathomable truth, it expresses the ever-changing nature of that truth and the absence of any predictive certainties in human affairs.[36]

Orlev describes an event where Jews are forced into trains against their will, while concentrating on both painful external events and the conscious space of the figures that seem to preserve full autonomy. He elaborates on the childish or civilian side of the soldier at the very moment that he is pushing the child and his mother. This perspective requires distance from the conventional hegemonic plot of the war between good and evil and also distance from the pathos that normally eliminates refinement, variety, humor, and the ability to observe, in short – art.

Sideshadowing is a somewhat simplistic concept, as it assumes that fullness is hidden in a pastless and futureless present, one that is not fettered by ideological and literary narratives. It is appropriate to the choice of a childish perspective which explains its innocence, its lack of awareness of a chain of preceding commentaries and narratives, and its seemingly fresh perspective of reality. In Grossman's *See Under – Love*,[37] the first chapter describes the attempts of a nine-year-old boy to discover the untold past of his parents during the Holocaust. The story progresses in a circle around that which cannot be understood, with the circle consisting of different and ridiculous versions of the metaphor of 'the Nazi animal', a common expression in discussions of the Holocaust in the 1950s and 1960s. The childish perspective is used as a method of examining the figure of parents locked within their silence about the Holocaust, but it is, primarily, a parodying view of the known ways of commentary that are available and their lack of validity in the case of events such as the Holocaust.

Baudrillard, in his *Simulacres et Simulation,* notes the amnesia and lack of reality of the Holocaust, which stem not from a lack of knowledge but, paradoxi-

---

35. Orlev, *Lead Soldiers*, 67.

36. M. Bernstein, *Foregone Conclusions – Against Apocalyptic History* (Berkeley, CA: California University Press, 1994), 4.

37. D. Grossman, *See Under – Love* (Tel Aviv: Hakkibutz Hameuchad, 1987) (Hebrew).

cally, from an inflation of knowledge and the vast number of representations of the Holocaust. He distinguishes between the 'artificial memory' that surrounds us (through mass media, especially television) and the 'real memory' that is expunged by the former and forgotten.[38] This sort of sensitivity to the tension between memory that is socially constructed and a different memory that is already beyond our reach, is common to writers of the 1980s. Parody is a way of expressing doubt about the validity of memory, and in this context evil is also represented in a parodying way:

> They forced her to bathe naked before the soldiers. They pushed her into the gas chamber but took her out at the last moment, before they closed the doors on her. They whipped her back with a whip made of iron wire with braided leather on it; she was given twenty-five strokes and made to count them aloud, and when she made a mistake they started over. They ordered her '*Muetzen ab und muetzen auf!*', and thus for hours she had to take off and put on her ragged hat again and again. They made a circle around her and stabbed her. They held onto her various parts and cut them from her body living and painfully. They cut her hair and pulled out one of her teeth with no anesthetic, with no warning. They brought many bottles of medicine from the camp clinic and ordered her to drink them all... They wrapped a strangulation cord around her neck and started to slowly pull her up, until they hung her. They injected gasoline into her heart... Between tortures Naomi joined the camp underground. She learned to use weapons.[39]

In his article on this book, which had been attacked because of its amoral stance, Yigal Schwarz wrote that '[the author] does not directly discuss the Holocaust but rather a large number of texts which did indeed try to describe evil, to imagine, to give it form, and even to give reasons for it'.[40] From this point of view Itamar Levi's book seems to Schwarz to be a parody of the norms of writing that had developed in Hebrew literature. This parody is meant to indicate their melodramatic rhetoric and the fact that they prevent understanding instead of serving it. Is there 'real' memory, and in what language can it be expressed – these are unanswerable questions. This change shows to what extent the Holocaust has evolved from being a close and immediate experience to a topic through which one can learn, not about a historical event, but rather about the narrative mechanisms that construct Israeli society even today. Levi's book seeks to demonstrate, *inter alia*, what the Israeli knows about the Holocaust. Its trivialization is not only an intentional esthetic distortion; it reflects a rather dreary cultural reality:

> What do our children know about their past? Demjanjuk is a prisoner of Zion. Mordechai Anilevich is a Jewish sculptor, he is the man who caught Eichmann. Eichmann himself, according to our children, is a doctor who experimented on the Jewish race. Treblinka is the capital of the Nazis. The swastika is a Christian symbol... 'Yad Vashem' is a neighborhood in Jerusalem. Janusz Korczak is a Nazi writer. The Final Solution is the creation of the State of Israel.[41]

38. J. Baudrillard, *Simulacres et Simulation* (Paris: Galilee, 1981), 77–80.
39. I. Levi, *The Legend of the Sad Lakes* (Jerusalem: Keter, 1989), 28–29 (Hebrew).
40. Y. Schwarz, 'Utterly Moral Mission', *Efes Shtayim* 1 (1992), 122 (Hebrew).
41. Levi, *Legend of the Sad Lakes*, 59–60.

The interest young Israelis show in visiting the death camps in Poland, the Ministry of Education orientation of the trips as the climax of learning about the Holocaust, and the many books published on the topic, are phenomena that began in the late 1980s. The attraction to the actual place of extermination and an unwillingness to accept museum-like replacements to a great extent parallel the ways in which recent Israeli literature approaches the Holocaust. These move between two poles: documentation and preservation of clear realistic boundaries of dealing with the subject, on the one hand, and contending with the topic of the Holocaust through imagination and fantasy, on the other. The search for the actual place, as well as the inability of the written word to impart a definite form to what happened and transmit it as a tradition, have given birth to the cathartic trip to the memorial sites in Poland. However, this short catharsis, which is usually accompanied by an unequivocal Zionist message, successfully hides the emptiness of the site, the fact that evil cannot be seen or visually actualized. The tension between what we know about the place and what can be seen there has inspired most of the books about these trips that have been written in recent years.

The pastoral landscape along the narrow road to Treblinka provided Yehudit Hendel (in *By Quiet Villages*)[42] with the background for an imaginary recreation of history in which trains full of Jews all follow the same route. The death camp, which was completely destroyed before the end of the war, turns out to be a place which must be imagined, where signs in several languages, tapes, and tour guides are supposed to tell its history. The paradoxical turning to this place and the discovery that it does not fill the role of witness built from the shattered and broken memories and stories of others, from heterogeneous and often conflicting representations – all of these are shown in a remarkable way in the literature of the trips to Poland. The first such book, in this case of a trip to Germany, was *Not from Now, Not from Here* by Yehuda Amihai.[43] The hero of the story, a veteran of the Israeli War of Independence, goes to his birthplace in Germany to wreak revenge for Ruth, his childhood love, who was murdered in the Holocaust. This hero, who plans his capture of the city and the finding of the guilty as if it was a military operation, discovers that revenge is impossible and evil cannot be identified. The grotesque situations which he encounters make it clear how dubious are the discourse of retaliation and the ability to judge and incriminate: ' "Do you see this young man?", said the hero, "he is the son of one of the most important Nazis of Weinburg. His father ran away to another country and his son is black-haired, nervous, and resembles a young Jewish intellectual".'[44] The knowledge of the past that the Israeli returning to Germany has acquired forces him to sort people 'into SS and SA companies. And this is a Gestapo agent. And this one, the bald one, was a guard in a concentration camp, and the fat, satisfied one was responsible for the fire in the crematoria so that it wouldn't go out.'[45] However, this sorting is not conducted so that he can implement the revenge he has so wanted, but rather to

42.   Y. Hendel, *By Quiet Villages* (Tel Aviv: Hakkibutz Hameuchad, 1987) (Hebrew).
43.   Jerusalem and Tel Aviv: Schocken Books, 1963 (Hebrew).
44.   Amihai, *Not from Now*, 187.
45.   Amihai, *Not from Now*, 591.

mark evil as missing or absent. As such, he must contend with it in a sober, inward way, and not in a judgemental or power-hungry fashion.

7. Conclusion

Sidra Ezrahi has drawn an important distinction between two different approaches to Auschwitz. The first, static approach represents it as a hermetically sealed place, destroying even the tools of measurement and recovery, and above all the ability to imagine life beyond it. The second, dynamic approach relates to the recreation of Auschwitz as an opportunity to maintain constant negotiation with history. For Ezrahi, the past changes when it comes to terms with the present by the literary conventions used to represent it.[46]

Independent of the periodization of Israeli Holocaust literature and the change in literary norms that it underwent, the representation of evil in Israeli fiction can be located in 'the grey zone'. It thereby expresses its opposition to stereotypes of Nazi evil, shows a lack of confidence in the static approach that separates unequivocally between opposites such as inside and outside, human and inhuman, Germans and Jews, and prefers the dynamic approach that identifies complexity with ambiguity. The refusal to give evil a mythological, demonic dimension, as well as the lack of interest in any discourse of revenge, are derived from a stance that strives for a sober way of dealing with the burden of memory, as part of a process of developing post-Holocaust identity. The dynamic approach rejects every safe perspective for making any essential distinction between criminals and their victims – a perspective that does not allow room for reversal, change, surprise which undermines every solid distinction.

By refraining from contending with evil and its cultural and social origins, Israeli literature has limited itself to the immediate contact between the Nazis and their Jewish victims. The organization of evil, its ideology, rhetoric, and methods of operation, the attraction to the leader figure – these are topics that were not of interest to Israeli fiction.

The absence of the multidimensional reality of Nazi evil signifies a deep structure or tendency in Israeli literature, namely, that of transforming national and historical conflicts into psychological ones. In this context I would like to mention another, similar transformation: that of the figure of the Arab in Hebrew fiction. Arabs, just like Germans, lose their national identity by being turned into a complex and ambivalent mirror, reflecting the tension between humanistic and nationalistic perspectives within the Israeli search for identity.

The overall approach willing to identify 'grey zones' indicates distance from evil, but not, at the same time, distance from the trauma. I am using the overworked term 'trauma' as a linguistic-mental state. Lawrence Langer[47] has analyzed the authentic report which Holocaust survivors have given of their experiences as a traumatic expression, one which was not capable of placing what was told within

---

46. S. Ezrahi, 'Representing Auschwitz', *History and Memory* 7.2 (Winter 1996), 122–23.

47. L. Langer, *Holocaust Testimonies: The Ruins of Memory* (New Haven and London: Yale University Press, 1991).

the chronological order and context of their lives. This expression lacks the perspective of distance and the ability to overcome fear and shock. The need to document and narrate becomes, mainly in the case of authors who were not themselves Holocaust survivors, an urgent need to recreate the Holocaust by demonstrating the inability to recover from its heritage, as a private and familial experience. The attention of the reader is normally split between the gruesome, shadowy past in the background, and the painful present of Holocaust survivors that is ruined either by repression or by insanity. To modern Israeli writers, historical evils are less important than their present psychological repercussions. In this framework the absence or marginality of a historically accurate description of evil in fiction does not exclude the fact that trauma remains a crucial factor in post-Holocaust experience, beyond any therapeutic perspective.[48]

48.   Gilead Morag came to a similar conclusion: 'The incorporation of fantastic elements into Israeli works of Holocaust fiction acknowledges the impossibility of an authentic representation of the concentration experience. At the same time, the fantastic enables an authentic response to this experience, which, although unrepresentable, continues to be powerfully present in the lives of Jews, including those who were not even born at the time.' G. Morag, 'Breaking Silence: Israel's Fantastic Fiction of the Holocaust', in A. Mintz (ed.), *The Boom in Contemporary Israeli Fiction* (Hanover, NH and London: Brandeis University Press, 1997), 163.

BIBLIOGRAPHY

Adorno, Theodor, 'Commitment', in *idem*, *Notes to Literature*, II (trans. S. Weber Nicholsen; New York: Columbia University Press 1992), 76–94.

—*Minima Moralia; Reflections from Damaged Life* (trans. E.F. Jephcott; London: Verso, 1978).

Albrektson, B., 'The Background and Origin of the Theology of Lamentations', *Studies in the Text and Theology of the Book of Lamentations* (Studia Theologica Lundensia, 21; Lund: C.W.K. Gleerup, 1963), pp. 214–39.

Alexander, P.S., 'Physiognomy, Initiation, and Rank in the Qumran Community', in P. Schäfer (ed.), *Geschichte-Tradition-Reflexion: Festschrift für Martin Hengel zum 70. Geburstag* (Tübingen: Mohr–Siebeck, 1996), I, 385.

Alt, K., *Weltflucht und Weltbejahung: Zur Frage des Dualismus bei Plutarch, Numenios, Plotin* (Abhandlungen der Akademie der Wissenschaften und der Literatur. Geistes- und Sozialwissenschaftliche Klasse zu Mainz 1993, 8; Stuttgart: Franz Steiner Verlag, 1993).

Alterman, Nathan, 'Dark Time's Eyes', in *idem*, *In the Circle* (Tel Aviv: Hakkibutz Hameuchad, 1975 [1964]), 87–89 (Hebrew).

Amihai, Yehuda, *Not from Now, Not from Here* (Jerusalem and Tel Aviv: Schocken Books, 1963).

Anders, G., *Die Antiquiertheit des Menschen*. II. *Über die Zerstörung des Lebens im Zeitalter der dritten industriellen Revolution* (Munich: Beck, 1986).

Appelfeld, Aharon, *Smoke* (Jerusalem: Akhshav, 1962) (Hebrew).

Aquinas, Thomas, *Summa theologiae* (Cambridge: Cambridge University Press, 1964).

Arendt, H., *Eichmann in Jerusalem: A Report on the Banality of Evil* (New York: Penguin Books, 1977 [1963]).

—*Elemente und Ursprünge totaler Herrschaft*: *Antisemitismus, Imperialismus, totale Herrschaft* (Munich and Zürich: Piper, 6th edn, 1998).

—*The Human Condition* (Garden City, NY: Doubleday; Anchor Books, 1959).

—*The Origins of Totalitarianism* (New York: Harcourt, Brace & World, 1951).

—*Vita activa oder Vom tätigen Leben* (Munich: Piper, 10th edn, 1998).

Aristotle, *Nicomachean Ethics* (Cambridge: Cambridge University Press, 2000).

Armstrong, A.H., 'Plotinus', in A.H. Armstrong (ed.), *The Cambridge History of Later Greek and Early Medieval Philosophy* (Cambridge: Cambridge University Press, 1970), 193–268.

Assmann, Jan, *Ma'at. Gerechtigkeit und Unsterblichkeit im Alten Ägypten* (Munich: Beck, 1990).

Attridge, H., and J. Strugnell, '369. 4QPrayer of Enosh', *Qumran Cave 4.VIII. Parabiblical Texts, Part H. 1* (DJD, 13; Oxford: Clarendon Press, 1994), 353–56.

Augustinus, A., *Confessiones*, ed. L. Verheijen (CChrSL, 27; Tournhout: Brepols, 1981).

—*Contra adversarium legis et prophetarum* (ed. K.-D. Daur; CChrSL, 49; Turnhout: Brepols, 1985).

—*Contra epistulam Manichaei* (ed. R. Jolivet and M. Jourjon; Bibliothèque Augustinienne, 17; Paris: Desclée de Brouwer, 1961).

—*Contra Faustum* (ed. J. Zycha; CSEL, 25/1; Vienna: Tempski, 1891).

—*Contra Felicem* (ed. J. Zycha; CSEL, 25/2; Vienna: Tempski, 1892).

—*Contra secundam Juliani responsionem imperfectum Opus* (ed. J.-P. Migne; PL, 45; Paris, 1865).

—*De beata vita. La vie heureuse* (ed. J. Doignon; Bibliothèque Augustinienne, 4/1; Paris: Desclée de Brouwer, 1986).

—*De civitate Dei* (ed. B. Dombart and A. Kalb; CChrSL, 47, 48; Turnhout: Brepols, 1955).

—*De diversis quaestionibus ad Simplicianum* (ed. A. Mutzenbecher; CChrSL, 44; Turnhout: Brepols, 1970).

—*De duabus animabus* (ed. J. Zycha; CSEL, 25/1; Vienna: Hölder-Pichler-Tempsky, 1891).

—*De genesi ad litteram* (ed. J. Zycha; CSEL, 28,1; Vienna: Hölder-Pichler-Tempsky, 1884).

—*De moribus ecclesiae catholicae et de moribus Manichaeorum* (ed. J.B. Bauer; CSEL, 90; Vienna: Hölder-Pichler-Tempsky, 1992).

—*De natura boni* (ed. J. Zycha; CSEL, 25/2; Vienna: Hölder-Pichler-Tempsky, 1892).

—*Enarrationes in Psalmos* (ed. E. Dekkers and J. Fraipont; CChrSL, 39.40; Turnhout: Brepols, 1956).

—*Enchiridion ad Laurentium de fide et spe et caritat* (ed. E. Evans; CChrSL, 46; Turnhout: Brepols, 1969).

—*Sermones* (ed. J.-P. Migne; PL, 38; Paris, 1845).

—*Tractatus in Iohannis Evangelium* (ed. M.-F. Berrouard; Bibliothèque Augustinienne, 72; Paris: Desclée de Brouwer, 1977).

Babut, J.-M., 'Que son sang soit sur sa tête!', *VT* 36 (1986), 474–80.

Baier, K., *The Moral Point of View* (Ithaca, NY: Cornell University Press, 1958).

Balentine, S.E., *The Hidden God: The Hiding of the Face of God in the Old Testament* (Oxford: Oxford University Press, 1983).

Barth, H.-M., *Der Teufel und Jesus Christus in der Theologie Martin Luthers* (FKDG, 19; Göttingen: Vandenhoeck & Ruprecht, 1969).

—'Zur inneren Entwicklung von Luthers Teufelsglauben', *KD* 13 (1967), 201–11.

Barth, K., *Kirchliche Dogmatik* II/1 (Zollikon–Zürich: Evangelischer Verlag, 1940).

—*Kirchliche Dogmatik* III/3 (Zollikon–Zürich: Evangelischer Verlag, 1950).

Barton, John, 'Canon and Old Testament Interpretation', in Edward Ball (ed.), *In Search of True Wisdom: Essays in Old Testament Interpretation in Honour of Ronald E. Clements* (JSOTSup, 300; Sheffield: Sheffield Academic Press, 1999), 37–52.

Baudelaire, Ch., *Les fleurs du mal* (ed. J. Delabroy; Paris: Poulet-Malassis et de Broise, 1986 [1857]).

Baudrillard, Jean, *Simulacres et Simulation* (Paris: Galilee, 1981).

Baumgarten, J.M., '4Q503 (Daily Prayers) and the Lunar Calendar', *RevQ* 12 (1987), 399–407.

—*Qumran Cave 4.XIII: The Damascus Document (4Q266–273)* (DJD, 18; Oxford: Clarendon Press, 1996).

Becking, B., *Een magisch ritueel in jahwistisch perspektief* (Utrechtse theologische reeks, 17; Utrecht: Faculteit der Godgeleerdheid, Rijksuniversiteit Utrecht, 1992).

Bentham, J., *An Introduction to the Principles of Morals and Legislation* (ed. J.H. Burns and H.L.A. Hart; rev. edn, ed. F. Rosen; Oxford: Oxford University Press, 1996 [1789]).

Berkovitz, E., 'Das Verbergen Gottes', in M. Brocke and H. Jochum (eds.), *Wolkensäule und Feuerschein: Jüdische Theologie des Holocaust* (Gütersloh: Kaiser, 1993).

Berlin, A., *Lamentations: A Commentary* (OTL; Louisville, KY, and London: Westminster/ John Knox Press, 2002).

Bernstein, Michael A., *Foregone Conclusions – Against Apocalyptic History* (Berkeley, CA: California University Press, 1994).

Beutel, A., *Im Anfang war das Wort: Studien zu Luthers Sprachverständnis* (Tübingen: Mohr, 1991).

Biddle, M., 'The Figure of Lady Jerusalem: Identification, Deification, and Personification of Cities in the Ancient Near East', in K.L. Younger, Jr, *et al.* (eds.), *Scripture in Context 4: The Biblical Canon in Comparative Perspective* (Lewiston, NY: Edwin Mellen Press, 1991), 173–94.

Birnbaum, D., *God and Evil* (Hoboken, NJ: Ktav, 1989).

Bogaert, Pierre-Maurice, 'Versions, ancient (Latin)', *ABD* 6, 799–803.

Bonhoeffer, D., *Ethik* (ed. H.E. Tödt *et al.*; Munich: Christian Kaiser, 1992).

Bornkamm, H., *Martin Luther in der Mitte seines Lebens: Das Jahrzehnt zwischen dem Wormser und dem Augsburger Reichstag* (Göttingen: Vandenhoeck & Ruprecht, 1979).

Bouzard, Jr, W.C., *We Have Heard with Our Ears, O God: Sources of the Communal Lament in the Psalms* (SBLDS, 159; Atlanta: Scholars Press, 1997).

Briggs, C.A., and E.G. Briggs, *A Critical and Exegetical Commentary on the Book of Psalms* (ICC; Edinburgh: T. & T. Clark, 1906–1907).

Bright, J., *Jeremiah* (AB; Garden City, NY: Doubleday, 1965).

Brown, F., S.R. Driver and C.A. Briggs, *Hebrew and English Dictionary of the Old Testament* (Oxford: Clarendon Press, 1966).

Brunner, H., 'Seth und Apophis – Gegengötter im ägyptischen Pantheon?', *Saeculum* 34 (1983), 226–34.

Buber, M., 'Right and Wrong: An Interpretation of Some Psalms', in *Darko shel Mikra* (Jerusalem: The Bialik Institute, 1978), 139–62 (Hebrew).

—*Torat Haneviim* (Tel Aviv: Bialik Institute and Dvir, 1950) (Hebrew).

Cagni, L., *The Poem of Erra* (Sources from the Ancient Near East, 1/3; Malibu: Undena, 1977).

Carroll, R.P., *Jeremiah* (OTL; London: SCM Press, 1986).

Cassuto, U., 'Nahash' (EB; Jerusalem: The Bialik Institute, 1968), V, 823–24 (Hebrew).

—'Serpent in Paradise' (EB; Jerusalem: The Bialik Institute, 1968), V, 823–25 (Hebrew).

Chadwick, H., *Augustine* (Oxford: Oxford University Press, 1986).

Charlesworth, J.H., 'A Critical Comparison of the Dualism in 1QS 3.13–4.26 and the "Dualism" Contained in the Gospel of John', in *idem* (ed.), *John and Qumran* (London: Geoffrey Chapman, 1971), 76–106.

Chazon, E., '444. 4QIncantation', in *idem et al.*, *Qumran Cave 4.XX* (DJD, 29; Oxford: Clarendon Press, 1999), 367–78.

Childs, B.S., *Biblical Theology of the Old and New Testaments* (London: SCM Press, 1992).

—*Introduction to the Old Testament as Scripture* (Philadelphia: Fortress Press; London: SCM Press, 1979).

—*Old Testament Theology in a Canonical Context* (London: SCM Press, 1985).

Cohen, C., 'The "Widowed" City', *JANESCU* 5 (*The Gaster Festschrift*; 1973), 75–81.

Cohen, M.E., *The Canonical Lamentations of Ancient Mesopotamia* (2 vols.; Potomac, MD: Capital Decisions Limited, 1988).

Cohn, G.H., *Studies in the Five Scrolls: The Scroll of Lamentations* (Jerusalem: Ministry of Education, 1975), 52–56 (Hebrew).

Collins, J.J., 'The Origin of Evil in Apocalyptic Literature and the Dead Sea Scrolls', in J. Emerton (ed.), *Congress Volume Paris 1992* (VTSup, 61; Leiden: E.J. Brill, 1995), 25–38.

Colpe, C., and W. Schmidt-Biggemann (ed.), *Das Böse. Eine historische Phänomenologie des Unerklärlichen* (Frankfurt a.M.: Suhrkamp, 1993).

Considine, P., 'The Theme of Divine Wrath in Ancient Mediterranean Literature', *Studi micenei ed egeo-anatolici* 8 (1969), 85–159.

Cook, Johann *The Septuagint of Proverbs: Jewish and/or Hellenistic Proverbs?* (VTSup, 69; Leiden: E.J. Brill, 1997).

Cooper, A., 'The Message of Lamentations', *JANESCU* 28 (2001), 1–18.

Cooper, J.S., *The Curse of Agade* (Baltimore and London: The Johns Hopkins University Press, 1983).

Cornill, D.C.H., *Das Buch Jeremia* (Leipzig: Tauchnitz, 1905).

Courcelle, P., 'Luther interprète des Confessions de Saint Augustin', *RHPR* 39 (1959), 235–50.

—*Recherches sur les confessions de Saint Augustin* (Paris: de Boccard, 1968).

Cress, D.A., 'Augustine's Privation Account of Evil. A Defense', *Augustinian Studies* 20 (1989), 109–128.

Dahood, M., 'Ugaritic-Hebrew Parallel Pairs', in L.R. Fisher (ed.), *Ras Shamra Parallels*, 1 (AnOr, 49; Rome: Pontifical Biblical Institute, 1972), 323–24.

Daiches, S., 'Zu II. Kön. IV, 34', *OLZ* 11 (1908), 492–93.

Dan, J., *'Al haQedusha* (Jerusalem, 1997).

—' "No Evil Descends from Heaven" ', in B.D. Cooperman (ed.), *Jewish Thought in the Sixteenth Century* (Cambridge, MA, 1983), 89–105.

—'Samael, Lilith and the Concept of Evil in Early Kabbala', *AJSReview* 5 (1980), 17–40.

Debus, J., *Die Sünde Jerobeams* (FRLANT, 93; Göttingen: Vandenhoeck & Ruprecht, 1967).

Delicostopoulos, A., 'Major Greek Translations of the Bible', in J. Krašovec (ed.), *Interpretation of the Bible. Interpretation der Bibel. Interprétation de la Bible. Interpretacija Svetega Pisma.* (Lubljana: Slovenska adademija znanosti in umetnosti; Sheffield: Sheffield Academic Press, 1998), 297–316.

Delius, H.-U., *Augustin als Quelle Luthers: Eine Materialsammlung* (Berlin: Evangelische Verlagsanstalt, 1984).

Des Pres, T., *The Survivor: An Anatomy of Life in the Death Camps* (New York: Oxford University Press, 1976).

Dietrich, W., and Chr. Link, *Die dunklen Seiten Gottes* (2 vols.; Neukirchen–Vluyn: Neukirchener Verlag, 2000).

Dimant, D., 'Dualism in Qumran: New Perspectives', in J.H. Charlesworth (ed.), *Caves of Enlightenment* (North Richland Hills: Bibal Press, 1998), 55–73.

—'The Pesher on the Periods', *IOS* 9 (1979), 77–102.

Dobbs-Allsopp, F.W., 'Darwinism, Genre Theory, and City Laments', *JAOS* 120 (2000), 625–30.

—*Lamentations* (Interpretation; Louisville, KY: John Knox Press, 2002).

—'Linguistic Evidence for the Date of Lamentations', *JANESCU* 26 (1998), 1–36.

—'Rethinking Historical Criticism', *BibInt* 7 (1999), 235–71.

—'Tragedy, Tradition, and Theology in the Book of Lamentations', *JSOT* 74 (1997), 29–60.

—*Weep, O Daughter of Zion: A Study of the City-Lament Genre in the Hebrew Bible* (BibOr, 44; Rome: Pontifical Biblical Institute, 1993).

Doerne, M., 'Gottes Ehre am gebundenen Willen. Evangelische Grundlagen und theologische Spitzensätze in De servo arbitrio', *Luther-Jahrbuch* 20 (Weimar: Böhlau, 1938), 45–92.

Dohmen, C., and D. Rick, 'רעע', *ThWAT* VII (Stuttgart/Berlin/Cologne: W. Kohlhammer, 1993), 582–612.

Dressler, B.. 'Vom Protest gegen das Böse zum Bösen als Protestmedium. Wie Jugendliche mit dem Bösen spielen', in *Das Böse* (Glaube und Leben, 12; Göttingen: Vandenhoeck & Ruprecht, 1997), 57–71.

Driver S.R., and G.B. Gray, *The Book of Job* (ICC; Edinburgh: T. & T. Clark, 1921).

Duhaime, J., 'Dualistic Reworking in the Scrolls from Qumran', *CBQ* 49 (1987), 32–56.

Duhm, B., *Das Buch Jesaia* (HAT; Göttingen: Vandenhoeck & Ruprecht, 4th edn, 1922).

—*Jeremia* (KHAT; Tübingen–Leipzig: J.C.B. Mohr [Paul Siebeck], 1901).

—*Die Psalmen erklart* (KHAT, 14; Tübingen: J.C.B. Mohr, 2nd edn, 1922).

Ebeling, G., *Luther: Einführung in sein Denken* (Tübingen: Mohr, 1964).

—*Lutherstudien* (vol. 2. Disputatio de homine. Part 3. Die theologische Definition des Menschen: Kommentar zu These 20–40; Tübingen: Mohr, 1989).

Ehrlich, A.B., *Mikrâ Ki-Pheschutô* (repr.; New York: Ktav, 1969) (Hebrew).

Eliade, M., *Patterns in Comparative Religion* (Lincoln, NE, and London: University of Nebraska, 1996).

Emmendörffer, M., *Der ferne Gott: Eine Untersuchung der alttestamentlichen Volksklagelieder vor dem Hintergrund der mesopotamischen Literatur* (Forschungen zum Alten Testament, 21; Tübingen: Mohr Siebeck, 1998).

Eph'al, I., *Siege and its Ancient Near Eastern Manifestations* (Jerusalem: Magnes Press, 1996) (Hebrew).

Evans, G.R., *Augustine on Evil* (Cambridge: Cambridge University Press, 1982).

Ezrahi, Sidra DeKoven, 'Representing Auschwitz', *History and Memory* 7.2 (1996), 121–55.

Fahlgren, K.H., *ṣᵉdaqā nahestehende und entgegengesetzte Begriffe im Alten Testament* (Uppsala: Almquist & Wiksell, 1932)= *idem*, 'Die Gegensätze von *ṣᵉdaqā* im Alten Testament', in K. Koch (ed.), *Um das Prinzip der Vergeltung in Religion und Recht des Alten Testaments* (WdF, 125; Darmstadt: Wissenschaftliche Buchgesellschaft, 1972), 87–129.

Falk, D.K., *Daily, Sabbath, and Festival Prayers in the Dead Sea Scrolls* (STDJ, 27; Leiden: E.J. Brill, 1998).

Farber-Ginat, A., ' "The Shell Precedes the Fruit" – On the Origin of Metaphysical Evil in Early Kabbalistic Thought' [Hebrew], *Eshel Be'er Sheva* 4 (1996), 118–42.

Feldman, Y., 'Whose Story Is It, Anyway? Ideology and Pschology in the Representation of the Shoah in Israeli Literature', in Saul Friedlander (ed.), *Probing the Limits of Representation: Nazism and the Final Solution* (Cambridge, MA: Harvard University Press), 223–39.

Fensham, F.C., 'A Possible Origin of the Concept of the Day of the Lord', *Biblical Essays: Die Oud Testamentiese Werkgemeenskap in Suid Afrika* (Potchefstroom: Rege-Pers Beparte, 1966), 90–97.

Ferris, Jr, P.W., *The Genre of Communal Lament in the Bible and the Ancient Near East* (SBLDS, 127; Atlanta: Scholars Press, 1992).

Fierer, Ruth, *Agents of Holocaust Lesson* (Tel Aviv: Hakkibutz Hameuchad, 1989) (Hebrew).

Fitzmyer, J.A., *The Aramaic Inscriptions of Sefire* (BibOr, 19; Rome: Pontifical Biblical Institute, 1967).

Frame, G., 'A Siege Document from Babylon Dating to 649 B.C.', *JCS* 51 (1999), 101–106.

Fredriksson, H., *Jahwe als Krieger: Studien zum alttestamentlichen Gottesbild* (Lund: C.W.K. Gleerup, 1945).

Freedman, D.H., 'Man as the Subject of the Theogony in the Lurianic Cabala' (Dissertation, University College London, 2001).

Frei, J., 'Different Patterns of Dualistic Thought in the Qumran Library. Reflections on their Background and History', in M. Bernstein *et al.* (eds.), *Legal Texts and Legal Issues* (STDJ, 23; Leiden: E.J. Brill, 1997), 275–335.

Frey, C., *Die Theologie Karl Barths: Eine Einführung* ([Waltrop: Hartmut Spenner] Frankfurt a. M.: Athenäum, 1994).

Friedlander, Saul, 'Roundtable Discussion', in B. Lang (ed.), *Writing and the Holocaust*, (New York: Holmes and Meier, 1988), 287–89.

García Martínez, F., 'Encore l'Apocalyptique', *JSJ* 17 (1987), 231.

García Martínez, F., and W.G.E. Watson, *The Dead Sea Scrolls Translated* (Leiden: E.J. Brill, 1994).

Gammie, J.G., 'Sapiential and Ethical Dualism in Jewish Wisdom and Apocalyptic Literature', *JBL* 93 (1974), 356–85.

Gerstenberger, E.S., *Psalms, Part 2, and Lamentations* (FOTL, 15; Grand Rapids, MI: Eerdmans, 2001).

Gikatilla, J., *Sha'arei Orah* (ed. J. Ben-Shlomo; 2 vols.; Jerusalem, 1971).

Gitay, Y., 'The Poetics of National Disaster: The Rhetorical Presentation of Lamentations', in *idem* (ed.), *Literary Responses to the Holocaust 1945–1995* (San Francisco: International Scholars Press, 1998), 1–11.

Gottleib, E. (ed.), *Mehqarim beSifrut haKabbalah* (Jerusalem, 1976).

Gottwald, N.K., 'The Book of Lamentations Reconsidered', in *idem*, *The Hebrew Bible in its Social World and in Ours* (SBLSS; Atlanta: Scholars Press, 1993), 165–73.

—'The Key to the Theology of Lamentations', in *idem*, *Studies in the Book of Lamentations* (SBT, 14; Chicago: Allenson, 1954), 47–62.

—'The Theology of Doom', in *idem*, *Studies in the Book of Lamentations* (SBT, 14; Chicago: Allenson, 1954), 63–89.

Graetz, N., 'Jerusalem the Widow', *Shofar* 17.2 (Winter1999), 16–24.

Gray, J., *I & II Kings* (OTL; London: SCM Press, 3rd edn, 1977).

Grayson, A.K. *Assyrian Rulers of the Early First Millennium BC, II (858–745 BC)* (Royal Inscriptions of Mesopotamia, Assyrian Periods, 3; Toronto: University of Toronto Press, 1996).

Green, M.W., 'The Eridu Lament', *JCS* 30 (1978), 127–67.

—'The Uruk Lament', *JAOS* 104 (1984), 253–79.

Greenberg, M., 'Psalm 140', in *Eretz Israel* 14 (1978), 88–99 (Hebrew).

Greenberg, U.Z., *Streets of the River* (Tel Aviv and Jerusalem: Schocken Books, 1951).

Greenstein, E.L., 'Lament over the Destruction of City and Temple in Early Israelite Literature', in Z. Talshir *et al.* (eds), *Homage to Shmuel: Studies in the World of the Bible* (S. Ahituv Festschrift; Beersheva: Ben-Gurion University of the Negev Press; Jerusalem: Bialik Institute, 2001), 88–97 (Hebrew).

Grossman, David, *See Under – Love* (Tel Aviv: Hakkibutz Hameuchad, 1986).

—Dalia Karpel, interview with David Grossman, *Ha'ir,* 10 January 1986 (Hebrew).

Gruenwald, I., 'Further Jewish Physiognomic and Chiromantic Fragments', *Tarbiz* 40 (1971), 301–19 (Hebrew).

Gwaltney, Jr, W.C., 'The Biblical Book of Lamentations in the Context of Near Eastern Literature', in W.W. Hallo *et al.* (eds.), *Scripture in Context II: More Essays on the Comparative Method* (Winona Lake, IN: Eisenbrauns, 1983), 191–211.

Hakham, A., *Job* (Da'at Miqra'; Jerusalem: Mossad Ha-Rav Kook, 1984) (Hebrew).

Hallo, W.W., 'Lamentations and Prayers in Sumer and Akkad', in J.M. Sasson (ed.), *Civilizations of the Ancient Near East* (New York: Charles Scribner's Sons, 1995), III, 1871–81.

Harrison, R.K., *Jeremiah and Lamentations* (TOTC; Leicester and Downers Grove, IL: Inter-Varsity, 1973).

Hasan-Rokem, G., *The Web of Life: Folklore and Midrash in Rabbinic Literature* (trans. B. Stein; Stanford: Stanford University Press, 2000).

Hasenfratz, H.-P. *Der indische Weg* (Freiburg i. Br.: Herder, 1994).

—'Iran: Antagonismus als Universalprinzip', *Saeculum* 34 (1983), 235–47.

—'Das Menschenbild des Islam', *Spectrum Iran* 12 (1999), 47–55 (49).

Hatch, E., and H.A. Redpath (ed.), *Concordance to the Septuagint and the Other Greek Versions of the Old Testament* (2 vols.; Oxford: Clarendon Press, 1897; reprinted Graz: Akademische Druck- und Verlangsanstalt, 1954).

Helsper, W. *(Neo)religiöse Orientierungen Jugendlicher in der 'postmodernen Moderne'*, in W. Ferchhoff (ed.), *Jugendkulturen – Faszination und Ambivalenz. Einblicke in jugendliche Lebenswelten* (Weinheim: Juventa, 1995), 66–81.

Hendel, Yehudit, *By Quiet Villages* (Tel Aviv: Hakkibutz Hameuchad, 1987) (Hebrew).

Herion, G.A., 'Wrath of God (OT)', *ABD* (New York: Doubleday, 1992), VI, 991–96.

Heschel, A.J., 'The Meaning and Mystery of Wrath', in *idem, The Prophets* (Philadelphia: Jewish Publication Society, 1962), 279–98.

Hick, John, *Evil and the God of Love* (New York: Harper & Row, 2nd edn, 1978).

Hillers, D.R., *Lamentations* (AB; Doubleday: New York, 2nd edn, 1992).

—*Treaty-Curses and the Old Testament Prophets* (BibOr, 16; Rome: Pontifical Biblical Institute, 1964).

Hoffman, Y., *Blemished Perfection: The Book of Job in Its Context* (Jerusalem: The Bialik Institute, 1995 [Hebrew]; Sheffield: Sheffield Academic Press, 1996).

—'The Day of the Lord as a Concept and a Term in the Prophetic Literature', *ZAW* 93 (1981), 37–50.

—'The First Creation Story', in H. Graf Reventlow and Y. Hoffman (eds.), *Creation in Jewish and Christian Tradition* (JSOTSup, 319; Sheffield: Sheffield Academic Press, 2002), 45–66.

—*Jeremiah* (Mikra Leyisrael; Jerusalem and Tel Aviv: Am Oved and Magnes, 2001).

—'Psalm 104', in M. Fishbane and E. Tov (eds.), *Sha'arei Talmon* (Winona Lake, IN: Eisenbrauns, 1992), 13*–24*.

Holladay, W. *Jeremiah* (2 vols.; Hermeneia; Minneapolis: Fortress Press, 1989).

Holtzman, A., 1994, 'Contemporary Trends in Israeli Fiction of the Holocaust', *Dappim: Research in Literature* 10 (1994), 131–58 (Hebrew).

Hunter, J., *Faces of a Lamenting City: The Development and Coherence of the Book of Lamentations* (Frankfurt: Lang, 1996).

Ibn Gabbai, M., *Avodat haQodesh* (2 vols.; Jerusalem, 1992).

Idel, M. ' "The Evil Thought" of God' [Hebrew], *Tarbiz* 49 (1989), 356–64.

Irenaeus [of Lyon], *Adversus Haereses*, III 7,1 (ed. A. Rousseau and L. Doutreleau; SC, 211; Paris: Cerf, 1974); IV 29,1 (ed. A. Rousseau, B. Hemmerdinger, L. Doutreleau and C.H. Mercier; SC, 100; Paris/Lyon: Cerf, 1965).

Iwand, H.J., Theologische Einführung, in Martin Luther, *Daß der freie Wille nichts sei. Antwort D. Martin Luthers an Erasmus von Rotterdam*, in Martin Luther, *Ausgewählte Werke* (ed. H.H. Borcherdt and G. Merz; Ergänzungsreihe 1, 3d edn Kaiser: Munich, 1975 [1954]), 253–64.

Jacobsen, T., Review of *Lamentation over the Destruction of Ur* by S.N. Kramer, *AJSL* 58 (1941), 219–24.

Jacobson, Y., 'The Aspect of the Feminine in Lurianic Kabbalah', in P. Schäfer and J. Dan (eds.), *Gershom Scholem's Major Trends in Jewish Mysticism, 50 Years After* (Tübingen, 1993), 241–43.

—'The Final Redemption from the Viewpoint of Adam according to Italian Sages during the Renaissance', *Da'at* 11 (1983) (Hebrew).

—'The Image of God, as the Source of Man's Evil according to the Maharal of Prague', *Da'at* 19 (1987), 112–23.

Jenni, E., [in E. Jenni] and D. Vetter, 'עָ י ר', *THAT* II (Munich: Chr. Kaiser; Zürich: Theolo-gischer Verlag, 1976), 259–68.

Jeremias, J., *Die Reue Gottes* (BTSt, 31; Neukirchen–Vluyn: Neukirchener Verlag, 2nd edn, 1997).

Johnson, B., 'Form and Message in Lamentations', *ZAW* 97 (1985), 58–73.

Jolivet, R., *La problème du mal d'après St Augustin* (Paris: Beauchesne, 1936).

Jonas, H., *Der Gottesbegriff nach Auschwitz: Eine jüdische Stimme* (Frankfurt a. M.: Suhrkamp, 1987).

Joyce, P., 'Lamentations and the Grief Process: A Psychological Reading', *BibInt* 1 (1993), 304–20.

Jüngel, E., *Quae supra nos, nihil ad nos. Eine Kurzformel der Lehre vom verborgenen Gott – im Anschluß an Luther interpretiert* (EvT, 32; Munich: Kaiser, 1972), 197–240.

Kaminsky, J.S., *Corporate Responsibility in the Hebrew Bible* (JSOTSup, 196; Sheffield: Sheffield Academic Press, 1995).

Katzetnik, *Piepel* (Tel Aviv: Hakkibutz Hameuchad, 1988) (Hebrew).

—*Salamandra* (Haifa: Shikmona, 1971) (Hebrew).

Kaufmann, Y., *The History of the Religion of Israel from its Beginnings to the End of the Second Temple Period* (Jerusalem and Tel Aviv: The Bialik Institute and Dvir, 1976).

—*Toledot Ha-Emumah ha-Yisraelit* (Jerusalem and Tel Aviv: Dvir, 1960) (Hebrew).

Kern, P.B., *Ancient Siege Warfare* (Bloomington and Indianapolis: Indiana University Press, 1999).

Kierkegaard, S., 'Sygdommen til Døden', in *Samlede Værker* (ed. A.B. Drachmann *et al.*; Copenhagen: Gyldendal, 1962–64, vol. XV) = *The Sickness Unto Death* (Princeton, NJ: Princeton University Press, 1980).

Kirkpatrick, A.F., *The Book of Psalms* (Cambridge: Cambridge University Press, 1951).

Kissane, E.J., *The Book of Psalms: Translated from a Critically Revised Hebrew Text with a Commentary* (Dublin: Browne and Nolan, 1964).

Klein, J., 'Lamentation over Ur', in W.W. Hallo and K.L. Younger, Jr (eds.), *The Context of Scripture 1: Canonical Compositions from the Biblical World. II. Monumental Inscrip-tions from the Biblical World* (Leiden: E.J. Brill, 1997. 2000).

Knierim, R., *Die Hauptbegriffe für Sünde im Alten Testament* (Gütersloh: Gütersloher Verlagshaus Gerd Mohn, 1965, 2nd edn, 1967).

Knuth, H.-C., 'Zwischen Gott und Teufel – Martin Luther über den Menschen', *Luther* 64 (1993), 10–23.

Kobelski, P.J., *Melchizedek and Melchiresa* (CBQMS, 10; Washington DC: The Catholic Biblical Association of America, 1981).

Koch, K., 'Gibt es ein Vergeltungsdogma im Alten Testament?', *ZTK* 52 (1955), 1–42 = reprinted in *Um das Prinzip der Vergeltung in Religion und Recht des Alten Testa-ments* (WdF, 12; Darmstadt: Wissenschaftliche Buchgesellschaft, 1972), 130–80 = *idem, Spuren des hebräischen Denkens: Gesammelte Aufsätze 1* (Neukirchen–Vluyn: Neukirchener Verlag, 1991), 65–103; ET: 'Is there a Doctrine of Retribution in the Old Testament?', in J.L. Crenshaw (ed.), *Theodicy in the Old Testament* (Issues in Theology and Religion, 4; Philadelphia: Fortress Press; London: SPCK, 1983), 57–87.

—'Der Spruch "Sein Blut bleibe auf seinem Haupt" und die israelitische Auffassung vom vergossenen Blut', *VT* 12 (1962), 396–416 = reprinted in *Um das Prinzip der Vergeltung in Religion und Recht des Alten Testaments* (WdF, 12; Darmstadt: Wissenschaftliche Buchgesellschaft, 1972), 432–56 = *idem, Spuren des hebräischen Denkens*, 128–45.

Koslowski, P., 'Sündenfälle. Theorien der Wandelbarkeit der Welt', in *Die Wirklichkeit des Bösen* (ed. F. Hermanni and P. Koslowski; Munich: Fink, 1998), 99–132.

Kramer, S.N., 'BM 98396: A Sumerian Prototype of the *Mater-Dolorosa*', *Eretz-Israel* 16 (Orlinsky Volume; 1982), 141*–46*.

—*Lamentation over the Destruction of Ur* (Assyriological Studies, 12; Chicago: University of Chicago Press, 1940).

—'The Weeping Goddess: Sumerian Prototypes of the *Mater Dolorosa*', *BA* 46.2 (Spring 1983), 69–80.

Krašovec, J., 'The Source of Hope in the Book of Lamentations', *VT* 42 (1992), 223–33.

Kraus, H.-J., *Klagelieder (Threni)* (BKAT; Neukirchen–Vluyn: Neukirchener Verlag, 2nd edn, 1960), 15–18.

—*Psalms 1–59, 60–150: A Commentary* (trans. H.C. Oswald; Minneapolis: Augsburg, 1988–89).

—*Theology of the Psalms* (trans. K. Crim; Minneapolis: Augsburg, 1986).

Künneth, W., *Politik zwischen Dämon und Gott* (Berlin: Lutherisches Verlagshaus, 1954).

Kutscher, R., *Oh Angry Sea (a-ab-ba hu-luh-ha): The History of a Sumerian Congregational Lament* (Yale Near Eastern Researches, 6; New Haven and London: Yale University Press, 1975).

Landy, F., 'Lamentations', in R. Alter and F. Kermode (eds.), *The Literary Guide to the Bible* (Cambridge, MA: Harvard University Press, 1987), 329–34.

Lang, Berel, *Act and Idea in the Nazi Genocide* (Chicago: University of Chicago Press, 1990).

Langer, Lawrence, *Holocaust Testimonies: The Ruins of Memory* (New Haven and London: Yale University Press, 1991).

Lee, N.C., *The Singers of Lamentations: Cities under Siege, from Ur to Jerusalem to Sarajevo* (Biblical Interpretation, 60; Leiden: E.J. Brill, 2002).

Leibniz, G.W., *Essais de Théodicée sur la bonté de Dieu, la liberté de l'homme et l'origine du mal* (Frankfurt a.M.: Insel, 1965).

—'Causa Dei asserta per justitiam ejus...', in *idem*, *Essais de Théodicée sur la bonté de Dieu, la liberté de l'homme et l'origine du mal*, vol. II (Frankfurt a. M.: Insel, 1965).

—*Theodicy: Essays on the Goodness of God, the Freedom of Man, and the Origin of Evil* (trans. E.M. Huggard; La Salle, IL: Open Court, 1985).

Lemaire, A., 'L'inscription araméenne de Bukân et son intérêt historique', *CRAIBL* (January–March 1998), 293–99.

Levenson, J.D., *Creation and the Persistence of Evil: The Jewish Drama of Divine Omnipotence* (San Francisco: Harper & Row, 1988).

Levi, I., *The Legend of the Sad Lakes* (Jerusalem: Keter, 1989) (Hebrew).

Levi, P., *The Drowned and the Saved* (New York: Summit Books, 1988).

Lewis, J.P., 'Versions, English (pre-1960)', *ABD* 6, 816–29.

Licht, J., *The Rule Scroll* (Jerusalem: The Bialik Institute, 1965).

—'Satan', EB (Jerusalem, 1982), VIII, 281–82.

—'Time and Eschatology in the Apocalyptic Literature and the Dead Sea Scrolls', *JJS* 16 (1965), 177–82.

—*The Thanksgiving Scroll* (Jerusalem: The Bialik Institute, 1957).

Liebes, Y., 'The Kabbalistic Myth of Orpheus' [Hebrew], in M. Idel, Z. Harvey and E. Schweid (eds.), *Shlomo Pines Jubilee Volume* (Jerusalem, 1988), I, 425–59.

Liebrecht, S.,'Strawberry's Girl', in *eadem*, *Chinese I Talk to You* (Jerusalem: Keter, 1993), 61–82 (Hebrew).

Linafelt, T., 'The Refusal of a Conclusion in the Book of Lamentations', *JBL* 120 (2001), 340–43.

—*Surviving Lamentations: Catastrophe, Lament, and Protest in the Afterlife of a Biblical Book* (Chicago and London: University of Chicago Press, 2000).

—'Zion's Cause: The Presentation of Pain in the Book of Lamentations', in *idem* (ed.), *Strange Fire: Reading the Bible after the Holocaust* (New York: New York University Press, 2000), 267–79.

Lindström, F., *God and the Origin of Evil* (ConBOT, 21; Lund: C.W.K. Gleerup, 1983).

Littell, F.H., and H.G. Locke, *The German Church Struggle and the Holocaust* (Detroit: Wayne State University Press, 1974).

Loewenstamm, S.E., 'Notes on the Origin of Some Biblical Figures of Speech', in J.M. Grintz, J. and J. Liver (eds.), *Studies in the Bible Presented to Professor M.H. Segal* (Jerusalem: Kiryat Sepher, 1964), 180–87 (182–83) (Hebrew).

Lohse, B., *Luthers Theologie in ihrer historischen Entwicklung und in ihrem systematischen Zusammenhang* (Göttingen: Vandenhoeck & Ruprecht, 1995).

Lorenz, K., *Das sogenannte Böse* (Vienna: Borotha-Schoeler, 29th edn, 1971).

Lorenz, R.,'Das vierte bis sechste Jahrhundert', in K.D. Schmidt and E. Wolf (eds.), *Die Kirche in ihrer Geschichte 1*, C1 (Göttingen: Vandenhoeck & Ruprecht, 1970).

Luhmann N., 'Einführende Bemerkungen zu einer Theorie symbolisch generalisierter Kommunikationsmedien', in *idem, Soziologische Aufklärung*, vol. II (Opladen: Westdeutscher Verlag, 1975), 170–92.

—'Komplexität und politische Planung', in *Politische Planung* (Opladen: Westdeutscher Verlag, 1971).

Luther, M., *Brief Nr. 3162, Luther an Wolfgang Capito in Straßburg 9. Juli 1537* (WABR 8; Weimar: Böhlau, 1938).

—*De servo arbitrio (1525)* (WA 18; Weimar: Böhlau, 1908).

—*Dictata super Psalterium (1513–1516)* (WA 3; Weimar: Böhlau, 1885).

—*Eine kurze Form der zehn Gebote, eine kurze Form des Glaubens, eine kurze Form des Vaterunsers (1520)* (WA 7; Weimar: Böhlau, 1897).

—*Genesisvorlesung (1535–1545)* (WA 42; Weimar: Böhlau, 1911).

—*Katechismuspredigten (1528)* (WA 30 I; Weimar: Böhlau, 1910).

—*Predigten des Jahres 1524* (WA 15; Weimar: Böhlau, 1899).

—*Predigten des Jahres 1531* (WA 34 II; Weimar: Böhlau, 1908).

—*Predigten des Jahres 1537* (WA 23; Weimar: Böhlau, 1901).

—*Predigten über das zweite Buch Mose* (WA 16; Weimar: Böhlau, 1904).

—*Randbemerkungen zu Augustini opuscula (1509)* (WA 9; Weimar: Böhlau, 1893).

—*Rationis Latomianae confutatio (1521)* (WA 8; Weimar: Böhlau, 1889).

—*Tischreden* vol. 5 (WAT 5; Weimar: Böhlau, 1919).

—*Vom Abendmahl Christi, Bekenntnis* (WA 26; Weimar: Böhlau, 1909).

—*Von den guten Werken (1520)* (WA 7; Weimar: Böhlau, 1888).

—*Vorlesung über das zweite Buch Mose* (WA 16; Weimar: Böhlau, 1904).

—*Vorlesung über den Römerbrief (1515/1516)* (WA 56; Weimar: Böhlau, 1938).

—*Vorlesung über Jesaja* (1527/1534) (WA 25; Weimar: Böhlau, 1902).

—*Vorrede zu Wider die gottlosen blutdürstigen Sauliten und Doegiten...ausgelegt durch D. Urbanum Regium (1541)* (WA 51; Weimar: Böhlau, 1914).

—*Wider die Antinomer (1539)* (WA 50; Weimar: Böhlau, 1914).

Lyotard, J.F., *The Differend: Phrases in Dispute* (Minneapolis: Minnesota University Press, 1988).

Maaser, W., *Die schöpferische Kraft des Wortes: Die Bedeutung der Rhetorik für Luthers Schöpfungs- und Ethikverständnis* (Neukirchen–Vluyn: Neukirchener Verlag, 1999).

Mackie, J.L., 'Evil and Omnipotence', in Michael L. Peterson (ed.), *The Problem of Evil: Selected Readings* (Indiana: University of Notre Dame Press, 1992), 89–101.

Mandolfo, C., *God in the Dock: Dialogic Tension in the Psalms of Lament* (JSOTSup, 357; Sheffield: Sheffield Academic Press, 2002).

McCann, J.C., *Psalm 73: An Interpretation Emphasizing Rhetorical and Canonical Criticism* (PhD dissertation, Duke University, 1985; Ann Arbor: University Microfilms International, 1991).

McDaniel, T.F., 'The Alleged Sumerian Influence upon Lamentations', *VT* 18 (1968), 198–209.

McKane, W., *Jeremiah* (2 vols.; ICC; Edinburgh: T. & T. Clark, 1996).

—*Prophets and Wise Men* (SBT, 44; London: SCM Press, 1965).

—*Proverbs* (OTL; London: SCM Press, 1970).

McSorley, H.J., *Luthers Lehre vom unfreien Willen: Nach seiner Hauptschrift De servo arbitrio im Lichte der biblischen und kirchlichen Tradition* (BÖT, 1; Munich: Hueber, 1967).

Meyer, J., *Historischer Kommentar zu Luthers kleinem Katechismus* (Gütersloh: Bertelsmann, 1929).

Michalowski, P., *The Lamentation over the Destruction of Sumer and Ur* (Winona Lake, IN: Eisenbrauns, 1989).

Milik, J.T., '4Q Visions de 'Amram et une citation d'Origine', *RB* 79 (1972), 77–97.

—'Le travail d'édition des manuscrits du Désert de Juda', *Volume de Congrès. Strasbourg 1956* (VTSup 4, 1957), 17–26.

—'Milki-sedeq et Milki-resa' dans les anciens écrits juifs et chrétiens' I, *JJS* 23 (1972), 95–144.

Millard, A., 'Hadad-Yith'i', in W.W. Hallo and K.L. Younger, Jr (eds.), *The Context of Scripture 2: Monumental Inscriptions from the Biblical World* (Leiden: E.J. Brill, 2000), 154b.

Mintz, Alan, 'The Rhetoric of Lamentations', in *idem, Hurban: Responses to Catastrophe in Hebrew Literature* (New York: Columbia University Press, 1984), 17–48.

Miodovnik, Y., 'The Motif of Famine in the Book of Lamentations and its Notional Setting in the Light of Ancient Near Eastern Literature' (MA thesis, Tel Aviv University, 2001) (Hebrew).

Miron, D., 'Between Ashes and Books', *Alpayim* 10 (1994) 196–224 (Hebrew).

Moore, G.E., *Principia Ethica* (1903) (ed. T. Baldwin; Cambridge: Cambridge University Press, rev. edn, 1993).

Moore, M.S., 'Human Suffering in Lamentations', *RB* 90 (1983), 534–55.

Morag, G., 'Breaking Silence: Israel's Fantastic Fiction of the Holocaust', in Alan Mintz, (ed.), *The Boom in Contemporary Israeli Fiction* (Hanover, NH, and London: Brandeis University Press, 1997), 143–83.

Mowinckel, S., *The Psalms in Israel's Worship* (2 vols.; trans. D.R. Ap-Thomas; Oxford: Basil Blackwell, 1962).

Müller, K., *Schamanismus* (Munich: C.H. Beck, 1997).

Nietzsche, F., 'Jenseits von Gut und Böse/Zur Genealogie der Moral', in *Sämtliche Werke. Studienausgabe* (ed. G. Colli and M. Montinari; vol. V Munich: Deutscher Taschenbuch Verlag, 1980).

Nitzan, B., '280. 4QCurses', *Qumran Cave 4.XX, Poetical and Liturgical Texts. Part 2* (DJD, 29; Oxford: Clarendon Press, 1999), 1–8.

—'286. 4QBerakhot[a]'; '287. 4QBerakhot[b]', in E. Eshel *et al.* (eds.), *Qumran Cave 4.VI, Poetical and Liturgical Texts, Part 1* (DJD, 11; Oxford: Clarendon Press, 1998), 27–30; 57-58.

—'Apocalyptic Historiosophy in Qumran Literature: Its Origins and Perspectives in the Legacy of Jacob Licht', in G. Brin and B. Nitzan (eds.), *Fifty Years of Dead Sea Scrolls Research: Studies in Memory of Jaacob Licht* (Jerusalem: Yad Ben-Zvi, 2001), 37–56 (Hebrew).

—*Qumran Prayer and Religious Poetry* (STDJ, 12; Leiden: E.J. Brill, 1994).

Noble, P.R., *The Canonical Approach: A Critical Reconstruction of the Hermeneutics of Brevard S. Childs* (Biblical Interpretation Series, 16; Leiden: E.J. Brill, 1995).

Noort, E., 'JHWH und das Böse', in *Prophets, Worship and Theodicy* (*OTS*, 23; Leiden: E.J. Brill, 1984), 120–36.

Oberman, H.A., *Luther: Man between God and Devil* (New Haven: Yale University Press, 1989).

O'Connor, K.M., *The Book of Lamentations: Introduction, Commentary, and Reflections* (New Interpreter's Bible, 6; Nashville: Abingdon Press, 2001).

—'Lamentations', in C.A. Newsom and S.H. Ringe (eds.), *The Women's Bible Commentary* (London: SPCK; Louisville, KY: Westminster/John Knox Press, 1992), 178–82.

—'The Tears of God: Divine Character in Jeremiah 2:9', in T. Linafelt and T.K. Beal (eds.), *God in the Fray: A Tribute to Walter Brueggemann* (Minneapolis, Fortress, 1998), 172–85.

Olyan, S.M., 'Honor, Shame, and Covenant Relations in Ancient Israel and its Environment', *JBL* 115 (1996), 201–18.

Oppenheim, A.L., ' "Siege Documents" from Nippur', *Iraq* 17 (1955), 69–89.

Orlev, Uri, *Lead Soldiers* (Jerusalem: Keter 1989 [1956]) (Hebrew).

Osten-Sacken, Peter von der, *Gott und Belial* (Göttingen: Vandenhoeck & Ruprecht, 1968).

Parpola, S., and K. Watanabe, *Neo-Assyrian Treaties and Loyalty Oaths* (State Archives of Assyria, 2; Helsinki: Helsinki University Press, 1988).

Paul, S.M., *Amos* (Hermeneia; Minneapolis: Fortress Press, 1991).

Pham, X.H.T., *Mourning in the Ancient Near East and the Hebrew Bible* (JSOTSup, 302; Sheffield: Sheffield Academic Press, 1999).

Philips, G., 'La raison d'être du mal d'après St Augustin' (Louvain Diss.; Univ. Grégorienne de Rome, 1927).

Plöger, O., *Sprüche Salomos* (BKAT, 17; Neukirchen–Vluyn: Neukirchener Verlag, 1984).

Plotinus, *Enneades* (ed. P. Henry; Oxford: Clarendon Press, 1964).

Pope, M.H., *Job* (AB; Garden City, NY: Doubleday, 3rd edn, 1973).

Provan, I. *Lamentations* (NCB; London: Pickering; Grand Rapids, MI: Eerdmans, 1991).

Puech, E., '11QPsAp^a: Un ritual d'exorcismes. Essai de reconstruction', *RevQ* 14 (1990), 377–408.

Rad G. von, *Weisheit in Israel* (Neukirchen–Vluyn: Neukirchener Verlag, 1970; ET *Wisdom in Israel* [London: SCM Press, 1972]).

Raz-Krakozkin, A., 'Exile within Sovereignty: Towards a Critique of the "Negation of Exile" in Israeli Culture', part 2, *Theory and Criticism* 5 (1994), 113–32 (Hebrew).

Re'emi, S.P., 'The Theology of Hope: A Commentary on the Book of Lamentations', in R. Martin-Achard and S.P. Re'emi, *God's People in Crisis: Amos and Lamentations* (International Theological Commentary; Edinburgh: Handsel Press; Grand Rapids, MI: Eerdmans, 1984), 73–134.

Reinhuber, Th., *Kämpfender Glaube: Studien zu Luthers Bekenntnis am Ende von De servo arbitrio* (Berlin and New York: de Gruyter, 2000).

Renkema, J., *Lamentations* (trans. B. Doyle; Historical Commentary on the Old Testament; Leuven: Peeters, 1998).

Reventlow, H. Graf, ' "Sein Blut komme über sein Haupt" ', *VT* 10 (1960), 311–27 = K. Koch (ed.), *Um das Prinzip der Vergeltung*, 412–31.

Reventlow, H. Graf, and Y. Hoffman (eds.), *Justice and Righteousness* (JSOTSup, 137; Sheffield: JSOT Press, 1992).

Rietschel, G., and P. Graff, *Lehrbuch der Liturgik* (Göttingen: Vandenhoeck & Ruprecht, 1951).

Roberts, J.J.M., 'The Motif of the Weeping God in Jeremiah and its Background in the Laments of the Ancient Near East', *Old Testament Essays* 5 (1992), 361–74.

Roskies, David G., *Against Apocalypse: Responses to Catastrophe in Modern Jewish Culture* (Cambridge, MA, and London: Harvard University Press, 1984).

Ross, W.D., *The Right and the Good* (Oxford: Clarendon Press, 1930).

Rudolph, W., *Jeremia* (HAT, I, 12; Tübingen: J.C.B. Mohr [Paul Siebeck], 1968).

Rüterswörden, U., 'Das Böse in der deuteronomischen Schultheologie', in T. Veijola (ed.), *Das Deuteronomium und seine Querbeziehungen* (Schriften der Finnischen Exegetischen Gesellschaft, 62; Helsinki: Finnische Exegetische Gesellschaft; Göttingen: Vandenhoeck & Ruprecht, 1996), 223–41.

Sacchi, P., *Jewish Apocalyptic and its History* (Sheffield: Sheffield Academic Press, 1996).

Salters, R.B., *Jonah and Lamentations* (OTG; Sheffield: Sheffield Academic Press, 1994).

Sarna, N., 'Rahab', *EB* (Jerusalem, 1976), VII, 328–29 (Hebrew).

Schäfer, C., *Unde malum. Die Frage nach dem Bösen bei Plotin, Augustinus und Dionysius* (Würzburg: Königshausen & Neumann, 2002).

Schaefer, K., *Psalms* (Berit Olam: Studies in Hebrew Narrative & Poetry; Collegeville, MN: Liturgical Press, 2001).

Scherer, A., *Das weise Wort und seine Wirkung: Eine Untersuchung zur Komposition und Redaktion von Proverbia 10,1–22,16* (WMANT, 83; Neukirchen–Vluyn: Neukirchener Verlag, 1999).

Schiffman, L.H., '299. 4QMysteris', in T. Elgvin *et al.* (eds.), *Qumran Cave 4.XV: Sapiential Texts, Part 1* (DJD, 20; Oxford: Clarendon Press, 1997), 36.

Schleiermacher, F., *Der christliche Glaube nach den Grundsätzen der evangelischen Kirche im Zusammenhange dargestellt von Dr. Friedrich Schleiermacher* (ed. M. Redecker; Berlin: W. de Gruyter, 7th edn of the 2nd version, 1960).

Schmid, H.H., *Gerechtigkeit als Weltordnung* (BHT, 40; Tübingen: Mohr Siebeck, 1968).

Schmid, Herbert, '«Gottlose» und Gottlosigkeit im Alten Testament', *Judaica* 33 (1977), 75–85, 127–35.

Schmidt, H., *Die Psalmen* (HAT, 15; Tübingen: J.C.B. Mohr, 1934).

Schmidt, K.D., and E. Wolf (eds.), *Die Kirche in ihrer Geschichte 1*, C1 (Göttingen: Vandenhoeck & Ruprecht, 1970).

Schmidt, W.H., 'Gott und Böses', *EvT* 52 (1992), 7–22 = *Vielfalt und Einheit alttestamentlichen Glaubens II* (Neukirchen–Vluyn: Neukirchener Verlag, 1995).

Scholem, G., *Major Trends in Jewish Mysticism* (New York, 1961).

—'Schöpfung aus dem Nichts und Selbstverschränkung Gottes', *Eranos-Jahrbuch* 25 (1956), 87–119.

—*Shabbetai Zevi vehaTenu'ah haShabbeta'it biYemei Hayyav* (Tel Aviv, 1988) [ET: *Sabbatai Sevi: The Mystical Messiah* 1626–1676, Princeton, 1973].

—'Sitra Ahra: Good and Evil in the Kabbalah', in *Pirqei Yesod beHavanat haKabbalah uSemaleha* (trans. J. Ben-Shlomo; Jerusalem, 1981), 187–212; English: *On the Mystical Shape of the Godhead: Basic Concepts in the Kabbalah* (trans. J. Chipman; New York, 1991), 56–87.

Schuller, A., and W.V. Rahden (eds.), *Die andere Kraft: Zur Renaissance des Bösen* (Berlin: Akademie-Verlag, 1993).

Schwartz, B., 'Psalm 50, Its Subject, Form and Place', in *Shnaton – An Annual for Biblical and Ancient Near Eastern Studies*, III (1978–79), 77–106 (Hebrew).

Schwarz, H., *Im Fangnetz des Bösen: Sünde-Übel-Schuld* (Göttingen: Vandenhoeck & Ruprecht, 1993).

Schwarz, Yigal, 'Utterly Moral Mission', *Efes Shtayim* 1 (1992), 121–24 (Hebrew).

Scott, R.B.Y.,'Wise and Foolish, Righteous and Wicked', in *Studies in the Religion of Ancient Israel* (VTSup, 23; Leiden: E.J. Brill, 1972), 146–65.

Seeberg, E., *Luthers Theologie: Motive und Ideen I* (Göttingen: Vandenhoeck & Ruprecht, 1929).

Segev, T., *The Seventh Million* (Jerusalem: Keter, 1983) (Hebrew).

Semel, N., 'A Trip to Two Berlins', in *eadem, A Hat of Glass* (Tel Aviv: Sifriat Poalim, 1988), 145–72 (Hebrew).

Sened, Y., and A. Sened, *Between the Living and the Dead* (Tel Aviv: Hakkibutz Hameuchad, 1964) (Hebrew).

Shaked, S., 'Persia', *EB* (Jerusalem, 1972), VI, 609.

—'Qumran and Iran: Further Consideration', *Israel Oriental Studies* 2 (1972), 433–46.

Shapira, A., 'The Holocaust: Private Memory and Collective Memory', in *eadem, New Jews Old Jews* (Tel Aviv: Am Oved, 1997), 86–103 (Hebrew).

Shaw, G.B., 'Man and Superman. Maxims for Revolutionists', in *The Complete Prefaces of G.B. Shaw* (London: Paul Hamlyn, 1965), 188–195.

Sidgwick, H., *The Methods of Ethics* (1874) (London: Macmillan and Company, 7th edn, 1907).

Skladny, U., *Die ältesten Spruchsammlungen in Israel* (Göttingen: Vandenhoeck & Ruprecht, 1962).

Smith, M., '462. 4QNarrative C', in M. Broshi *et al.* (eds.), *Qumran Cave 4.XIV: Parabiblical Texts, Part 2* (DJD, 19; Oxford: Clarendon Press, 1995), 195–208.

Sobol, Yehoshua, *Ghetto* (Tel Aviv: Or-Am, 1992 [1984]) (Hebrew).

Sperber, M., *Churban oder Die unfaßbare Gewißheit* (Vienna: Europaverlag, 1979).

Stern, D., *Parables in Midrash* (Cambridge, MA: Harvard University Press, 1991), 124–30.

Strauss, A.L., *Studies in Literature* (Jerusalem: The Bialik Institute, 1970), 89–94 (Hebrew).

Streib, H., 'Teufel VII, Praktisch-theologisch', in *TRE* 33 (2001), 137–40.

Strugnell, J., *et al.* (eds.), *Qumran Cave 4.XXIV: Sapiential Texts, Part 2* (DJD, 34; Oxford: Clarendon Press, 1999).

Talmon, S., and I. Knohl, 'A Calendrical Scroll from a Qumran Cave: Mishmarot Ba, 4Q321', in D.P. Wright *et al.* (eds.), *Pomegranates and Golden Bells: Studies in Biblical, Jewish and Near Eastern Ritual, Law, and Literature in Honor of Jacob Milgrom* (Winona Lake, MI: Eisenbrauns, 1995), 276–302.

Tate, M.E., *Psalms 51–100* (WBC, 20; Waco, TX: Word Books, 1990).

Tertullian, *Adversus Marcionem* (ed. E. Evans; Oxford: Oxford University Press, 1972).

Thiel, W., *Die deuteronomistische Redaktion von Jeremia 1–25* (WMANT, 41; Neukirchen–Vluyn: Neukirchener Verlag, 1973).

—*Die deuteronomistische Redaktion von Jeremia 26–45* (WMANT, 52; Neukirchen–Vluyn: Neukirchener Verlag, 1981).

—'Deuteronomistische Redaktionsarbeit in den Elia-Erzählungen', in *Congress Volume Leuven 1989* (VTSup, 43; Leiden: E.J. Brill, 1991), 148–71 = *Gelebte Geschichte* (Neukirchen–Vluyn: Neukirchener Verlag, 2000), 139–60.

—*Könige. 2. Teilband. Lfg. 1* (BKAT, IX/2,1; Neukirchen–Vluyn: Neukirchener Verlag, 2000).

Tigay, J.H., 'Lamentations, Book of', *EncJud* (1971), X, 1368–75.

Tinney, S., *The Nippur Lament* (Philadelphia: S.N. Kramer Fund, 1996).

Tishby, I., *Mishnat haZohar* (Jerusalem, 1957), I, 285–377; ET: *The Wisdom of the Zohar* (3 vols.; trans. D. Goldstein; Oxford, 1989).

—*Torat haRa' vehaQelippah beKabbalat haAri* (Jerusalem, 1963).

Tur-Sinai, N., 'Belial', EB (Jerusalem, 1965), II, 132–33 (Hebrew).

Uffenheimer, B., *The Visions of Zechariah* (Jerusalem: Kiryat Sepher, 1961) (Hebrew).

van der Ploeg, J., 'Le Psaume XCI dans une recension de Qumran', *RB* 72 (1965), 210–17.

—'Un petit rouleau de Psaumes apocryphes (11QPsAp^a)', in G. Jeremias *et al.* (eds.), *Tradition und Glaube: Das Frühe Christentum in seiner Umwelt. Festgabe für K.G. Kuhn* (Göttingen: Vandenhoeck und Ruprecht, 1971), 128–39.

van der Toorn, K., B. Becking and P.W. van der Horst (eds.), *Dictionary of Deities and Demons in the Bible* (Leiden: E.J. Brill; Grand Rapids, MI; Cambridge, UK: Eerdmans, 2nd edn, 1999).

Vermes, G. (trans.), *The Dead Sea Scrolls in English* (Sheffield: JSOT Press, 3rd edn, 1987).

Vierzig, S., *Das Böse* (Stuttgart: W. Kohlhammer, 1984).

Vital, R. Hayyim, *'Etz Hayyim* (Jerusalem, 1988).

—*Mevo She'arim* (Jerusalem, 1988).

—*Sefer Ta'amei haMizvot* (Jerusalem, 1988).

—*Sha'ar Ma'amarei Rashbi* (Jerusalem, 1988).

—*Sha'ar Ma'amarei Razal* (Jerusalem, 1988), Masekhet Shabbat.

—*Sha'ar haMizvot* (Jerusalem, 1988).

Vogelsang, W., *Videocliquen. Action- und Horrorvideos als Kristallisationspunkte von jugendlichen Fangemeinschaften*, in W. Ferchhoff (ed.), *Jugendkulturen – Faszination und Ambivalenz. Einblicke in jugendliche Lebenswelten* (Weinheim: Juventa, 1995), 120–32.

Wacholder, B.Z., and M.G. Abegg, *A Preliminary Edition of the Unpublished Dead Sea Scrolls* (Washington, DC: BAS, 1995).

Wanke, G., 'Dämonen II. Altes Testament', *TRE* 8 (Berlin; New York: W. de Gruyter, 1981), 275–77.

Weier, R., *Das Thema vom verborgenen Gott von Nikolaus von Kues zu Martin Luther* (Buchreihe der Cusanus-Gesellschaft, 2; Münster: Aschendorff, 1967).

Weinfeld, M., 'God the Creator in Gen. 1 and in the Prophecy of Second Isaiah', *Tarbiz* 37 (1968), 105–132 (Hebrew).

—'Instructions for Temple Visitors in the Bible and in Ancient Egypt', in S. Groll (ed.), *Egyptological Studies* (Scripta Hierosolymitana, 28; Jerusalem: Magnes Press, 1982), 224–50.

—*Justice and Righteousness in Israel and the Nations: Equality and Freedom in Ancient Israel in Light of Social Justice in the Ancient Near East* (Jerusalem: Magnes Press, 1985)

—'The Uniqueness of the Decalogue and its Place in Jewish Tradition', in *The Ten Commandments as Reflected in Tradition and Literature Throughout the Ages* (ed. B. Segal; Z. Jerusalem: Magnes Press, 1985), 1–34, esp. 17–21 (Hebrew).

Weiser, A. *The Psalms: A Commentary* (trans. H. Hartwell; OTL; London: SCM Press, 1962).

Weiss, M., 'On the Book of Lamentations', שורר ישורון 3 (1966), 11–16.

—*The Bible from Within: The Method of Total Interpretation* (Jerusalem: Magnes Press, 1984).

—*Scriptures in their Own Light: Collected Essays* (Jerusalem: The Bialik Institute, 1987) (Hebrew).

Weizsäcker, C.F. von, 'Modelle des Gesunden und Kranken, Guten und Bösen, Wahren und Falschen', in *idem, Die Einheit der Natur* (Munich: Hanser, 1971), 320–41.

Weizsäcker, V. von, *Der Begriff sittlicher Wissenschaft* (Frankfurt/M.: Schulte-Bulmke 1948).

Westermann, C., *Isaiah 40–66* (OTL; London: SCM Press, 1969).

—*Lamentations: Issues and Interpretation* (trans. C. Muenchow; Minneapolis: Fortress Press, 1994).

Williams, R., 'Creation', in A.D. Fitzgerald (ed.), *Augustine through the Ages: An Encyclopedia* (Grand Rapids/Cambridge: Eerdmans, 1999).

Winston, D., 'The Iranian Component in the Bible, Apocrypha, and Qumran', *History and Religion* 5 (1965), 183–216.

Würthwein, E., *Das erste Buch der Könige Kapitel 1–16* (ATD, 11.1; Göttingen; Zürich: Vandenhoeck & Ruprecht, 2nd edn, 1985).

Yates, W., 'An Introduction to the Grotesque', in J.L. Adams and W. Yates (eds.), *The Grotesque in Art and Literature: Theological Reflections* (Grand Rapids, MI: Eerdmans, 1997).

Yehoshua, A.B., *The Wall and the Mountain: The Extra-Literary Reality of the Writer in Israel* (Tel Aviv: Zmora Bitan, 1989) (Hebrew).

Zaehner, R.C., *Dawn and Twilight of Zoroastrianism* (London: Weidenfeld and Nicholson; New York: Putnam's Sons, 1961 [2nd edn, 1975]).

von Zahn-Harnack, A., *Adolf von Harnack* (Berlin: Hans Bott Verlag, 1936).

Ziehe, T., 'Vom vorläufigen Ende der Erregung – Die Normalität kultureller Modernisierungen hat die Jugend-Subkulturen entmächtigt', in W. Helsper (ed.), *Jugend zwischen Moderne und Postmoderne* (Opladen: Leske + Budrich, 1991), 57–73.

Zukerman, Y., and M. Basok, *The Book of the Wars of the Ghettos* (Tel Aviv: Hakkibutz Hameuchad, 1954) (Hebrew).

MSWWF [Ministerium für Schulen, Wissenschaft und Forschung] des Landes Nordrhein-Westphalen (ed.), *Sekundarstufe II Gymnasium/Gesamtschule, Richtlinien und Lehrpläne* (Frechen: Ritterbach, 1999).

Issues of periodicals dealing with evil:
'Geheimnisvolle Kräfte', *RU* 29 (1999).
'Das Böse', *Religion Heute(M)* 1 (1989).
'Das Böse – eine oft verdrängte Herausforderung', *Glauben und Lernen* 12 (1997).
'Wohin mit dem Teufel?', *EvT* 52 (1992).

INDEX

INDEX OF REFERENCES

OLD TESTAMENT